Facial Attractiveness

Evolutionary, Cognitive, and Social Perspectives

Edited by Gillian Rhodes and
Leslie A. Zebrowitz

Advances in Visual Cognition
Gillian Rhodes, Series Editor

ABLEX
Westport, Connecticut • London

Library of Congress Cataloging-in-Publication Data

Facial attractiveness : evolutionary, cognitive, and social perspectives /
edited by Gillian Rhodes and Leslie A. Zebrowitz.
p. cm.—(Advances in visual cognition, ISSN 1534–746X ; v. 1)
Includes bibliographical references and index.
ISBN 1–56750–636–4 (alk. paper)—ISBN 1–56750–637–2 (pbk. : alk. paper)
1. Physiognomy. 2. Face—Social aspects. 3. Interpersonal attraction. I. Rhodes, Gillian. II. Zebrowitz, Leslie A., 1944– III. Series.
BF859.F33 2002
153.7′5—dc21 2001016045

British Library Cataloguing in Publication Data is available.

Library of Congress Catalog Card Number: 2001016045
ISBN: 1–56750–636–4
1–56750–637–2 (pbk.)
ISSN: 1534–746X

First published in 2002

Ablex Publishing, 88 Post Road West, Westport, CT 06881
An imprint of Greenwood Publishing Group, Inc.
www.ablexbooks.com

Printed in the United States of America

The paper used in this book complies with the
Permanent Paper Standard issued by the National
Information Standards Organization (Z39.48–1984).

10 9 8 7 6 5 4 3 2 1

Contents

Introduction vii

1 What Makes a Face Attractive and Why: The Role of Averageness in Defining Facial Beauty
Adam J. Rubenstein, Judith H. Langlois, and Lori A. Roggman 1

2 The Attractiveness of Average Faces: Cross-Cultural Evidence and Possible Biological Basis
Gillian Rhodes, Kate Harwood, Sakiko Yoshikawa, Miwa Nishitani, and Ian McLean 35

3 Evolution and Individual Differences in the Perception of Attractiveness: How Cyclic Hormonal Changes and Self-Perceived Attractiveness Influence Female Preferences for Male Faces
Anthony C. Little, Ian S. Penton-Voak, D. Michael Burt, and David I. Perrett 59

4 Female Faces and Bodies: N-Dimensional Feature Space and Attractiveness
Karl Grammer, Bernhard Fink, Astrid Juette, Gudrun Ronzal, and Randy Thornhill 91

5 An Ethological Theory of Attractiveness
Magnus Enquist, Stefano Ghirlanda, Daniel Lundqvist, and Carl-Adam Wachtmeister 127

6 Charismatic Faces: Social Status Cues Put Face Appeal in Context
Caroline F. Keating 153

7 Dimensions of Facial Physical Attractiveness: The Intersection of Biology and Culture
Michael R. Cunningham, Anita P. Barbee, and Correna L. Philhower 193

8 Cultural Perspectives on Facial Attractiveness
Karen K. Dion 239

9 Nature Let a Hundred Flowers Bloom: The Multiple Ways and Wherefores of Attractiveness
Leslie A. Zebrowitz and Gillian Rhodes 261

Index 295

About the Editors and Contributors 307

Introduction

The last decade has seen an exciting change in our understanding of what makes a face attractive, and why we have the preferences we do. The old idea that beauty is in the eye of the beholder, with preferences varying idiosyncratically from person to person or culture to culture, has been challenged by recent evidence for close agreement about which faces are attractive, both across and within cultures (Langlois & Roggman, 1990; Zebrowitz, 1997). These findings suggest instead that we all share an eye for beauty. Moreover, our preferences emerge early in development, with infants as young as 2–3 months in age preferring to look at faces that adults find attractive (Langlois et al., 1987; Rubenstein, Kalakanis & Langlois, 1999). These findings raise the intriguing possibility that some preferences may be innate. So just what are these preferences, why do we have them, and how did we get them?

In this volume we bring together seminal work from cognitive, evolutionary, social, and developmental perspectives, which explores these questions, and the psychological and biological mechanisms underlying our preferences. Much of this research has used sophisticated computer-imaging techniques to manipulate facial images, taking researchers beyond a correlational approach and allowing experimental tests of what makes a face attractive. Some of the results are surprising, some are controversial, and some are even paradoxical, but together they bring a new perspective to understanding the perception of attractiveness, in its evolutionary, cognitive, cultural, and motivational contexts.

One surprising answer to the question of what makes a face attractive is that averageness is attractive (Rubenstein et al., Chapter 1; Rhodes et al., Chapter 2; Enquist et al., Chapter 5, all in this volume). Rubenstein and his colleagues (Chapter 1) take a strong position, arguing that averageness is the key to attractiveness. Others agree that average faces are attractive, but disagree that averageness provides a complete answer to what makes a face attractive. Little and his colleagues (Chapter 3) examine whether extreme sexually dimorphic traits might be more attractive than average traits. They find that feminized traits are attractive in female faces, and Grammer and colleagues (Chapter 4) suggest that the same is true for the female body. The evidence that masculinized traits are attractive in male faces, however, is more controversial (see chapters by Little et al., Chapter 3; Keating et al., Chapter 6; Cunningham et al., Chapter 7; Zebrowitz & Rhodes, Chapter 9). Keating (Chapter 6) suggests that attractive faces have a balance of dominance and warmth cues, which may explain why masculinized male faces are not always optimally attractive. Symmetry also appears to be attractive (Little et al., Chapter 3). Perhaps the most striking conclusion to emerge from these chapters, however, is that there is no single gold standard of attractiveness (Cunningham et al., Chapter 7; Zebrowitz & Rhodes, Chapter 9). Averageness, certain extremes, symmetry, youthfulness, pleasant expressions, and familiarity all contribute.

Another important point to emerge from these chapters is that, despite considerable agreement among people about which faces are attractive, interesting individual and cultural differences in preferences remain. Little and colleagues (Chapter 3) provide a fascinating discussion of how individual differences in hormonal status and self-rated attractiveness can affect preferences, and Dion (Chapter 8) discusses how different cultural perspectives can affect the attributions that are made about people based on their attractiveness.

The most challenging question addressed by the contributors is, why do we have the preferences we do? One suggestion is that our preferences evolved as an adaptation to the problem of mate choice. On this view, attractive traits signal aspects of mate quality, such as fertility, youthfulness, or health, and so the preferences evolved because they enhanced reproductive success (Rhodes et al., Chapter 2; Little et al., Chapter 3; Grammer et al., Chapter 4; Keating, Chapter 6). Others disagree, suggesting instead that preferences reflect the operation of general perceptual or cognitive mechanisms, such as the ability to abstract prototypes (Rubenstein et al., Chapter 1) or discriminate between male and female faces (Enquist et al., Chapter 5). On this view, the attractive traits need not directly signal mate quality. These accounts attempt to explain preferences that are widely shared and that persist over time. Preferences are not, however, identical for different individuals or at different times, and these variations must also be explained. Several contributors speculate that individual learning histories and social goals may account for these variations (Enquist et al., Chapter 5; Zebrowitz & Rhodes, Chapter 9).

All these attempts to explain our preferences focus on sexual attractiveness, but people can also be attractive as friends or mentors. These preferences are also discussed (Keating, Chapter 6; Cunningham, Chapter 7; Zebrowitz & Rhodes, Chapter 9), but it is an open question how the different kinds of attractiveness relate to one another. If preferences reflect the operation of general cognitive or perceptual mechanisms, then similar traits should be attractive in all cases. In contrast, if preferences evolved as an adaptation to mate choice, then there is no reason to expect the same preferences for friends and mates. An investigation of similarities and differences in the traits preferred in friends, mates, and mentors may, therefore, tell us something about how we came to have the preferences we do.

This volume is the first in a new series, *Advances in Visual Cognition.* Visual cognition encompasses a huge range of topics, including face and object perception; attention; visual memory; visual imagery; spatial cognition; modularity; frames of reference for recognition; visual-motor control; perceptual organization; reading and lexical access; and the perception of form, depth, motion, color, texture, symmetry and surfaces. We chose the perception of facial attractiveness as the topic for our first volume because research in this area has been enormously productive, resulting in a radical shift in our understanding of what makes a face attractive and why. Twenty years ago, standards of beauty were thought to be idiosyncratic and arbitrary, the products of culture and the media, and certainly of little interest to students of the human mind. Today, the picture looks very different. Instead of being idiosyncratic, many standards of beauty appear to be highly consistent across individuals, cultures, and even species. Instead of being arbitrary, they appear to reflect the operation of basic perceptual and cognitive mechanisms and the selection pressures operating during human evolutionary history. At the same time, they can also be fine-tuned by individual learning histories and social goals. The chapters in the present volume illustrate the productive combination of cognitive, evolutionary, cultural, and motivational perspectives that has led to this new view.

REFERENCES

Langlois, J. H., & Roggman, L. A. (1990). Attractive faces are only average. *Psychological Science, 1*, 115–121.

Langlois, J. H., Roggman, L. A., Casey, R. J., Ritter, J. M., Reiser-Danner, L. A., & Jenkins, V. Y. (1987). Infant preferences for attractive faces: Rudiments of a stereotype? *Developmental Psychology, 23*, 363–369.

Rubenstein, A. J., Kalakanis, L., & Langlois, J. H. (1999). Infant preferences for attractive faces: A cognitive explanation. *Developmental Psychology, 15*, 848–855.

Zebrowitz, L. A. (1997). *Reading faces.* Boulder, CO: Westview Press.

ACKNOWLEDGMENTS

We would like to thank the following individuals for reviewing drafts of the chapters: Tom Alley, Nalini Ambady, Diane Berry, Jamin Halberstadt, Don Kalick, Linda Mealey, Jim McKnight, Joann Montepare, and Leigh Simmons.

CHAPTER 1

What Makes a Face Attractive and Why: The Role of Averageness in Defining Facial Beauty

Adam J. Rubenstein, Judith H. Langlois, and Lori A. Roggman

Scientists and philosophers have written and conjectured about beauty for centuries. Today one can find over 2,500 different research studies by using the search terms *physical attractiveness* (which includes the term *beauty*) and *physical appearance* in psychological journals alone. Yet, much of this research has been conducted without a conceptual definition of what attractiveness is or why judges seem to agree about it. This chapter will discuss facial attractiveness, our theory of what characterizes facial attractiveness, and why certain faces have more appeal than others, even to young infants. Findings from both adult and infant research suggest that there may be a universal standard of attractiveness, and we will discuss what aspect of faces seems to be universally perceived as attractive. We will also speculate about the mechanisms that could account for the development of attractiveness preferences and for the surprising fact that even young infants seem to recognize attractiveness in faces.

UNIVERSAL PREFERENCES FOR ATTRACTIVENESS?

Before we begin, however, it is necessary to dismiss a myth about facial attractiveness, "Beauty is in the eye of the beholder." This adage dates back at least to the third century BC, "Beauty is not judged objectively, but according to the beholder's estimation" (Theocritus, *The Idyll*). The adage is commonly heard, taught to children by almost all mothers and grandmothers, and is part of received wisdom. Simply put, the adage states that "different people have different ideas about what is beautiful" (Spears, 1993, p. 45)—based on individual experiences, we each develop idiosyncratic opinions about attractiveness and about who is and isn't attractive. Thus, using this adage to predict human behavior, even people raised in common environments should encounter unique faces that would affect their concept of attractiveness. Furthermore, if the adage is true, people from different backgrounds and experiences, such as those from different cultures, should develop very different definitions of attractiveness. And, if the adage is true, there is no point to this chapter or even to this volume because there is no common ground for discussion.

Empirical evidence, however, has shown the adage to be false. Using meta-analysis, we examined 130 samples of attractiveness ratings from 94 different studies in the face perception literature (Langlois et al., 2000). This meta-analysis quantitatively assessed the agreement (or disagreement) of thousands of people, both young and old, male and female. The primary studies examined in the meta-analysis largely used Likert-type ratings to assess both the agreement of adults and the agreement of children from within the same culture as well as agreement among adults from different ethnic and cultural groups. Contrary to the adage, the results indicated high agreement about attractiveness from even very different types of raters (see Table 1.1). Effective reliabilities, which assess the reliability of the mean of the judges' ratings and, thus, can be generalized to random raters (Langlois et al., 2000; Rosenthal, 1991), were analyzed in four separate analyses.[1] The average within-culture effective reliability was $r = .90$ for ratings of adult faces and $r = .85$ for ratings of child faces, both $ps < .05$. The average cross-ethnic (ratings of different ethnic groups by raters living in the same culture) effective reliability was $r = .88$. Cross-cultural (ratings of different ethnic groups by raters from different cultures) effective reliability was even higher, $r = .94$. These reliabilities for cross-ethnic and cross-cultural ratings of attractiveness were statistically significant, meaningful, and show consistent agreement among raters regardless of particular experience with different types of faces.

Our meta-analysis also examined variables that might moderate agreement, such as year of publication, sample size, gender of the person being judged, and the situation in which the person was judged (e.g., rating photographs vs. *in situ* ratings). Somewhat to our surprise, not a single moderator variable had consistent or substantial effects on levels of agreement. While one might assume that methodological differences or group membership could influence attractiveness ratings, it instead appears that a fundamental characteristic of the human face is primarily responsible for agreement regarding facial attractiveness.

These results indicate that beauty is not simply in the eye of the beholder. Rather, raters agree about the attractiveness of both adults and children, even across cultures. Our findings are consistent with those of Feingold (1992), who did a meta-analysis of reliability coefficients from samples of U.S. and Ca-

Population	Number of rated samples	Number of attractiveness raters	r
Within-culture ratings of adults	88	1694	.90
Within-culture ratings of children	28	1182	.85
Cross-cultural ratings of Adults	17	12146	.94
Cross-Ethnic ratings of Adults	9	659	.88

Table 1.1 Effective reliability of attractiveness ratings (Langlois et al., 2000).

nadian adults and obtained an average effective reliability of $r = .83$. Together, the meta-analyses of Feingold and Langlois and colleagues (2000) suggest a possibly universal standard by which attractiveness is judged. They also seriously question the common assumption that attractiveness ratings are culturally unique and merely represent media-induced standards.

Agreement regarding attractiveness is not limited to ratings made by adults and school-age children. Research conducted within the past 15 years has demonstrated a previously inconceivable fact: Young infants are aware of attractiveness and exhibit preferences for attractive faces that mirror those of adults (Kramer, Zebrowitz, 1995; Langlois et al, 1987; Langlois, et al 1991; Rubenstein, Kalakanis, & Langlois, 1999; Samuels & Ewy, 1985; Samuels, Butterworth, Roberts, Graupner, & Hole, 1994; Slater, Von der Schulenburg, Brown, & Badenoch, 1998). These studies (which used children ranging from newborns up to 25 months of age) use a method of investigation called the *visual preference design* in which infants are simultaneously presented with two faces, one attractive and one unattractive. The time the infant spends looking at each face is measured. The assumption underlying the paradigm is that looking longer to one face over another indicates a preference for that face on the part of the infant. The results of these visual preference studies with infants are impressively consistent: Infants as young as a few days of age prefer to look longer at faces adults judge as attractive. These findings are also robust, having been replicated numerous times using different samples of faces (e.g., multiple samples of female Caucasian faces) and faces from different groups (e.g., female and male Caucasian faces, female African American faces, infant faces).

Do the visual preferences of infants really represent a preference? This is an important question and should not be left to assumption. Therefore, Langlois, Roggman, and Rieser-Danner (1990) asked whether or not the visual preferences displayed by infants extended to other infant behaviors. In the first study, they asked a professional theatrical mask maker to design and construct attractive and unattractive masks for a woman who would later interact with infants as a "stranger." The masks were very lifelike and thin so that they moved with the stranger's face—she could smile, blink her eyes, and so on. The stranger played with 60 one-year-old infants using a strict, rehearsed script so that her behavior would be consistent for all infants. These interactions between the stranger and the babies were coded by observers who could not see the stranger's face and who, therefore, could not be biased by the attractiveness manipulation. In addition, the stranger was not aware of which mask she was wearing—all shiny surfaces were occluded and the masks were identical on the inside—so she could not behave differently based on how she believed she looked. Furthermore, coders evaluated the stranger's behavior in the two conditions and there were no significant differences in her behavior toward the infants. The results showed that infants' preferences for attractiveness extend beyond visual preferences. The infants more frequently avoided the stranger when she was unattractive than when she was attractive and they showed more negative emotion and distress in the unattractive than in the attractive condition. Furthermore, boys (but not girls) approached the female stranger more often in the attractive than in the unattractive condition, perhaps foreshadowing the types of interactions that will occur later when the boys are older!

In a second study, Langlois et al. (1991a) created dolls that were identical except for their faces. One doll had an attractive face while the other doll had an unattractive face. Twelve-month-olds were given dolls to play with and the length of time they played with each doll was recorded. The results revealed that the infants played with the attractive doll for almost twice the amount of time as they played with the unattractive doll. These two studies combined strongly indicate that infants' preferences for attractiveness are not limited to looking behavior. The quantity of visual responses and attention to attractive and unattractive faces is consistent with the frequency and duration of other behaviors toward faces, indicating that longer looking is a valid measure of preference.

Prior to the discovery that even young infants prefer attractive faces, it was widely assumed that preferences for attractive faces were learned. Received wisdom declared that attractiveness preferences were gradually developed through exposure to the preferences of our parents and peers as well as to the concept of beauty idealized by the media. However, studies showing that preferences for attractive faces are evident early in life and studies showing near universal preferences for attractive faces in adults seemingly eliminate the gradual socialization perspective. Both adults and infants appear to possess a common standard by which they judge attractiveness. Either infants are innately attracted to certain faces more than others or infants acquire their attractiveness preferences very early in life as part of basic processes of perceptual development.

The need for identifying *how* we develop attractiveness preferences becomes obvious when we look at the strong impact it has on our lives. Langlois and colleagues (2000) found in a meta-analysis of the attractiveness literature that attractive people have an advantage over unattractive people because they are viewed as having better social skills (e.g., Kuhlenschmidt & Conger, 1988), more competence at their jobs (e.g., Shapiro, Struening, Shapiro, & Barten, 1976), and as possessing leadership qualities that are lacking in others (e.g., Cherulnik, 1989). These differing opinions of attractive and unattractive people are manifested in actual treatment: attractive people receive higher salaries (e.g., Hamermesh & Biddle, 1994), elicit more cooperation (e.g., West & Brown, 1975), are rewarded more often (e.g., Raza & Carpenter, 1987), and in general have more positive interactions than unattractive people (e.g., Langlois, Roggman, & Rieser-Danner, 1990). There even seem to be differences in actual behavior in that attractive individuals are better adjusted (e.g., Cash & Smith, 1982), possess higher self-esteem (e.g., O'Grady, 1989), have more dating experience (e.g., Curran & Lippold, 1975), and are more extroverted than unattractive individuals (e.g., Garcia, Stinson, Ickes, Bisonette, & Briggs, 1991). How do these behavioral differences come about? Are they the results of attractiveness-based differential treatment? By understanding the pathway by which attractiveness preferences are developed, we may better understand how and when attractiveness is used as a cue in social interactions, and, subsequently, better understand how to ameliorate attractiveness biases and stereotypes.

The need to more fully understand the mechanism through which attractiveness preferences form is intensified by research investigating the early development of attractiveness stereotypes. Physical attractiveness may have an effect on the formation of stereotypes during infancy, even before socialization influences can become significant. Recent research has demonstrated that infants as young as 12 months of age are sensitive to the fact that positive valence is associated with attractive people and negative valence is associated with unattractive people (Rubenstein, 1999). Using an intermodal matching procedure, 12-month-olds were simultaneously shown video clips of attractive and unattractive faces while listening to voices speaking in either a pleasant or an unpleasant tone of voice. The infants looked longer at the attractive face when listening to the positive voice and looked longer at the unattractive face when listening to the negative voice. These results indicate that by the end of the first year of life infants associate pleasantness with attractive faces and unpleasantness with unattractive faces. Thus, by 12 months of age, the rudiments of the "beauty is good" stereotype that pervades our society seems to be in place.

WHAT MAKES A FACE ATTRACTIVE?

If standards and preferences for facial attractiveness are innate or acquired very early in life, and if there is considerable agreement about attractiveness both within and across cultures, then what exactly is facial attractiveness and why should it be so preferred by infants, children, and adults alike? The question of what makes a face attractive is an important one. One of the first attempts to define facial attractiveness came from the ancient Greeks who believed that aesthetic preferences could have their origins in mathematics. Specifically, the Greeks focused on the mathematical concept of the "Golden Proportion," a ratio of roughly 1:1.6 that is used to describe the relationship between different parts of physical structures (Huntley, 1970). Natural objects such as the structure of flowers or the spiral in a seashell exemplify the existence of the golden ratio in nature (see Figure 1.1). The ratio has been used by architects to create structures that are pleasing to the eye, such as the Parthenon of ancient Greece. Even Renaissance artists such as Leonardo Da Vinci attempted to put the Golden Proportion to work in painting the human face by using it as a guide for the placement of facial features.

Research conducted in the late 1800s provided a first hint of another way to conceptualize facial attractiveness. Francis Galton (1833, 1888) wondered if certain groups of people had certain facial characteristics. To find the answer, he created photographic composite images of the faces of vegetarians and criminals to see if there was a "typical" facial appearance of the vegetarian or the criminal (although we can speculate about Galton's reasons for creating the "criminal" face, we must leave to the reader's imagination his reasons for

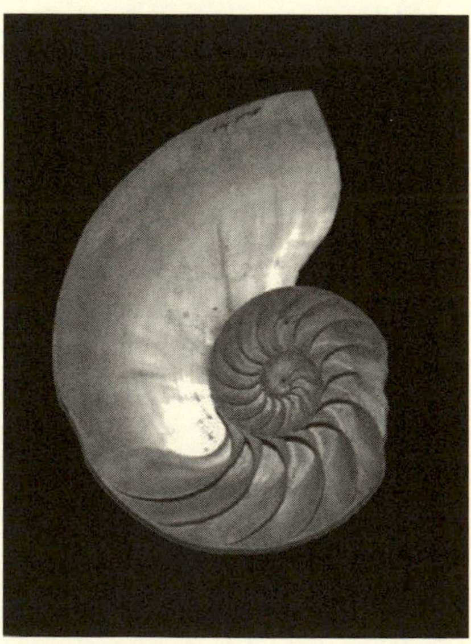

Figure 1.1. Golden Proportion in nature.

creating the "vegetarian" face!). Galton overlaid multiple images of faces onto a single photographic plate so that each individual face contributed roughly equally to a final composite face. While the resulting "averaged" faces did little to allow the *a priori* identification of either criminals or vegetarians, Galton observed that the composite image was more attractive than the component faces. Similar observations were made in 1886 and 1887 by Stoddard, who created composite faces of members of the National Academy of Sciences and graduating seniors of Smith College.

These anecdotal observations of a nineteenth-century English anthropologist and an American psychologist proved insightful. Langlois and Roggman (1990) systematically examined whether mathematical averageness is linked with facial attractiveness. Langlois and Roggman randomly selected photographs of 96 female Caucasian faces and 96 male Caucasian faces that were then divided into three different groups (for generalization purposes) of 32 faces for each gender. Each of 32 photographs in a group were computer scanned and digitized. Although perceived as a perceptual whole, facial images actually are composed of multiple rows and columns of small dots (pixels) that vary in values of brightness and color. When mathematically averaging two images, pixel values are added and divided so that the resulting composite image represents the mathematical average of the individual faces (see Figure 1.2). In this manner, composite images of 2-, 4-, 8-, 16-, and 32 faces were created for each group (see Figure 1.3). These mathematically averaged faces and their component faces were rated for attractiveness by 300 judges on a 5–point

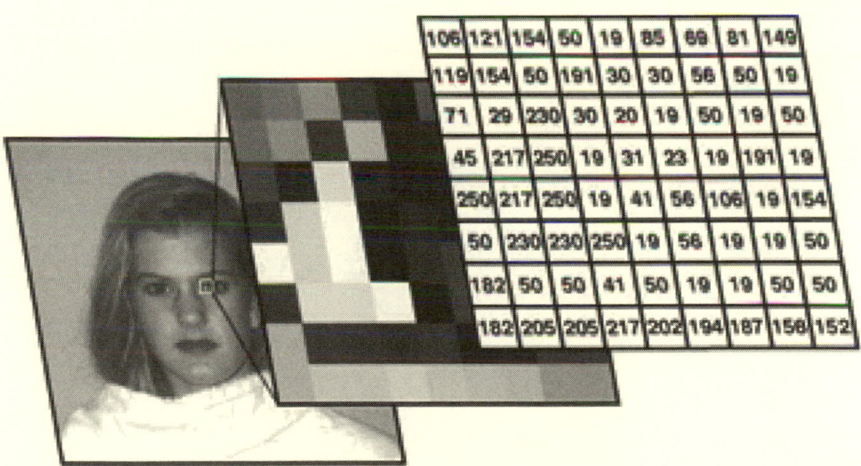

Figure 1.2 Pixel values of faces from Langlois et al. (1994). The box represents the numerical values of the individual pixels on the black-and-white image. The shading of each pixel has a corresponding numerical value, called a gray value. When mathematically averaging faces, overlapping pixels from the two images are averaged to produce a mathematically average image.

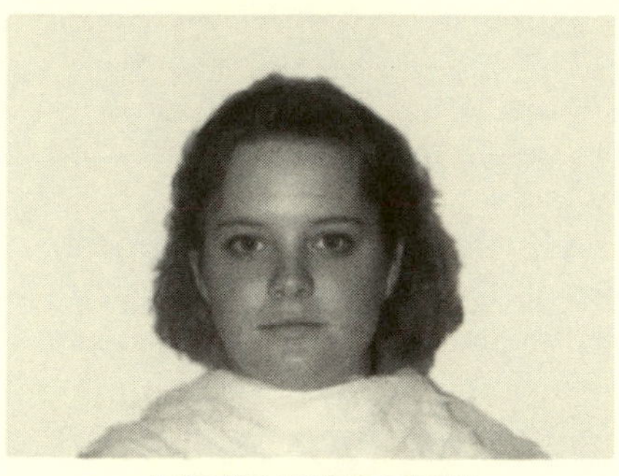

2-FACE COMPOSITE

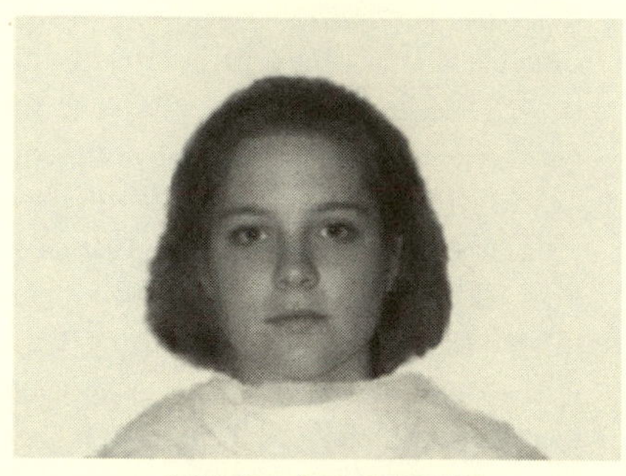

4-FACE COMPOSITE

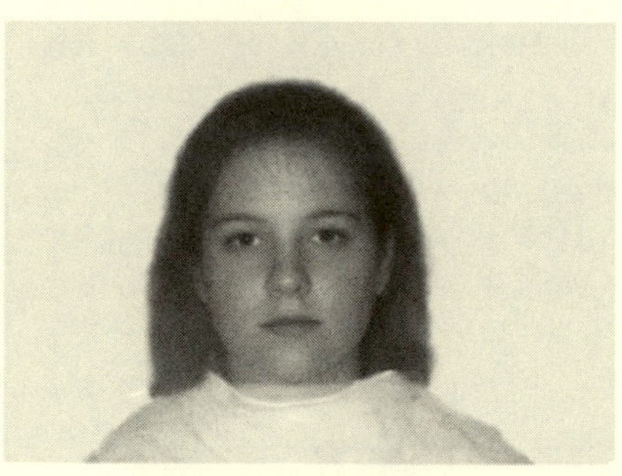

8-FACE COMPOSITE

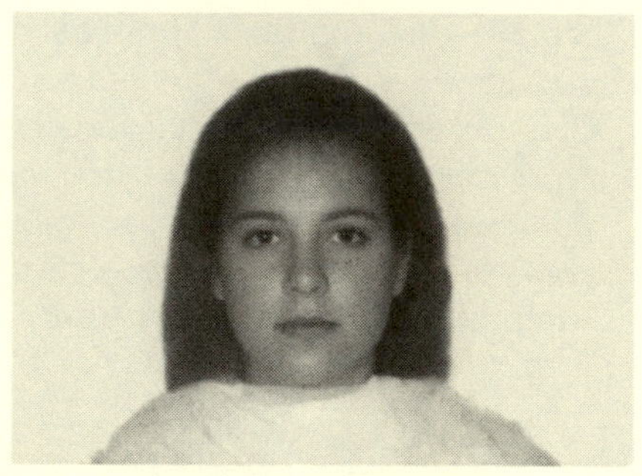

16-FACE COMPOSITE

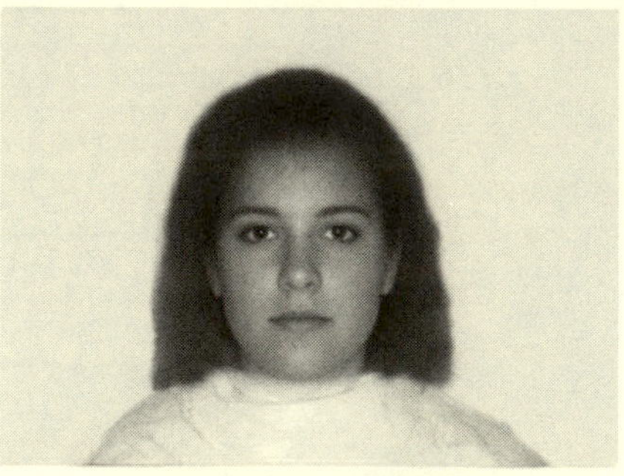

32-FACE COMPOSITE

Figure 1.3. Progression of mathematically averaged faces from 2 faces to 32 faces.

Likert scale (1 = very unattractive, 5 = very attractive). The findings were statistically significant and robust. For each of the groups of male and female faces, the 16-and 32-face averaged faces were rated as higher in attractiveness than the mean attractiveness ratings of the component faces and as more attractive than the composites consisting of fewer faces. These results illustrate that a face representing the central tendency or average of a population is attractive.

Current research into the attractiveness of averaged faces has moved from a computer overlaying procedure in which pixel values are averaged to a computer morphing procedure. Keypoint markers are placed on an image of the face to designate the location, size, and configuration of the facial features (e.g., Benson & Perrett, 1993; see Figure 1.4). Facial images are then combined based upon the average of the keypoint locations to create averaged faces. The keypoint morphing technique produces averaged faces that lack the "ghosting" due to blur or soft focus often associated with the original averaging studies of Langlois and Roggman (1990). While the morphing procedure is still a form of mathematical averaging, it has the benefit over the pixel averaging procedure that it allows for more accurate alignment of facial features in order to create higher quality images. Using this methodology, Rhodes and Tremewan (1996) digitized photographs of faces and extracted line drawings from the images. The line drawings were mathematically averaged together. The resulting averaged line drawings were rated as higher in attractiveness than were the individual nonaveraged faces. Rubenstein, Langlois, and Kalakanis (1999) went beyond line drawings of faces and applied the morphing technique to real faces. Like the Langlois and Roggman study, a

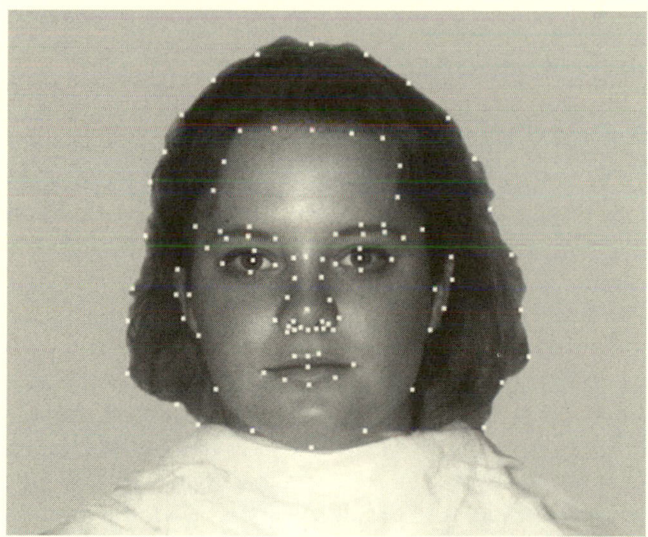

Figure 1.4. Example of keypoint placement on the human face.

sample of 32 female Caucasian faces was randomly selected from a large database of faces. These faces were then averaged using the keypoint technique to create 2-, 4-, 8-, 16-, and 32-face averages that were rated for attractiveness along with their component faces. The results indicated a strong pattern of preference for the averaged faces that mirrored the findings of the earlier Langlois and Roggman study.

Up to this point, the research described has focused on the attractiveness of Caucasian faces. It is clear, however, that preferences for mathematically averaged faces go beyond Caucasian faces to faces from other ethnic groups. Pollard (1995) generalized the finding that averaged faces are attractive from primarily Caucasian to a cross-cultural sample of judges. Pollard created mathematically averaged faces of male Caucasian and female Caucasian faces by creating photographic overlays using timed exposures. These faces were then rated for attractiveness by judges from four different countries: New Zealand, India, China, and Nigeria. Despite the differences in cultural backgrounds, high cross-cultural agreement was found for the attractiveness ratings of the faces. However, the use of photographic overlays is not the best methodology to create mathematically averaged faces because of the inherent imprecision involved in the timing of photographic exposure. In contrast, Rhodes, Harwood, Yoshikawa, and Nishitani (Chapter 2, this volume) used the morphing procedure described above and also found cross-cultural preferences for mathematically averaged faces. Rubenstein, Langlois, Kalakanis, Larson, and Hallam (1997) extended the finding that averaged faces are attractive faces to a sample of female Asian faces. Using a morphing procedure, samples of 32 female Caucasian faces and 32 female Asian faces were separately combined to form a mathematically averaged face for each ethnic group. The averaged faces and their component faces were evaluated by Caucasian and Asian judges. High cross-cultural agreement was found in the attractiveness ratings from both ethnic groups, indicating that the Caucasian and Asian judges considered the same faces to be attractive, regardless of the ethnicity of the faces being judged. Both the averaged female Caucasian faces and averaged female Asian faces were rated as attractive, demonstrating that the average of a population is attractive regardless of the ethnicity of the faces from which they are created and regardless of the ethnicity of the raters. Thus, adults from different cultural backgrounds consider averaged faces to be attractive.

The finding that averaged faces are attractive and preferred is not limited to just preferences of adults. Even 6-month-old infants consider averaged faces to be attractive (Rubenstein et al., 1999). In a study parallel to Langlois and colleagues (1987, 1990), infants were shown pairs of a female Caucasian 32–face averaged composite face and a female Caucasian unattractive individual face. The attractiveness of the faces was determined by adult judges. The infants' looking time to each face was measured and the results showed that infants look significantly longer at averaged faces compared to unattractive faces.

Thus young infants demonstrate a preference for averaged faces just as adults do.

It is important to be clear about what we mean by an "average" face. A mathematically averaged face is not an average or common face. It is not average in facial attractiveness. The term "average" (more accurately referred to as "averaged" face) refers only to the physical configurations of faces created by averaging multiple individual faces together mathematically. These mathematically averaged faces have features and a configuration representative of the population average. A mathematically averaged face is *not* average in perceived attractiveness or other psychological dimensions associated with faces. Rather, these averaged faces and any individual faces that are close in configuration to the mathematical average are extreme, not average, in attractiveness.

CRITICISMS OF THE AVERAGE HYPOTHESIS

The explanation of facial attractiveness as the average of the population is not without criticism. Pittenger (1991) argued that averaging pixel values of a matrix of the whole face as we did rather than averaging spatial locations of anatomically defined features does not preserve the shapes and locations of anatomical features. Langlois, Roggman, Musselman, and Acton (1991b) showed that averaging matrices of gray values in effect creates a frequency map that is similar to a contour map in which contrast information is preserved. Such a map clearly does preserve the shape and location of anatomical features, as much work has previously shown (Ballard & Brown, 1982; Marr, 1977; Ramachandran, 1988). Furthermore, the keypoint average method, discussed above, does average anatomical features, and produces the exact same results as the pixel matrix averaging procedure with respect to judgments of attractiveness.

Pittenger's (1991) second complaint was that, by averaging two-dimensional representations of faces normally perceived in three dimensions, we distorted distances along lines not perpendicular to the viewing direction. In a mathematical proof, Langlois and colleagues (1991b) showed that this concern was trivial and inconsequential, as has also been proven in other research (Acton & Bovick, 1990; Barrow & Tennebaum, 1981; Marr, 1982).

Pittenger's (1991) final criticism was that he believed that a functional "optimal value" was preferable to using a measure of central tendency to understand what explains facial attractiveness. We replied then (Langlois et al., 1991b) and still believe today that such an argument about "optimal" values is circular and lacks both parsimony and scientific rigor: How is "optimal" to be defined and operationalized? Optimal with respect to what? Very widely spaced eyes might provide superior binocular vision and protruding ears might provide superior sound localization but neither are considered to be very attractive on a face. Likewise, by what set of weights are we to judge whether "optimal" eye width is more or less important than "optimal" ear protrusion? Until the proponents of an "optimal" definition of attractiveness specify their construct, it cannot be falsified and we, therefore, do not see its utility.

Artifacts of Averaging

Other early criticisms of our theory that "averageness" produces attractive faces claimed that artifacts of the averaging process were better explanations for the attractiveness of mathematically averaged faces than was "averageness." For example, Alley and Cunningham (1991) suggested several artifacts of the averaging process that could result in increased attractiveness of averaged faces: blurring and smoothing that would remove blemishes, softening of focus that would increase the appearance of youthfulness, and an increase in symmetry that would remove unattractive asymmetries. Both logic and empirical testing show that these artifacts do not explain the attractiveness of averaged faces.

Blurring and Smoothing

Blurring and smoothing of faces result when faces are averaged together and, therefore, composite faces can have a "soft focus," as well as smooth, uniform skin tones, free of blemishes. In our facial averaging studies, however, individual faces are always "smoothed and blurred" to match any smoothing and blurring that occurs in averaged faces as a result of the computer manipulation (Langlois & Roggman, 1990; Langlois et al., 1994; Rubenstein et al., 1999). Therefore, any differences documented between averaged and individual faces cannot be due to smoothing or blurring because the faces are equivalent on these dimensions. Second, we (Langlois et al., 1994) further examined artifacts of the averaging process by photographing the same individual multiple times and creating an averaged face from these different images of the same person. Thus, individual faces were image-processed in exactly the same manner as a mathematically averaged face consisting of multiple different faces. If "smoothing and blurring" and other artifacts of computer averaging procedures are responsible for attractiveness, rather than averaging together different faces, the face resulting from averaging together multiple images of the same person should also be attractive. However, this is not what we found. Averaging together multiple images of the same person did not produce an attractive face, whereas averaging together multiple faces does (Langlois et al., 1994). Thus, the smoothing and blurring aspects of the averaging process cannot explain the attractiveness of the face. An averaged facial configuration is necessary and sufficient to create an attractive face.

Youthfulness

Youthfulness, although certainly related to perceived attractiveness, also is not adequate to explain the findings of Langlois and Roggman (1990). It is clear that, in general, young people are rated as more attractive than old people (e.g., Alley, 1988; Henss, 1991; Mathes, Brennan, Haugen, & Rice, 1985; Zebrowitz, Olson, & Hoffman, 1993). However, all the faces in the Langlois and Roggman sample were young college students. Thus, for youthfulness to account for the results of averaging, youthfulness would have to be correlated with attractiveness within this young sample. Langlois and colleagues (1994), therefore, had judges rate the perceived age of averaged faces as well as the age of the individual faces that comprised the averaged faces. There was no significant relation between youthfulness and attractiveness for either male or female faces ($r = .04$, n.s.; $r = .13$, n.s., respectively), demonstrating that the perceived youthfulness of the faces was not a criterion in determining the attractiveness of this particular sample of faces. Thus, although we certainly agree that young faces are generally rated as more attractive than old faces (e.g., Zebrowitz et al., 1993), youthfulness *per se* does not account for the attractiveness of averaged faces when they are derived from young faces. To reiterate, although we agree that youthfulness is a component of attractiveness when different age cohorts of faces are compared with each other, we disagree that youthfulness accounts for the attractiveness of averaged faces within age cohorts.

Symmetry

A number of critics have argued that symmetry, not averageness, accounts for the attractiveness of averaged faces. Alley and Cunningham (1991) claimed (but provided no empirical data in support of their claim) that the symmetry created by averaging faces together is what accounts for their attractiveness. Of course, symmetry in a face is important—no reasonable person would deny that severely distorted, asymmetrical faces are not attractive. Many craniofacial deformities involve severe distortions of symmetry in faces. It is also true that mathematically averaged faces are high in symmetry, indicating a relationship of some sort between averageness and symmetry. However, the real issue is as follows: Can symmetry *explain* the attractiveness of mathematically averaged faces? And, is symmetry *sufficient* to produce attractiveness in faces? Like youthfulness, to conclude that symmetry is the defining factor of attractiveness in normal faces, there must be a strong relationship between symmetry and attractiveness in normal faces. Furthermore, if symmetry is defining, perfectly symmetrical faces should be more attractive than faces that are not perfectly symmetrical.

To test whether or not symmetry defines attractiveness, Langlois and colleagues (1994) evaluated the attractiveness of symmetrical faces in two different ways. First, they evaluated the attractiveness of perfectly symmetrical, mirror-image faces (chimeras). Chimeras were created on a computer by dividing a face down a central, vertical line and replacing one side with a mirror image of the other (i.e., replacing the left side of the face with a mirror image of the right side). Both "left" and "right" chimerical faces were created. The chimerical faces and the original faces from which they were created were rated for physical attractiveness on a 5-point Likert scale. The results showed that the original (asymmetrical) faces were rated as significantly higher in attractiveness than the perfectly symmetrical chimerical faces. Inspection of the faces confirmed the validity of the statistics: Some perfectly symmetrical faces can be quite unattractive and some asymmetrical (within the normal range) can be quite attractive. (See Figure 1.5.)

Second, because the chimeric method of creating symmetrical faces can introduce structural abnormalities that create faces abnormal in appearance (Rhodes, Roberts, & Simmons, 1999), Langlois and colleagues (1994) created symmetric faces by averaging together a normal face and its mirror image. If the greater attractiveness of averaged faces is due simply to the symmetry produced by the averaging procedure, the mirror-image averaging technique of producing symmetrical faces should also produce highly attractive faces. However, this not what the results showed. Rather, composite faces made by averaging together many faces were judged to be significantly more attractive than composite symmetrical faces made by averaging together the same individual and its mirror image. This evidence refutes the claim that averaged faces are attractive because they are symmetrical rather than because they represent the central tendency of the population.

Grammer and Thornhill (1994) investigated both symmetry and averageness as potential explanations of attractive faces, and, like Alley and Cunningham (1991), claimed that attractiveness is defined by symmetry, not averageness. They created four composite faces made from four faces each, two composite faces made from eight faces each, and one composite face made

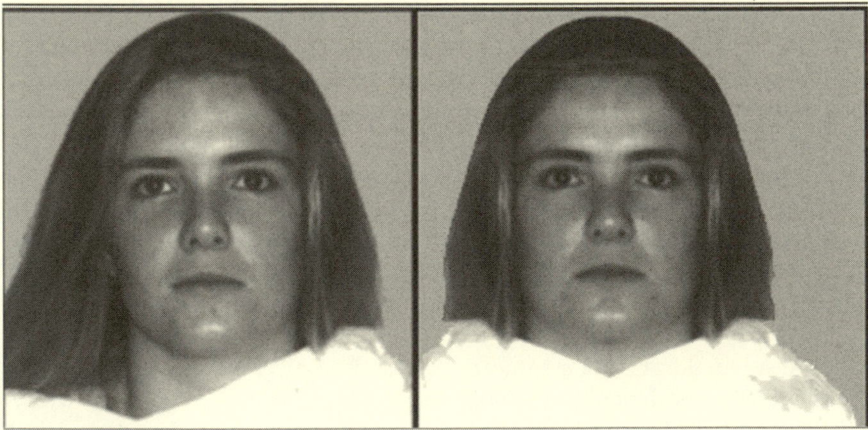

Figure 1.5. Example of individual face (left) and the corresponding symmetrical chimera (right). Used with permission.

from 16 faces for both male and female faces. After correlating level of averageness (4-, 8-, or 16-faces) with attractiveness ratings, Grammer and Thornhill concluded that averageness was not associated with high attractiveness. In contrast, after removing the impact of averageness on the face, facial symmetry was related to perceived facial attractiveness. Thus, Grammer and Thornhill concluded that symmetry was more important than averageness in facial attractiveness. However, by creating primarily low-level averaged faces (four 4-face composites, two 8-face composites, and only one 16-face composite), Grammer and Thornhill analyzed the effect of averageness in a sample of averaged faces that did not approach the population average. No statistician would agree that sampling four or eight items from a large population is sufficient to approach the population mean and any impact of an averageness effect from the 16–face composite (the only face that would begin to approach a representation of the population average) would have been negated by analyzing the averaged faces as a group. Langlois and Roggman (1990) and Langlois and colleagues (1994) claim only that faces close in configuration to the mathematical average of a population are attractive, not that averaging together any small sample of faces will produce either attractiveness or averageness. Indeed, Langlois and Roggman found that attractiveness was highest for 32-face composites, whereas the lower-level composites were not significantly different in attractiveness from individual faces. By using faces that were primarily low-level composites (4- and 8-faces), Grammer and Thornhill failed to test the averageness hypothesis as proposed by Langlois and Roggman.

Rhodes, Sumich, and Byatt (1999) directly manipulated both the symmetry and averageness of faces, creating images of high and low mathematical averageness by warping individual faces so that their configurations were made closer to that of a mathematically average face or further from that of a mathematically average face. They also created perfectly symmetrical versions of the images by morphing each face with its mirror image. Their findings indicated that symmetry impacted attractiveness independently of averageness. However, the impact of averageness on facial attractiveness appeared to be more robust than that of symmetry. Furthermore, recent research (Rhodes et al., 1999) has demonstrated that two-face morphs rated high in averageness were rated as being more attractive than symmetrical images of faces, lending strength to the claim that averageness has a robust impact on the perception of facial attractiveness.

Finally, the importance of symmetry is also called into question by infant research. Using a visual preference paradigm, Samuels and colleagues (1994) presented infants with normal faces and with symmetrical chimerical faces. Infants ranging in age from 4 to 25 months of age preferred adult-rated attractive faces over merely symmetrical faces. If symmetry defines attractiveness, the infants should have preferred the symmetrical faces. However, given the questionable findings using chimerical faces in adult studies, research utilizing mirror-image averaging will be necessary to confirm that infants prefer attractive faces over symmetrical faces.

Thus, although it appears that symmetry is related to the attractiveness of a human face, it is not essential. Although a mathematically averaged face will be symmetrical, a symmetrical face is not necessarily highly attractive or close to the mathematical average of a population of faces. Furthermore, a highly attractive face is not necessarily highly symmetrical. This conclusion is consistent with the oft-heard comment of movie stars that insist on being photographed only from their "good side."

Facial Extremes

Some critics of the averaging hypothesis claim that extreme facial features rather than averageness account for attractiveness. The exaggerated feature argument rests in evolutionary theory and observation in which certain characteristics of males, such as large antlers or bright colors, are "attractive" to females of the species (almost always, nonhuman species). Presumably, as a result of female preferences, features like large antlers are subject to positive selection pressures. Interestingly, however, there are many differences and contradictions between the human and nonhuman literatures. In nonhumans, it is the male rather than the female who possesses these "extreme" features. In humans, in contrast, evolutionary theory posits that attractiveness and "extremes" are more important for females than males (Buss & Barnes, 1986; Buss & Schmitt, 1993; Jackson, 1992).

Furthermore, the logic of the exaggerated feature position is suspect because the "extreme/exaggerated" argument suffers from the same problem of circularity as the "optimal" argument discussed earlier. The exaggerated features theory does not specify how large the features must be or when a feature changes from being "exaggerated" to "abnormal" in human faces. Furthermore, even within the normal range of feature sizes, eyes that may be large for one face may appear as "small" for another face (see Figure 1.6). What is crucial is not the size of any individual feature but rather the entire configuration of the face and all its constituent parts. For human faces, exaggerated or large features in and of themselves cannot be a parsimonious explanation of attractiveness because one can easily imagine a face with huge eyes or a huge nose or a huge mouth that would not be attractive. Thus, the generalization from nonhumans to humans of the exaggerated feature hypothesis is dubious, at least with respect to the face. Furthermore, as we will see in the next section, the averageness hypothesis is not inconsistent with evolutionary theory.

Nonetheless, using evolutionary theory as the underlying theoretical rationale, Perrett, May, and Yoshikawa (1994) created a mathematically averaged face from a group of 16 highly attractive faces taken from a population of 60 faces. Perrett and his colleagues then exaggerated the facial features of the 16-face composite by calculating differences between it and a mathematically

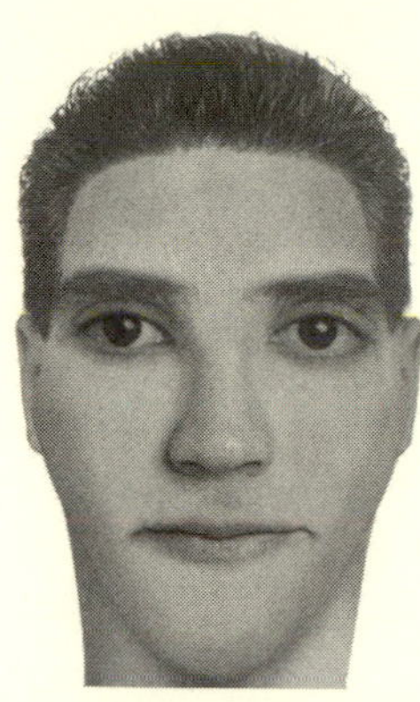

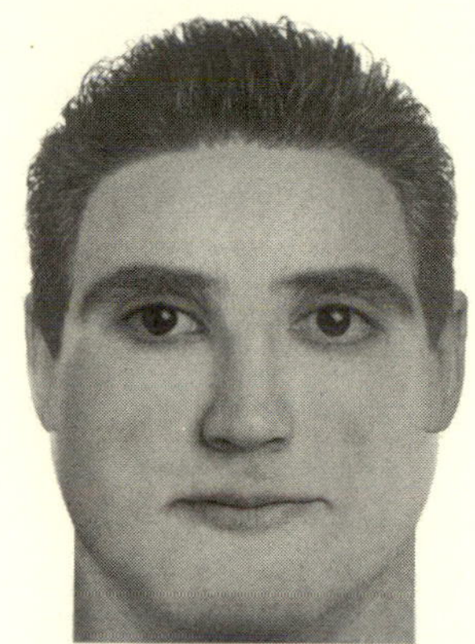

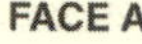

FACE A FACE B

Figure 1.6. Do extreme features produce attractive faces? Faces A and B have the exact same internal features but placed within a different head size. Most raters judge Face A as having eyes too large (bulging), a nose too large, and too large a mouth. They judge the entire face as unattractive, demonstrating that extreme features such as large eyes are not necessarily attractive. Most raters judge Face B, with identical features as Face A, to have eyes that are about average in size, and both a small nose and mouth. They judge the configuration of Face B to be more attractive (although not highly attractive) than Face A despite having identically sized internal features. Thus, it is the configuration of the entire face not the size of individual features that determines facial attractiveness.

averaged face created from all 60 faces. Keypoints on the "high attractive" averaged face were selected and compared to the corresponding keypoints on a mathematically averaged face representative of the population. From this comparison, the differences between the two faces were then exaggerated by 50%, creating a "caricature" face. Thus, if the eyes of the "high attractive" composite face were normally larger than the population average, the size of the eyes would be further exaggerated through the caricaturing process. Perrett and colleagues reported that Caucasian and Asian female faces with extreme facial features were more attractive than composite faces created by averaging together only very attractive female faces or composite faces comprised of female faces of all attractiveness levels (this last type being analogous to the Rubenstein et al. [1999], methodology). Their conclusions, however, were more likely due to artifacts of their methodology than evidence against the averaging hypothesis.

First, note that averaged faces were exaggerated to create the caricature faces, making averageness the foundation of the caricature faces. Thus, logically, creating faces that are deviations from this base or creating averaged faces from only very attractive faces cannot disconfirm our theory. Because more attractive faces are closer to the mathematical average of the population, creating averaged faces from only attractive faces merely yields a face even closer to the average because exclusion of unattractive faces reduces variation in the population. Second, note that Perrett's claims were overgeneralized: their results for female faces were not replicated by their own results for male faces. Finally, Perrett and colleagues (1994) used a forced-choice task that emphasized very small differences in facial appearance because judges were not allowed to rate faces as equally attractive. Research in the judgment and decision-making literature shows that forced-choice measures (such as that used by Perrett) and Likert-scale judgment measures (such as that used by Langlois) can, and quite frequently do, yield different results dependent on the judgment situation (see Payne, Bettmann, & Johnson, 1993, for a review). The debate concerning the more appropriate measure of true preferences is long-running (Guilford, 1954; Torgerson, 1958). Although far from resolved, some evidence indicates that forced-choice measures are more appropriate for judgments of highly specific characteristics based on highly specific dimensions such as which pair of eyes are further apart. In contrast, Likert-scale judgments are more appropriate when holistic judgments, such as attractiveness, are made (e.g., Acredolo, O'Connor, Banks, & Horobin, 1989). Because most face perception research indicates that we process faces as wholes instead of processing individual features (e.g., Ellis, Burton, Young, & Flude, 1997; Tanaka, Kay, Grinnell, Stansfield, & Szechter, 1998), a Likert scale may be more appropriate for judging attractiveness.

Nevertheless, to evaluate empirically Perrett and colleagues' (1994) claims, we created computer-generated faces in an identical fashion. Thus, we created the following types of Caucasian (male and female) and Asian (female) faces: Individual nonaveraged faces, population averaged (made from randomly selected faces of all levels of attractiveness, as per Rubenstein et al. [1999]), high averaged (made from only very attractive faces, as per Perrett et al.), and caricature (made by exaggerating facial features, as per Perrett et al.)

Unlike Perrett, we used several different methods of evaluating attractiveness. First, a group of judges (N = 135) rated the faces for attractiveness using a nonforced-choice task in which one choice allowed judges to indicate that the two faces were equally attractive. Another group of judges (N = 135) rated the faces on a Likert scale (1 = very unattractive, 5 = very attractive), the standard method of assessing attractiveness. A third group of judges (N = 300) indicated whether or not they believed the images depicted two different people or different photographs of the same person (see Figure 1.7).

Analyses of the Likert ratings showed that there were *no* significant differences in attractiveness among the caricatures, high averaged faces, and population averaged faces ($F(2,264) = 2.72$, n.s.). Furthermore, *a priori* power analyses ensured that these null results were not due to low statistical power (recall also that a large number of raters participated so that even small differences could have proved significant). Planned comparisons of the caricature faces with the high averaged and population averaged faces revealed no significant differences in the perceived attractiveness of the faces. When judges were

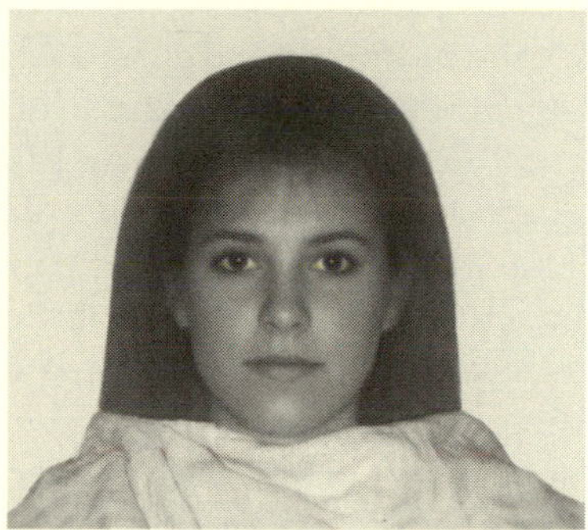
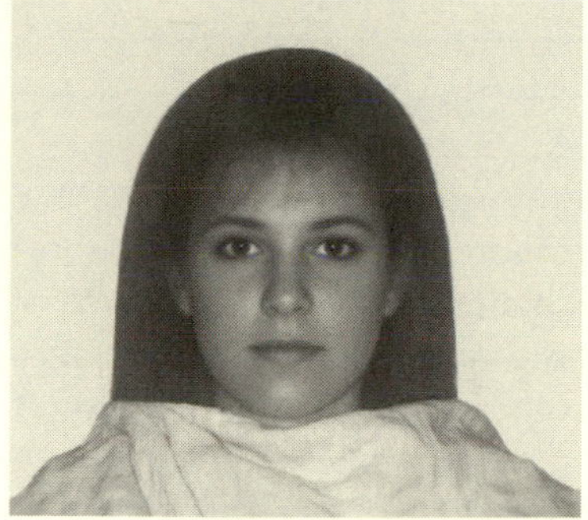

Figure 1.7. Comparison of mathematically average face (left) and caricature face.

asked to evaluate the faces with the extreme features (caricature faces) versus the averaged faces made from only very attractive faces (high averaged), they did not prefer either to the other. Instead they selected the "equally attractive" option more often than chance ($X^2(1) = 90.32$, $p < .001$). Indeed, judges believed these faces were merely different pictures of the same individual ($X^2(1) = 180.62$, $p < .001$). When judges were asked to evaluate the faces made from only very attractive faces (high averaged) versus faces made from randomly selected faces of all levels of attractiveness (population averaged), they did not prefer either to the other. Instead, they again selected the "equally attractive" option more often than chance ($X^2(1) = 14.03$, $p < .001$), and were more likely to believe that these faces were pictures of the same individual, although this pattern was not significant.

These results do not support Perrett and colleagues' (1994) findings and instead argue against the "extreme" view of attractiveness. Furthermore, visual inspection of the faces in Figure 1.6 shows that the differences between our averaged faces and Perrett and colleagues' caricature/extreme faces are trivial: The faces look much more alike than different. This should not be surprising given that the Perrett faces with "exaggerated" features used averaged faces as the foundation for creating exaggerated faces. Thus, although it may be possible to modestly enhance the attractiveness of a mathematically average face, Perrett's results support rather than refute our theory. This same logic extends to other work in which averaged faces are "feminized," such as Perrett and colleagues (1998) and Rhodes, Hickford, and Jeffery (2000).

Differences between Physical and Psychological Representations

In the most recent published criticism of averaging, Busey (1998) reported on differences between actual and predicted locations of morphed (averaged) faces in psychological face space. He reasoned that, because the morph of the images of two parent faces is represented by the average *physical* locations of the two parents (in terms of pixel locations), the morph should also be represented by the centroid of the *psychological* dimensions (e.g., perceived youthfulness, pudginess, etc.) associated with the parent faces as extracted from similarity ratings. Thus, a morph should represent 50% of each parent's physical attributes and judges should rate morphs as equally similar to each parent. Instead, Busey found deviations between the actual and "predicted" locations. That is, raters did not judge the morphs to be exactly in between the parent faces on the psychological dimensions. His report concluded that these deviations posed significant problems for research using image-processing techniques to derive a face that represents the centroid of a population.

Busey (1998) had raters judge the similarity between pairs of faces, including some morphed faces, and used multidimensional scaling (MDS) procedures to determine psychological dimensions of the morphs, their parent faces, and random pairs of faces. He converted these similarity ratings into a Euclidean space, where the distance between points represented the degree of psychological disparity between faces. He then interpreted the resulting clusters of points by inferring six "psychological" dimensions, such as age and adiposity, on which raters seemed to have differentiated the faces. This multidimensional space, based on similarity ratings, converted to Euclidian space, is what Busey termed "psychological face space."

We note several problems with these procedures and conclusions. First, the major thesis that physical and psychological space should be equivalent is inconsistent with our theory. Following such an argument, for example, would lead to the prediction that morphs should be judged to be in between their two parents in attractiveness. However, it is clear that when many faces are averaged or morphed together, the composite is more attractive than the individual "parents." This "deviance" or discrepancy between mathematical averaging and psychological dimensions is in fact the very basis for our hypothesis that Euclidean averageness is a major component in psychological attractiveness. Thus, Busey's (1998) findings confirm, not undermine, what we reported in 1990 and 1994.

Second, by making claims such as "age appears to be the primary dimension along which people organize faces," Busey (1998) implies that his face space can be generalized to all faces and all types of judgments about faces. The article argues that this particular psychological face space can be used to evaluate "experiments in which the physical prototype created by combining faces is assumed to correspond to a psychological prototype created by unknown psychological combination mechanisms" (p. 476). Yet, Busey used only bald men as stimuli. What if women's faces had been included? Wouldn't gender emerge as a primary dimension? Indeed, in other MDS studies of psychological space, different sets of dimensions emerge showing that MDS solutions are highly dependent on input (Hirschberg, Jones, & Haggerty, 1978; Pedelty, Levine, & Shevell, 1985). Other studies have shown that faces are represented differently depending upon the psychological task at hand (Gerrig, Maloney, & Tversky, 1991; Markman, 1999). It is very unlikely that facial representation is a stored, fixed "thing" that is timeless and divorced from context and task. Any single MDS solution is only one of many possible representations of how the human mind represents faces.

Summary

We end this section by reiterating what we claim and what we do not claim about the importance of averageness in human faces. Our claim is that averageness is essential to facial attractiveness. Without averageness, a face will not be judged as attractive. However, we do not claim that averageness is exclusive. Other factors influence the perceived attractiveness of the human face. Youthfulness and symmetry, among others, have all been shown to enhance the attractiveness of a face in certain situations. However, although these factors can enhance attractiveness, none are sufficient causes of attractiveness. For example, a face can be both youthful and unattractive. It is only in combination with averageness that youthfulness creates a highly attractive face. Averageness is the only characteristic discovered to date that is both necessary and sufficient to ensure facial attractiveness—without a facial configuration close to the average of the population, a face will not be attractive no matter how smooth, youthful, or symmetrical. Averageness is *fundamental.*

MECHANISMS

We turn now to a discussion of the mechanisms underlying preferences for attractive faces. Why do people prefer attractive faces and how might various explanatory mechanisms relate to averageness? Given that even young infants prefer attractive faces, it is very unlikely preferences are socialized, gradually learned, and due merely to media exposure. Instead, two other theoretical accounts suggest potential answers.

Evolution and Innate Preferences for Attractive Faces

Very young infants exhibit preferences for attractive faces. Are such preferences innate or acquired? Evolutionary theory provides an explanation for how preferences for attractive faces might be built into the young organism from birth. Indeed, the averageness hypothesis does not oppose an evolutionary point of view and is in fact quite compatible with it. Stabilizing or normalizing selection is more ubiquitous than directional selection in evolution. Normalizing selection selects for average-size physical characteristics in the species-typical range and selects against extremes (e.g., Barash, 1982). Average physical characteristics, according to this view, are indicative of health and genetic fitness (Thornhill, 1998). Mating with healthy attractive partners would increase the probability of successful reproduction and genetic transmission: Potential offspring from such a union would have a higher chance of survival. Thus, an evolved tendency to prefer average physical characteristics may underlie preferences for attractive "averaged" faces. If such preferences have evolved, perhaps they are also innate and present at birth.

The evidence on whether or not contemporary attractive people are healthier than unattractive people is mixed. When strangers are asked to make attributions of health based solely on a photograph of the face, attractive people are consistently assumed to be healthier than unattractive people (Buss & Barnes, 1986). However, studies using only impressions of strangers based on photographs are not adequate to test the health hypothesis. Because of the well-known "beauty is good" stereotype, judges have a positive bias toward attractive individuals. Therefore, associations between perceptions of facial attractiveness and perceptions of health in these rating studies probably reflect a positive halo effect rather than a true relation between attractiveness and real health.

To investigate whether or not health and facial attractiveness are related, studies must examine objective measures of health. Only a few have done so, probably because of the difficulty of obtaining samples for which actual (as opposed to perceived) measures of health are available. We were able to locate five studies in which some kind of nonattributional measure of health as a function of facial attractiveness was available. Reis, Wheeler, Nezlek, Kernis, and Spiegel (1985) collected a number of health indices but found few significant associations between attractiveness and health in college students. A single moderate relation was found in which unattractive students visited the student health center more frequently than did attractive students. Hansell, Sparacino, and Ronchi (1982) found a relation between attractiveness and health as assessed by blood pressure. Unattractive people had higher blood pressure than attractive people. However, the interpretation of both visits to a student health center and blood pressure are problematic. Are less attractive people fundamentally less healthy than attractive people? Or do unattractive people visit the health center and have higher blood pressure because life is more stressful for them because they are judged and treated less favorably than attractive people are (Langlois et al., 2000)?

Shackelford and Larsen (1999) obtained self-reports of health and objectively assessed heart rate recovery in a study of 66 undergraduate women and 34 undergraduate men. Self-reported symptoms of the minor complaints assessed in this study (headache, stuffy nose, muscle soreness) are neither objective nor important measures of real health and should not be used to evaluate "health." For heart rate recovery, a single significant correlation emerged for the small sample of males but not for the larger sample of females. Thus, the results of this study provide weak and equivocal support for the proposed link between health and attractiveness.

Using the archival records of a longitudinal sample ranging in age from 11 to 66, Kalick, Zebrowitz, Langlois, and Johnson (1998) found that, if anything, adolescent attractiveness *falsely* advertised health: Although raters who made health attributions judged attractive individuals to be more healthy than unattractive individuals, the correlation between facial attractiveness and a variety of objective composite health scores (derived from physician and hospital records) was actually slightly negative. The study, which benefited from a large sample size, also found no significant relation between attractiveness and the number of offspring. Thus, the results of the Kalick and colleagues study question the evolutionary assumption that attractiveness is related to actual health, at least in individuals born between 1920 and 1929.

Finally, Cronin, Spirduso, Langlois, and Freedman (1999) separated adult health and physical fitness into different components and obtained actual performance measures for each. Like the results of Kalick and colleagues (1998), no significant relation between attractiveness and health emerged. Interestingly, however, there was a statistically significant relation between facial attractiveness and physical fitness. Fitness (endurance, strength, balance, and flexibility) was defined as "the ability to carry out daily tasks with vigor and alertness, without undue fatigue, and with ample energy to enjoy leisure-time pursuits and to meet unforeseen emergencies" (U.S. Department of Health and Human Services, 1996). Health (resting heart rate, blood pressure rankings, and body fat percentages) was defined as a positive state of physical, mental, and social well-being or the absence of disease and illness (U.S. Department of Health and Human Services, 1996). Health status and fitness may differ in their relation to attractiveness ratings because they represent two different dimensions of performance. Health status, for example, is not the highest range of physical potential for a person; the average person may have adequate health, but the fit individual surpasses "good" or average health. Thus, a level of fitness beyond adequate health may be required to observe a relationship between physical function and attractiveness, at least in our modern, primarily healthy society. Obviously, very poor health would contribute to a person's appearance, but, within the normal range of older adults, attractiveness predicts fitness better than resting heart rate, blood pressure rankings, and body fat percentages.

Another approach to testing mechanisms underlying the preference for attractiveness is to determine whether or not such preferences are innate. The term *innate* is used in different ways by different people. Here, we use the term as many developmental psychologists do and consistent with the preferred dictionary definition: present at birth, and not requiring any experience to be manifested. Logically, if preferences for attractive faces are *not* present at birth, evolutionary mechanisms cannot be ruled out because many innate characteristics are not expressed until later in development (i.e., puberty). However, if preferences for attractive faces *are* present at birth, many experiential accounts of how preferences for attractiveness develop can be ruled out. Thus, studying newborn infants can yield insight into the mechanism responsible for the ubiquitous preferences for attractive faces.

Some research suggests that preferences for *faces* over nonfacial patterns are evident in newborns prior to any direct visual experience with faces (Goren, Sarty, & Wu, 1975; Morton & Johnston, 1991). In these newborn studies, infants are presented with geometric shapes configured in the shape of a human face or in a scrambled configuration. Infants pay significantly more attention to stimuli representing a facial configuration, indicating an innate predisposition to pay attention to the human face. Indeed, there may be a selective advantage for infants to prefer faces. Attending to facial stimuli is important for social interaction, so infants may have a built-in preference for faces (e.g., Linn, Reznick, Kagan, & Hans, 1982). Perhaps if infants are born with preferences for faces over nonfaces, they also are born with preferences for attractive over unattractive faces, given that attractive faces are better "examples" of faces than are unattractive faces.

To determine whether preferences for attractiveness are innate, it is necessary to conduct research with newborns that have no experience with faces. Needless to say, such research is very difficult to conduct. Some research has been conducted with newborns, but the evidence from these studies for an innate attractiveness preference is mixed. Slater and colleagues (1998) used a visual preference paradigm and measured looking times toward pairs of attractive and unattractive female faces in very young infants (average age = 72 hours). The infants looked longer at the attractive faces. However, two limitations of the study make innateness a questionable interpretation of the data. The first is that the infants in the study ranged in age from 14 hours to 151 hours and it is therefore likely that they had substantial experience with faces prior to participating in the study. Early and rapid *learning* about faces based on experience has previously been demonstrated by Walton and Bower (1994). Walton and Bower showed newborn infants individual faces and then presented them with a face that was the mathematical average of the individual faces. The newborns reacted to the averaged face as a familiar face, indicating that the infants were encoding facial information from very brief exposures. Thus, innate preferences for attractive faces can be claimed only if such rapid learning is controlled or eliminated.

The second limitation of the Slater and colleagues (1998) study is that the infants were held by an experimenter who supported the infant's head and body and was not blindfolded, or in some other way prevented from seeing the stimuli, as is typical in most studies involving infant looking times (e.g., Langlois et al., 1987; Quinn, 1987; Younger, 1985). It also is possible, therefore, that the infants' looking behavior was subtly affected by preferences of the experimenter who was holding the infant at the time of the study.

In her dissertation work at the University of Texas, Lisa Kalakanis (1997) tested two different samples of infants who were only about 15 minutes old. Kalakanis was present in the delivery room and recorded the infants' experience with faces. Unlike Slater and colleagues, she used a visual tracking procedure like that of Morton and Johnson (1991). In this procedure, the infant is lying on a crib and follows a moving photograph of either an attractive or unattractive face. The experimenter has no opportunity to influence infant looking behavior. Furthermore, all tracking was videotaped and coded by observers who could not see which face the infant was following, a procedure that thereby eliminated the possibility of experimenter/observer bias. The results of the study were mixed: Although the infants did seem to track attractive faces further than unattractive faces in some pairs, most of the time they did not. Given the methodological problems of the Slater and colleagues study and the mixed results of the Kalakanis study, it is premature to conclude that preferences for attractive faces are innate and do not require exposure or experience. Additional studies with newborns are critical to resolve the issue.

Cognitive Theory and Experience-Based Preferences for Attractive Faces

The literature in cognitive psychology suggests another mechanism underlying the preferences of both infants and adults for attractive faces. Cognitive representations, called prototypes, may be defined as a central exemplar or "average" of a category. Preferences for prototypes have been shown in several studies using a variety of categories of stimuli: color categories (Martindale & Moore, 1988), object categories (Whitfield & Slatter, 1979), and musical categories (Smith & Melara, 1990). Prototypes are perceived as "typical" and are "good" examples of a category of stimuli (Evans, 1967). Furthermore, faces rated as more attractive are also rated as more typical than less attractive faces (Light, Hollander, & Kayra-Stuart, 1981). Averaged faces, therefore, which are attractive, might be prototypic of the human face.

Prototypes are recognized as familiar even when never seen before—perhaps this is why both adults and infants prefer prototypical faces. Posner and Keele (1968) generated families of dot patterns, in which each dot varied in distance from a prototype (averaged from the examples) pattern of dots. Adults identified the prototype as familiar even when they saw it for the first time, indicating that they had cognitively "averaged" across the individual exemplars to form a prototype. Likewise, Bomba and Siqueland (1983) showed dot patterns to infants and found that they also responded to an averaged prototype as if familiar despite having never seen it before. Similar results have been found in infants viewing schematic drawings of faces. When shown a novel face with features that were averaged feature values from faces previously shown, infants looked longer at the face. Thus, the new face was treated as a familiar member of the category, or a prototype, even though they had not previously seen that particular configuration of facial features (Strauss, 1979).

Can infants extract a prototype face from complex images of real faces? Can infants cognitively average across faces they experience to form a prototype? If they cannot, an information processing or cognitive averaging account is an unlikely explanation for their preferences for attractive faces.

We empirically evaluated the viability of a cognitive averaging explanation for attractiveness preferences (Rubenstein et al., 1999). Six-month-olds were tested in a familiarization procedure, similar to that used by Bomba and Siqueland (1983). In this paradigm, infants are familiarized to a group of category exemplars, in our case, normal faces. After they are familiarized, they are shown multiple test comparisons in which looking time is measured. The general idea is that the infants' preference for novel stimuli, after a familiarization procedure, will reveal which test stimuli seem familiar to them and which do not.

In our research, the infants were familiarized to eight unfamiliar, attractive female faces, presented sequentially and repeatedly. Once the infants were familiarized with the faces, they were shown test comparisons in which different types of individual faces were paired with the prototype face created by averaging together the familiarization faces. The test faces were all equal in attractiveness to ensure that, in this case, infants were responding to novelty or familiarity, not attractiveness. Both familiar and novel faces were paired with each other and with the prototype/averaged face in the test trials. If infants can and do abstract the averaged representation from multiple exemplars of faces, the average of those faces should seem familiar to them, even though they have never seen it before, because it would match their internal representation formed during familiarization. Thus, according to the assumptions of this procedure, if infants are capable of averaging across faces to form prototypes, they will demonstrate a preference for *novel* faces over the averaged face because the never-before-seen averaged face would be experienced as familiar.

The infants in this study demonstrated a pattern of looking showing that they perceived the averaged face as familiar, even though they had never previously seen this face. Thus, cognitive averaging can explain both preferences for attractive faces (prototype faces) and why averageness is attractive. Through exposure to facial exemplars, even young infants can form a prototypical representation of the face.

The finding that infants look longer at novel, individual faces than at averaged faces is not contradictory with previous research showing that infants prefer both averaged and attractive faces (e.g., Langlois et al., 1991a; Rubenstein et al., 1999). First, recall that in the familiarization study, all the faces were equal in attractiveness, as judged by adults, so that the infants were selecting their preferred face based on it's familiarity, not on it's attractiveness. Second, the logic of the familiarization procedure is very different from that of the visual preference procedure. In the visual preference procedure, infants see two *novel* faces simultaneously. Babies, therefore, can choose to look at the novel face they prefer. In the familiarization procedure, the experimenter deliberately exposes infants to faces until the babies become *bored* with them—the faces become excessively *familiar* to the infants. Once bored with a particular stimulus, infants will look at something novel, assuming they remember the previous, overly familiar stimuli. If babies are shown the face of their own mothers over and over again, they will become bored and look longer at a subsequently shown novel face. This does not mean they do not prefer their mother to the novel face. It merely means that they are able to recognize and remember something very familiar in this experimental context. Thus, the different predictions about infant looking behavior in these two different experimental paradigms are logically consistent and not contradictory (see Hunter & Ames, 1988, for a review of infant preferences for familiarity and novelty).

The proximal cognitive averaging account can nicely account for race and ethnic differences in preferences for attractiveness. Although raters from many different cultures and ethnic groups significantly agree about who is and isn't attractive, and their rank orders of individual faces are highly similar, there are still group differences evident in the literature. Many studies demonstrate an in-group bias in which the in-group evaluates their own group as more attractive than an out-group (e.g. Moss, Miller, & Page, 1975). In-group bias would follow from different experience with different kinds of faces—the faces that are averaged together are different from group to group. Thus, although averaged faces (of 32 or more faces) from different ethnic groups are judged as attractive, ethnic differences in the facial features of the averaged face may still be preserved and preferred by the in-group. The reason that there is so much cross-group similarity in ranking the attractiveness of different types of faces is because faces from different ethnic groups are much more similar than they are different. And, any face, regardless of unique ethnic features, will be judged as attractive if it is close to the average of the central tendency of the population, according to our point of view.

The work showing that averaged faces are attractive, together with the work showing that infants form prototypes (averages) of faces, suggest that cognitive averaging may be the proximal ontogenetic mechanism underlying preferences for facial attractiveness. The work also suggests that preferences for attractive faces are not innate but rather that experience with faces is necessary for these preferences to develop. The amount of experience required, however, is not extensive because the brain of the human infant has probably evolved to process faces efficiently and to average across many different types of experienced stimuli. Thus, the work on cognitive averaging does not suggest that evolution is irrelevant to or in conflict with the proximal cognitive account. Cognitive averaging is an efficient information-processing strategy with likely adaptive consequences.

CONCLUSION

At the beginning of this chapter, we introduced a popular maxim concerning physical attractiveness: "Beauty is in the eye of the beholder." We now know through empirical research that this maxim is false. Furthermore, the theoretical perspective described in this chapter can parsimoniously explain why beauty is *not* in the eye of the beholder. Mathematical averageness is a necessary and fundamental characteristic of perceived attractiveness in the human face and the concept of averageness has theoretical deep roots in both evolutionary and cognitive psychology. The explanatory power of averageness theory is robust. Although other characteristics of the human face may be in some way associated with attractiveness (e.g., symmetry, youthfulness), none of these competing explanations can fully explain attractiveness preferences when averageness is removed from the equation nor can they explain the attractiveness of averaged faces.

Think of averageness like a cake—there are basic ingredients that are required before a cake can be a cake. Flour, sugar, eggs, and butter are fundamental—they are both necessary and sufficient to make a cake. There are other ingredients, however, that create cakes with individual identities: adding carrots produces carrot cake, adding chocolate produces chocolate cake. And finally, adding icing to the cake will make a sweeter cake. But without the flour, sugar, eggs, and butter, all you have is icing; without the flour, sugar, eggs, and butter, all you have is a carrot. For faces, characteristics like youthfulness and symmetry are analogous to icing and carrots—they are nice but not necessary. And, although we agree that adding youthfulness to averageness is surely better than adding wrinkles, without averageness, you are left with something that is nice but neither necessary nor sufficient.

What is the benefit of identifying the fundamental characteristic of a human face that makes it attractive and what is the benefit to understanding the manner in which attractiveness preferences are formed? Although averageness can explain how and why we prefer attractive faces, we must also focus on why it is important to understand what makes a face attractive. "Beauty is in the eye of the beholder" is not the only commonly heard piece of conventional wisdom that concerns attractiveness. For instance, "beauty is only skin deep" indicates that an individual's appearance is not a sincere reflection of their internal personality traits. "Never judge a book by its cover" dictates that we should not base our treatment of others upon their outward physical appearance. As the first maxim was proven false, these two additional sayings are also not supported empirically—they imply truisms that are not true. People are judged by their covers as if their beauty reflected inner characteristics deeper than their skin. Physical attractiveness is a salient piece of information that helps define our social interactions.

Through investigating the characteristics that cause a face to be perceived as attractive, we may gain greater insight as to how the physical attractiveness stereotypes that so greatly affect our social interactions are formed and how they may be attenuated. We believe that our conception of attractiveness in terms of mathematical averageness and our explanation of the evolutionary and cognitive mechanisms behind the development of attractiveness preferences can provide a substantial and necessary stepping stone to further address the impact of attractiveness on our society.

NOTE

1. Rosenthal (1991) indicates that two types of reliability statistics can be analyzed using meta-analysis: mean interrater reliabilities (used to estimate agreement between specific pairs of judges) and effective reliabilities (used to estimate the reliability of the mean of the judges' ratings). In our analysis of effective reliabilities, mean interrater reliabilities were converted to effective reliabilities in order to investigate general agreement about facial attractiveness.

REFERENCES

Acredolo, C., O'Conner, J., Banks, L., & Horobin, K. (1989). Children's ability to make probability estimates: Skills revealed through application of Anderson's functional measurement methodology. *Child Development, 60*, 933–945.

Acton, S. T., & Bovick, A. C. (1990). *GRUPO: A 3–D structure recognition system.* Paper presented at the Proceedings of the International Society for Optical Engineers (SPIE) Conference on Visual Communication and Image Processing, Lausanne, Switzerland.

Alley, T. R. (1988). The effects of growth and aging on facial aesthetics. In T. R. Alley (Ed.), *Social and applied aspects of perceiving faces* (pp. 51–62). Mahwah, NJ: Erlbaum.

Alley, T. R., & Cunningham, M. R. (1991). Averaged faces are attractive, but very attractive faces are not average. *Psychological Science, 2*, 123–125.

Ballard, D. H., & Brown, C. M. (1982). *Computer vision.* Upper Saddle River, NJ: Prentice-Hall.

Barash, D. P. (1982). *Sociobiology and behavior.* New York: Elsevier North Holland.

Barrow, H. G., & Tennebaum, J. M. (1981). Interpreting line drawings as three-dimensional surfaces. *Artificial Intelligence, 17*, 75–116.

Benson, P. J., & Perrett, D. I. (1993). Extracting prototypical facial images from exemplars. *Perception, 22*, 257–262.

Bomba, P. C., & Siqueland, E. R. (1983). The nature and structure of infant form categories. *Journal of Experimental Child Psychology, 35*, 294–328.

Busey, T. A. (1998). Physical and psychological representations of faces: Evidence from morphing. *Psychological Science, 9*, 476–483.

Buss, D. M., & Barnes, M. (1986). Preferences in human mate selection. *Journal of Personality and Social Psychology, 50*, 559–570.

Buss, D. M., & Schmitt, D. P. (1993). Sexual strategies theory: An evolutionary perspective on human mating. *Psychological Review, 100*, 204–232.

Cash, T. F., & Smith, E. (1982). Physical attractiveness and personality among American college students. *Journal of Psychology, 111*, 183–191.

Cherulnik, P. D. (1989, May). *Physical attractiveness and judged suitability for leadership.* Paper presented at the annual meeting of the Midwestern Psychological Association, Chicago.

Cronin, D. L., Spirduso, W. W., Langlois, J. H., & Freedman, G. (1999). *Health, Physical fitness, and Facial Attractiveness in Older Adults.* Unpublished manuscript.

Curran, J. P., & Lippold, S. (1975). The effects of physical attraction and attitude similarity on attraction in dating dyads. *Journal of Personality, 43,* 528–539.

Ellis, A. W., Burton, A. M., Young, A., & Flude, B. M. (1997). Repetition priming between parts and wholes: Tests of a computational model of familiar face recognition. *British Journal of Psychology, 88,* 579–608.

Evans, S. H. (1967). A brief statement of schema theory. *Psychonomic Science, 8,* 87–88.

Feingold, A. (1992). Good-looking people are not what we think. *Psychological Bulletin, 111,* 304–341.

Galton, F. (1883). *Inquiries into human faculty and its development.* New York: Macmillan.

Galton, F. (1888). Personal identification and description. *Proceedings of the Royal Institution of Great Britain, 12,* 346–360.

Garcia, S., Stinson, L., Ickes, W., Bisonette, V., & Briggs, S. R. (1991). Shyness and physical attractiveness in mixed sex dyads. *Journal of Personality and Social Psychology, 61,* 35–49.

Gerrig, R. J., Maloney, L. T., & Tversky, A. (1991). Validating the dimensional structure of psychological spaces: Applications to personality and emotions. In D. R. Brown & J. E. K. Smith (Eds.), *Frontiers of mathematical psychology: Essays in honor of Clyde Coombs.* New York: Springer-Verlag.

Goren, C., Sarty, M., & Wu, P. (1975). Visual following and pattern discrimination of face-like stimuli by newborn infants. *Pediatrics, 56,* 544–549.

Grammer, K., & Thornhill, R. (1994). Human (*Homo sapiens*) facial attractiveness and sexual selection: The role of symmetry and averageness. *Journal of Comparative Psychology, 108,* 233—242.

Guilford, J. P. (1954). *Psychometric methods* (2nd ed.). New York: McGraw-Hill.

Hamermesh, D. S., & Biddle, J. E. (1994). Beauty and the labor market. *American Economic Review, 84,* 1174–1194.

Hansell, S. J., Sparacino, J., & Ronchi, D. (1982). Physical attractiveness and blood pressure: Sex and age differences. *Personality and Social Psychology Bulletin, 8,* 113–121.

Henss, R. (1991). Perceiving age and attractiveness in facial photographs. *Journal of Applied Psychology, 21,* 933–946.

Hirschberg, N., Jones, L. E., & Haggerty, M. (1978). What's in a face?: Individual differences in face perception. *Journal of Research in Personality, 12,* 488–499.

Hunter, M. A., & Ames, E. W. (1988). A multifactor model of infant preferences for novel and familiar stimuli. *Advances in Infancy Research, 5,* 69–95.

Huntley, H. E. (1970). *The divine proportion: A study in mathematical beauty.* New York: Dover.

Jackson, L. A. (1992). *Physical appearance and gender: Sociobiological and sociocultural perspectives.* Albany: State University of New York Press.

Kalakanis, L. (1997). *Newborn preferences for attractive faces.* Unpublished doctoral dissertation, University of Texas at Austin.

Kalick, S. M., Zebrowitz, L. A., Langlois, J. H., & Johnson, R. M. (1998). Does human facial attractiveness honestly advertise health? Longitudinal data on an evolutionary question. *Psychological Science, 9*, 8–13.

Kramer, S., Zebrowitz, L. A., San Giovanni, J. P., & Sherak, B. (1995). Infants' preferences for attractiveness and babyfaceness. In B. G. Bardy, R. J. Bootsma, & Y. Guiard (Eds.), *Studies in perception and action: III* (pp. 389–392). Mahwah, NJ: Erlbaum.

Kuhlenschmidt, S., & Conger, J. C. (1988). Behavioral components of social competence in females. *Sex Roles, 18*, 107–112.

Langlois, J. H., Kalakanis, L. E., Rubenstein, A. J., Larson, A. D., Hallam, M. J., & Smoot, M. T. (2000). Maxims or myths of beauty: A meta-analytic and theoretical review. *Psychological Bulletin, 126*, 390–423.

Langlois, J. H., Ritter, J. M., Roggman, L. A., & Vaughn, L. S. (1991a). Facial diversity and infant preferences for attractive faces. *Developmental Psychology, 27*, 79–84.

Langlois, J. H., & Roggman, L. A. (1990). Attractive faces are only average. *Psychological Science, 1*, 115–121.

Langlois, J.H., Roggman, L. A., Casey, R. J., Ritter, J. M., Rieser-Danner, L. A., & Jenkins, V. Y. (1987). Infant preferences for attractive faces: Rudiments of a stereotype? *Developmental Psychology, 23*, 363–369.

Langlois, J. H., Roggman, L. A., & Musselman, L. (1994). What is average and what is not average about attractive faces? *Psychological Science, 5*, 214–220.

Langlois, J. H., Roggman, L. A., Musselman, L., Acton, S. (1991b). A picture is worth a thousand words: Reply to "On the difficulty of averaging faces." *Psychological Science. 2*, 354–357.

Langlois, J. H., Roggman, L. A., & Rieser-Danner, L. A. (1990). Infants' differential social responses to attractive and unattractive faces. *Developmental Psychology, 26*, 153–159.

Light, L. L., Hollander, S., & Kayra-Stuart, F. (1981). Why attractive people are harder to remember. *Personality and Social Psychology Bulletin, 7*, 269–276.

Linn, S., Reznick, J. S., Kagan, J., & Hans, S. (1982). Salience of visual patterns in the human infant. *Developmental Psychology, 18*, 651–657.

Markman, A. B. (1999). *Knowledge representation.* Mahwah, NJ: Erlbaum.

Marr, D. (1977). Analysis of occluding contour. *Proceedings of the Royal Society of London, B 197*, 441–475.

Marr, D. (1982). *Vision.* San Francisco: W. H. Freeman.

Martindale, C., & Moore, K. (1988). Priming, prototypicality, and preference. *Journal of Experimental Psychology: Human Perception and Performance, 14*, 661–670.

Mathes, E. W., Brennan, S. M., Haugen, P. M., & Rice, H. B. (1985). Ratings of physical attractiveness as a function of age. *Journal of Social Psychology, 125*, 157–168.

Morton, J., & Johnson, M. H. (1991). CONSPEC and CONLERN: A two-process theory of infant face recognition. *Psychological Review, 98*, 164–181.

Moss, M.K., Miller, R., & Page, R. A. (1975). The effects of racial context on the perception of physical attractiveness. *Sociometry, 38*, 525–535.

O'Grady, K. E. (1989). Physical attractiveness, need for approval, social self-esteem, and maladjustment. *Journal of Social and Clinical Psychology, 8*, 62–69.

Payne, J.W., Bettman, J. R., & Johnson, E. J. (1993). *The adaptive decision maker.* New York: Cambridge University Press.

Pedelty, L., Levine, S. C., Shevell, S. K. (1985). Developmental changes in face processing: Results from multidimensional scaling. *Journal of Experimental Child Psychology, 39,* 421–436.

Perrett, D. I., Lee, K. J., Penton-Voak, I., Rowland, D., Yoshikawa, S., Burt, D. M., Henzi, S. P., Castles, D. L., & Akamatsu, S. (1998). Effects of sexual dimorphism on facial attractiveness. *Nature, 394,* 884–887.

Perrett, D. I., May, K. A., & Yoshikawa, S. (1994). Facial shape and judgments of female attractiveness. *Nature, 368,* 239–242.

Pittenger, J. B. (1991). On the difficulty of averaging faces: Comments on Langlois and Roggman. *Psychological Science, 2,* 351–353.

Pollard, J. S. (1995). Attractiveness of composite faces: A comparative study. *International Journal of Comparative Psychology, 8,* 77–83.

Posner, M. I., & Keele, S. W. (1968). On the genesis of abstract ideas. *Journal of Experimental Psychology, 77,* 155–158.

Posner, M. I., & Keele, S. W. (1970). Retention of abstract ideas. *Journal of Experimental Psychology, 83,* 304–308.

Quinn, P. C. (1987). The categorical representation of visual pattern information by young infants. *Cognition, 27,* 145–179.

Ramachandran, V. S. (1988). Perceiving shape from shading. *Scientific American, 259,* 76–83.

Raza, S. M., & Carpenter, B. N. (1987). A model of hiring decisions in real employment interviews. *Journal of Applied Psychology, 72,* 596–603.

Reis, H. T., Wheeler, L., Nezlek, J., Kernis, M. H., & Spiegel, N. (1985). On specificity in the impact of social participation on physical and psychological health. *Journal of Personality and Social Psychology, 48,* 456–471.

Rhodes, G., Hickford, C., & Jeffery, L. (2000). Sex-typicality and attractiveness: Are supermale and superfemale faces super-attractive? *British Journal of Psychology, 91,* 125–140.

Rhodes, G., Roberts, J., & Simmons, L. (1999). Reflections on symmetry and attractiveness. *Psychology, Evolution, and Gender, 1,* 279–295.

Rhodes, G., Sumich, A., & Byatt, G. (1999). Are average facial configurations attractive only because of their symmetry? *Psychological Science, 10,* 52–58.

Rhodes, G., & Tremewan, T. (1996). Averageness, exaggeration, and facial attractiveness. *Psychological Science, 7,* 105–110.

Rosenthal, R. (1991). *Meta-analytic procedures for social research.* Newbury Park, CA: Sage.

Rubenstein, A. J. (1999). *The ability to form stereotypic associations during infancy: A cognitive look at the basis of the "Beauty is good" stereotype.* Unpublished doctoral dissertation, University of Texas at Austin.

Rubenstein, A. J., Langlois, J. H., & Kalakanis, L. E. (1999). Infant preferences for attractive faces: A cognitive explanation. *Developmental Psychology, 35,* 848–855.

Rubenstein, A. J., Langlois, J. H., Kalakanis, L. E., Larson, A. D., & Hallam, M. J. (1997, March). *Why do infants prefer attractive faces?* Poster presented at the biennial meeting of the Society for Research in Child Development, Washington, DC.

Samuels, C. A., Butterworth, G., Roberts, T., Graupner, L., & Hole, G. (1994). Facial aesthetics: Babies prefer attractiveness to symmetry. *Perception, 23,* 823–831.

Samuels, C. A., & Ewy, R. (1985). Aesthetic perception of faces during infancy. *British Journal of Developmental Psychology, 3,* 221–228.

Shackelford, T. K., & Larsen, R. J. (1999). Facial attractiveness and physical health. *Evolution and Human Behavior, 20,* 71–76.

Shapiro, A. K., Struening, E., Shapiro, E., & Barten, H. (1976). Prognostic correlates of psychotherapy in psychiatric outpatients. *American Journal of Psychiatry, 133,* 802–808.

Slater, A., Von der Schulennurg, C., Brown, E., Badenoch, M., Butterworth, G., Parsons, S., & Samuels, C. (1998). Newborn infants prefer attractive faces. *Infant Behavior and Development, 21,* 345–354.

Smith, D. J., & Melara, R. J. (1990). Aesthetic preference and syntactic prototypicality in music: 'Tis the gift to be simple. *Cognition, 34,* 279–298.

Spears, R. A. (Ed.). (1993). *NTC's (National Textbook Company's) dictionary of proverbs and cliches.* Lincolnwood, IL: National Textbook Company.

Stoddard, J. T. (1886). Composite portraiture. *Science, 8*(182), 89–91.

Stoddard, J. T. (1887). Composite photography. *Century, 33,* 750–757.

Strauss, M. S. (1979). Abstraction of prototypical information by adults and 10-month-old infants. *Journal of Experimental Psychology: Human Learning and Memory, 5,* 618–632.

Tanaka, J. W., Kay, J. B., Grinnell, E., Stansfield, B., & Szechter, L. (1998). Face recognition in young children: When the whole is greater than the sum of its parts. *Visual Cognition, 5,* 479–496.

Thornhill, R. (1998). Darwinian aesthetics. In C. Crawford & D. L. Krebs (Eds.), *Handbook of evolutionary psychology* (pp. 543–572). Mahwah, NJ: Erlbaum.

Thornhill, R., & Gangestad, S. W. (1993). Human facial beauty: Averageness, symmetry and parasite resistance. *Human Nature, 4,* 237–269.

Torgerson, W. S. (1958). *Theory and methods of scaling.* New York: Wiley.

U. S. Department of Health and Human Services (1996). Surgeon General's Report on Physical Activity and Health. Washington, DC. (NTIS No. AD-A329 047/5INT).

Walton, G. E., & Bower, T. G. (1994). Newborns form "prototypes" in less than 1 minute. *Psychological Science, 4,* 203–205.

West, S. G., & Brown, T. J. (1975). Physical attractiveness, the severity of the emergency and helping: A field experiment and interpersonal simulation. *Journal of Experimental Social Psychology, 11,* 531–538.

Whitfield, T. W., & Slatter, P. E. (1979). The effects of categorization and prototypicality on aesthetic choice in a furniture selection task. *British Journal of Psychology, 70,* 65–75.

Younger, B. A. (1985). The segregation of items into categories by ten-month-old infants. *Child Development, 56,* 1574–1583.

Zebrowitz, L. A., Olson, K., & Hoffman, K. (1993) Stability of babyfaceness and attractiveness across the life span. *Journal of Personality and Social Psychology, 64,* 453–466.

CHAPTER 2

The Attractiveness of Average Faces: Cross-Cultural Evidence and Possible Biological Basis

Gillian Rhodes, Kate Harwood, Sakiko Yoshikawa, Miwa Nishitani, and Ian McLean

After considering the cultural diversity of beautification practices, Charles Darwin concluded that, "It is certainly not true that there is in the mind . . . any universal standard of beauty" (1998, p. 890), the implication being that humans lack species-typical, biologically based, standards of beauty.[1] Many psychologists have held a similar view, believing that standards of beauty are set, perhaps quite arbitrarily, by our culture (for reviews, see Berry, 2000; Cunningham, Chapter 7, this volume; Zebrowitz, 1997).

Recent evidence, however, challenges this view, suggesting instead that some standards of beauty may reflect our biological rather than our cultural heritage. First, there is considerable cross-cultural agreement about which faces are attractive and which are unattractive (for reviews, see Cunningham, this volume; Dion, Chapter 8, this volume; Langlois & Roggman, 1990; Zebrowitz, 1997). Second, preferences emerge very early in development, before cultural standards of beauty are likely to have been assimilated (Langlois et al., 1987; Rubenstein, Kalakanis, & Langlois, 1999; Rubenstein, Langlois, & Roggman, Chapter 1, this volume).

As a result, close attention is now being paid to the possibility that some standards of beauty may be part of our biological heritage, and to how such preferences could have evolved (Enquist et al., Chapter 5, this volume; Etcoff, 1999; Grammer et al., Chapter 4, this volume; Halberstadt & Rhodes, 2000; Jones, 1996; Kalick, Zebrowitz, Langlois, & Johnson, 1998; Little et al., Chapter 3, this volume; Miller & Todd, 1998; Simpson & Kenrick, 1996;

Thornhill & Gangestad, 1993, 1994, 1999). One view is that they evolved as adaptations to the problem of finding a good mate (for reviews, see Cronin, 1991; Etcoff, 1999; Grammer et al., this volume; Jones, 1996; Little et al., this volume; Miller & Todd, 1998; Møller & Swaddle, 1997). On this view, the preferred traits provide information about mate quality (e.g., health, fertility, or intelligence), giving individuals who find these traits attractive a reproductive advantage over those without these preferences.

Another possibility is that preferences evolved because the offspring of attractive individuals are themselves attractive. Fisher (1915, 1930) noted that the offspring of individuals with idiosyncratic preferences would be relatively unpopular as mates (Fisher, 1915, 1930), giving those with the popular preference more descendants. On this "good taste" view, the preferred traits need not provide any information about mate quality.

Finally, preferences could be by-products of general perceptual biases or information-processing mechanisms, such as the need to recognize individuals or objects from different viewpoints or to abstract prototypes from structurally distinct sets of objects (Endler & Basolo, 1998; Enquist & Arak, 1994; Enquist & Johnstone, 1997; Enquist et al., Chapter 5, this volume; Johnstone, 1994; Kalick et al., 1998; Rubenstein et al., this volume). On this view, the preferred traits would not signal mate quality.

Of course these evolutionary mechanisms are not mutually exclusive. Different preferences could have been shaped by different mechanisms or by a combination of mechanisms, operating at different stages of the evolution of a preference. For example, a perceptual bias to look at eyes could preadapt an organism to attend to facial (rather than body) cues to mate quality.

In this chapter we focus on the attractiveness of average faces, and whether such a preference has some biological basis. First, we review evidence that average facial configurations are attractive. Second, we consider two possible evolutionary mechanisms for this preference, arguing that average traits plausibly signal mate quality (see below) and that cognitive prototype abstraction mechanisms could also contribute to the attractiveness of average faces. Then, we consider whether developmental and cross-cultural evidence supports a biological basis for the attractiveness of average faces. Finally, we present some new cross-cultural data with interesting implications for understanding why average faces are attractive.

EVIDENCE THAT AVERAGE FACIAL CONFIGURATIONS ARE ATTRACTIVE

The first hint that average faces are attractive came from Sir Francis Galton's (1878) observation that composite photographs, from which the "peculiarities" of individual faces have been eliminated, are strikingly beautiful. Strictly speaking, photographic composites are not mathematical averages, but Galton's observation has been confirmed for computer-averaged composite faces, which are more attractive than their component faces (Langlois & Roggman, 1990; Rhodes, Sumich, & Byatt, 1999b). The attractiveness of these averaged composites cannot be completely explained by their smooth complexions, because line drawing composites are also attractive (Rhodes & Tremewan, 1996). Furthermore, individual faces can be made more attractive by reducing their spatial differences from an average configuration (by anticaricaturing), and less attractive by exaggerating those differences (by caricaturing) (Rhodes & Tremewan, 1996; Rhodes et al., 1999b). These results also show that the attractiveness of averageness is not an artifact of blending faces together, because none of the images were blends. Furthermore, changes in attractiveness produced by altering the averageness of faces cannot be fully explained by accompanying changes in symmetry or expression (Rhodes et al., 1999b). A question that remains unresolved is whether the youthful appearance of averaged composites (Langlois, Roggman, & Musselman, 1994) accounts for their appeal.

The studies described so far have shown that artificially generated average configurations are attractive, but what about natural variations in averageness? Are more average faces more attractive than less average ones? The answer appears to be yes. Several studies have shown that the attractiveness of normal, undistorted faces correlates positively with ratings of averageness and typicality, and negatively with ratings of distinctiveness (the converse of averageness) and unusualness (Light, Hollander, & Kayra-Stuart, 1981; Rhodes & Tremewan, 1996; Rhodes et al., 1999b; see also Grammer & Thornhill, 1994).[2] One study has also found a significant relationship between objective measurements of facial averageness and attractiveness (Jones & Hill, 1993).

Although there is now good evidence, from a variety of methodologies, that average facial configurations are attractive, they may not be optimally attractive (Alley & Cunningham, 1991; Perrett, May, & Yoshikawa, 1994). For example, average configurations of both male and female faces can sometimes be made even more attractive by exaggerating female traits (Little et al., Chapter 3, this volume; Penton-Voak et al., 1999; Perrett et al., 1998; Rhodes, Hickford, & Jeffery, 2000; see Penton-Voak & Perrett, 2000; Keating, Chapter 6, this volume), and faces that happen to deviate from averageness in precisely this way may be more attractive than average configurations. Nevertheless, average configurations are still more attractive than most real faces, and their appeal must be explained.

TWO POSSIBLE EVOLUTIONARY MECHANISMS

Several theorists have conjectured that a preference for averageness is an adaptation to the problem of mate choice, which evolved because average facial traits signal a high-quality mate (Gangestad & Buss, 1993; Thornhill & Gangestad, 1993). On this "good genes" view, average traits would signal (at least some) qualities of a desirable mate, such as health, fertility, intelligence, social competence, and so on. Facial averageness may reflect developmental stability, that is, the ability to maintain normal development in spite of environmental and genetic stress (Thornhill & Møller, 1997). More speculatively, it may reflect protein (and ultimately genetic) heterozygosity, which enhances parasite resistance (Gangestad & Buss, 1993; Thornhill & Gangestad, 1993). Finally, if stabilizing selection operates on facial traits, as on many other traits (so that average facial traits are best suited for carrying out their functions, for example, an average jaw configuration may be optimal for chewing), then individuals with average traits would have higher fitness than others, as would their mates (Koeslag, 1990; Symons, 1979).

Genetic and environmental stress can certainly produce deviations from the normal phenotype of the face and body (Hoyme, 1994; Thornhill & Møller, 1997). In a recent review, Thornhill and Møller (1997) identified links between minor physical anomalies and a variety of disorders (Down's syndrome, autism, schizophenia, and learning disability) and with poor academic performance and hyperactivity (in boys). These results support the view that deviations from the average phenotype reflect developmental instability, and that averageness signals mate quality.

We note, however, that not all deviations from averageness reflect developmental instability and poor mate quality. For example, the most extreme and flamboyant peacock tails are likely to have the healthiest owners (Cronin, 1991). In general, extreme sexual ornaments are attractive (Andersson, 1994), and can signal health by indicating low parasite loadings (Hamilton & Zuk, 1982; Møller, 1990; Wedekind, 1992), high fertility (Symons, 1995; Thornhill & Gangestad, 1996), and/or a strong immune system (Folstad & Karter, 1992; Thornhill & Gangestad, 1993; Thornhill & Møller, 1997). The attractiveness of feminized features in human male faces, discussed above, may be an exception to the general attractiveness of extreme secondary sexual characteristics.

There are good theoretical reasons to think that averageness signals mate quality, but is there any direct evidence for a link between facial averageness and mate quality in normal human populations? Some studies have looked for a more general link between facial attractiveness and health, with little success (Kalick et al., 1998; Shackelford & Larsen, 1999). Kalick and colleagues (1998) found no correlation between attractiveness and health scores, derived from detailed medical assessments, in a large sample of young adults. Shackelford and Larsen (1997, 1999) found very few significant correlations between attractiveness and health, or symmetry and health, out of a large set of examined health measures. Recently, however, Rhodes et al. (2000) have shown that facial distinctiveness (a converse measure of averageness) at age 17 is associated with poor childhood health in males and poor current health in females. These results indicate that facial averageness may signal an important aspect of mate quality—namely health.

Let us turn now to another mechanism by which a preference for averageness could evolve, namely as a by-product of some general information-processing mechanism that has nothing particularly to do with mate choice. On this account, a preference for averageness is not an adaptation to the problem of mate choice and should not be restricted to faces. Recent support for this account comes from the finding that averageness is attractive for a variety of nonface stimuli (Halberstadt & Rhodes, 2000).

One possibility is that an innate prototype abstraction mechanism, which is tuned by experience, results in a preference for average faces (Langlois & Roggman, 1990; Langlois et al., 1994; Rubenstein et al., 1999; Rubenstein et al., Chapter 1, this volume; Symons, 1979). Humans certainly have such a mechanism (or one that closely mimics the operation of one), because familiarity with exemplars from a category makes the (unseen) prototype or average of those exemplars appear very familiar (for reviews, see Rhodes, 1996; Rubenstein et al., this volume). It may also be innate, because newborns abstract prototypes within minutes of birth, preferring to look at a composite of presented faces rather than a composite of unseen faces (Walton & Bower, 1993).

What this account lacks, however, and the "good genes" account provides, is an explanation of why averages are *attractive*. We may abstract prototypes, but why do we find them attractive? One possibility is that their familiarity makes them attractive (Langlois et al., 1994). Interestingly, however, correlations between attractiveness and averageness for some nonface stimuli remain significant when familiarity is partialled out, suggesting that familiarity may not fully account for the attractiveness of averageness (Halberstadt & Rhodes, 2000). It remains to be seen whether the same is true for faces.

The preceding discussion suggests that there are good theoretical grounds to hypothesize that a preference for averageness is part of our evolutionary heritage, and some modest empirical support for the hypothesis. We turn now to two other lines of evidence that are relevant to any debate about whether a preference is biologically based: developmental and cross-cultural.

DEVELOPMENTAL EVIDENCE

Perhaps the strongest indication that a preference is biologically based would be evidence that it emerges early in development. Although it is well established that preferences emerge early (for a review, see Rubenstein et al., Chapter 1, this volume), researchers have just begun to study when a preference for average faces emerges. Initial results suggest that it emerges early in development (Rubenstein et al., 1999; Rubenstein et al., Chapter 1, this volume). Rubenstein and his colleagues showed 6-month-old infants an averaged composite of 32 female faces, paired with a face judged by adults to be unattractive. Four different unattractive faces were used, giving four average–unattractive pairs (between subjects). For three of the four pairs, infants looked slightly, but significantly, longer at the composite ($M = 7.8$ seconds) than the unattractive faces (M = 6.3 seconds). Although it is not always straightforward to interpret looking preferences in infants, this result is consistent with the possibility that the babies preferred more average faces.

Future studies will need to examine whether infants also prefer averaged composites over more attractive individual faces than were used in this initial study. Also, given that averaged composites generally look a little different from real faces, and that infants often favor the unusual in a selective looking paradigm, it will be important to determine whether infants prefer the more average image when neither is a composite (e.g., when viewing anticaricature–caricature pairs).

CROSS-CULTURAL EVIDENCE

Historically, cross-cultural evidence has played an important role in theories of beauty, with cross-cultural diversity motivating culturally-based theories and cross-cultural agreement motivating biologically-based theories. If a preference for averageness is biologically based, then it should be found in many cultures. The study of isolated cultural groups is of special interest in this context, because their preferences are unlikely to be explained by cultural transmission of standards of beauty.

One study examined the preferences of an isolated group of Paraguayan Ache Indians, and found that attractiveness was negatively correlated with deviations from averageness for Ache faces (Jones & Hill, 1993).[3] They note, however, that deviations from averageness were confounded with age, so the attractiveness of younger faces could have inflated the observed relationship between averageness and attractiveness. This study does not, therefore, clearly show that averageness is attractive in this isolated group.

Truly isolated groups are rare in the modern world, however, and most cross-cultural studies of attractiveness have examined less culturally isolated groups. Two such studies have looked for a preference for average facial traits and failed to find one (Cunningham, Roberts, Wu, Barbee, & Druen, 1995; Jones & Hill, 1993). However, neither found the preference for Western participants, so that the negative results with non-Western participants may have been due to low power or some other weakness of the design.

THE PRESENT EXPERIMENTS

We carried out two experiments to determine whether a preference for average own-race facial configurations occurs in non-Western groups. One study tested ethnic Chinese individuals who had recently arrived in a Western country (Experiment 1) and the other tested Japanese individuals living in Japan (Experiment 2). If a preference for average facial configurations is biologically based, we would expect to find it in these two non-Western cultures.

A general problem with such studies is the difficulty of ruling out cultural transmission accounts of cross-cultural agreement. This problem may, however, be minimal in the case of a preference for averageness, which is defined relative to a particular population. Average faces from visually distinct populations (e.g., Caucasian and Chinese) will look different, and so adopting the standards of beauty of the other group (e.g., finding average configurations for that population attractive) would seem unlikely to generate a preference for average own-race faces.

This argument supposes that average facial configurations are attractive because they represent the central tendency of a population of faces, that is, because they display typical or familiar feature values for that population. This view has been defended by Langlois and her colleagues. An alternative possibility, however, is that the attractiveness of average faces results from properties, or combinations of properties, that do not require experience with the relevant population, such as a youthful appearance, a pleasant expression, or a healthy complexion. Preferences for such "absolute" properties could readily transfer between cultures. Some of these properties have been ruled out as sole accounts of the attractiveness of average faces (see earlier discussion), but others (e.g., youthfulness) have not, and nor has the possibility that a combination of such properties accounts for the attractiveness of average faces.

We attempted to address the issue of why average faces are attractive by examining the preferences of nonexpert (mostly Caucasian) as well as expert Chinese raters of Chinese faces in Experiment 1. If average faces are attractive because they represent the central tendency of a population, then expertise with that population should be required for average configurations to be attractive. Alternatively, if people are responding to absolute properties of average images, then expertise should not be needed to find the average configurations attractive.

Previous cross-cultural studies have not resolved this issue. Jones and Hill (1993) found little consistent difference between expert (Ache Indians) and nonexpert raters (from other ethnic groups) in the correlations of attractiveness and deviations from averageness, suggesting that expertise with the relevant population may not be needed to find averageness attractive. As noted above, however, their correlations are difficult to interpret because deviations from averageness were confounded with age. Pollard (1995) reported a stronger preference for composite Caucasian faces, by more expert (Caucasian and Chinese New Zealanders) than less expert (Nigerians and Indians living in their home countries) raters. However, formal statistical comparisons were not carried out, and the composites were made using multiple exposure photography, which produces large rather than average-sized features (as acknowledged by the author; see also Pittenger, 1991).

EXPERIMENT 1

The main aim was to determine whether averageness is attractive in a non-Western culture. A second aim was to investigate the effect of expertise with a population of faces on the preference for averageness in that population.

We examined whether attractiveness increases with the number of component faces in Chinese averaged composite faces (cf. Langlois & Roggman, 1990) for Chinese and non-Chinese individuals. We also investigated whether ratings of distinctiveness (the converse of averageness) correlate negatively with attractiveness, as found for Caucasian faces (e.g., Rhodes et al., 1999b; Rhodes & Tremewan, 1996).

Averaged composites differ from component faces in texture (shading), as well as shape, typically having smoother complexions and a softer look. Studies with Caucasian faces have shown that these textural properties are attractive (Benson & Perrett, 1992), but that they do not fully account for the attractiveness of averaged composites (Rhodes et al., 1999b; Rhodes & Tremewan, 1996). Averageness of shape also appears to be important. We attempted to replicate this finding with Chinese composites by producing texture-matched composites that varied only in shape, as well as normal composites, which vary in both shape and texture. We predicted that both types of composites would be attractive.

Method

Participants

Thirty-two Chinese (16 males [M], 16 females [F]) and 32 non-Chinese (16M, 16F) individuals participated. All the Chinese participants were born in Asian countries (Indonesia, N = 8; Malaysia, N = 7; People's Republic of China, N = 4; Taiwan, N = 4; Hong Kong, N = 3; Singapore, N = 3; Philippines, N = 2; Thailand, N = 1). They had been in Australia for an average of 6 months (range 1–18 months), attending local high schools (mean age 16.8 yrs, SD = 1.5 yrs). They knew few Caucasians (M = 1.5, SD = 0.6), but did watch Western television (M = 1.4 hours per day, SD = 0.6) and movies (M = 1.8 per week, SD = 0.7).

The non-Chinese participants were recruited from an Introductory Psychology course (mean age 19.9 yrs, SD = 6.8 yrs). All but two were Caucasian (1 Caucasian/Middle Eastern, 1 Caucasian/Filipino). Twenty-five were born in Australia and the others had lived in Australia for at least 5 years (mean 17.8 years). None were from an Asian country.

Stimuli

Thirty-two, front-view, black and white photographs (11.5 x 14.5 cm) of young Chinese adults (16M, 16F) displaying neutral expressions were digitized and used to make composite faces. No clothing or jewelry were visible. Prior to making composites, blemishes and hair on the forehead were removed using the cloning tool in Adobe Photoshop, a computer program. The faces were scaled to a standard interpupil distance of 80 pixels, and rotated (if necessary) so that the eyes were horizontally aligned.

Composites were made using Gryphon's Morph program. To make a composite, a set of 169 landmark points was found by eye on each face, and their locations marked using a mouse-click. The program then calculated the mean location of each landmark point for the set of component faces, warped each face onto this average configuration, and averaged the grey levels in corresponding small regions of the face (for details, see Beale & Keil, 1995). For each sex of face, we created a 2–face (Av2), 4–face (Av4), 8–face (Av8), and 16–face (Av16) composite (Figure 2.1, top row). We also created a second set of composites, using different component faces for the 2–face, 4–face, and 8–face composites, and using the same set for the 16 faces, but with component faces entered in the opposite order (Morph creates composites incrementally, adding one face at a time, weighted appropriately). The two 2–face, 4–face, and 8–face composites look different, but the two 16–face composites look virtually identical. We minimized textural differences between the composites and the individual component faces by sharpening the composites and slightly blurring the component faces in Photoshop.

We also created texture-matched "shape composites," in which only the averageness of shape varied. The shape composites (Av2/16, Av4/16, Av8/16) were created by mapping the texture of each 16–face composite onto its corresponding 2–face, 4–face, and 8–face composite (Figure 2.1, bottom row).

All the images (16 individual faces, 8 composites, and 6 shape composites for each sex; N = 60 in total) were displayed in oval masks that hid most of the hair but showed the face outline, chin, and ears.

Procedure

After providing demographic information, each participant rated all 60 images on both attractiveness and distinctiveness, using 7–point scales. The images were blocked by sex of face and both sexes were rated on one scale before being rated on the other scale. Two different random orders of faces were used, counterbalanced with scale order and face-sex order. Images were presented individually on a Power Macintosh computer and remained on until the rating was made. Distinctiveness was explained as the ease with which a face could be picked out of a crowd (1 = very difficult to pick out of a Chinese crowd, 7 = very easy to pick out of a Chinese crowd), as in previous studies (e.g., Rhodes & Tremewan, 1996; Valentine, 1991).

Finally, participants completed a forced-choice task in which they chose the more attractive image for each of the 48 pairs of texture-matched composites (all with the Av16 texture). For each set and each sex of face, all six possible pairs of composites with matching texture (Av2/16, Av4/16, Av8/16, Av16) were presented twice (N = 48), once with the more average image on top and once with the more average image on the bottom.

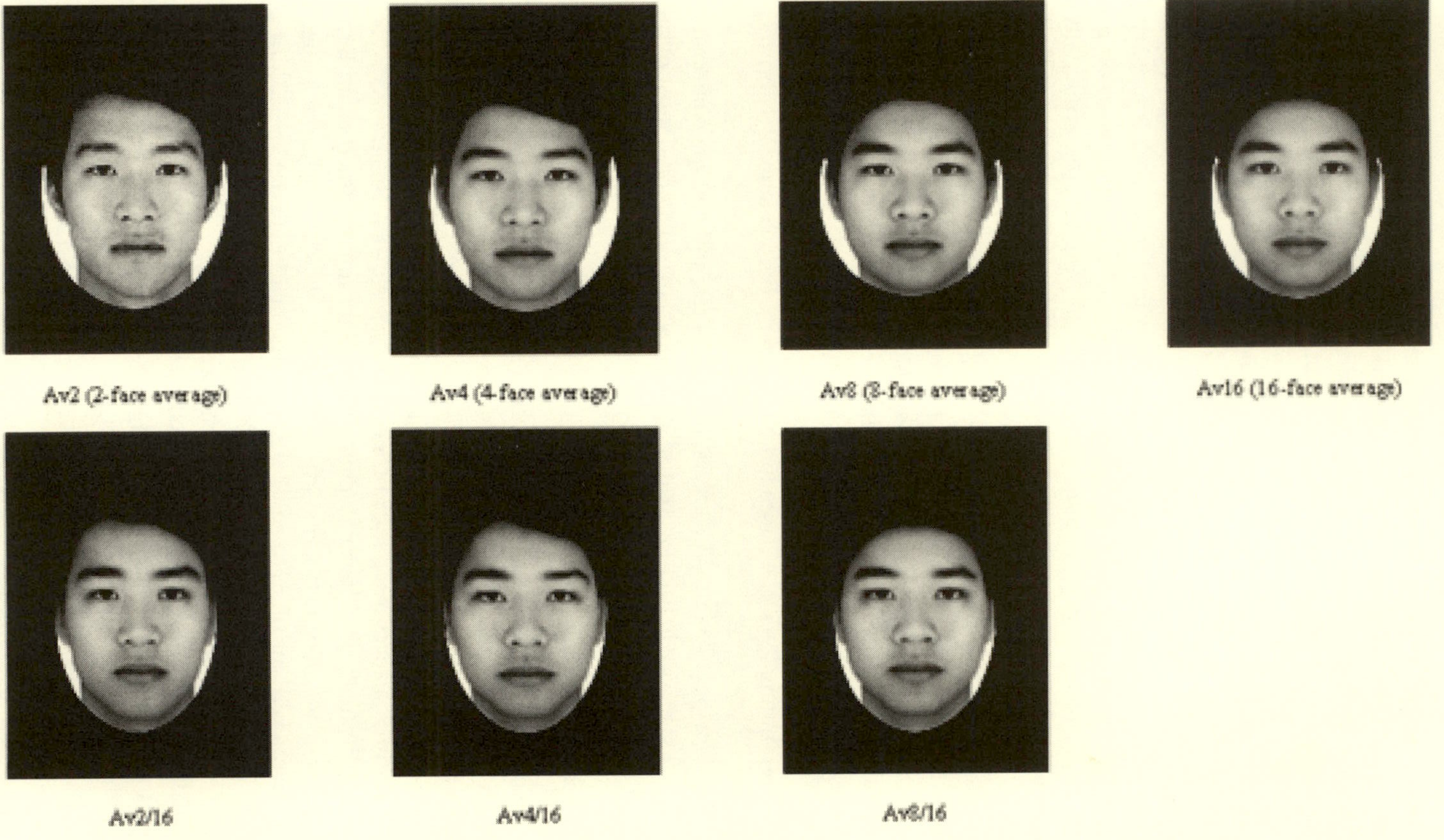

Figure 2.1. Example of average Chinese composites used in Experiment 1. *Top row*: normal composites of 2, 4, 8, and 16 Chinese male faces. *Bottom row*: shape (texture-matched) composites, with Av16 texture warped into the shapes of the Av2, Av4, and Av8 composites.

In the rating and forced-choice tasks, participants were told to try to ignore differences in picture quality produced by computer-generation of the images. All instructions were given in English.

Results and Discussion

Attractiveness

Ratings. A four-way ANOVA was carried out with sex and race (Chinese, non-Chinese) of rater as between-participant factors, and sex of face and image type (individual face, Av2, Av4, Av8, Av16, Av2/16, Av4/16, Av8/16) as repeated measures factors. An alternative design would be to have type of composite (normal, shape) as an additional factor, but, because the data for individual faces and Av16 composites are identical for both types of composites, we prefer to use a single image-type factor.[4] Planned t-tests, with Bonferroni corrections for multiple comparisons, were used to test for predicted increases in attractiveness with increases in number of component faces. An initial 5–way ANOVA with the additional factor of rating scale order (attractiveness first or distinctiveness first) showed that order did not modify any of the theoretically significant results, so we report the results of the simpler 4–way ANOVA.

There was a significant main effect of image type, $F(7,420) = 147.49$, $p < .0001$, which interacted with race of participant, $F(7,420) = 3.04$, $p <.004$. Inspection of Figure 2.2 shows that attractiveness generally increased with the number of component faces, for both Chinese and non-Chinese participants. Planned, one-tailed t-tests were carried out separately for Chinese and non-Chinese participants to determine whether attractiveness increased with the number of component faces for the normal composites (Indiv vs. Av2, Av2 vs. Av4, Av4 vs. Av8, Av8 vs. Av16) and the shape (texture-matched) composites (Av2/16 vs. Av4/16, Av4/16 vs. Av8/16, Av8/16 vs. Av16). A Bonferroni correction for multiple comparisons ($N = 14$) gave a significance level of .004. For Chinese participants, attractiveness increased significantly with increments from Av2 to Av4, and Av8 to Av16, both t's > 3.51, p's < .0005, 1–tailed. For non-Chinese participants, attractiveness increased with increments from Individual to Av2, and Av2 to Av4, all t's > 4.35, p's < .0005, 1–tailed. For both races, there was a significant increase in attractiveness for the shape composites from Av8/16 to Av16, both t's > 3.79, p's < .0005, 1–tailed. Therefore, the attractiveness of averaged composites is not due solely to changes in texture.

There were significant linear effects of number of component faces on attractiveness for both groups of raters and both types of composites: Chinese raters, $F(1, 31) = 82.15$, $p < .0001$ (normal composites), $F(1, 31) = 64.46$, $p < .0001$ (shape composites); non-Chinese raters, $F(1, 31) = 273.10$, $p < .0001$ (normal composites), $F(1, 31) = 229.35$, $p < .0001$ (shape composites). These findings parallel results for Caucasian faces and raters (Langlois & Roggman,

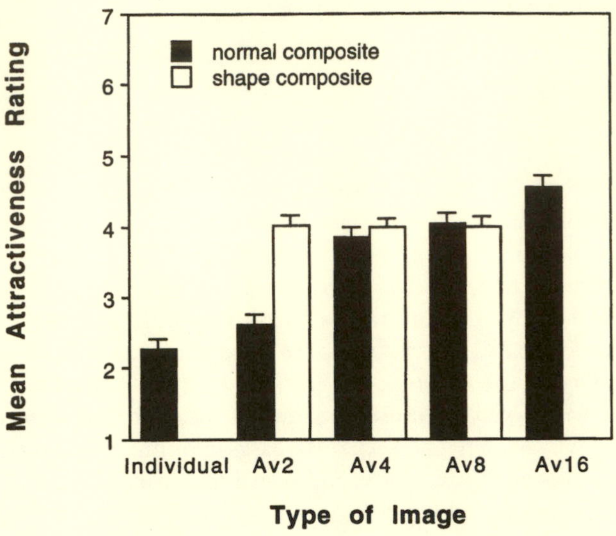

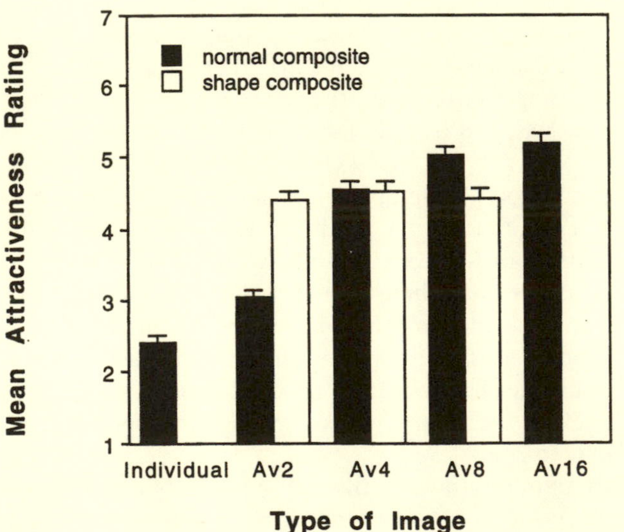

Figure 2.2. Attractiveness of Chinese faces as a function of type of image for Chinese (top) and non-Chinese (bottom) participants in Experiment 1. SE bars are shown.

1990) and provide further evidence that averageness is attractive in Chinese faces.

Overall, we found no evidence that averaged Chinese composites were more attractive for Chinese than non-Chinese raters. Instead, the increase in attractiveness with increasing numbers of component faces appeared to be larger for non-Chinese than Chinese raters.

Image type interacted with sex of face, $F(7,420) = 4.73$, $p < .0001$, but the attractiveness of male and female composites both increased with the number of component faces. Female composites increased in attractiveness for all increments (Ms = 2.3, 2.9, 4.3, 4.6, 5.1) and male composites increased for increments up to, but not beyond, 8 component faces (Ms = 2.5, 2.8, 4.1, 4.5, 4.6). For the shape composites, the biggest increases occurred with increments from 1 to 2, and 8 to 16 component faces for both male (Ms = 2.5, 4.0, 4.1, 4.0, 4.6) and female faces (Ms = 2.3, 4.4, 4.4, 4.4, 5.1).

Curiously, non-Chinese participants rated the images (all Chinese) as more attractive ($M = 4.2$) than the Chinese participants ($M = 3.7$), $F(1, 60) = 6.96$, $p < .02$. There was also a main effect of sex of participant, $F(1, 60) = 8.47$, $p < .006$, which interacted with sex of face, $F(1, 60) = 8.22$, $p < .006$. Males rated male and female faces as equally attractive (both Ms = 3.9), whereas females rated female faces as more attractive ($M = 4.2$) than male faces ($M = 3.7$).

Forced-Choice. The dependent variable was the proportion of trials on which the more average shape composite was preferred (no preference = .5). A four-way ANOVA was carried out on these data, with race and sex of participant as between-participants factors and sex of face and type of pair (Av2/16 vs. Av4/16, Av4/16 vs. Av8/16, Av8/16 vs. Av16)[5] as repeated measures factors. This analysis provides a very sensitive test of preferences for averageness when only shape information is varied.

There was a significant main effect of type of pair, $F(2,120) = 61.44$, $p < .0001$, which was qualified by an interaction with race of participant and sex of face, $F(2,120) = 5.25$, $p < .007$ (Table 2.1). Planned comparisons were carried out for each race of participant and sex of face to determine which proportions were significantly greater than 0.50, indicating a preference for the more average image. A Bonferroni correction for multiple comparisons ($N = 12$) was made, giving a significance level of .004. As shown in Table 2.1, Chinese and non-Chinese participants both preferred the more average image when choosing between the 8– and 16–face male and female shape composites, all t's > 4.58, p's < .0005, 1–tailed. The non-Chinese participants also preferred the more average image when choosing between the male 4– and 8–face composites, $t = 3.37$, $p < .0005$, 1–tailed. These results closely parallel the attractiveness rating results, and indicate that Chinese and non-Chinese participants preferred more average-shaped Chinese faces, even when the same texture was displayed in all the images. This preference was, however, restricted to the choice between 8–face and 16–face composites. The differences in shape be-

	Chinese Participants	Non-Chinese Participants
Female Faces		
Av2/16 vs Av4/16	0.31	0.46
Av4/16 vs Av8/16	0.60	0.53
Av8/16 vs Av16	0.77*	0.82*
Male Faces		
Av2/16 vs Av4/16	0.52	0.46
Av4/16 vs Av8/16	0.60	0.70*
Av8/16 vs Av16	0.77*	0.90*

Table 2.1. Proportion of trials on which the more average shape composite was chosen as the more attractive image in Experiment 1. Asterisks indicate a significant preference for the more average shape composite.

tween the 2–face, 4–face, and 8–face shape composites may have been too subtle to generate differences in attractiveness.

There was a significant main effect of sex of face, $F(1, 60) = 11.07, p < .001$, with a stronger preference for more average shapes in male faces ($M = 0.65$) than female faces ($M = 0.58$).

There was a significant main effect of race of participant, $F(1, 60) = 4.16, p < .05$ ($M = 0.60$, Chinese; $M = 0.65$, non-Chinese), but it was non-Chinese, not Chinese, participants who showed a stronger preference for more average shapes. This result suggests that a high level of expertise with Chinese is not required for average Chinese faces to be attractive, and that subjects are either responding to some absolute property of the images or that relatively little expertise is needed to respond to the statistical property of averageness.

Correlations between Attractiveness and Distinctiveness

Reliability of attractiveness and distinctiveness ratings for the full set of 60 images (composites and shape composites as well as individual faces) was assessed separately for Chinese and non-Chinese raters, using Cronbach's coefficient alpha. Attractiveness ratings were highly reliable for both Chinese (alpha = .96) and non-Chinese (alpha = .98) raters. Interestingly, the mean ratings from Chinese and non-Chinese participants correlated very highly ($r = .96$, $df = 58$), indicating strong cross-cultural agreement in attractiveness judgments.

Distinctiveness ratings were reliable for the non-Chinese raters (alpha = .96), but not the Chinese raters (alpha = -.11). It is possible that Chinese raters, whose first language was not English, were confused by the distinctiveness instructions, which were more complex than the attractiveness instructions.

For the non-Chinese raters, attractiveness and distinctiveness were highly negatively correlated, $r = -.91$, $df = 58$, $p < .0001$, replicating previous findings with Caucasian faces (Rhodes et al., 1999b). When only the normal faces were included (no normal composites or shape-composites), the correlation remained high, $r = -.76$, $df = 30$, $p < .0001$. We could not sensibly examine these correlations for Chinese raters, because their distinctiveness ratings were not reliable.

Composites versus Component Faces

Attractiveness ratings were averaged across raters (separately for Chinese and non-Chinese raters) to provide a mean rating for each image. Except for 2–face composites, all composites were more attractive than all individual component faces for both Chinese and non-Chinese raters.

EXPERIMENT 2

In Experiment 2 we examined whether raters from another non-Western country, Japan, find average own-race faces attractive. These raters were living in their native country and had much less contact with Western individuals and culture than the Chinese participants in Experiment 1.

Method

Participants

Twenty-five Japanese university students (12M, mean age 22.6 yrs; 13F, mean age 23.0 years), living in Japan, participated in the experiment. Amount of contact with Western culture was not formally assessed, but Japanese students normally learn English in school and have access to Western movies and dramas on television (about 15–20 hours a month). Personal contact with Western people is unusual, however, except in English classes.

Stimuli

One hundred and twenty (60M, 60F) front-view, color photographs of young Japanese adults displaying neutral expressions were used to make the composites. No clothing or jewelry was visible. The faces were scaled to a standard interpupil distance of 80 pixels, and rotated (if necessary) so that the eyes were horizontally aligned. Averaged composites of 2 (10 versions), 5 (10 versions), 10 (6 versions), 20 (2 versions) and 30 (2 versions) same-sex faces were generated by randomly selecting (without replacement) same-sex faces (Figure 2.3). Composites were made using the FUTON system, which is similar to

Gryphon's Morph (Kamachi et al., 1998). All the images were displayed in a rectangular-shaped mask that hid the outer hairline.

Procedure

Each participant rated all 30 composites and 10 individual faces (the same for all raters) for each sex (80 images in total) on attractiveness and distinctiveness using 5–point scales. Attractiveness was always rated first. All 80 images were presented in a different random order for each task. Distinctiveness was explained in the same way as in Experiment 1. All instructions were given in Japanese.

Results and Discussion

Attractiveness

A three-way ANOVA was carried out with sex of rater as a between-participants factor and image type (Individual, Av2, Av5, Av10, Av20, Av30) and sex of face as repeated measures factors. There was a significant main effect of image type, $F(5,115) = 46.78$, $p < .0001$, and a significant linear increase in attractiveness as the number of component faces increased, $F(1,24) = 61.32$, $p < .0001$ (Figure 2.4). Planned, one-tailed t-tests (with Bonferroni correction for multiple comparisons) showed that attractiveness increased significantly with increments from Individual faces to Av2, from Av2 to Av5, and from Av5 to Av20, all t's > 2.97, p's < .004. Composites containing 10 or more images did not differ significantly in attractiveness, t's < 1. There were no other significant main effects or interactions.

Correlations between Attractiveness and Distinctiveness

Both attractiveness and distinctiveness ratings were highly reliable, with Cronbach coefficient alphas of .94 and .93, respectively. Attractiveness and distinctiveness ratings were negatively correlated in the full set of images, $r = -.68$, $df = 78$, $p < .0001$. For the 20 individual faces, the correlation was close to zero, $r = .03$, ns. Additional distinctiveness ratings were obtained to provide ratings for the full set of 120 faces (rated in small sets, with 16–20 raters per set). With this larger set, the correlation was -.33, $df = 118$, $p < .0001$.

Composites versus Component Faces

A mean attractiveness rating was obtained for each image, by averaging across raters. Except for 2–face composites, almost all the composites were more attractive than the component faces. Only one male (5–face) composite was less attractive than the most attractive male face, and two female composites (one 5–face and one 10–face) were less attractive than the most attractive female face.

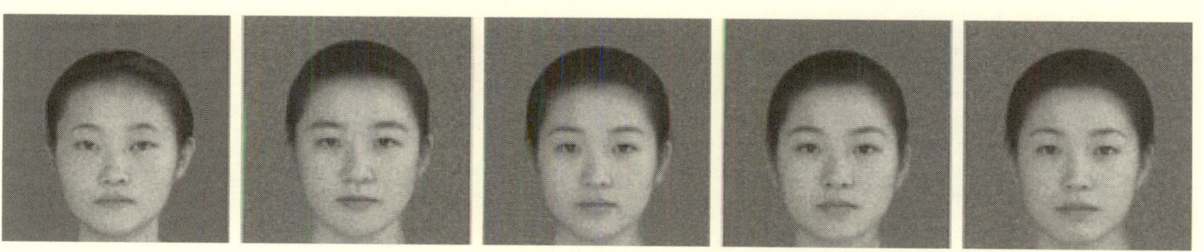

Figure 2.3. Example of averaged Japanese composites used in Experiment 2. *From left to right*: Composites of 2, 5, 10, 20, and 30 Japanese female faces.

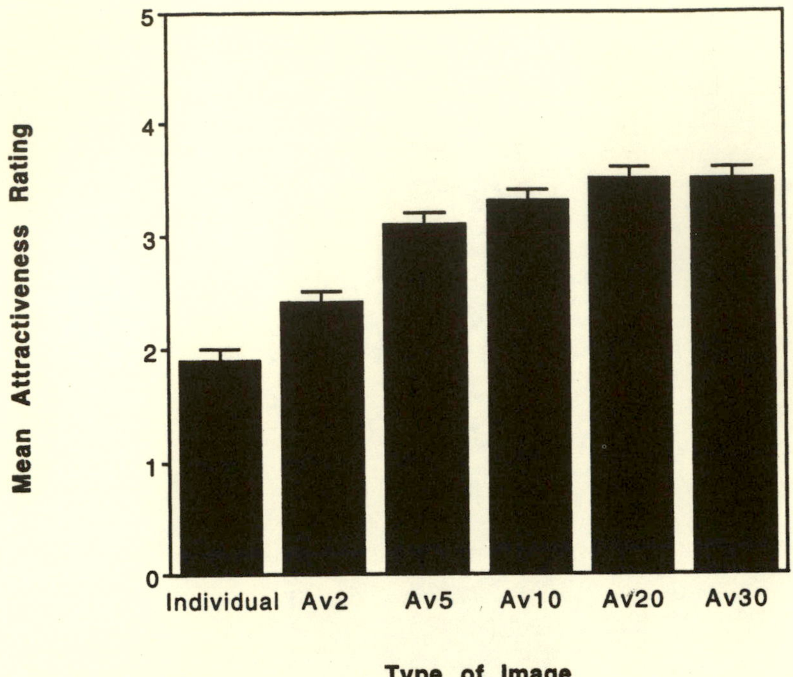

Figure 2.4. Attractiveness of Japanese faces as a function of type of image for Japanese participants in Experiment 2. SE bars are shown.

CONCLUSIONS

Our results extend previous findings that averageness is attractive in Western cultures (Langlois & Roggman, 1990; Rhodes et al., 1999b; Rhodes & Tremewan, 1996), to two non-Western cultures. Both Chinese and Japanese individuals found average, own-race facial configurations attractive. Attractiveness increased with the number of component faces, up to the maximum of 16 for Chinese composites, and up to 10 for Japanese composites. Almost all the composites, except for 2–face composites, were more attractive than any of the component faces. For Chinese faces, we showed that the attractiveness of averaged composites was not due solely to their morphed textures (which gives smoother complexions and soft-focus appearance), with the 16–face composite preferred to the same image warped into less average shapes.

For Japanese raters and faces, attractiveness was significantly negatively correlated with distinctiveness (the converse of averageness), as it is for Caucasian raters and faces (Rhodes et al., 1999b). For Chinese faces, we could not examine this correlation for Chinese raters, because their distinctiveness ratings were unreliable. For non-Chinese (mostly Caucasian) raters, however, attractiveness of Chinese faces was significantly negatively correlated with distinctiveness.

There was very high agreement between Chinese and non-Chinese raters on the attractiveness of the Chinese images, with both groups finding averaged composites of Chinese faces attractive. This result corroborates the high levels of cross-cultural agreement reported in other studies of facial attractiveness (Cunningham et al., 1995; Jones & Hill, 1993; Rubenstein et al., Chapter 1, this volume; Zebrowitz, Montepare, & Lee, 1993; for reviews see Langlois & Roggman, 1990; Zebrowitz, 1997). Cross-cultural agreement was not examined for Japanese faces, because non-Japanese raters were not tested.

Cross-cultural agreement is a hallmark of biologically-based preferences, and these results are precisely as expected if a preference for average facial configurations is biologically based. To provide strong support for a biological preference, however, cross-cultural agreement must not be due to cultural transmission of standards of beauty. At the outset we argued that such an account would be unlikely to explain a preference for averageness, if people are responding to averageness as the central tendency of own-race faces, which are visually distinct from other-race faces.

We investigated whether people were responding to averageness per se by examining the effect of expertise on preferences for averaged Chinese composites. If averaged composites are attractive because of their averageness, we expected that more expert raters would show a stronger preference for the composites than less expert raters. This was not what we found. The less expert, non-Chinese raters found averageness just as attractive in Chinese faces as the expert Chinese raters did. This result suggests that raters may not be responding to averageness per se, but to absolute properties of the images.[6] If they are, then we cannot rule out the possibility of an influence by Western standards of beauty. Future studies with more culturally isolated groups are needed.

If people are responding to absolute properties of averaged composites, what might they be? Studies with Caucasian faces and raters have shown that neither smoothness of complexion, nor symmetry, nor pleasantness of expression can explain the attractiveness of averageness (e.g., Rhodes & Tremewan, 1996; Rhodes et al., 1999b). It remains to be seen, however, whether a *combination* of such variables might account for the attractiveness of averaged composite faces. Another good candidate to examine would be youthfulness, because averaged composites and blended faces look younger than the component faces (Burt & Perrett, 1995; Langlois et al., 1994).[7] Furthermore, anticaricatures (high in averageness) tend to look younger and caricatures (low in averageness) tend to look older than the original faces (Burt & Perrett, 1995; O'Toole, Vetter, Volz, & Salter, 1997). To fully understand what makes average faces attractive, we need to consider all the potentially important variables together, and see which ones contribute independently to the attractiveness of averageness.

In this chapter, we have argued that there are good theoretical reasons to think that the attractiveness of average facial configurations may have some biological basis. The findings that average faces are attractive in non-Western cultures, presented here, and evidence that the preference may emerge early in development (Rubenstein et al., 1999), provide initial converging support for this view. Evidence that more culturally isolated groups also find average faces attractive and confirmation that average faces are indeed attractive to young infants would strengthen the case that a preference for average facial configurations is biologically based.

Future research is needed to investigate the evolutionary mechanisms that may have shaped our preference for average faces. More research is needed on whether average facial traits signal health and other aspects of mate quality, as predicted by the "good genes" account (e.g., Thornhill & Gangestad, 1993). The attractiveness of average nonface objects, which are unrelated to mate choice, suggests an alternative view, namely that the appeal of average faces may reflect general information-processing mechanisms rather than being a specific adaptation to the mate choice problem (Halberstadt & Rhodes, 2000). We should, therefore, investigate what general perceptual or learning mechanisms, such as prototype abstraction and the need to generalize across visually similar exemplars, might contribute to the attractiveness of averageness.

NOTES

This work was supported by grants from the Australian Research Council and the University of Western Australia. Experiment 1 formed part of an honors thesis submitted to the University of Western Australia by the second author. Some of the results from Experiment 2 are described in Nishitani, Yoshikawa, and Akamatsu (1999). We thank Leigh Simmons for helpful discussion about the issues addressed in this chapter.

1. Darwin himself speculated that culturally diverse preferences might be innate.

2. Ratings of averageness and distinctiveness change systematically with experimental manipulations of geometric averageness, confirming their validity as indicators of the spatial averageness of faces (Rhodes & Tremewan, 1996; Rhodes et al., 1999b).

3. Two measures of deviation from averageness were used, both based on the variability of deviations of distances between facial landmarks in a face from median values for faces of that race.

4. The means for individual faces and the various composites had similar variances, despite the greater number of data points in the individual face means, so that including them all as levels of the same factor does not violate the homogeneity of variance assumption.

5. This is the subset of pairs most relevant for determining whether attractiveness increased as more component faces were added. We also did the analysis with all pair types included, and found that Chinese participants preferred the shape composite with more component faces in all pairs except for the 2–face versus 4–face male and female pairs and the 2–face versus 8–face female pairs. Non-Chinese participants also preferred the shape composite with more component faces, except for the 2–face versus 4–face male and female pairs and the 4–face versus 8–face female pairs.

6. We note, however, that this result does not rule out the possibility that people were responding to averageness per se, because relatively little experience may be needed to abstract the central tendency of a class of stimuli (for a review, see Rhodes, 1996).

7. Langlois and colleagues (1994) argued that youthfulness does not provide an adequate account of attractiveness because it did not correlate with attractiveness in their set of component faces. Nevertheless, it may still contribute to the appeal of averaged composites.

REFERENCES

Alley, T. R., & Cunningham, M. R. (1991). Averaged faces are attractive, but very attractive faces are not average. *Psychological Science, 2*, 123–125.

Andersson, M. (1994). *Sexual selection.* Princeton, NJ: Princeton University Press.

Beale, J. M., & Keil, F. C. (1995). Categorical effects in the perception of faces. *Cognition, 57*, 217–239.

Benson, P., & Perrett, D. (1992). Face to face with the perfect image. *New Scientist, 1809*, 32–35.

Berry, D. S. (2000). Attractiveness, attraction, and sexual selection: Evolutionary perspectives on the form and function of physical attractiveness. In M. P. Zanna (ed.), *Advances in experimental social psychology (Vol 32)*. San Diego, CA: Academic Press.

Burt, D. M., & Perrett, D. I. (1995). Perception of age in adult Caucasian male faces: Computer graphic manipulation of shape and color information. *Proceedings of the Royal Society of London, Series B, 259*, 137–143.

Cronin, H., (1991). *The ant and the peacock: Altruism and sexual selection from Darwin to today.* Cambridge, UK: Cambridge University Press.

Cunningham, M. R., Roberts, A. R., Wu, C.-H., Barbee, A. P., & Druen, P. B. (1995). "Their ideas of beauty are, on the whole, the same as ours": Consistency and variability in the cross-cultural perception of female physical attractiveness. *Journal of Personality and Social Psychology, 68*, 261–279.

Darwin, C. (1998). *The descent of man.* Amherst, NY: Prometheus Books. (Original work published 1874.)

Endler, J. A., & Basolo, A. L. (1998). Sensory ecology, receiver biases and sexual selection. *Trends in Ecology and Evolution, 13*, 415–420.

Enquist, M., & Arak, A. (1994). Symmetry, beauty and evolution. *Nature, 372*, 169–172.

Enquist, M., & Johnstone, R. A. (1997). Generalization and the evolution of symmetry preferences. *Proceedings of the Royal Society of London, Series B, 264*, 1345–1348.

Etcoff, N. (1999). *Survival of the prettiest: The science of beauty.* New York: Doubleday.

Fisher, R. A. (1915). The evolution of sexual preference. *Eugenics Review, 7*, 184–192.

Fisher, R. A. (1930). *The genetical theory of natural selection.* Oxford, UK: Clarendon Press.

Folstad, I., & Karter, A. J. (1992). Parasites, bright males, and the immunocompetence handicap. *American Naturalist, 139*, 603–622.

Galton, F. (1878). Composite portraits. *Journal of the Anthropological Institute of Great Britain and Ireland, 8*, 132–142.

Gangestad, S., & Buss, D. M. (1993). Pathogen prevalence and human mate preferences. *Ethology and Sociobiology, 14*, 89–96.

Grammer, K., & Thornhill, R. (1994). Human (*Homo sapiens*) facial attractiveness and sexual selection: The role of symmetry and averageness. *Journal of Comparative Psychology, 108*, 233–242.

Halberstadt, J., & Rhodes, G. (2000). The attractiveness of non-face averages: Implications for an evolutionary explanation of the attractiveness of average faces. *Psychological Science, 11*, 285–289.

Hamilton, W. D., & Zuk, M. (1982). Heritable true fitness and bright birds: A role for parasites? *Science, 218*, 384–387.

Hoyme, H. E. (1994). Minor anomalies: Diagnostic clues to aberrant human morphogenesis. In T. A. Markow (Ed.), *Developmental instability: Its origins and evolutionary implications* (pp. 309–317). Dordrecht, Netherlands: Kluwer.

Johnstone, R. A. (1994). Female preference for symmetrical males as a by-product of mate recognition. *Nature, 372*, 172–175.

Jones, D. (1996). *Facial attractiveness and the theory of sexual selection.* Ann Arbor: Museum of Anthropology, University of Michigan.

Jones, D., & Hill, K. (1993). Criteria of facial attractiveness in five populations. *Human Nature, 4*, 271–296.

Kalick, S. M., Zebrowitz, L. A., Langlois, J. H., & Johnson, R. M. (1998). Does human facial attractiveness honestly advertise health? Longitudinal data on an evolutionary question. *Psychological Science, 9*, 8–13.

Kamachi, M., Mukaida, S., Yoshikawa, S., Kato, T., Oda, M., & Akamatsu, S. (1998). Facial image manipulation system for psychological research on face processing [in Japanese]. *Technical Report of IEICE, HIP, 97 (No. 39)*, 73–80.

Koeslag, J. H. (1990). Koinophilia groups sexual creatures into species, promotes stasis, and stabilizes social behaviour. *Journal of Theoretical Biology, 144*, 15–35.

Langlois, J. H., & Roggman, L. A. (1990). Attractive faces are only average. *Psychological Science, 1*, 115–121.

Langlois, J. H., Roggman, L. A., Casey, R. J., Ritter, J. M., Reiser-Danner, L. A., & Jenkins, V. Y. (1987). Infant preferences for attractive faces: Rudiments of a stereotype? *Developmental Psychology, 23*, 363–369.

Langlois, J. H., Roggman, L. A., & Musselman, L. (1994). What is average and what is not average about attractive faces? *Psychological Science, 5*, 214–220.

Light, L. L., Hollander, S., & Kayra-Stuart, F. (1981). Why attractive people are harder to remember. *Personality and Social Psychology Bulletin, 7*, 269–276.

Miller, G. F., & Todd, P. M. (1998). Mate choice turns cognitive. *Trends in Cognitive Sciences, 2*, 190–198.

Møller, A. P. (1990). Effects of a haematophagus mite on the barn swallow (*Hirundo rustica*): A test of the Hamiltion and Zuk hypothesis. *Evolution, 44*, 771–784.

Møller, A. P., & Swaddle, J. P. (1997). *Asymmetry, developmental stability and evolution.* Oxford, UK: Oxford University Press.

Møller, A. P., & Thornhill, R. (1997). A meta-analysis of the heritability of developmental stability. *Journal of Evolutionary Biology, 10*, 1–16.

Nishitani, M., Yoshikawa, S., & Akamatsu, S. (1999). Characteristics of average faces [in Japanese]. *Technical Report of the Institute of Electronics, Information and Communication Engineers, 1*, 23–30.

O'Toole, A. J., Vetter, T., Volz, H., & Salter, E. M. (1997). Three-dimensional caricatures of human heads: Distinctiveness and the perception of facial age. *Perception, 26*, 719–732.

Palmer, A. C. & Strobeck, C. (1986). Fluctuating asymmetry: Measurement, analysis, pattern. *Ann. Rev. Ecol. Syst., 17*, 391–421.

Penton-Voak, I. S., & Perrett, D. I. (2000). Female preference for male faces changes cyclically: Further evidence. *Evolution and Human Behavior, 21*, 39–48.

Penton-Voak, I. S., Perrett, D. I., Castles, D. L., Kobayashi, T., Burt, D. M., Murray, L. K., & Rinamisawa, R. (1999). Menstrual cycle alters face preference. *Nature, 399*, 741–742.

Perrett, D. I., Lee, K. J., Penton-Voak, I., Rowland, D., Yoshikawa, S., Burt, D. M., Henzi, S. P., Castles, D., & Akamatsu, S. (1998). Effects of sexual dimorphism on facial attractiveness. *Nature, 394*, 884–887.

Perrett, D. I., May, K. A., & Yoshikawa, S. (1994). Facial shape and judgements of female attractiveness. *Nature, 368*, 239–242.

Pittenger, J. B. (1991). On the difficulty of averaging faces: Comments on Langlois and Roggman. *Psychological Science, 2*, 351–353.

Pollard, J. (1995). Attractiveness of composite faces: A comparative study. *International Journal of Comparative Psychology, 8*, 77–83.

Rhodes, G. (1996). *Superportraits: Caricatures and recognition.* Hove, UK: Psychology Press.

Rhodes, G., Hickford, C., & Jeffery, L. (2000). Sex-typicality and attractiveness: Are supermale and superfemale faces super-attractive? *British Journal of Psychology, 91*, 125–140.

Rhodes, G., Roberts, J., & Simmons, L. (1999a). Reflections on symmetry and atttractiveness. *Psychology, Evolution and Gender, 1*, 279–295.

Rhodes, G., Sumich, A., & Byatt, G. (1999b). Are average facial configurations attractive only because of their symmetry? *Psychological Science, 10*, 52–58.

Rhodes, G., & Tremewan, T. (1996). Averageness, exaggeration, and facial attractiveness. *Psychological Science, 7*, 105–110.

Rhodes, G., Zebrowitz, L. A., Clark, A., Kalick, S. M., Hightower, A., & McKay, R. (2000). Do facial averageness and symmetry signal health? *Evolution and Human Behavior, 22*, 31–46.

Rubenstein, A. J., Kalakanis, L., & Langlois, J. H. (1999). Infant preferences for attractive faces: A cognitive explanation. *Developmental Psychology, 15*, 848–855.

Samuels, C. A., Butterworth, G., Roberts, T., Graupner, L., & Hole, G. (1994). Facial aesthetics: Babies prefer attractiveness to symmetry. *Perception, 23*, 823–831.

Shackelford, T. K., & Larsen, R. J. (1997). Facial asymmetry as an indicator of psychological, emotional, and physiological distress. *Journal of Personality and Social Psychology*, 72, 456–466.

Shackelford, T. K., & Larsen, R. J. (1999). Facial attractiveness and physical health. *Evolution and Human Behavior, 20*, 71–76.

Simpson, J. A., & Kenrick, D.(Eds). (1996). *Evolutionary social psychology*. Mahwah, NJ: Erlbaum.

Symons, D. (1979). *The evolution of human sexuality*. Oxford, UK: Oxford University Press.

Symons, D. (1995). Beauty is in the adaptations of the beholder: The evolutionary psychology of human female sexual attractiveness. In P. R. Abrahamson & S. D. Pinkerton (Eds.), *Sexual nature, sexual culture* (pp. 80–118). Chicago and London: University of Chicago Press.

Thornhill, R., & Gangestad, S. W. (1993). Human facial beauty. *Human Nature, 4*, 237–269.

Thornhill, R., & Gangestad, S. W. (1994). Human fluctuating asymmetry and sexual behavior. *Psychological Science, 5*, 297–302.

Thornhill, R., & Gangestad, S. W. (1996). The evolution of human sexuality. *Trends in Ecology and Evolution, 11*, 98–102.

Thornhill, R., & Gangestad, S. W. (1999). Facial attractiveness. *Trends in Cognitive Science, 3*, 452–460.

Thornhill, T., & Møller, A. P. (1997). Developmental stability, disease and medicine. *Biological Reviews, 72*, 497–548.

Valentine, T. (1991). A unified account of the effects of distinctiveness, inversion, and race in face recognition. *Quarterly Journal of Experimental Psychology, 43A*, 161–204.

Walton, G. E., & Bower, T. G. R. (1993). Newborns form "prototypes" in less than 1 minute. *Psychological Science, 4*, 203–205.

Wedekind, C. (1992). Detailed information about parasites revealed by sexual ornamentation. *Proceedings of the Royal Society, Series B, 247*, 169–174.

Zebrowitz, L. A. (1997). *Reading faces: Window to the Soul?* Boulder, CO: Westview Press.

Zebrowitz, L. A., Montepare, J. M., & Lee, H. K. (1993). They don't all look alike: Individuated impressions of other racial groups. *Journal of Personality and Social Psychology, 65*, 85–101.

CHAPTER 3

Evolution and Individual Differences in the Perception of Attractiveness: How Cyclic Hormonal Changes and Self-Perceived Attractiveness Influence Female Preferences for Male Faces

Anthony C. Little, Ian S. Penton-Voak, D. Michael Burt, and David I. Perrett

INTRODUCTION: AN EVOLUTIONARY VIEW OF FACIAL ATTRACTIVENESS

What makes a face beautiful? What makes people seek out and desire to mate with the owners of beautiful faces? Individual males and females differ in their attractiveness to members of the opposite gender: there appears to be no human culture yet found in which individuals do not express a preference for some members of the opposite sex over others (Buss, 1989; Symons, 1979). In recent years an evolutionary view has been proposed to help us understand why some faces are perceived to be more attractive than others (e.g., Cunningham, Barbee, & Pike, 1990; Grammer & Thornhill, 1994; Jones, 1995; Perrett et al., 1998; Thornhill & Gangestad, 1993).

An evolutionary view posits that the attractiveness of individuals is directly linked to their value as mates (Symons, 1987); high value mates are those who can best enhance the reproductive success of the judge. Females and males should both be sensitive to cues that indicate higher mate value. Individuals who were attentive to cues of high mate value, and based mate choice decisions on them, left behind healthier and more fecund children than those who failed to attend to these cues. For example, males, more than females, value youth in a partner (Buss, 1989) and one explanation for the attractiveness of youth is that fertility, which has a direct impact on reproductive success, decreases with age in females more steeply than it does in males (Buss & Schmitt, 1993). In other words, younger women are proposed to have a higher mate value than older women if youth and fertility are linked. Over our evolutionary history, men with a genetic predisposition to prefer younger partners produced more offspring than men who were predisposed to choose older partners. This differential reproduction would continue until a preference for younger partners became universal and species typical in the male population. A preference for younger females does indeed appear to be in place in the human male psyche: males report valuing relative youth in a potential partner more than females do in 37 different cultures (Buss, 1989). Of course, there is more to mate choice than just age and this leaves those interested in the study of attractiveness the task of finding out which characteristics are associated with high and low mate value.

Although behavior and personality are integral to the perception of mate value (Buss, 1989), this chapter focuses on the physical characteristics associated with mate value. Women and men are both concerned with good looks in a mate. Although both genders do not place physical attractiveness at the top of a list of criteria they claim to employ when choosing a partner (Buss, 1989), Walster, Aronson, Abrahams, and Rottman (1966) have shown that the single best predictor of young adults' satisfaction with an artificial "blind date" is facial attractiveness for both men and women. An evolutionary view may be able to help us to understand why physical characteristics matter so much.

There is a diversity of non-human species that relies on external factors, such as the sizes, shape, and color of feathers, fur, and antlers, to attract mates. A variety of mechanisms have been proposed to account for the evolution of these characteristics. One of the most pervasive of these mechanisms, and the focus of this chapter, is that traits influencing attractiveness are associated with either phenotypic or genotypic quality (e.g., Møller, 1990a, 1992). The advantages associated with such characteristics are often thought to be heritable, and so the attractiveness of these traits is considered an advertisement of "good genes." The evolutionary view of human facial attractiveness is most influenced by this good genes theory of sexual selection. The owners of attractive facial features are therefore expected to be chosen preferentially as mates because of the potential direct benefits that a healthy partner can bring to an individual (e.g., decreased risk of disease contagion) and the heritable benefits to potential offspring that these facial traits advertise. Many studies have highlighted the importance of the heritable benefits of mating based on facial attractiveness (e.g., Grammer & Thornhill, 1994; Thornhill & Gangestad, 1993).

The purpose of this review is to explore female preferences for male faces. In the first part we examine theories and studies of human male facial attractiveness. We focus on the three major factors proposed to be honest indicators of phenotypic quality. This part paves the way for understanding the logic behind the experiments described in the second part, where we describe experiments that allow participants to manipulate two key factors proposed to be linked to male phenotypic quality: symmetry and secondary sexual characteristics. Before discussing these experiments it is therefore important to look at what symmetry and sexual secondary characteristics are proposed to signify in the human male face and examine some of the evidence for their importance in attractiveness decisions.

THEORIES OF HUMAN FACIAL ATTRACTIVENESS

The three main factors that have been proposed to advertise the biological quality of an individual in human faces, and hence to influence attractiveness as a mate, are averageness, symmetry, and secondary sexual characteristics. These factors are not necessarily mutually exclusive and theories for the influence of each factor on facial attractiveness have received empirical support (briefly reviewed below).

Facial Averageness

The averageness of faces is related to how closely they resemble the majority of other faces within a population; nonaverage faces have more extreme characteristics than the average of a population. Average faces are proposed to be attractive because an alignment of features that is close to a population average is linked to genetic heterozygosity (diversity) (Mitton & Grant, 1984; Thornhill & Gangestad, 1993). Thornhill and Gangestad have argued that average faces may be preferred to less average faces because owners of average faces possess a more diverse set of genes, which may result in less common proteins to which pathogens are poorly adapted. Parasites are generally best adapted to proteins that are common in the host population, hence parasites are adapted to the genes that code for the production of these proteins. This would mean that those possessing average faces would be less susceptible to parasitism than those with less average features. A second theory in support of the attractiveness of averageness in faces is that extreme (nonaverage) genotypes are more likely to be homozygous for deleterious alleles, that is, to be more likely to possess genes that are detrimental to an individual than those with more average genotypes (Thornhill & Gangestad, 1993). Both of these theories propose evolutionary benefits to mating with those possessing average faces.

Evidence for averageness in faces being attractive, "the averageness hypothesis," comes from several sources. Light, Hollander, and Kayra-Stuart (1981) studied real faces and found, for male faces, more attractive faces were rated as less distinctive, and less distinctive faces rated as more average in a population of faces. A second line of evidence comes from studies that manipulate the averageness of faces. Francis Galton (1878) was one of the first experimenters to propose that facial attractiveness may relate to facial averageness. Using photographic superimposing techniques, he noted that the faces created from this blending were more attractive than the constituent faces. Recent studies have improved upon these techniques, using computers to create digitally blended composite faces (the features of several individual faces are lined up before the images are superimposed). Langlois and Roggman (1990; see also Langlois, Roggman, & Musselman, 1994) found that these composite faces were judged to be more attractive than the individual faces from which they were made up.

Another line of evidence in favor of averageness relating to attractiveness comes from studies using caricatures. A caricature exaggerates the differences between an individual face and an average face, thereby reducing the averageness of the original, making it more extreme in its features. An anticaricature performs the opposite change, moving a face closer to the average of the population. Using three levels of averageness (caricature or low averageness, original or medium averageness, and anticaricature or high averageness), Rhodes and Tremewan (1996) found that as averageness increased, distinctiveness decreased and that, consistent with the averageness hypothesis, attractiveness showed the opposite pattern, with higher attractiveness being associated with higher averageness. In agreement with Light and colleagues (1981), a significant negative correlation between distinctiveness and attractiveness was also found. These studies show that, despite some findings to the contrary (e.g., Grammer & Thornhill, 1994), there appears to be increasing evidence that the averageness of faces does influence their attractiveness.

Dissociating averageness from other factors is, however, problematic. Alley and Cunningham (1991) have pointed out that composite faces possess a high degree of bilateral symmetry as well as possessing features that are close to a population average. As no reliable directional asymmetries have been found in human faces at rest (e.g., Perrett et al., 1999; see Rhodes, Proffitt, Grady, & Sumich, 1998), average faces are by definition symmetric and symmetry is proposed to be found attractive in faces (see below). Rhodes, Sumich, and Byatt (1999) independently manipulated averageness and symmetry and concluded that both positively and independently influence attractiveness judgments, providing some clarification of the situation. Averageness also appears to be inextricably linked with sexually dimorphic facial features. As male faces are made increasingly more average, by increasing the number of faces present in a composite, their perceived masculinity decreases (Little & Hancock, 2001). Facial masculinity is also proposed to influence the attractiveness of faces (see below). It is important for future research on facial averageness to look at how these covariates (symmetry and facial masculinity) influence the attractiveness of averageness in real faces.

Facial Symmetry

Symmetry refers to the extent that one half of an image (organism, etc.) is the same as the other half. A character demonstrates fluctuating asymmetry

(FA) when symmetry is the outcome of normal development and deviations from this symmetry are randomly distributed within a population (Ludwig, 1932; Van Valen, 1962). Most morphological features of plants and animals demonstrate FA. FA is a particularly useful measure of the ability of an organism to cope with developmental stress (both genetic and environmental) because we know that the optimal developmental outcome of most characters is symmetry. Any deviation from perfect symmetry can be considered a reflection of imperfect development (e.g., Møller, 1990a; Thornhill & Gangestad, 1993).

Only high-quality individuals can maintain symmetric development under environmental and genetic stress and therefore symmetry can serve as an indicator of phenotypic quality as well as genotypic quality (e.g., the ability to resist disease, Møller, 1997; Møller & Thornhill, 1997). This would lead to a preference for mates with low FA. Indeed, morphological symmetry appears to be related to reproductive success in many species, including humans (Gangestad & Thornhill, 1997b; Manning, Scutt, Whitehouse, & Leinster, 1997; Møller & Thornhill, 1998).

Studies of naturally occurring human facial asymmetries provide evidence that symmetry is found attractive. Grammer and Thornhill (1994) estimated the overall asymmetry in male and female faces by marking lateral feature points on a face and connecting them with six horizontal lines. On a perfectly symmetrical face the midpoint of each line (calculated as [(left point-right point)/2 + right point) should be in line with the midpoint of all the other lines and so the sum of midpoint differences would be zero. Numbers greater than zero therefore provide a measure of the asymmetry present in a face. Using this method it was found that the horizontal symmetry of the faces was correlated with attractiveness judgments of both male and female faces (Grammer & Thornhill, 1994). Using a similar technique, Scheib, Gangestad, and Thornhill (1999) also found that symmetry and rated attractiveness correlated in male faces. Interestingly, the relationship between symmetry and facial attractiveness was still observed when only the left or right half of each face was presented. While this technique does not remove all cues to symmetry, the authors note that some covariant of symmetry that can be ascertained from half-faces may influence attractiveness judgements. Mealy, Bridgestock, and Townsend (1999) studied symmetry and attractiveness in monozygotic twin pairs. Such twins are genetically but not developmentally identical, and hence manifest differing levels of facial symmetry when adult. Symmetry was assessed by having left-left and right-right chimearic image pairs of each of the two twins rated for similarity. Separate raters were then asked to judge the most attractive twin of the pairs using the original images. A significant correlation was found between ratings of symmetry and attractiveness for both male and female twins. These three studies of real faces therefore support the notion that symmetry in faces is attractive.

It is surprising then that several studies directly manipulating human facial images have found that asymmetry is generally preferred to symmetry (Kowner, 1996; Langlois, Roggman, & Musselman, 1994; Samuels, Butterworth, Roberts, Graupner, & Hole, 1994; Swaddle & Cuthill, 1995). Most of these studies have created symmetric face images by aligning one vertically bisected half-face with its mirror reflection (Kowner, 1996; Langlois et al., 1994; Samuels et al., 1994). These techniques may induce additional stimulus differences unrelated to symmetry. For example, a mouth of normal width displaced to the right of the midline will assume atypical widths in left-mirrored and right-mirrored chimearic face images (see Figure 3.1, a, c, d).

Despite results from experiments using chimearic stimuli failing to detect a preference for symmetry, several studies have demonstrated that symmetry can have a positive influence on attractiveness. Rhodes, Proffitt, Grady, and Sumich (1998) and Hume and Montgomerie (2001) have examined symmetry by blending an original face and a mirror image to create more symmetrical versions of original faces. Symmetrical images were retouched to remove artifacts. Both of these studies have provided evidence that symmetry is found attractive in faces.

Perrett and colleagues (1999) have also examined the role of symmetry in facial attractiveness and three experiments manipulating symmetry are briefly described below. In Experiment 1, symmetry in face shape was improved without changing the symmetry of face textures; natural asymmetries in skin pigmentation were present in both the original and more symmetric remapped versions of the same face (Figure 3.1). Adults' responses to pair-wise presentation of these two versions of each face indicated a clear preference for the symmetrically remapped stimuli. Experiment 2 used stimuli with average texture information generated from a set of faces. This average texture was rendered into both the original face shapes and symmetrically remapped shapes of the set of individual faces, giving perfect symmetry in the remapped version. Pair-wise presentation showed a preference for perfectly symmetrical face stimuli. Experiment 3 used a rating task rather than a forced-choice paradigm (stimuli were presented one at a time rather than in pairs), and again participants showed a preference for symmetry in faces, rating symmetric faces as more attractive than more asymmetric faces.

Thus, the three most recent, and perhaps methodologically superior, computer graphic studies (Hume & Montgomerie, 2001; Perrett et al., 1999; Rhodes et al., 1998) parallel the findings of investigations into naturally occurring facial asymmetries (Grammer & Thornhill, 1994; Mealy et al., 1999; Scheib et al., 1999): all these studies report that symmetry is indeed attractive. It is also worth noting that the increased attractiveness of symmetrical faces is separable from the effects of increasing averageness (Rhodes et al., 1999).

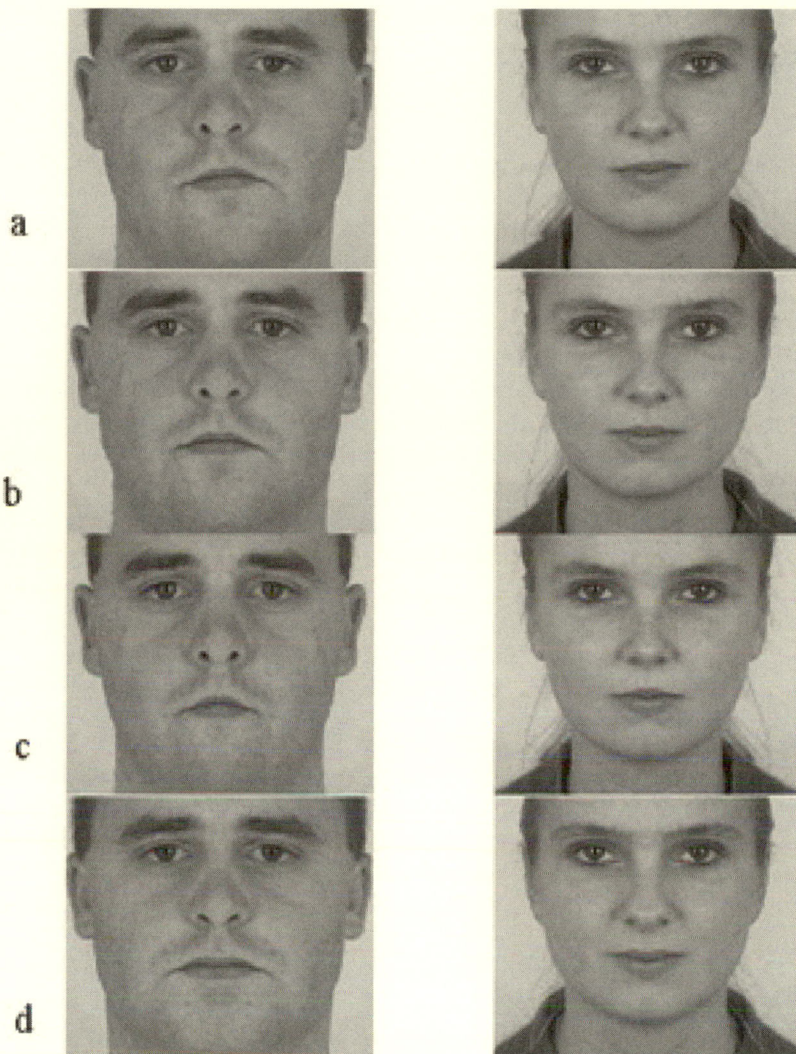

Figure 3.1. Symmetry manipulation for facial images with natural skin textures. A male face on the left and a female face on the right. The original faces (a) and their symmetric counterparts (b), were made using the technique of Perrett and colleagues (1999) outlined above. Note that asymmetries in pigmentation and shadows present in the original faces (a) remain in the more symmetrically shaped versions (b); (c) and (d) are chimearic faces made by combining the left sides (c) and right sides (d) of the original face with their mirror reflections. These images illustrate the shape abnormalities that this technique induces.

Reprinted from Perrett et al., "Symmetry and Human Facial Attractiveness," Evolution and Human Behavior (1999), pp. 295–307, with permission from Elsevier Science.

Secondary Sexual Characteristics and Sexual Dimorphism

Male and female faces differ in their shape. Mature features in adult human faces reflect the masculinization or feminization of secondary sexual characteristics that occurs at puberty. These face shape differences in part arise because of the action of hormones such as testosterone. Larger jawbones, more prominent cheekbones, and thinner cheeks are all features of male faces that differentiate them from female faces (e.g., Enlow, 1990).

Extremes of secondary sexual characteristics are proposed to be attractive because they advertise the quality of an individual in terms of heritable benefits: they indicate that the owners of such characteristics possess good genes. The favored explanation of the importance of these facial traits is that they represent a handicap to an organism (Zahavi, 1975) and the costs of growing the trait means that only healthy individuals can produce them. In this way, these "honest" handicaps are proposed to indicate the fitness of the owner. For example, secondary sexual characteristics are proposed to be linked to parasite resistance because the sex hormones that influence their growth, particularly testosterone, lower immunocompetence. Testosterone has been linked to the suppression of immune function in many species (see Hillgarth & Wingfield, 1997, for a review), including humans (Kanda, Tsuchida, & Tamaki, 1996; Yesilova et al., 2000). Larger secondary sexual characteristics should be related to a healthier immune system because only healthy organisms can afford the high sex hormone handicap on the immune system that is necessary to produce these characteristics (e.g., Folstad & Karter, 1992). For example, in roaches (*Rutilus rutilus*) it has been shown that the size of certain sexual characteristics varies according to parasitic infection, which is related to immune system quality (Wedekind, 1992). Females may use these features to accurately judge infection and immune system quality in males.

In females, estrogen dependent characteristics of the female body correlate with health and reproductive fitness and are found attractive (e.g., breast asymmetry, Manning, Scutt, Whitehouse, & Leinster, 1997; and body shape, Singh, 1993). Increasing the sexual dimorphism of female faces should therefore enhance attractiveness, as estrogen also affects facial growth (Enlow, 1990), and indeed there is considerable evidence that feminine female faces are considered attractive. Studies measuring facial features from photographs of women (Cunningham, 1986; Grammer & Thornhill, 1994; Jones & Hill, 1993) and studies of manipulating facial composites (Perrett et al., 1994, 1998) all indicate that feminine features increase the attractiveness of female faces across different cultures. If estrogenized female faces provide cues to fertility and health, then male preferences for such features are potentially adaptive.

The link between sexual dimorphism and attractiveness in male faces is less clear. Cunningham and colleagues (1990) and Grammer and Thornhill (1994) used facial measurements and found that females preferred large jaws in males. "Masculine" features, such as a large jaw and a prominent brow ridge, are reliably associated with ratings of dominance in photographic, identi-kit, and composite stimuli (Berry & Brownlow, 1989; Berry & Wero, 1993; Keating, 1985; McArthur & Apatow, 1983–1984; McArthur & Berry, 1987; Montepare & Zebrowitz, 1998; Perrett et al., 1998). The relationship between facial attractiveness and facial masculinity is unclear however. Despite findings showing a preference for more masculine and dominant faces (e.g., Keating, 1985), several studies have shown that feminine characteristics and faces of low dominance are of increased attractiveness (Berry & McArthur, 1985; Cunningham et al., 1990; Perrett et al., 1998). Cunningham and colleagues have suggested that a resolution to this conflict could be that very attractive male faces possess a combination of both masculine and feminine features, and so reflect "multiple motives" in female mate choice (i.e., the desire for a dominant and a cooperative partner).

Computer graphic techniques can be used to construct "average" male and female faces by digitally blending photographs of individuals of one sex. Sexual dimorphism in face shape can then be enhanced or diminished by taking the geometrical differences between male and female face shapes and either exaggerating or decreasing them (e.g., Perrett et al., 1998). This process simultaneously changes all dimorphic shape characteristics in the face. For example, "masculinizing" a male face shape by increasing the differences between a male and female average increases the size of the jaw and reduces lip thickness because male jaws are larger than female jaws and the lips of men are thinner than those of women.

The shape differences between male and female faces are described by a set of vectors between marked delineation points on the features of the male and female averages (172 landmark points define the outline of the face, eyes, mouth, nose, etc.). Transforms are expressed as a percentage of the distance traveled along these vectors: in a 25% "feminized" male face shape, each delineation point is moved 25% of the way along the vector to the female average face. The color information from the original male average is then warped into this new shape. To "masculinize" male face shapes, the direction of the male-female vector is reversed before the points are moved along it (see Figure 3.2 for examples of "masculinized" and "feminized" male face stimuli).

Perrett and colleagues (1998) presented both Japanese and Caucasian face stimuli (average ages for all faces, male and female, was around 21 years) to 42 Japanese and 50 Caucasian adult males and females (mean age for all participants, male and female, was around 22) in their country of origin. Participants could alter the appearance of a face (increasing the masculinity or femininity of the shape) on a computer monitor by using a computer mouse. For the male face stimuli, the shape selected by Caucasians as most attractive (from the shape range available) was significantly feminized for both the Caucasian male face and the Japanese male face continua. Similarly, Japanese participants also selected significantly feminized versions of the male stimuli for both the Japa-

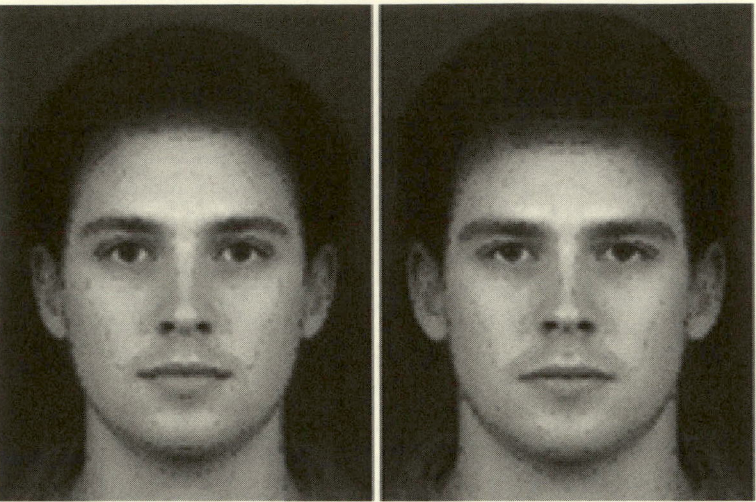

Figure 3.2. *Left*: 50% feminized male composite; *right*: 50% masculinized male composite.

nese and Caucasian male face continua. Thus, in both cultures it was found that participants showed a preference for feminized male faces.

This preference for "feminized" male faces seems contrary to predictions from a "good genes" view of sexual selection and to some other published studies of male facial attractiveness reviewed briefly above. Rather than preferring typically masculine faces (with prominent brow ridges and large jaws), which are associated with possible immunocompetence benefits, both male and female adults appear to favor a small amount of femininity in men's faces. To assess whether personality attributions influenced the attractiveness judgments, Caucasian and Japanese male composite stimuli (in masculinized, average, or feminized versions) were presented to new participants. Increasing the masculinity of face shape increased perceptions of dominance, masculinity, and age but decreased perceptions of warmth, emotionality, honesty, cooperativeness, and quality as a parent (Perrett et al., 1998).

It appears then that "socially valued" traits such as honesty, warmth, cooperation, and skill as a parent are associated with feminized versions of male faces, while traits such as dominance are associated with masculinized face shapes. Feminization of male face shape may increase attractiveness because it "softens" particular features that are perceived to be associated with negative personality traits.

Given the importance of personality in a partner (Buss, 1989), it is reasonable to expect that personality inferences from faces may influence that face's attractiveness. Furthermore, personality attributions, though stereotypic, may, to some extent, predict actual behavior (Albright, Kenny, & Malloy,

1988; Berry & Wero, 1993; Borkenau & Liebler, 1992; Kenny, Horner, Kashy, & Chu, 1992; Zebrowitz, 1997; Zebrowitz & Collins, 1997). Female face choice may thus represent a trade-off between the desire for good genes and the desire for a cooperative partner.

ACQUIRING GOOD GENES: CYCLICAL AND SELF-PERCEIVED ATTRACTIVENESS INFLUENCES ON MALE FACE PREFERENCE

Despite a focus on what is universal in attractiveness judgments, there are likely to exist interesting individual differences in what people are looking for in a partner's face. The complexity of adding the influence of individual differences in observers to an already complicated research field, with its sometimes contradictory findings (e.g., femininity versus masculinity preferences), may have acted to discourage researchers from exploring these variables. In this section, we outline some of our work indicating that preferences can change in an individual over time and also examine data that suggest differences between individual observers.

Menstrual Cycle Shifts in Face Preferences

Women's menstrual cycles last between 21 and 35 days and most standard models of the menstrual cycle are based on a mean duration of 28 days. In such models, ovulation occurs on approximately day 14 at the end of the follicular phase (Regan, 1996). Days 11–14 (the late follicular phase) are characterized by a rise in androgen, progesterone, and a rapid increase of estrogen levels, which peak approximately 2 days before ovulation. This estrogen peak causes a surge of lutenizing hormone, which in turn leads the follicle to rupture and the ovum to be released on day 14 in standard models. During the 14 days following ovulation, the luteal phase, progesterone and estrogen levels rise until a drop in both hormone levels occurs before the onset of menstruation (the beginning of the next cycle). Human sperm may survive in the female reproductive tract for around 5 days (Baker & Bellis, 1995), and so copulations in the 5 days preceding ovulation (mid- to late-follicular phase) are most likely to result in conception. Once ovulation has taken place, copulation is unlikely to lead to pregnancy.

Peaks in sexual desire and activity have been reported at different stages across the menstrual cycle (e.g., around ovulation, Urdy & Morris, 1968; in the mid-follicular phase, Urdy & Morris, 1977; see Regan, 1996, for a review). Despite confusion as to exactly when peaks in sexual interest occur, two studies report that women with partners may be more inclined to seek sex outside the pair bond when conception following sex is most likely to occur. Bellis and Baker (1990; Baker & Bellis, 1995) present data indicating that the rate of human female extra-pair copulations is around 2.5 times higher during the follicular phase than in the luteal phase, possibly to promote sperm competition when conception is likely. In agreement with these findings, studies of women's clothing in Viennese discotheques (Grammer, Jutte, & Fischmann, 1997) indicate that in the follicular phase of the menstrual cycle (as revealed by estradiol assays), women tended to dress in tighter, more revealing clothing. This may be an example of an unconscious action in females to increase the likelihood of copulation at peak fertility.

Changes in Female Preferences for Male Scent Across the Menstrual Cycle

Odor is thought to influence mate choice and there is some evidence that women are able to make biologically significant judgments of male odor that may be fitness relevant. The major histocompatability complex (MHC) is a set of genes that play an important role in immune function (Klein, 1986). MHC differences can be detected in body odors produced by humans and influence preference judgments of these body odors (Wedekind, Seebeck, Bettens, & Paepke, 1995). Wedekind and Furi (1997) examined the influence of MHC on male odor attractiveness using worn T-shirts. Males wore the same T-shirts for a week. These shirts were presented to male and female subjects who smelled the T-shirts and rated the odor for "pleasantness." Both women and men rated the odors of men who had dissimilar MHC genes to themselves as preferable to MHC-similar men.

A preference for dissimilar MHC may serve to maximize immune system function in offspring by increasing heterozygosity in MHC and so lead to greater parasite resistance, or it may decrease preferences for close relations and so prevent inbreeding (Wedekind & Furi, 1997). Comparisons were not made between phases of the menstrual cycle, but all women were tested around the 12th day of their menstrual cycle, coinciding with the occurrence of peak fertility. Interestingly, these preferences for men differing in immune system genotypes were reversed in women using oral contraception, implying that the hormonal changes associated with ovulation play an important role in modulating preferences for potential genetic benefits based on odor.

Three further studies of odor preferences present similar findings to Wedekind and Furi (Gangestad & Thornhill, 1998; Rikowski & Grammer, 1999; Thornhill & Gangestad, 1999). These studies employ similar methodologies but do not propose any specific chemical as a signal and instead concentrate on the bodily and facial symmetry of the male T-shirt wearers. All three studies demonstrate that women are sensitive to and prefer the scent of males who are symmetrical, through some as-yet-undetermined chemical signal. Importantly, these female preferences for odor appear to have a cyclic component. The discrimination of high-and low-quality males is influenced by hormonal status across the menstrual cycle. Females preferred the scent of males proposed to be of high genetic quality only when the risk of conception was highest.

Interpretation of Cyclic Preferences

These cyclic changes have been interpreted from a "good genes" perspective. The possible benefits of symmetrical mates are outlined in the first part of this chapter and so a preference for symmetric men when conception is most likely may be adaptive, increasing offspring viability. In combination with other evidence, such a mechanism may be especially important in extra-pair sexual activity. Females prefer symmetrical men as extra-pair copulation (EPC) partners (Gangestad & Thornhill, 1997a; Thornhill & Gangestad, 1994), and evidence reviewed above indicates that EPC activity peaks in the follicular phase (Baker & Bellis, 1995).

Cyclic Preferences for Masculinity in Male Face Shapes

Given that odor traits relating to possible male gene quality are apparently more attractive to women at high fertility phases of the menstrual cycle, the same could be true for female preferences for male facial shape. Females may be attracted to more "masculine" faces with exaggerated secondary sexual facial characteristics when conception is most likely, that is, in the follicular phase of the menstrual cycle. Three studies, presented below, have assessed this.

Five male stimuli with differing levels of masculinity/femininity (50% and 30% feminized, the average, and 30% and 50% masculinized) were presented in the *BBC Tomorrow's World* magazine. Participants were also asked to complete a short questionnaire with details of the female respondents' age, use of oral contraception, and number of days since the onset of their last period. Participants were 178 women, 39 of which used oral contraception. Following Gangestad and Thornhill (1998), a standard 28-day model of the female menstrual cycle was used to assign the 139 remaining female respondents (mean age of 30.7 years with a range of 14–50) to one of two groups based on their chance of conception. This was estimated from the number of days since the onset of the participants' last menses: "high conception risk" (N = 55; the follicular phase, days 6–14) or "low conception risk" (N = 84; days 0–5 and 15–28, menses and the luteal phase). Those in the low conception risk did not show a preference for faces of different levels of masculinity that was different from that expected by chance (though there was a trend to prefer feminized faces, a greater proportion of participants choosing the 30% feminized face), whereas the "high conception risk" group showed a significant preference for masculinized faces (the greatest proportion of participants choosing the +30% masculinized face, Penton-Voak & Perrett, 2000). The finding that masculinized faces were preferred in this study at high risk differed from the relative shift found by Penton-Voak and colleagues (1999a), which showed a shift to a lower preference for femininity at high risk. This may be due to either the different face stimuli used or the broader range of participants. These data indicated that women are attracted to exaggerated male traits when conception following coitus is most likely (the follicular phase), and not at other times of the menstrual cycle.

If cyclic preferences are an adaptation to maximize fitness in offspring through extra-pair copulations and such shifts represent the interaction of hormonal and social factors, it is possible that women within relationships may manifest different patterns of response than those without a partner. Once women have secured a partner, those seeking extra-pair partners may be more attentive to cues to possible heritable quality (as signaled by androgenic effects on face shape) than those not in a relationship, cuckolding her current partner and providing better genes for their children. For females not in a relationship, maximizing offspring fitness and raising the child alone may not be as successful a strategy as securing a long-term investment from a male.

Two sets (derived from a Caucasian and a Japanese male average) of five stimuli (40% and 20% masculinized, the average, and 20% and 40% feminized) were presented to 39 Japanese students (Penton-Voak et al., 1999a). The participants took part in two experimental sessions, one in the follicular phase of their menstrual cycle, and one in the luteal phase, as estimated from self-reports of average cycle length. In addition, participants reported whether they were currently in a "steady" heterosexual relationship. Overall, subjects preferred feminized faces (a replication of Perrett et al., 1998), and the origin of stimuli (Japanese or Caucasian) had no effect. Women in the follicular phase showed a preference for significantly less feminized faces (Figure 3.3).

While no significant effects or interactions were found when the relationships of participants were analyzed, there were trends that women in relationships preferred more masculine faces in general ($p = 0.07$) and showed a greater follicular phase shift toward masculinity than women without partners ($p = 0.08$). Both of these trends are consistent with an extra-pair copulation interpretation of cyclic preferences: once a main partner has been acquired, women may be less concerned with perceived personality indicating beneficial paternal behavior, and more concerned with cues to genetic quality in possible extra-pair partners (i.e., those features associated with testosterone). Note that there is no need to postulate conscious awareness of the reasons behind these preference changes and the preference change itself.

Another laboratory-based within-subjects experiment tested the preferences of British female students across their menstrual cycles (Penton-Voak et al., 1999a). An interactive methodology was used allowing female undergraduates to alter the apparent masculinity and femininity of five male facial continua (four Caucasian and one Japanese). To investigate the possible role of cyclic preference changes in short-term or possibly extra-pair sexual relationships, participants were asked to make one of two attractiveness judgments: to pick a face that would be attractive in a "long-term partner" (N = 26, not using oral contraception), or a face that would be attractive in a "short-term sexual partner" (N = 23, not using oral contraception). In this sample, cyclic shifts favoring relative masculinity in the follicular phase only occurred in females judging attractiveness for a "short-term sexual partner"; preferences for a

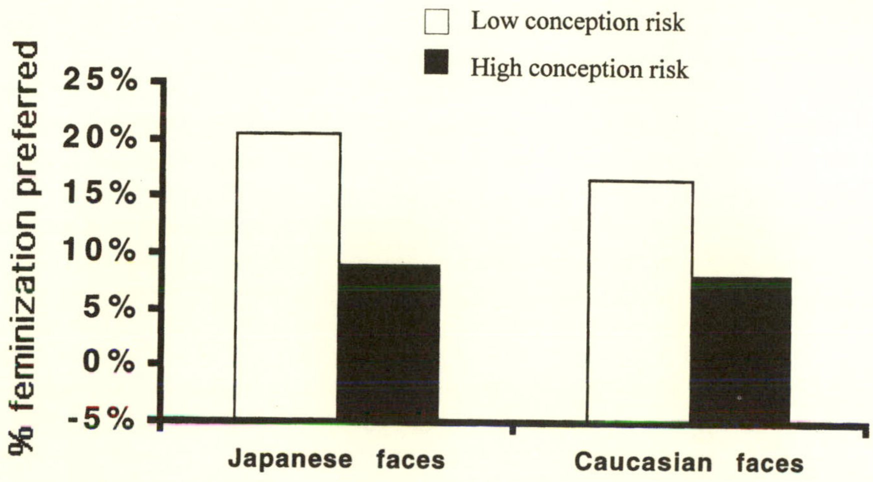

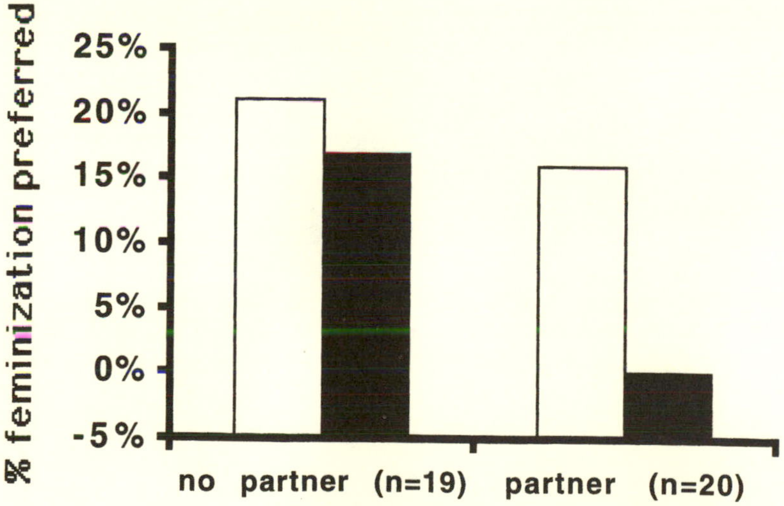

Figure 3.3. Effects of conception risk on femininity preferred in male faces by Japanese females in Japanese and Caucasian faces (top, from Penton-Voak et al., 1999a). Preferences during high and low conception risk phases for subjects with (n = 20) and without (n = 19) a partner (bottom), data for Japanese and Caucasian faces combined.

"long-term partner" remained constant across the cycle (Penton-Voak et al., 1999a).

Cyclic Preferences, Mixed Female Mating Strategies, and "Good Genes"

The experiments summarized above found evidence of a cyclic preference for male face shape: women exhibit preferences for biologically relevant aspects of facial structure that may signal heritable immunocompetence benefits when conception is most likely. The results are also consistent with other cyclic preferences relevant to mate choice reviewed earlier.

Masculine faces and feminine faces are associated with behaviors that have potential costs and benefits to the reproductive success of an individual (Berry & Wero, 1993; Perrett et al., 1998). Heritable immunocompetence benefits may be acquired from the owners of masculine faces (proposed high testosterone). Other factors are also linked to masculinity, however. With a masculine partner there is the cost of a potential lowering of paternal investment. Femininity in male faces may be associated with an opposite collection of characteristics (i.e., low heritable immunocompetence benefits but high parental investment). Female sexual behavior may thus serve multiple functions in addition to fertilization. It is possible that some females may choose a primary partner whose relatively low masculine appearance suggests cooperation and extended parental care. Occasionally pursuing extra-pair copulations with males with a relatively masculine appearance when conception is most likely would provide heritable immunocompetence benefits to offspring. Potentially, then, sexual behavior arising from cyclic preferences may provide the benefits of multiple mates (genetic diversity in offspring, "good-genes" benefits in offspring, encouraging competition at the level of sperm) without losing the advantages of a primary partner (such as extended paternal investment). It must be stressed that there is no cause to believe that individuals need be consciously aware of the possible evolutionary advantages that this strategy may confer or for the behavior it may bring about to be considered moral.

Self-Perceived Attractiveness and Proposed Markers of Good Genes

In the animal literature there has been much interest in the influence of parasites on male ornaments (e.g., Houde & Torio, 1992; Millinski & Bakker, 1990; Møller, 1990b). These studies are based on Hamilton and Zuk's (1982) theory of parasite-driven sexual selection of traits, which suggests that certain traits in males honestly advertise immunocompetence and are consequently selected for by females in mate choice. Those with lower-quality immune systems are proposed to be more prone to parasites than those with high-quality immune systems. This theory has recently been expanded to predict the attractiveness of secondary sexual characteristics and symmetry in male faces (e.g., Grammer & Thornhill, 1994; Thornhill & Gangestad, 1993).

The question of how parasites influence females' preferences for such male "ornaments" has often been neglected (Lopez, 1999; Poulin & Vickery, 1996). In humans both males and females vary in their mate value (Symons, 1987). If immune system quality and resistance to parasites is advertised by facial traits such as symmetry and secondary sexual characteristics (Thornhill & Gangestad, 1993) and these traits are in turn related to attractiveness (see earlier review), we can expect them to relate to mate value in both males and females.

Parasites and Assortative Mating for Parasite Load

In a variety of animals it has been shown that parasites can bring about changes in a host's attractiveness and competitiveness, the general finding being that parasite load has a negative influence on the host's mating success (Borgia & Collis, 1989; Millinski & Bakker, 1990; Zuk, 1992). Assortative mating refers to a pattern of mating. Positive assortative mating occurs when individuals possessing similar phenotypes pair up more often than would be expected by chance. Negative assortative mating refers to the reverse condition, where individuals of dissimilar phenotypes pair up more often than would be expected by chance (Burley, 1983). When both males and females of a species are choosy (as in humans) and are attempting to avoid infected individuals, we would expect to find positive assortative mating for parasite immunity, with males and females of high immune system quality and males and females of lower immune system quality forming partnerships (Møller, 1994; Møller & Hoglund, 1991).

A tendency for matching for parasite load in mating pairs has been demonstrated in beetles (*Timarcha maritama*; Thomas, Oget, Gente, Desmots, & Renaud, 1999) and the pairing of individuals with similar parasite loads is also seen in other species. For example, Thomas, Renaud, and Cezilly (1996) have shown assortative mating for parasite load in amphipods *(Gammarus insensibilis)* and Møller (1994) presents evidence that a similar matching for parasite load is also found in barn swallows (*Hirundo rustica*). It is difficult to separate out the causes of assortative mating in these studies. One of the suggestions of Thomas and colleagues (1999) is that the assortative mating in the beetles they studied could be due to the detrimental effect of parasites on breeding condition. If parasitized males and females are delayed in the start of their breeding cycle, then they will mate associatively, as unparasitized males and females will have paired up earlier. Given that females are usually the "choosy" gender, it is possible that female preferences play a role in this assortative mating. Indeed, Møller (1994) has argued that the matching for parasite load observed in swallows may be due to mutual mate choice based on tail length (a secondary sexual characteristic negatively associated with parasite infection).

Condition-Dependent Mate Choice

A second line of evidence suggests that animals are attentive to phenotypic markers of quality in others. Work by Millinski and Bakker (1990) has shown that in three-spined sticklebacks (*Gasterosteus aculeatus*), parasites reduce the intensity of the red coloration around males' throats. This coloration is important to female mate choice and females preferentially mate with males with more intense color. When cues to color were removed (by using green light to make the differences in red coloration invisible) males that were previously preferred were chosen at levels around chance, although males' courtship displays remained the same. Thus, females use the intensity of red coloration to avoid parasitized males and therefore select males with good immune systems. Importantly, the phenotypic quality of an individual affects their preferences for members of the opposite gender. Bakker, Kunzler, and Mazzi (1999) allowed female three-spined sticklebacks to choose between computer animations of courting males. The two males differed only in the intensity of red coloration (red versus orange) around the throat and so represented an "attractive" versus "unattractive" phenotype. A significant correlation was found between female condition (condition measured as body weight/body size) and mate choice. Females who were in better condition showed a greater preference for the red-throated male and those in worse condition showed a preference for the orange male. As these females were raised in laboratory conditions and isolated from males before becoming reproductively active, these preferences are not dependent on experience of competition in mating.

Another example of condition-dependent mate choice comes from Lopez (1999). The parasite *Gyrodactylus turnbulli* reduces the sexual display and color intensity of male guppies (*Poecilia reticulata*), which makes them less attractive to females (Houde & Torio, 1992). Lopez examined how this same parasite influences female mate-choice decisions. Infected and uninfected females were presented with a choice of two males, one attractive (high display rate, high color intensity) and one unattractive (low display rate, low color intensity). When presented with these two males, uninfected females were significantly more likely to choose the attractive male over the less attractive male. By contrast, infected females were less discriminative in their choice of mates and showed no preference for the more attractive male over the less attractive male. Females were raised in laboratory conditions in same-gender groups and were virgin when presented with males to choose between, thereby minimizing the possibility that learning played any role in the acquisition of these preferences.

Interpreting Condition-Dependent Mate Choice

Why should some females not show a preference for phenotypic signs in males that provide cues to higher-quality immune systems? There are some provocative studies in the animal literature showing that in certain species with bi-parental care, high phenotypic quality males invest less in each female than males of lower phenotypic quality. Male pine engraver beetles (*Ips pini*) assist the female in creating tunnels for her brood and defend these nests from potential predators. Studies indicate that large males left the female and her nest (i.e., stopped investing) sooner than smaller males (field study, Robertson, 1998; laboratory study, Reid & Roitberg, 1995). Robertson and Roitberg (1998) note that larger, and therefore higher-quality males in terms of flying capabilities, had a greater potential for further reproduction than did smaller males. Larger males therefore benefited by leaving earlier in terms of increased likelihood of achieving a greater number of mates. Conversely, smaller males had less potential for further reproduction and because the duration of paternal care in a given brood was positively related to relative success of that brood, once a small male has a mate he benefits by staying with the female longer.

It may therefore be adaptive for females in poor condition to show a preference for males displaying cues to poorer heritable parasite resistance, as the greater parental investment may be of greater benefit to them and their offspring than the heritable immunocompetence acquired from high-quality males. High immune quality females may be able to extract more investment from high-quality males than low immune quality females. This hypothesis remains to be addressed. Even if this is not the case, high immune quality females may be better able to cope with decreased parental investment (or gain little from increased male investment).

"Market-Value" as a Measure of Condition in Humans

These findings in the animal literature, that a variety of species demonstrate condition-dependent mate choice, suggest that humans might also show different preferences based on condition or self-perceptions of their value as mates. Humans differ in their attractiveness as mates. Pawlowski and Dunbar (1999) use the term "market-value" to specify how much demand there is for a particular individual as a mate, and this will prove useful in our discussion. High market-value (or value) females should be more attentive than lower value females to male traits, such as symmetry and secondary sexual characteristics, which are thought to be phenotypic signals linked to heritable immune system quality. Conversely, females who perceive themselves as less competitive in the mating market may lack these preferences or actively prefer cues to nonimmunocompetence-related benefits in faces, such as the likelihood of increased parental investment (e.g., feminine-faced males are seen as more cooperative and as more likely to make better parents than masculine-faced males, Perrett et al., 1998).

Two Face Preference Experiments

Heterosexual female participants were asked to rate themselves on a 5–point scale for physical attractiveness. We assume that self-perceived physical attractiveness of a female relates to how attractive males will find that female, and that this in turn relates to their market-value (Pawlowski & Dunbar, 1999). Below, for simplicity we use the term "value" or mate value but we acknowledge that value has multiple dimensions. Participants were also asked to rate the importance of physical attractiveness in a partner of the opposite sex, also on a 5–point scale. The participant's preference for both facial masculinity and symmetry was then measured.

Self-Rated Physical Attractiveness and Masculinity

To measure preferences for masculinity, participants were asked to judge a series of five faces for their attractiveness as long-term partners. Participants were able to alter the level of preferred masculinity in the face using the interactive techniques employed by Perrett and colleagues (1998), which are outlined in the first part of this chapter. Preferences for each participant were estimated from the average percentage masculinity or femininity chosen for the five faces.

Seventy-one participants (aged 16–64, mean age = 24.1 yrs, SD = 8.8) took part in this experiment. It was found that self-rated physical attractiveness was positively and significantly related to a preference for masculinity in male faces, controlling for participant age (r = .32, p = .006). Figure 3.4 illustrates this relationship, dividing participants by score into low (self-rated attractiveness 1–2, n = 15), average (self-rated attractiveness 3, n = 29), and high self-rated attractiveness groups (self-rated attractiveness 4–5, n = 27).

From Figure 3.4 it can be seen that self-rated physical attractiveness influences the level of masculinity preferred in male faces. Those rating themselves as less attractive preferred comparatively more feminine male faces. Although females who consider themselves above average in attractiveness appear to prefer "average" male face shapes, this is evidence suggesting that they are relatively more attentive to a proposed marker of immune system quality in males than those females rating themselves as less attractive.

Self-Rated Physical Attractiveness and Symmetry

A measure of preference for symmetry was obtained by presenting participants with 13 pairs of male faces and 13 pairs of female faces, one of each pair was the original face, the other having been transformed to possess symmetry in shape, retaining the original skin textures. The symmetrical faces were created using the same techniques as used by Perrett and colleagues (1999), in Experiment 1, which were outlined in the first part of this chapter and were only subtly different from the original faces (see Figure 3.1). Participants were asked to choose the most attractive face from these pairs and the number of times the symmetric face was chosen over the original face was taken as a measure of a preference for symmetrical faces.

Ninety-seven female participants (aged 17–46, mean = 20.8 yrs, SD = 4.7) took part in the study. In line with previous studies, an overall preference for symmetry was found for both male (symmetrical male face chosen 61.5% of the time, one-sample t-test, $t_{96} = 7.2$, p .001) and female (symmetrical female face chosen 57.5% of the time, one-sample t-test, $t_{96} = 4.1$, $p < .001$) faces. A

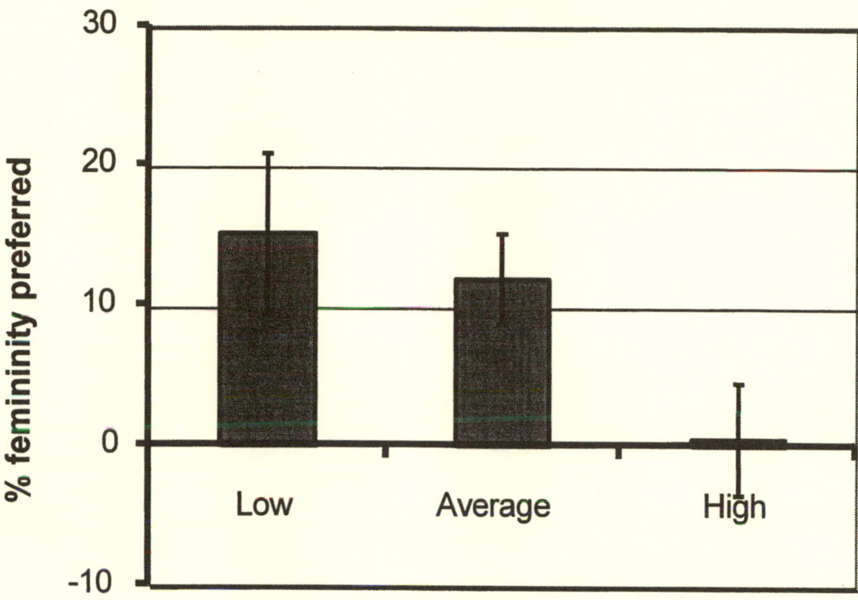

Figure 3.4. Preference for femininity in male faces as a function of female self-rated attractiveness. Preference was measured as the average % masculinity/femininity (+/1 SE) chosen from interactive continua of five faces (see first part of this Chapter).

positive relationship was found between a preference for symmetry in male faces and self-rated physical attractiveness (Pearson product moment correlation, r_{97}= .24, p= .017). Importantly, no such relationship was found between self-rated physical attractiveness and a preference for symmetry in female faces (Pearson product moment correlation, r_{97} = .01, p = .85).

Figure 3.5 illustrates this relationship, dividing participants by score into low (n = 20), average (n = 54), and high self-rated attractiveness groups (n = 21). From Figure 3.5 it can be seen that those females who rated themselves as high in physical attractiveness showed a preference for more symmetric male faces, a preference that was not evident in those who rated themselves as low in attractiveness or when any of the females were choosing female faces. The percentage symmetry preferred refers to the proportion of symmetric faces chosen from a set of 13 faces. These results indicate that a self-perceived "high mate-value" is related to an enhanced preference for a second proposed indicator of "good genes" (although it is possible that facial masculinity and symmetry may in fact covary in real male faces, Scheib et al., 1999). The finding that self-rated physical attractiveness had no influence on a preference for symmetry when judging female faces indicates that the change in preference found

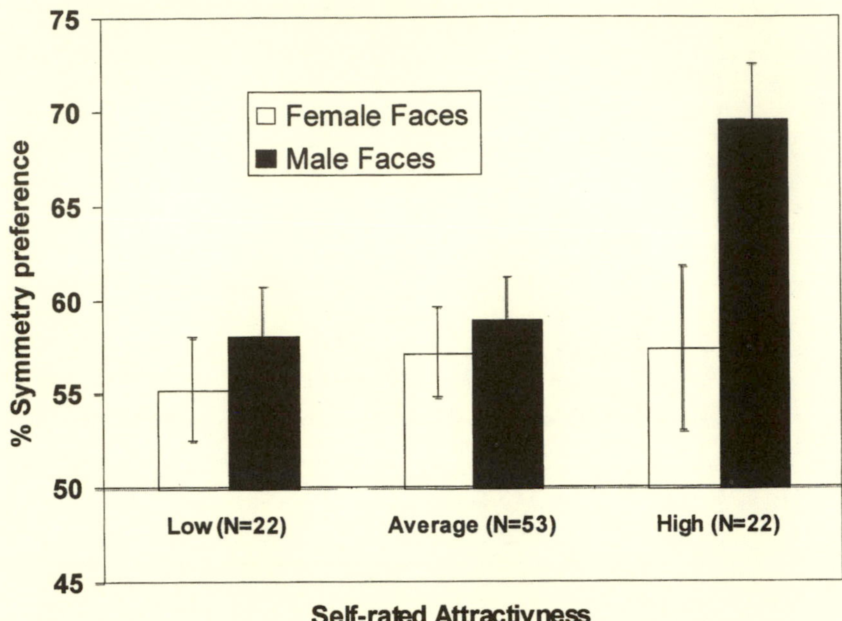

Figure 3.5. Preference for facial symmetry as a function of female self-rated attractiveness. Preference was measured as the number of symmetrical faces chosen from 13 pairs and is expressed as a percentage (+/- 1 SE).

when judging male faces relates only to choice of mate and not to attractiveness judgments in general.

Phenotypic Quality-Dependent Mate Choice, Individual Mating Strategies, and "Good Genes"

One possible outcome of condition-dependent face preference is positive assortative mating for perceived phenotypic quality. In humans there are studies showing that individuals pair up with others of similar attractiveness, matching for attractiveness (Shepherd & Ellis, 1972), and there is also evidence that couples possess faces that are perceived to be similar to each other (Hinsz, 1989; but see Penton-Voak, Perrett, & Pierce, 1999b). Positive assortative mating may reflect pairing with respect to immunocompetence, which has been demonstrated in beetles (Thomas et al., 1999). In our survey a significant positive relationship was found between self-rated attractiveness and the physical attractiveness of a male partner that the females indicated they desired ($r = .30$, $p < .001$, with 194 participants). This is also evidence that females who viewed their market-value as high were more interested in the physical attractiveness of a partner than those who believed their market-value to be lower.

Assortative mating can come about by means other than specific preferences, such as "like prefers like," or "opposites attract." One of the most favored explanations is that organisms do not want to mate in this way but are forced to because of market pressures: their own attractiveness limits the attractiveness of the mates they can acquire (e.g., Burley, 1983; Feingold, 1988; Kalick & Hamilton, 1986). High attractiveness individuals are able to acquire high attractiveness mates and, as they pair up, less attractive individuals are left to pair up with less attractive mates. In this way a species-wide preference for high-quality mates can result in a positive assortative mating pattern. This view, then, posits that we are each struggling to find the most "attractive" mate, attractive in the sense of highest phenotypic quality that signals good immunity genes. If our attractiveness is low we may be unable to acquire such individuals as partners in reality, but nonetheless we should judge those highest in phenotypic quality as most attractive.

In the above experiment we showed something different: participants demonstrated a preference for faces that are greater in femininity when the perceivers believed themselves to be of low attractiveness. Evidence that individuals differ in their preferences for faces based on self-rated attractiveness is therefore some evidence against the traditional explanation of positive assortative mating. It is possible that these preferences are the result of individuals learning their mate value through competition, and this learning results in a change of preference within the individual.

As well as a learning component, it is also possible that this preference may have a genetic and/or condition-dependent component. Bakker and colleagues (1999), in their study of stickleback preferences, found that the genetic lineage of the groups influenced both the condition and the preferences of females. Groups sired by different fathers, despite standardized rearing conditions, differed significantly in both their overall condition and in their preferences for red-throated males. In sticklebacks, then, condition appears to be in part heritable and mate preferences may therefore have a genetic- or condition-dependent expression component, as no opportunities to learn mate value via competition or other means was available to the females. Genetic-and-condition-dependent expression of mate preferences are interrelated, as condition is in part heritable, condition-dependent expression of preferences would also appear to be heritable. Of course, positing a genetic/condition-dependent component in mate preference in humans does not preclude that competition, and other factors may also play a role in the attractiveness of mates that are acquired.

One speculative interpretation of different mate preferences is that these preferences may reflect different strategies for individuals between two extremes (with a continuum running between them). At one end females may obey the rule "If of high mate-value then look to maximize phenotypic quality, indicating immunocompetence, in prospective partners," and, at the other end "If of low market value maximize reproductive success by pursuing males most likely to invest/least likely to desert." Natural selection would be most likely to favor those females who provided the best genes for heritable immunocompetence for their offspring, and so such a rule could only arise if there existed advantages to low-value females not to be as attentive to cues to heritable immunocompetence in a partner as high-value females.

As noted earlier, male beetles of high phenotypic quality invest less in females than lower-quality males and this lower investment arises because larger males have a greater potential to acquire further mates than do smaller males (Robertson & Roitberg, 1998). Although the duration of paternal care in a given brood is positively related to the relative success of that brood, it appears that for larger males the benefits of seeking out additional mates are greater than increasing investment in each brood. For smaller males, the reverse might be true: increasing investment in each brood may increase success more than seeking additional mates.

Human males, like beetles, may balance the prospect of seeking further mating opportunities with the amount they invest (e.g., time, resources) in each mate. Males in possession of good immunity genes may spend more time seeking extra mating opportunities relative to males who do not possess these good genes. Thornhill and Gangestad (1994) have shown that more symmetric human males (i.e., those men proposed to be of higher phenotypic quality) have more sexual partners than less symmetric men. The acquisition of a greater number of mates implies that there is reduced investment in each individual mate from more symmetric males; these males must spend less time with each mate and spend more time actively seeking mates out in order to acquire more sexual encounters. There is also some evidence to suggest that males with enhanced secondary sexual characteristics are associated with lower parental investment. Perrett and colleagues (1998) have shown that feminized male faces are associated with attributions of "good parent" and that masculinized faces are not associated with the attribution of good parenting skills. A recent experiment we conducted on British television presented masculinized and feminized male faces with two dating adverts representing a male seeking a short-term and a long-term relationship. Participants were asked which face went with each advert. Over 18,000 viewers took part in the study and overwhelmingly the feminized face was more often associated with the long-term advert than the short-term advert and the masculinized face was more often associated with the short-term advert than the long-term advert (Little et al., 2000).

Evidence that a proposed marker of good genes is linked to a greater number of sexual encounters and that there appear to exist stereotypes linking masculine secondary sexual characteristics with poor parenting and a propensity for short-term relationships supports the notion that the possession of so-called good genes for immunocompetence may be linked to decreased parental investment. A preference for high phenotypic quality in males in low market-value females may thus have been maladaptive, as the cost of selecting a low investment male might outweigh the benefit of the good genes acquired from him, whereas high-quality females may be either more able to cope with lower paternal investment or be able to acquire both good genes and investment from a high-quality male.

Another point arising from this discussion is that condition-dependent mate preferences may mean that a male's attractiveness is not necessarily related to quality in terms of good genes for immunocompetence (see also Perrett et al., 1998). The perceived value of certain mates appears to be dependent on the judging females' mate value. For example, paradoxically, those males without good genes for immunocompetence may have the highest mate value when being judged by females of low mate value. Females of low mate value may be unable to acquire mates with good immunocompetence genes or else suffer from desertion/low investment by "attractive" male partners. This is a cautionary note that research into attractiveness should not look to heritable benefits of immuno-competence alone in its description of the adaptive nature of preferences.

SUMMARY AND CONCLUSIONS

Summary

Despite the speed with which we make attractiveness decisions, judging the attractiveness of faces represents a complex set of decision-making processes. In the first part of this chapter we presented a brief overview of the evolutionary approach to attractiveness, which suggests that the attractiveness of potential mates is linked to factors that are indicative of possible reproductive benefits. We also briefly reviewed the arguments and evidence for three of the main facial characteristics proposed to be linked to evolutionary success, averageness, symmetry, and secondary sexual characteristics.

Literature reviewed in the first part suggests that there are several factors that interact in making faces attractive and there appears to be growing consensus in what these factors are. For example, most studies have begun to agree that symmetry is a significant factor in judgments of facial attractiveness (e.g., Grammer & Thornhill, 1994; Perrett et al., 1999; Rhodes et al., 1998). For some factors the collected evidence is less clear, for example, the role of sexual dimorphism in determining facial attractiveness has been the source of much debate. The findings reported in Perrett and colleagues (1998; see also Cunningham et al., 1990) indicate that women do not have clear preferences for "masculinized" face shapes, which are proposed to be found attractive from a traditional good genes view of facial attractiveness (e.g. Grammer & Thornhill, 1994). Despite an overall preference for feminine male faces, the proposed indicators of "good genes" in masculine male faces have been found to be of increased attractiveness in two contexts, which are discussed in the second part of this chapter.

In the second part we presented two recent findings concerning the perception of male facial attractiveness that focus on differences in the observers. We examined whether the menstrual cycle influences female preferences for male face shape, reviewing studies that show that women's preferences do change across their menstrual cycle and that they exhibit relative preferences for proposed cues to favorable heritable genetic characteristics (facial masculinity) when conception is most likely (Penton-Voak et al., 1999a). A mixed strategy in female mate choice has been put forward as one explanation of this finding. Females may choose a long-term partner on the basis of cooperation and high parental care (indicated by a low masculine appearance), while occasionally pursuing extra-pair copulations with males with proposed markers of good genes for immunity (indicated by a relatively masculine appearance) when conception is most likely.

We also examined the role of mate value in attractiveness decisions showing that women differ in their preference for both symmetry and secondary sexual characteristics in male faces, depending on their self-perceived attractiveness. Females who rate themselves as above average in attractiveness prefer higher levels of both symmetry and secondary sexual characteristics in male faces than do women who rate themselves as low or average in attractiveness. These factors are both proposed to be markers of heritable fitness but are not necessarily independent of each other (e.g., Scheib et al., 1999). The differences in preference may in part arise from quality-dependent expression of mate preferences, resulting in strategies linked to female phenotypic quality. It is unlikely that high-quality males will invest equally in high- and low-quality females and this means that, despite equal heritable benefits, there are differential benefits for high- and low-quality females in selecting high-quality males. A preference for males of reduced genetic quality in low-quality females could be adaptive, if the costs of reduced paternal investment outweigh the proposed heritable immunity benefits.

Conclusions

Evolutionary theory has proved to be a powerful tool in exploring human facial attractiveness. Beauty increasingly appears to be ingrained in our biology: characteristics associated with evolutionarily relevant advantages to the choosing individual are perceived as attractive. Averageness, symmetry, and secondary sexual characteristics are facial factors that have been proposed to serve as indicators of the likelihood of survival and reproductive success and there is evidence that each is tied to our perceptions of facial attractiveness.

Demonstrations of the impact of the menstrual cycle and self-rated female quality on preferences for male faces highlight an often-ignored factor in studies of facial attractiveness: the role of individual differences in perceivers. Many studies examining attractiveness focus on what is being perceived and, although an assumption that perceivers are equal in their perceptions is both useful and justified in many areas, we hope that studies examining the role of the observers will help to place beauty back into the eye of the beholder.

NOTE

The authors would like to thank Gillian Rhodes, Leslie Zebrowitz, Randy Thornhill, and an anonymous reviewer for their thoughtful and helpful comments. This research was supported by the ESRC and Unilever Research.

REFERENCES

Albright, L., Kenny, D. A., & Malloy, T. E. (1988). Consensus in personality judgements at zero acquaintance. *Journal of Personality and Social Psychology, 55*, 387–395.

Alley, T. R., & Cunningham, M. R. (1991). Averaged faces are attractive, but very attractive faces are not average. *Psychological Science, 2*, 123–125.

Baker, R. R., & Bellis, M. A. (1995). *Human sperm competition: Copulation, masturbation, and infidelity.* London: Chapman and Hall.

Bakker, T. C., Kunzler, R., & Mazzi, K. (1999). Condition-related mate choice in sticklebacks. *Nature, 401*, 234.

Bellis, M. A., & Baker, R. R. (1990). Do females promote sperm competition? Data for humans. *Animal Behaviour, 40*, 997–999.

Berry, D. S., & Brownlow, S. (1989). Were the physiognomists right? Personality correlates of facial babyishness. *Personality and Social Psychology Bulletin, 15*, 266–279.

Berry, D. S., & McArthur, L. Z. (1985). Some components and consequences of a babyface. *Journal of Personality and Social Psychology, 48*, 312–323.

Berry, D. S., & Wero, J.L.F. (1993). Accuracy in face perception: A view from ecological psychology. *Journal of Personality, 61*, 497–520.

Borgia, G., & Collis, K. (1989). Female choice for parasite free male satin bowerbird *(Pitiloryhnchus violaceus). American Zoologist, 30*, 279–286.

Borkenau, P., & Liebler, A. (1992). Trait inferences: Sources of validity at zero acquaintance. *Journal of Personality and Social Psychology, 62*, 645–657.

Burley, N. (1983). The meaning of assortative mating. *Ethology and Sociobiology, 4*, 191–203.

Buss, D. M. (1989). Sex differences in human mate preferences: Evolutionary hypotheses tested in 37 cultures. *Behavioural and Brain Sciences, 12*, 1–49.

Buss, D. M., & Schmitt, D. (1993). Sexual strategies theory: An evolutionary perspective on human mating. *Psychological Review, 100*, 204–232.

Cunningham, M. R. (1986). Measuring the physical in physical attractiveness: Quasi-experiments on the sociobiology of female facial beauty. *Journal of Personality and Social Psychology, 50*, 925–935.

Cunningham, M. R., Barbee, A. P., & Pike, C. L. (1990). What do women want? Facialmetric assessment of multiple motives in the perception of male facial physical attractiveness. *Journal of Personality and Social Psychology, 59*, 61–72.

Enlow, D. H. (1990). *Facial growth* (3rd ed.). Philadelphia: Harcourt Brace Jovanovich.

Feingold, A. (1988). Matching for attractiveness in romantic partners and same-sex friends—a meta-analysis and theoretical critique. *Psychological Bulletin, 104*, 226–235.

Folstad, I., & Karter, A. J. (1992). Parasites, bright males and the immunocompetence handicap. *American Naturalist, 139*, 603–622.

Galton, F. (1878). Composite portraits. *Journal of the Anthropological Institute of Great Britain and Ireland, 8*, 132–142.

Gangestad, S. W., & Thornhill, R. (1998). Menstrual cycle variation in women's preferences for the scent of symmetrical men. *Proceedings of the Royal Society of London, Series B, 265*, 927–933.

Gangestad, S. W., & Thornhill, R. (1997a). The evolutionary psychology of extrapair sex: The role of fluctuating asymmetry. *Evolution and Human Behaviour, 18*, 69–88.

Gangestad, S. W., & Thornhill, R. (1997b). Human sexual selection and developmental stability. In J. A. Simpson & D. T. Kenrick (Eds.), *Evolutionary social psychology* (pp. 169–195). Mahwah, NJ: Erlbaum.

Grammer, K., & Thornhill, R. (1994). Human (*homo sapiens*) facial attractiveness and sexual selection: The role of symmetry and averageness. *Journal of Comparative Psychology, 108*, 233–242.

Grammer, K., Jutte, A., & Fischmann, B. (1997). Der Kampf der Geschlechter und der Krieg der Signale. In B. Kanitscheider (Ed.), *Liebe, Lust und Leidenschaft. Sexualitat im Spiegal der Wissenschaft.* Stuttgart, Germany: Hirzel.

Hamilton, W. D., & Zuk, M. (1992). Heritable true fitness and bright birds: A role for parasites? *Science, 218*, 384–387.

Hillgarth, N., & Wingfield, J. C. (1997). Testosterone and immunosuppression in vertebrates: Implications for parasite mediated sexual selection. In N. E. Beckage (Ed.), *Parasites and pathogens* New York: Chapman & Hall.

Hinsz, V. B. (1989). Facial resemblance in engaged and married couples. *Journal of Social and Personal Relationships, 6*, 223–229.

Houde, A. E., & Torio, A. J. (1992). Effect of parasitic infection on male colour pattern and female choice in guppies. *Behavioural Ecology, 3*, 346–351.

Hume, D. K., & Montgomerie, R. (2001). Facial attractiveness signals different aspects of "quality" in women and men. *Evolution and Human Behavior, 22*, 93–112.

Jones, D. (1995). Sexual selection, physical attractiveness, and facial neoteny. *Current Anthropology, 36*, 723–748.

Jones, D., & Hill, K. (1993). Criteria of facial attractiveness in five populations. *Human Nature, 4*, 271–296.

Kalick, S. M., & Hamilton, T. E. (1986). The matching hypothesis reexamined. *Journal of Personality and Social Psychology, 51*, 673–682.

Kanda, N., Tsuchida, T., & Tamaki, K. (1996). Testosterone inhibits immunoglobulin production by human peripheral blood mononuclear cells. *Clinical and Experimental Immunology, 106*, 410–415.

Keating, C. F. (1985). Gender and the physiognomy of dominance and attractiveness. *Social Psychology Quarterly, 48*, 61–70.

Kenny, D. A., Horner, C., Kashy, D. A., & Chu, L. (1992). Consensus at zero acquaintance: Replication, behavioural cues and stability. *Journal of Personality and Social Psychology, 62*, 88–97.

Klein, J. (1986). *Natural history of the major histocompatibility complex.* New York: Wiley.

Kowner, R. (1996). Facial asymmetry and attractiveness judgement in developmental perspective. *Journal of Experimental Psychology: Human Perception and Performance, 22*, 662–675.

Langlois, J. H., & Roggman, L. A. (1990). Attractive faces are only average. *Psychological Science, 1*, 115–121.

Langlois, J. H., Roggman, L. A., & Musselman, L. (1994). What is average and what is not average about attractive faces? *Psychological Science, 5*, 214–219.

Light, L. L., Hollander, S., & Kayra-Stuart, F. (1981). Why attractive people are harder to remember. *Personality and Social Psychology Bulletin, 7*, 269–276.

Little, A. C., & Hancock, P.J.B. (under review). *The role of masculinity and distinctiveness in judgements of human male facial attractiveness.*

Little, A. C., Penton-Voak, I., Burt, D. M., & Perrett, D. I. (in preparation). *Masculinity/femininity in male faces and the stereotypical attribution of preferred relationship length.*

Lopez, S. (1999). Parasitised female guppies do not prefer showy males. *Animal Behaviour, 57*, 1129–1134.

Ludwig, W. (1932). *Das Rechts-links problem im tierreich und beim menschen.* Berlin: Springer-Verlag.

Manning, J. T., Scutt, D., Whitehouse, G. H., & Leinster, S. J. (1997). Breast asymmetry and phenotypic quality in women. *Evolution and Human Behaviour, 18*, 223–236.

McArthur, L., & Apatow, K. (1983–1984). Impressions of baby-faced adults. *Social Cognition, 2*, 315–342.

McArthur, L. Z., & Berry, D. S. (1987). Cross-cultural agreement in perceptions of babyfaced adults. *Journal of Cross-Cultural Psychology, 18*, 165–192.

Mealy, L., Bridgestock, R., & Townsend, G. (1999). Symmetry and perceived facial attractiveness. *Journal of Personality and Social Psychology, 76*, 151–158.

Millinski, M., & Bakker, T. C. (1990). Female sticklebacks use male coloration in sticklebacks and therefore avoid parasitised males. *Nature, 344*, 330–333.

Mitton, J. B., & Grant, M. C. (1984). Associations among protein heterozygosity, growth rate, and developmental homeostasis. *Annual Review of Ecology and Systematics, 15*, 479–499.

Møller, A. P. (1990a). Fluctuating asymmetry in male sexual ornaments may reliably reveal mate quality. *Animal Behaviour, 40*, 1185–1187.

Møller, A. P. (1990b). Parasites, sexual ornaments, and mate choice in the barn swallow. In J. E. Loye & M. Zuk (Eds.), *Bird-parasite interactions: Ecology, evolution, and behaviour* (pp. 328–343). Oxford: Oxford University Press.

Møller, A. P. (1992). Female swallow preference for symmetrical male sexual ornaments. *Nature, 357*, 238–240.

Møller, A. P. (1994). *Sexual selection and the barn swallow.* Oxford: Oxford University Press.

Møller, A. P. (1997). Developmental stability and fitness: A review. *American Naturalist, 149*, 916–942.

Møller, A. P., & Hoglund, J. (1991). Patterns of fluctuating asymmetry in avian feather ornaments: Implications for models of sexual selection. *Proceedings of the Royal Society of London, Series B, 245*, 1–5.

Møller, A. P., & Thornhill, R. (1997). A meta-analysis of the heretability of developmental stability. *Journal of Evolutionary Biology, 10*, 1–16.

Møller, A. P., & Thornhill, R. (1998). Bilateral symmetry and sexual selection: A meta-analysis. *American Naturalist, 151*, 174–192.

Montepare, J. M., & Zebrowitz, L. A. (1998). Person perception comes of age: The salience and significance of age in social judgments. In M. P. Zanna (Ed.), *Advances in Experimental Social Psychology* (Vol. 30, pp. 93–163). San Diego, CA: Academic Press.

Pawlowski, B., & Dunbar, R. I. M. (1999). Impact of market value on human mate choice. *Proceedings of the Royal Society of London, Series B, 266*, 281–285.

Penton-Voak, I. S., & Perrett, D. I. (2000). Female preference for male faces changes cyclically—further evidence. *Evolution and Human Behaviour, 21*, 39–48.

Penton-Voak, I. S., Perrett, D., Castles, D., Burt, M., Koyabashi, T., & Murray, L. K. (1999a). Female preferences for male faces change cyclically. *Nature, 399*, 741–742.

Penton-Voak, I., Perrett, D., & Pierce, J. (1999b). Computer graphic studies of the role of facial similarity in attractiveness judgements. *Current Psychology, 18*, 104–117.

Perrett, D. I., Burt, D. M., Penton-Voak, I. S., Lee, K. J., Rowland, D. A., & Edwards R. (1999). Symmetry and human facial attractiveness. *Evolution and Human Behaviour, 20*, 295–307.

Perrett, D. I., Lee, K. J., Penton-Voak, I. S., Rowland, D. R., Yoshikawa, S., Burt, D. M., Henzi, S. P., Castles, D. L., & Akamatsu, S. (1998). Effects of sexual dimorphism on facial attractiveness. *Nature, 394*, 884–887.

Perrett, D. I., May, K. A., & Yoshikawa, S. (1994). Facial shape and judgments of female attractiveness. *Nature, 368*, 239–242.

Poulin, R., & Vickery, W. L. (1996). Parasite mediated sexual selection: Just how choosy are parasitised females? *Behavioural Ecology and Sociobiology, 38*, 43–49.

Regan, P. C. (1996). Rhythms of desire: The association between menstrual cycle phases and female sexual desire. *Canadian Journal of Human Sexuality, 5*, 145–156.

Reid, M. L., & Roitberg, B. D. (1995). Effects of body size on investment in individual broods by male pine engravers (*Coleoptera: Scolytidae*). *Canadian Journal of Zoology, 73*, 1396–1401.

Rhodes, G., Proffitt, F., Grady, J., & Sumich, A. (1998). Facial symmetry and the perception of beauty. *Psychonomic Bulletin and Review, 5*, 659–669.

Rhodes, G., Sumich, A., & Byatt, G. (1999). Are average facial configurations attractive only because of their symmetry? *Psychological Science, 10*, 52–58.

Rhodes, G., & Tremewan, T. (1996). Averageness, exaggeration and facial attractiveness. *Psychological Science, 7*, 105–110.

Rikowski, A., & Grammer, K. (1999). Human body odor, symmetry and attractiveness. *Proceedings of the Royal Society of London, Series B, 266*, 869–874.

Robertson, I. C. (1998). Paternal care enhances male reproductive success in pine engraver beetles. *Animal Behaviour, 56*, 595–602.

Robertson, I. C., & Roitberg, B. D. (1998). Duration of paternal care in pine engraver beetles: Why do larger males care less? *Behavioural Ecology and Sociobiology, 43*, 379–386.

Samuels, C. A., Butterworth, G., Roberts, T., Graupner, L., & Hole, G. (1994). Facial aesthetics: Babies prefer attractiveness to symmetry. *Perception, 23*, 823–831.

Scheib, J. E., Gangestad, S. W., & Thornhill, R. (1999). Facial attractiveness, symmetry, and cues to good genes. *Proceedings of the Royal Society of London, Series B, 266*, 1913–1917.

Shepherd, J. W., & Ellis, H. D. (1972). The role of physical attractiveness in selection of marriage partners. *Psychological Reports, 30*, 1004.

Singh, D. (1993). Body shape and women's attractiveness—the critical role of waist-to-hip ratio. *Human Nature, 4*, 297–321.

Swaddle, J. P., & Cuthill, I. C. (1995). Asymmetry and human facial attractiveness: Symmetry may not always be beautiful. *Proceedings of the Royal Society of London, Series B, 261*, 111–116.

Symons, D. (1979). *The evolution of human sexuality*. Oxford: Oxford University Press.

Symons, D. (1987). An evolutionary approach: Can Darwin's view of life shed light on human sexuality? In J. H. Greer & W. T. O'Donohoe (Eds.), *Theories of human sexuality* (pp. 91–126). New York: Plomin Press.

Thomas, F., Oget, E., Gente, P., Desmots, D., & Renaud, F. (1999). Assortative pairing with respect to parasite load in the beetle *Timarcha maritima* (Chrysomelidae). *Journal of Evolutionary Biology, 12*, 385–390.

Thomas, F., Renaud, F., & Cezilly, F. (1996). Assortative pairing by parasitic prevalence in *Gammarus insensibilis* (Amphipoda): Patterns and processes. *Animal Behaviour, 52*, 683–690.

Thornhill, R., & Gangestad, S. W. (1993). Human facial beauty: Averageness, symmetry, and parasite resistance. *Human Nature, 4*, 237–269.

Thornhill, R., & Gangestad, S. W. (1994). Human fluctuating asymmetry and sexual behaviour. *Psychological Science, 5*, 297–302.

Thornhill, R., & Gangestad, S. W. (1999). The scent of symmetry: A human sex pheromone that signals fitness? *Evolution and Human Behaviour, 20*, 175–201.

Udry, J. R., & Morris, N. (1968). Distribution of coitus in the menstrual cycle. *Nature, 200*, 593–596.

Urdy, R. J., & Morris, N. M. (1977). The distribution of events in the human menstrual cycle. *Journal of Reproduction and Fertility, 51*, 419–425.

Van Valen, L. (1962). A study of fluctuating asymmetry. *Evolution, 16*, 125–142.

Walster, E., Aronson, V., Abrahams, D., & Rottman, L. (1966). Importance of physical attractiveness in dating behaviour. *Journal of Personality and Social Psychology, 4*, 508–516.

Wedekind, C., & Furi, S. (1997). Body odor preferences in men and women: Do they aim for specific MHC combinations or simply heterozygosity? *Proceedings of the Royal Society of London, Series B, 264*, 1471–1479.

Wedekind, C., Seebeck, T., Bettens, F., & Paepke, A. J. (1995). MHC-dependent mate preferences in humans. *Proceedings of the Royal Society of London, Series B, 260*, 245–249.

Wedekind, C. (1992). Detailed information about parasites revealed by sexual ornamentation. *Proceedings of the Royal Society of London, Series B, 247,* 169–174.

Yesilova, Z., Ozata, M., Kocar, I. H., Turan, M., Pekel, A., Sengul, A., & Ozdemir, I. C. (2000). The effects of gonadotropin treatment on the immunological features of male patients with idiopathic hypogonadotropic hypogonadism. *Journal of Clinical Endocrinology and Metabolism, 85,* 66–70.

Zahavi, A. (1975). Mate selection: A selection for a handicap. *Journal of Theoretical Biology, 53,* 205–214.

Zebrowitz, L. A. (1997). *Reading faces: Window to the soul?* Boulder, CO: Westview Press.

Zebrowitz, L. A., & Collins M. A. (1997). Accurate social perception at zero acquaintance: The affordances of a Gibsonian approach. *Personality and Social Psychology Review, 1,* 203–222.

Zuk, M. (1992). The role of parasites in sexual selection: Current evidence and future directions. *Advances in the Study of Behaviour, 21,* 39–68.

CHAPTER 4

Female Faces and Bodies: N-Dimensional Feature Space and Attractiveness

Karl Grammer, Bernhard Fink, Astrid Juette, Gudrun Ronzal, and Randy Thornhill

BEAUTY PERCEPTION AND CULTURAL RELATIVISM

Charles Darwin wrote in 1872 in his book *The Descent of Man*: "It is certainly not true that there is in the mind of man any universal standard of beauty with respect to the human body" and "It is, however, possible that certain tastes may in the course of time become inherited, though I know of no evidence in favor of this belief" (p. 798).

Charles Darwin came to the conclusion that there are highly variable beauty standards in different cultures. He had asked missionaries and ethnographers to describe the beauty standards of different ethnic groups. The diversity of answers that he received made generality difficult. It still seems to many researchers that beauty standards are arbitrarily culturally determined. For example, Crogan (1999) points out that beauty standards vary highly over time and history and between (and even within) societies. This argument for a high degree of cultural relativism culminates in the following statement: "Evolutionary psychologists have failed to demonstrate convincingly that preferences for particular body shapes are biologically based. . . . Current data suggest that body satisfaction is largely determined by social factors, and is intimately tied to sexuality" (p. 164).

This argument, however, is contrasted with the fact that humans have a preoccupation with attractiveness, and it has been repeatedly shown that we treat people differently according to their physical appearance, preferring attractive others (Baugh & Parry, 1991; Hatfield & Sprecher, 1986; Zebrowitz, 1997).

Where does this obsessive preoccupation with beauty and attractiveness come from? If some psychological algorithms were able to process information and solve problems better than others, and thus result in more offspring by Darwinian selection, then humans are quite likely to have widespread, even universal, adaptations in our thinking and reasoning (Cosmides, Tooby, & Barkow, 1992). This logic also applies to attractiveness ratings and might explain the human obsession with looks. In this chapter we maintain that human attractiveness judgments have evolved by selection and are responsible for our perception of attractiveness and beauty.

Moreover, we argue that because beauty judgments are evolved, faces cannot be separated from bodies during judgments (Thornhill & Grammer, 1999). Attractiveness ratings seem to be an integral part of impression formation. When two people start to interact, this will typically take place from a distance. Thus, the perception of body shape might often be prior to the perception of faces. In this chapter we argue that much research on facial attractiveness has the severe shortcoming of reducing the perception of attractiveness to a simplistic, one-dimensional concept.

In order to illustrate our view, we will first review different approaches to the measurement of beauty. We start with feature measurement approaches, then proceed to descriptions of averageness and symmetry, and also review the background of possible evolutionary explanation. We do this in order to identify possible cues or signals, which could be used by raters in attractiveness judgments. Then we try to link the beauty measurement approaches to a more general theory of decision-making involving the concept of attractiveness as a unidirectional, n-dimensional feature space in which multiple ornaments are organized signals. We treat women's beauty only.

Finally, we empirically examine our approach in two different ways. One way is the consideration of single ornaments. The second approach involves examining naturally occurring groups of ornaments. We will test which of the approaches can produce the best prediction of actual attractiveness ratings.

WHAT IS PHYSICAL IN ATTRACTIVENESS?

Several rating studies, especially those by Iliffe (1960), have shown that people of the same ethnic group share common attractiveness standards. In these standards, ratings of pictures for beauty and sexual attractiveness seem to be the same over social class, age, and sex. This work has been replicated several times by Henss (1987, 1988). Thus, beauty standards are shared in a given population.

Moreover, recent studies (Cunningham, Roberts, Wu, Barbee, & Druen, 1995) suggest that the constituents of beauty are neither arbitrary nor culturally bound. The consensus, on which a female is considered to be good-looking or not, is quite high in four cultures (Asian, Hispanic, black, and white women all rated by males from all cultures, see Cunningham, Rhodes, Dion, this volume). Three-month-old children gaze longer at attractive faces than at unattractive faces, which led Langlois, Roggman, and Reiser-Danner (1990) to conclude that beauty standards are not learned and that there is an innate beauty detector. If humans possess a common standard in attractiveness, there must be common features that are used for its detection and classification.

SINGLE FEATURES APPROACH

The first question is: What are the features of attractiveness and is it possible to find single features that are correlated with attractiveness? If attractiveness has a relation to mate selection, then we would expect on theoretical grounds that the evaluation of traits in the opposite sex will include two categories of physical features: first, those traits should be valued that guarantee optimal reproduction and fertility (e.g., youth, Symons, 1979), and second, the features of certain sexual dimorphisms should be valued. Certain sexually dimorphic traits are expected to be valued under the assumption that both sexes are adapted to optimal survival and reproduction, but constraints are sex-specific. Thus, the signals that make a male typically "male" and a female typically "female" should be key signals for ratings of attractiveness in mate choice. Early approaches to measuring physical attractiveness were done by measuring various traits in faces and bodies, having these faces and bodies rated, and then comparing the traits to these ratings.

The almost automatic positive reaction to babyness proportions in faces (Fridlund & Loftis, 1990) has led to the assumption that babyness could be involved in attractiveness perception, because it could signal neoteny or youth and thereby promote care-taking behavior. A high forehead should be especially attractive because it is supposed to signal babyness and neoteny (Cunningham, 1986; Eibl-Eibesfeldt, 1997; Hess, Seltzer, & Shlien, 1965). Besides forehead height, brows situated high on the forehead and their curvature are supposed be an expressive signal, which signals a permanent "eyebrow-flash" and thus will give the face an attentive, open look (Cunningham, 1986; Eibl-Eibesfeldt, 1997). Jones (1996) shows that relatively neotenous female faces, that is, faces that appear to be younger than the actual age of the face, are rated as more attractive by male raters from five populations.

However, attractiveness and youth ratings could rely on the influence (presence or absence) of sex hormones. Wildt and Sir-Peterman (1999) showed that age ratings of female pictures are different than actual age, and female attractiveness in their sample was estrogen-dependent. A small chin, small nose, high forehead, and big eyes have been mentioned in many studies as traits of "babyness" (Cunningham, 1986; Johnston & Franklin, 1993; Rensch, 1963).

A small mouth and full lips are attractive, because they are supposed to demonstrate high estrogen levels and thus optimal fertility hormone profiles (Johnston & Franklin, 1993; Thornhill & Gangestad, 1993). Grammer and Atzwanger (1994), however, have shown that high cheekbones, as a sign of maturity, have to be added for a face to be viewed as attractive. These various traits appear to be the result of a high estrogen-to-testosterone ratio during puberty, with estrogen involved in capping the growth of bony structure in the face and body (Thornhill & Grammer, 1999).

The hormone argument can be applied to nose width and length, lower face length, chin length, and jaw width, which retain their small size in women under relatively low levels of male sex hormones (e.g., testosterone) and relatively high levels of estrogen, giving rise to sex-typical hormone markers (Thornhill & Gangestad, 1993). High estrogen-to-testosterone levels also result in the enlargement of lips and the fat pad in the upper cheek area. These enlargements are analogous to estrogen-mediated fat deposition in breasts, thighs, and buttocks.

Ellison (1999) has found that current estrogen levels in saliva correlate positively with conception probability across women when age is controlled. Thus, estrogen-based phenotypic effects like high cheekbones, a small lower face, and the female typical body shape may honestly signal fertility.

Some single features of the body depend on body fat distribution, for example, female breast and buttock size, and correlate with attractiveness for the other sex (Hess, Seltzer, & Shlien, 1965). In general, females have twice as much body fat as males and this fat is distributed differently on the body. Males have an android fat distribution in which fat is found preliminarily in the abdominal region. Females have a gynoid fat distribution with fat mainly found in the gluteofemoral region. In addition, female breasts consist of about 80% fat. Thus, fat distribution is highly sex-specific.

Firm breasts with small, lightly pigmented areolas, erect nipples, and the breast axis pointing upward and out in a V-angle are expected to be rated as attractive, because they are signs of young adulthood and therefore fertility (Symons, 1979). Compared to the adult male, the adult female body build is marked by relatively low values of shoulder width. Thus, the female-typical shoulder width is expected to be attractive, because shoulder girdle and associated musculature develop under the influence of testosterone.

On one hand, the distribution of body fat signals the ratio of estrogen to testosterone, since the dominance of one of these hormones is responsible for a typical female or male fat distribution and body shape. On the other hand, the amount of fat in the female body is important for a stable level of female sex steroids, and thereby affects female menstrual cycling (at least 25% of body weight is necessary for cycling, Frisch, 1975). Kirchengast and Huber (1999) showed that body fat distribution rather than the total amount of body fat correlates with the onset of pubertal hormonal activity as well as with the probability of successful conception in women participating in an artificial insemination program (see also Singh, 1993). Thus, sex-specific fat distribution (i.e., breast and buttock size) is directly related to reproductive success, and the amount of visible fat can predict whether a female is fertile or not. However, overall weight is linked to fertility as well: heavy mothers have more children. Appreciation of heavier women in various cultures seems to depend on environmental stability (Anderson, Crawford, Nadean, & Lindberg, 1992). In unstable environments, body weight is linked to status and to attractiveness (Furnham & Baguma, 1994).

Traits that are developed under the influence of sex hormones may not only signal optimal hormone levels for reproduction. They may also be "honest signals" of parasite resistance and general mate quality. The handicap principle (Zahavi, 1975) explains the evolution of extravagant and costly structures in terms of honest signals, which can be afforded only by high-quality individuals. With regard to sex hormones, Folstad and Karter (1992) provide evidence that they affect negatively an individual's immune system. It is likely that androgens and estrogens allocate energy and resources between reproductive functions and immunological defenses, giving rise to a tradeoff between reproduction and survival. To allocate energy into immunological defenses, infected individuals may be forced to reduce the costs of sexual displays by lowering their sex hormone levels (Wedekind & Folstad, 1994). Thus, traits that signal high sex hormone levels are honest in the sense that they impose an indirect handicap on the immune system.

Moreover, parasite resistance is a main theme in mate selection (Hamilton & Zuk, 1982). The battle that hosts wage against parasites cannot be won by permanent adaptation. Whenever a host develops an effective immunity against parasites, the parasites will evolve countermeasures. Parasites have an edge because they have shorter life cycles than hosts. This theoretical consideration also would provide a more parsimonious explanation for the attractiveness of certain babyness features in women. Because these features develop under sex hormones, they may be signals in the context of the handicap principle instead of stimuli promoting care taking.

Another signal is the absence and presence of body hair, which is also sexually dimorphic and therefore likely a feature of attractiveness. Removal of female body hair is more common than removal of male body hair. Females appreciate body hair developed under male sex hormones, but males prefer its absence. Cleanly shaved legs and armpits are a youthful trait (Symons, 1979).

Males seem to prefer long head hair in women (Ronzal, 1996) and female hair growth on the head is more stable. Indeed, hair loss and baldness are a result of male sex hormones. Long hair thus is sexually dimorphic.

The general function of hair (on the head, in the armpits, and pubic hair) may be the distribution of pheromones produced in the apocrine glands. Hair is expected to give a greater surface for pheromone distribution into the air. Thus, long female hair may be a "pheromone-distribution organ" correlated with optimal female sex hormone levels. The scalp (and all other regions of the human body that are covered with hair) has apocrine glands, which are thought to be responsible for pheromone production (Stoddart, 1995).

Female hair color is also a trait of attractiveness. Rich and Cash (1993) have shown that blonde hair, although infrequent in most populations, dominates in pictures of females presented in magazines for males. This gives rise to a completely different issue. Thelen (1983) showed that preference for any hair color (brunette, blonde, or red) depends on the distribution of hair color in a population. Males prefer the "rare" color. This leads to an unstable situation and a given color cannot be consistently selected as an attractive trait. The reason for this situation might be a preference for "rare" genes, which could help in the host–parasite race discussed above.

Skin color is also a feature of attractiveness. Van den Berghe and Frost's (1986) study indicates that, within an ethnic group, young women have lighter skin than older women and thus skin color distinguishes fertility among women. Accordingly, men seem to prefer lighter-skinned women, because they are presumably more fertile. One possible partial explanation of such selection is infantile mimicry: the imitation of infantile traits by one sex to reduce aggression and to elicit care-taking behavior in the other (Eibl-Eibesfeldt, 1997; Lorenz, 1943). This trend toward infantilization is more advanced in women than in men (Frost, 1988). Thus, skin traits may reliably indicate several aspects of female mate value.

THE ATTRACTIVE AVERAGE

There are, however, many objections to the approach of decoding attractiveness by using single features. One is methodological. Many researchers measure many features (up to a few hundred) and then correlate them with attractiveness. Oftentimes, there is no correction for the number of statistical tests done and hence the replication rate across studies is low. For many features, another objection against single-feature study for the assessment of attractiveness is that the relationship between the size of some features and attractiveness ratings sometimes is curvilinear. In the case of facial features, this has been shown using computer-generated averaged faces, an approach based on Galton's (1879) method of photographic averaging. Several studies have shown (Grammer & Thornhill, 1994; Kalkofen, Müller, & Strack, 1990; Langlois, Roggman, & Reiser-Danner, 1990; Müller, 1993; Rhodes & Tremewan, 1996) that computer-generated composite faces of women are more attractive than most of the single faces used for generating them.[1]

Curvilinear relations also can be found among nonfacial body features. A low waist-to-hip ratio (WHR) is judged most attractive in women (Singh, 1993). The range of waist-to-hip ratio is similar for the sexes before puberty (0.85 to 0.95). After puberty, women's hip fat deposits cause their WHRs to become significantly lower than men's. Healthy, reproductively capable women have WHRs between 0.67 and 0.80, whereas healthy men have a ratio in the range of 0.85 to 0.95.

The preference for averageness could be explained in terms of stabilizing selection where selection is against the extremes of a population (Langlois & Roggmann, 1990; Symons, 1979). Thornhill and Gangestad (1993) proposed that preference for average trait values could have evolved, because on continuously distributed heritable traits, the average connotes genetic heterozygosity. Heterozygosity could signal an outbred mate or provide genetic diversity in defense against parasites. Parasite resistance should be a valued signal in mate choice (Hamilton & Zuk, 1982).

Langlois and Roggman (1990) emphasized the importance of prototypes in human categorization and recognition as the basis for the attractiveness of averageness. Indeed, a basic feature of human cognition is the creation of "prototypes" (Rosch, 1978). This means that we constantly evaluate stimuli from our social and nonsocial environment and classify these stimuli into categories. This reduces the amount of information, increasing its usefulness and its economy of storage in memory. Composites look familiar precisely because they are average or representative faces, resembling many faces. It is still unclear whether average faces are prototypes—that is, are average representations of stimuli of one class, but if our brain uses prototypes, the averageness of composites made from each sex might well correspond with being a "prototypical" male or female.

In our view, one of the most interesting possibilities from attractiveness prototyping is that we may be able to adjust adaptively our beauty standards to the mean of the population. If average faces correspond to prototypes, attractive averageness expands our possibilities of mate choice. If we had an inflexible biological template (Suchbild) for attractiveness judgment, we could run the danger of either never meeting somebody fitting the template or being frustrated by the nonfitting mates we find. Through prototyping, our beauty standard could be adjusted to the population in which we live. In view of this, we should expect learning mechanisms to be involved in beauty standards, and an ability to adjust these standards to the population in which we live. This could also explain the apparently different standards of aspects of beauty over time and cultures (Grammer, 1995).

There are single faces, however, that are not average, but are rated very attractive (Grammer & Thornhill, 1994; Perrett, May, & Yoshikawa, 1994). These findings have provoked considerable debate, suggesting alternative explanations for the attractiveness of composites. The higher attractiveness ratings of computer-generated composites over many individual faces could be due to the fact that the prototypes lack skin blemishes and are much softer than normal pictures. Thus, higher attractiveness ratings for the composites could be caused by their apparent skin condition.

There is a relationship between dermatoses and elevated levels of sex hormones, which are often correlated with an ovarian dysfunction (e.g., "polycistic ovary syndrome," Schiavone, Rietschel, Sgoutas, & Harris 1983; Steinberger, Rodriguez-Rigau, Smith, & Held, 1981). To our knowledge, no one has reported a study that directly measured skin texture or experimentally changed skin texture by blurring or removing artifacts in order to examine its effects on attractiveness. Furthermore, the effects of image manipulation on the perception by raters are unknown, because the effects of the manipulations themselves on the surface of the face are not measured directly, and most researchers assume that the manipulations affect all stimuli in the same way. Fink and Grammer (2000) focused on these issues. They used female faces that were standardized for their shape and found that skin texture significantly influences attractiveness ratings. Langlois, Roggman, and Musselman (1994), however, argued against the blurring artifact by showing that a composite of different photographs of the same face is not particularly attractive. They also felt that composites look more familiar than individual component faces, but saw this as a part of their averageness explanation (Langlois et al., 1994).

In our view, the debate on the effect of averageness on attractiveness ratings is still unresolved. Another problem is that composite faces are more symmetric than most of the individual faces used for creating them.

THE ROLE OF SYMMETRY

Bodily and facial asymmetries manifested in normally bilaterally symmetric traits are the result of developmental instabilities during embryonic and subsequent development (Thornhill & Gangestad, 1996). Developmental instability arises during development as the result of environmental perturbations such as pathogens and of genetic perturbations such as deleterious mutations. As a consequence, symmetry may be an honest or reliable signal of an individual's genetic and phenotypic quality and thereby important in mate choice (Thornhill & Gangestad, 1993). Indeed, symmetry as a mate-selection criterion has been shown in many species, from scorpionflies (Thornhill, 1992) to birds (Møller & Pomiankowski, 1993) to humans.

Grammer and Thornhill (1994) provided the first evidence that facial symmetry may be a significant feature in facial attractiveness. These findings, which have been referred to as the "symmetry hypothesis" (Rhodes, Sumich, & Byatt, 1999), have been disputed. Langlois and colleagues (1994) were critical of the hypothesis after finding that symmetry did not correlate with attractiveness, and that perfectly symmetric faces were less attractive than the original ones. Other studies (Kowner, 1996; Samuels, Butterworth, Rogerts, Graupner, & Hole, 1994; Swaddle & Cuthill, 1995) also showed that asymmetric faces were judged more attractive than symmetric faces. Most of these studies have created stimulus faces by aligning one half of a face with its mirror reflection. Perrett and colleagues (1999) showed that this mirror reflection could introduce abnormal feature shapes. Swaddle and Cuthill (1995), as well as Rhodes, Proffitt, Grady, and Sumich (1998), produced their stimuli by combining a face with its mirror image. Perrett and colleagues (1999) criticized this method because it increases the amount of blemishes in the skin texture. They used a warping technique involving calculation of symmetrical landmarks. In a rating study, these faces were compared to the original asymmetric faces. They found that the more symmetrical faces were rated more attractive. Thornhill and Gangestad (1999a) have critically reviewed the research on facial symmetry and attractiveness and conclude that symmetry itself plays a significant role in attractiveness judgments. In addition, there is some evidence that bodily symmetry is correlated with ratings of facial attractiveness (see Thornhill & Gangestad, 1999a).

SENSORY EXPLOITATION

Preferences for symmetrical stimuli also could be subsumed under the concept of *sensory exploitation.* Recent research suggests that symmetry is one of the main factors in recognition of, and reaction to, stimuli. Several computer simulations have shown that neural networks, when confronted with various stimuli, respond strongly to symmetry (Enquist & Arak, 1994; Enquist, Ghirlanda, Lundquist, & Wachtmeister, Chapter 5, this volume; Johnstone, 1994). Symmetry in faces may lead to an easier encoding of faces. Also, symmetric faces may be easier to process because of their lower complexity. Thus, symmetrical stimuli may exploit the sensory system of the receiver and therefore be attractive in contexts unrelated to mate choice. Such general preferences for symmetry (Rensch, 1963) would serve no obvious mate-selection function.

Similarly, average or prototypical faces might have a better fit to prototypical neural templates. As a result, prototypes might be recognized faster, easier, and more completely, and thus might create higher nervous excitation. This could be the reason for a preference toward average stimuli. Maybe our brain accepts better-fitting stimuli more willingly. Müller (1993) has called this kind of process *neuroaesthetics.*

It remains unclear how features are combined and interact during attractiveness judgments. Considerable evidence has accumulated in recent years supporting the hypothesis that both facial and bodily physical attractiveness are health certifications and thus represent honest signals of phenotypic and genetic quality (Thornhill & Gangestad, 1999a; Thornhill & Grammer, 1999). The hypothesis that beauty connotes health was first proposed by Westermarck (1921) and later by Ellis (1926) as well as Symons (1979, 1995). There is no doubt, regardless of how variables are decoded, that attractiveness is a cognitive construct in the eye (brain, mind) of the beholder.

BEAUTY: AN N-DIMENSIONAL FEATURE SPACE?

On theoretical grounds, the many features in the female face and body that affect attractiveness can be reduced to three categories. The first is signals of optimal sex-hormone levels and/or immunocompetence handicap. The second is signals of developmental stability. These categories may be linked via parasite resistance. The third is youth and thus fertility.

A salient question is how the features that influence attractiveness are related to each other. These features are analogous to the multiple ornaments of birds that are involved in sexual attraction. Møller and Pomiankowski (1993) identify three hypotheses to explain multiple sexual ornaments among species. One is the *multiple message hypothesis*, which argues that each ornament signals a specific, unique property of the condition of an individual. This could be the case if one ornament signals resistance to disease X, another to disease Y, and neither disease or only one affects the overall condition and hence lifetime reproductive success. The second is the *redundant signal hypothesis* that multiple ornaments more reliably predict overall condition. In this case, mate choosers should pay attention to several sexual ornaments because, in combination, they provide a better estimate of general condition than does any single ornament. The third is the *unreliable signal hypothesis* that most ornaments of species with multiple sex traits do not signal condition.

Cunningham and his colleagues (1995, 1997) suggested a "multiple fitness model"—that attractiveness varies across multiple dimensions, rather than a single dimension, with each feature signaling a different aspect of mate value. This model corresponds with the first hypothesis above.

Thornhill and Grammer (1999) showed that independent attractiveness ratings in Austria and the United States of the same women in each of three poses (face, front nude with faces covered, and back nude) are significantly positively correlated, as predicted by the redundant signal hypothesis. Because of the connection of attractive features of the face, back, and front to estrogen, the correlation between the ratings of the different pictures implies that women's faces and bodies comprise a single ornament of honest mate value. The redundant signal hypothesis implies that features involved in different communicative channels should relate to overall condition. In order to test this claim, Rikowski and Grammer (1999) focused on the question of whether body scent signals general mate quality like other cues in sexual attraction. The results showed significant positive correlations between facial attractiveness and sexiness of body odor for female subjects (see also Thornhill & Gangestad, 1999b). Moreover, the more symmetric the body of a woman, the sexier is her smell (but see Thornhill & Gangestad, 1999b).

Schleidt and Crawley (1980) provided an approach that might solve the problem of integration of many features or signals into one meaning. They proposed an "n-dimensional vector approach" to multiple signal communication, where each signal is a single vector with size and direction. If such an n-dimensional feature space is present in the perception and attribution of attractiveness, its structure can be assessed to test hypotheses about multiple ornaments. If the redundant signal hypothesis is true, all attractiveness features will point in the same direction. Said differently, all the features will intercorrelate (e.g., small chin and big lips will co-occur with facial and breast symmetry). In this case, the receiver will be able to decode the signal of overall condition clearly and unmistakably by assessing multiple ornaments. The n-dimensional feature space would then be unidirectional with regard to condition and corresponding phenotypic and genetic quality. This will not be the case for the multiple message hypothesis. If the redundant signal hypothesis is true, a possible method for decoding attractiveness itself, given that the ornaments have the same signaling quality, would be to compare their magnitude. This is the simplest approach we can imagine, because it does not require any further processing like shape analysis or the detection of the relationship of one feature to another feature. This method would not work when all ornaments signal different qualities of condition, as in the multiple message hypothesis.

Gigerenzer and Goldstein (1996) suggest that people use fast and frugal algorithms, which produce the same results as more complex designs of decision-making algorithms in many everyday decision-making problems. One example of a simple algorithm in attractiveness judgments would be *the worst (or best) feature approach*. This means that signal receivers simply compare the size of the worst (least attractive) or best (most attractive) feature in an n-dimensional feature space (regardless of the feature's content) in order to come to a decision that one person is more attractive than another. Note that this method only takes the size of the feature into account, not its quality. Such fast and frugal algorithms would work only if the redundant signaling hypothesis is true. This would allow for subtle attractiveness discriminations, because the sizes of single features will differ in any n-dimensional space. Such an algorithm would suggest that beauty perception may not be a positive concept, but the reverse concept: *avoid ugliness*.

Yet even simpler methods are conceivable. When there is no direct comparison available, a simple threshold model could be used. Then the worst feature has to be over a certain threshold before the whole person is rated attractive. This method, too, would allow for fine-tuned discriminations according to the size of the feature that exceeds the threshold.

Basically, all cognitive models are constrained in two ways. The first is complexity, which is related to utility. The principle of parsimony would suggest that simpler models have a higher explanatory value than more complex models. Second, any model has to use knowledge in order to come to a decision. As with the first constraint, we can assume that the less knowledge a model uses, the higher is its utility.

In order to explore the possible existence of a unidirectional, n-dimensional feature space for the assessment of female beauty, we examine the following:

We evaluate the contributions of the physical features discussed above to attractiveness ratings of women. We will use traditional measuring techniques with landmarks and newly developed image analysis techniques.

We test how these features are organized either as multiple, different signals or as redundant signals. The multiple message hypothesis states that different ornaments signal different properties of the condition of an individual. The redundant signal hypothesis predicts that in multiply ornamented species all traits used in mate choice will show condition-dependent expression and will be correlated with overall condition (Møller & Pomiankowski, 1993).

We also examine these hypotheses by comparing the variability of the measured traits to the attractiveness ratings. A relation of low variability of the traits to high attractiveness would support the redundant signaling hypothesis.

Furthermore, we conduct a principal component analysis on the attractive traits. The resulting factors provide insight into the organization of the sexual traits in the n-dimensional feature space.

Finally, we try to build a model of how attractiveness ratings are reached by the brain, based on the assumption that simple fast and frugal algorithms are used for beauty ratings. This is done by simulating possible cognitive strategies and then examining their fit to the attractiveness ratings. This is a new approach to research in decision-making for attractiveness judgments. The basic assumption is that decoding is easier if there is a unidirectional, n-dimensional feature space with consistent stimuli (i.e., if one trait is attractive, all traits are attractive). It is exploratory and does not provide a final solution to the question of how attractiveness ratings map to decision-making in attractiveness judgments. It provides direction as to how future research might approach the questions of this decision-making.

METHODS

Subjects and Rating Procedure

Akira Gomi took nude photographs of 92 Caucasian women, ranging in age from 18 to 30. The women responded to Gomi's advertisement in the *Los Angeles Times*, were paid about $50 (U.S.), and signed a consent form allowing their photographs to be used commercially or in scientific studies. The photos were taken under constant light conditions with a digital camera and there was no color processing involved. Gomi standardized the photos for size and distance to the camera. Facial photos were with neutral expression and faces appeared to have little to no make-up on them. Body photos were with standardized posture (standing upright, arms extending down the sides of the body with the feet a few inches apart) and perpendicular orientation to the camera.

Three different picture poses of each subject were rated for attractiveness: face only, front of nude body from head to knee with head and hair blocked out, and nude back from head to knee bend. The photos (350 x 480 pixels in size, 72 dpi resolution, color control by Color Sync from Apple Computers) were presented to each rater on a 17-inch computer screen using presentation software developed by the first author. The pictures were first presented individually for five seconds and sequentially to each rater in order to give the rater an overview of the photos. Immediately after this preview, the photos were presented to the rater for rating. Each rater conducted ratings privately without anyone else in the room. Photo order in presentations was randomized initially, but all raters of a set of photos saw the same order in both the preview and actual rating aspects. Rating was on a 1–7 scale of attractiveness, where 7 is most attractive and 1 is least attractive. Opposite sex attractiveness ratings of facial photographs are known to be related positively to romantic and sexual interest in the person depicted (e.g., Grammer, 1995).

Each of the three sets of pictures of each subject were rated by men who self-reported their age (mean age = 25 yrs, range = 19–55) and ethnicity. Each rater rated only one of the three sets. Three groups of men (N = 10 per group) rated each set in each country; there were 30 raters in Vienna and 30 raters in New Mexico. The New Mexico ratings were used to examine the cross-cultural generality of the attractiveness ratings. All Viennese raters identified themselves as Caucasian, but U.S. raters showed a mixture of self-reported ethnic backgrounds: Oriental (3 raters), Hispanic (5 raters), Native American (3 raters), and Caucasian (19 raters). (For interrater reliability, see Results.)

In some pictures the visibility of focal body parts was restricted by hair. These photos were not usable for measurements and digital image analysis and therefore the final number of women used for this paper (n = 70) differs from that used by Thornhill and Grammer (1999).

Measurements

Standardization

Before image-processing operations were performed, the pictures were standardized to the same orientation. The faces were coded with 51 landmarks (source coordinates, see Figure 4.1). In a second step, the mean coordinates (destination coordinates) for all faces and the mean respective landmarks were calculated. A computer program for the size standardization of the faces and figures was developed following Bookstein (1997) and Wolberg (1990) using a simplified version of the procrustes approach. This program calculates the center of gravity of the source coordinates for each face. The face was then moved on the picture plane so that the center of gravity of the face fell on the center of gravity of the destination coordinates. Finally, each face was resized to 150% of its original size. Faces were then scaled down in one-pixel steps, until the square sum of the difference between source and destination coordinates reached a minimum (least square method). After scaling, the face was rotated about the center of gravity for 45°. Then the same method as above was applied for stepwise rotation. This resulted in nondistorted size- and orientation-optimized pictures in relation to the center of gravity of the face. The same procedure was applied to the front (46 landmarks) and the back views

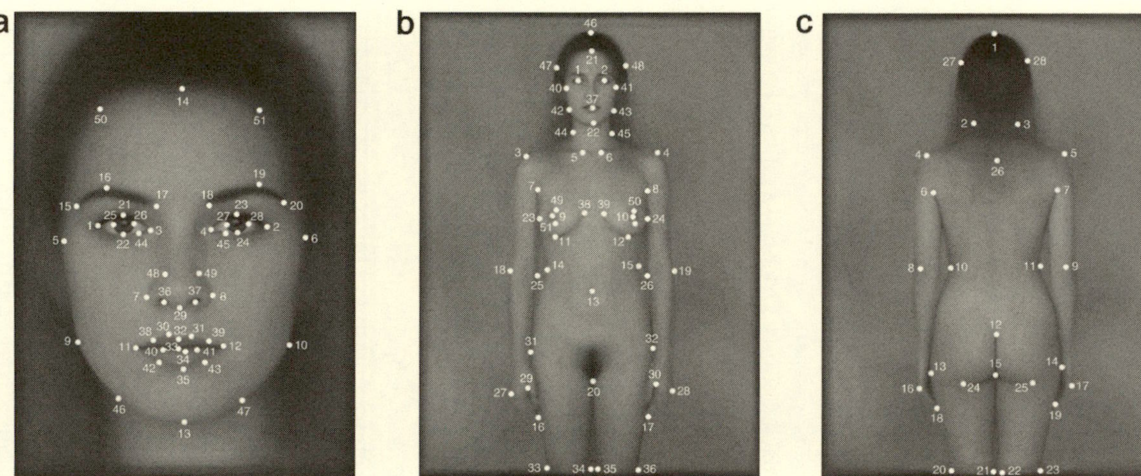

Figure 4.1. This figure shows the landmarks on the three views (face, front, and back) used in this study.

(28 landmarks) (Figure 4.1). Landmark placement reliability was tested with an untrained student and resulted in a mean error of 1.5 (SD = 0.8) pixels placement error. This is an error of 0.43% picture size in the horizontal direction and 0.31% in the vertical direction.

Feature Measurements

Thirty-six features were measured. Some basic measurements (height, weight, breast size, and waist and hip circumference) were taken directly by Akira Gomi. All other measurements were taken from the pictures themselves.

The features were all derived from the literature as having a potential influence on attractiveness ratings in faces or bodies. Thus, for each feature, we could predict the possible relationship to attractiveness (see Introduction and Appendix). The feature measurements were divided into three main categories: (a) direct pixel dimensions of features (see Appendix, numbers 1 to 10); (b) measurements analyzed automatically by digital image analysis features (see Appendix, numbers 11 to 16); and (c) global stimulus descriptors derived from digital image analysis features (see Appendix, numbers 17 to 18).

Direct pixel dimension measurement was used for those features in which the size of the feature is predicted to correlate either negatively or positively with attractiveness. This involved 19 features (forehead height, brow height and curvature, lower face length, nose width and length, chin length and jaw width, eye width and height, mouth width and height, cheekbone height, breast height, areolar size, angle of breast axis, buttock size, hair length, and shoulder width).

Digital image analysis methods were applied to the measurement of 11 additional features. These features are face, breast, and buttock asymmetry; skin texture homogeneity; skin color for face, front, and back; hair color and pubic hair color; nipple color; and lip color. For all eleven measurements predictions were derived from the literature (see Appendix).

Finally, we added six global stimulus descriptors to the measurements (averageness for face, front, and back; stimulus complexity for face, front, and back). The stimulus complexity features allow us to assess whether there is a global influence of complexity on the ratings of the stimulus itself as predicted by neuroaesthetic theory. The digital assessment of averageness allows us to avoid the pitfall of digital alterations of pictures in order to assess the influence of averageness (see Note 1).

RESULTS

Trait Measurements and Attractiveness

Thornhill and Grammer (1999) showed, using the same stimulus materials and attractiveness ratings as in this study, that there are significant correlations for the ratings of face with back and with front poses, as well as for the poses back and front. Austrian and American males agreed in their attractiveness ratings, both within and between countries. We calculated the reliability for the subsample ($n = 70$) used herein. The Austrian ratings for face, front, and back have a reliability of Cronbach's alpha = 0.71. The American ratings showed a comparably high reliability of alpha = 0.72. When all ratings are analyzed together (Americans, Austrians, faces, front, and back), alpha was 0.87. This indicates that the attractiveness ratings for all views and the two cultures are reliable. In the subsample, the raters judged the attractiveness of a face similarly to that of the front and the back view of the same person (Spearman correlations between the three views: face and front $r = 0.29$, $p < .05$; face and back $r = 0.37$, $p < .05$; front and back $r = 0.74$, $p < .05$). This suggests a unidirectional, n-dimensional feature space, as predicted by the redundant signal hypothesis. Thus, attractiveness was summed up for all views (total attractiveness, Table 4.1).

In order to test the contribution of the single measurements to the overall rating of attractiveness, we calculated the single correlations between each of the variables outlined above and total attractiveness (see Table 4.1); 12 of 36 correlations reached significance and 19 pointed in the predicted direction. Four of the significant correlations (breast circumference, eye height, back view color value, and front view color value) pointed in the opposite direction than predicted. Given the high number of correlations, their statistical significance is not the most salient issue. Instead, the size of a correlation coefficient has to be taken into account. Also, even when there is a weak relation between the size of the single measurements and attractiveness, it appears that facial and body traits, in general, contribute to the ratings in the same direction.

Next, we tested for the uniformity of the features. For this, the data were z-transformed in order to make the values for the different traits comparable in size. For subsequent interpretation of the results, this transformation means that we do not look anymore at the absolute size of a trait for one person compared to all the sizes of that trait for others in the sample. We correlated the variability of values of all traits with total attractiveness. The result was a small, but significant correlation, $r = -0.23$ ($n = 70, p = .05$). This means that a female who was rated attractive showed low variability in those traits we selected for the analysis. In a female who was rated unattractive, all traits tended to differ more in value and extremes occurred. This pattern is consistent with the existence of a unidirectional, n-dimensional feature space, where attractive features in the body and face are linked within women, and variable combinations of traits within women are rated unattractive. We turn now to the question of what heuristics a person might use for the assessment of attractiveness. There are several strategies possible and we simulate these strategies with our data.

Single Feature Measurements and Decision-Making

As discussed above, there is some evidence for the redundant signal hypothesis. Thus, we explored whether single traits could be the basis of deci-

	Attractiveness				
	Face	Front view	Back view	Total	Prediction
Height†	.02	.17	.31*	.24*	+
Breast circumference†	-.21	-.18	-.23	-.24*	+
Waist circumference†	-.05	-.31*	-.46*	-.36*	-
Hip circumference†	-.01	-.23	-.24*	-.20	+
Weight†	.01	-.14	-.18	-.14	-
Forehead height	-.18	-.14	-.19	-.22	+
Brow height	.07	.26*	.23	.23	+
Brow curvature	.13	.09	.02	.08	+
Lower face length	-.09	-.03	-.01	-.04	-
Nose length	-.10	.01	-.01	-.03	-
Nose width	-.13	-.02	.10	.02	-
Jaw width	.11	-.31*	-.18	-.15	-
Eye width	.25*	-.07	.05	.09	+
Eye height	-.29*	-.19	-.23	-.28*	+
Mouth width	.01	.10	.15	.12	-
Mouth height	.33*	.35*	.37*	.41*	+
Cheekbone height	-.08	-.06	-.20	-.12	+
Breast size	.06	.47*	.33*	.35*	+
Areolar size	-.16	-.45*	-.42*	-.41*	-
Angle of breast axis	.07	.10	-.01	.05	+
Buttock size	-.07	-.06	-.25*	-.18	+
Hair length	.18	.26*	.33*	.34*	+
Shoulder width	-.05	-.15	-.21	-.18	-
Face symmetry	.22	.25*	.32*	.34*	+
Breast symmetry	.14	.11	.18	.16	+
Buttock symmetry	-.09	.05	.03	-.01	+
Skin homogeneity	.16	.11	.03	.12	+
Face color value	-.02	-.09	-.09	-.10	+
Back view color value	-.19	-.26*	-.29*	-.31*	+
Front view color value	-.15	-.28*	-.20	-.25*	+
Hair color value	-.03	-.01	.00	-.01	+
Pubic hair color value	.21	.24*	.21	.26*	+
Areolar red color value	.18	.03	.09	.11	+
Areolar color value	-.19	-.03	-.11	-.11	+
Lip red color value	-.04	.00	-.03	-.02	+
Lip color value	-.07	-.14	-.10	-.13	+

*$p < 0.05$

Table 4.1. Pearson correlations of single features with assessed attractiveness of the face, the front view, the back view, and all together. For prediction of the direction of the correlation (+/-), see Introduction. Measurements, which were taken from the real person, are marked with †, otherwise measurements were taken from photographs (N = 70).

sion-making in attractiveness ratings. The first strategy we tested is *avoid the most extreme trait.* This is a simple decision strategy, which would work as follows. The rater would look at all traits, compare them, and then take the most extreme one (for instance, nose size) for rating and comparison between rated subjects. This strategy would not require a unidirectional, n-dimensional feature space, but it would require knowledge about the variation of all traits in order to decide which trait is of extreme size in comparison to all other traits. In order to test this, the maxims of the absolute values of the z-scores for each target were calculated, and the value of the trait with the highest absolute z-score was taken as the most extreme trait for the simulation. The results in Table 4.2 indicate that such a strategy would lead to poor decision accuracy. Although there was a tendency for the sizes of the trait with the highest z-score to be negatively correlated with attractiveness, none of the correlations were significant. Thus, attractiveness ratings do not appear to be attributed by an avoidance of extremes strategy.

The second strategy would be as simple as the strategy above. This strategy can be called an *idiosyncratic choice.* In this strategy, only one trait is looked at, a haphazard or random choice, but the rater has knowledge of the attractiveness distribution for this trait. In this case, a rater uses, for instance, only eye size, and another rater uses only mouth width. To examine this strategy, we multiplied all features' sizes that correlate negatively with attractiveness by -1, so that all correlations with attractiveness are positive. Then we selected for each rater one variable at random. Each rater would rely on just one of the features and use it to make his attractiveness decision. This was done in 15 simulations. The correlation between randomly selected trait size and attractiveness reached significance once out of 15 simulations. Table 4.2 shows the

	Attractiveness ratings			
Strategy	Face	Front	Back	Total
Avoid the most extreme trait	-.12	-.19	-.07	-.14
Idiosyncratic choice	-.24 -> .13	-23 -> .29	-.16 -> .36	-.20 -> .31
Use the best trait	.11	.19	.25*	.22
Avoid the worst trait	.20	.44*	.37*	.41*
Compare to average	-.13	-.28*	-.16	-.21
Use the least complex stimulus	-.15	-.19	-.21	-.24*
Use the best factor	.13	.44*	.55*	.48*
Use the worst factor	.35*	.49*	.45*	.53*

*p < 0.05

Table 4.2. Correlations between outcomes of decision strategies and attractiveness ratings (N = 70).

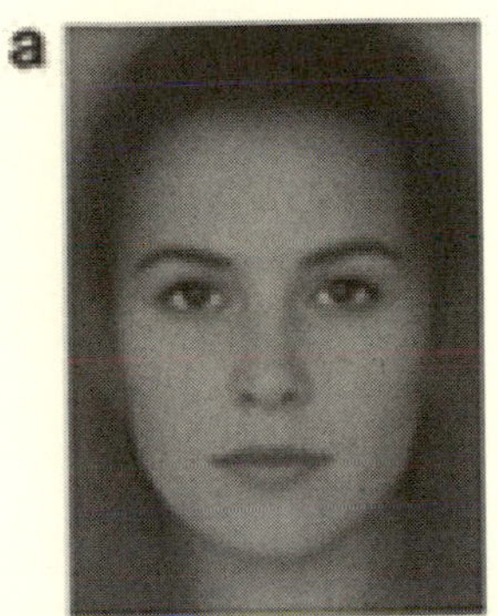

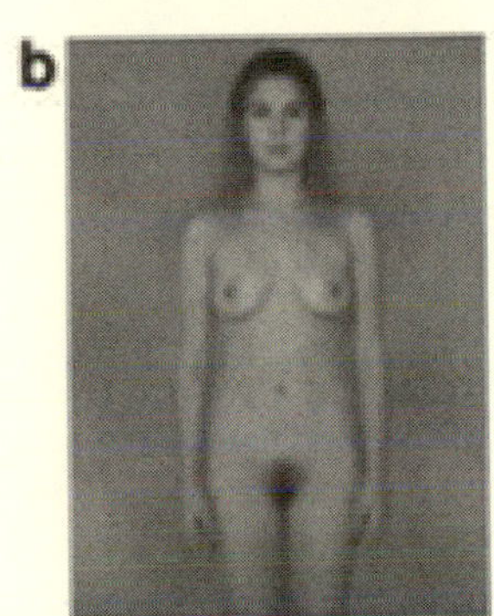

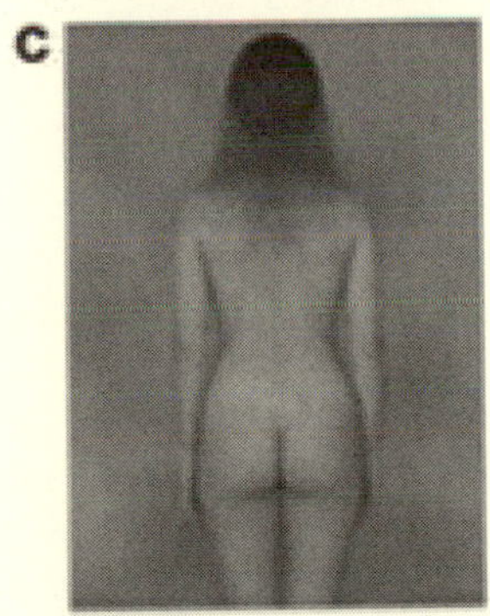

Figure 4.2. This is the average morph of all 70 females from this study. Pictures were morphed in one single pass for all 70 subjects.

results as a correlation range. This strategy also performed poorly in predicting attractiveness.

Another strategy can be called *use the best trait*. In contrast to the first strategy and like the second strategy, a unidirectional, n-dimensional feature space has to be present. This means that all traits are redundant signals with regard to attractiveness. In order to simulate this redundancy, all trait values correlating negatively with attractiveness were multiplied by -1. The strategy then would work as follows: compare all traits and then select the best one (i.e., trait with maximum cue value, the trait correlating highest with attractiveness), and use the cue value of this trait for the attractiveness decision. As shown in Table 4.2, the correlation between actual ratings and trait size by this method is higher than with the first strategy but is not significant.

Use the best represents a positive concept of attractiveness. In contrast, the fourth strategy we tested is an avoidance strategy. In this case, attractiveness ratings are perceived as negative concepts, not positive ones. Beauty judgment might not be an appraisal of positive stimuli, but an avoidance strategy, here called *avoid the worst*. It would use the same knowledge as the third strategy, but this time simply take the minimum size of the trait with the smallest value for a decision. In Table 4.2 we show that, with the exception of the face, such a strategy yields significant correlations between trait selection results and attractiveness ratings. Thus, so far, the avoidance strategy provides the best fit to data.

An alternative to the single-feature approach is one that subsumes single features for decision-making about attractiveness. Thus, we tried to identify one or more latent variables behind the single features by factor analysis. First, however, we will look at two other alternatives to a single feature approach: averageness and stimulus complexity.

The Role of Averageness

One objection against a strategy that involves examining many single features before decision-making is the amount of information that has to be assessed and used for decisions. Thus, we tried to simulate information reduction strategies of prototyping and determining stimulus complexity. The prototyping strategy is called *compare to averageness*. In order to asses averageness, each picture was morphed to the mean coordinates and then the amount of deviance from the mean was calculated. When a picture is warped to other coordinates, each pixel will move by a certain distance. These distances were summed up. The measure describes how far away a picture is from the mean of all pictures, that is, from the assumed prototype. Figure 4.2 shows morphed prototypes for the face, front, and back views.

In addition to examining the relation between prototypicality of a stimulus and attractiveness, we determined whether there is a correlation (rank-Spearman correlation, *rs*), between face, front, and back view deviance from the average. If so, this would be evidence for a unidirectional, n-dimensional feature space. There were indeed significant positive correlations between deviance of face and front ($n = 70$, $rs = .25$, $p = .04$), deviance of front and back ($n = 70$, $rs = .29$, $p = .01$), but there was no significant correlation between face and back ($n = 70$, $rs = .06$, n.s.). This result supports our assumptions only partially.

When we compared the three views with the respective ratings, we found negative correlations for deviance of face and facial attractiveness ($n = 70$, $rs = -.26$, $p = .05$), for deformation of front view and front attractiveness ($n = 70$, $rs = -.36$, $p = .002$), but again none for back view and back attractiveness ($n = 70$, $rs = -.02$, n.s.). Finally, we computed a complete deviance and correlated it with attractiveness, but only front attractiveness deviance from average reached significance (see Table 4.2).

These results suggest that an average appearance might be attractive, but there is probably more than a simple fitting on an average template. They also imply that attractiveness is more than just averageness.

Stimulus Complexity and Attractiveness

An assumption sometimes made about attractiveness ratings is that the mere complexity of a stimulus could be responsible for the ratings. Thus, we tested another strategy: *use the least complex stimulus*, and calculated the amount of image compression, which is possible for each picture. The more compression possible, the less complex the stimulus. As was the case for deviance from prototype, there were significant positive interrelations for compression of face, front, and back view ($n = 70$, face-back $rs = .25$, p = .03; face-front $rs = .11$, n.s.; back-front $rs = .54$, $p = .001$). Moreover, there was a positive correlation between variability (see above) and total complexity ($n = 70$, $rs = .41$, $p = .001$). When we looked for the correlations of the single complexity measures and attractiveness, there was only one significant correlation: the less complex the stimulus, the higher the total attractiveness (see Table 4.2).

Factor Analysis of the Traits and Attractiveness

So far, the analysis shows that one strategy (i.e., *avoid the worst*) accounts for the highest variance reduction in attractiveness ratings. The disadvantage of this strategy is that it requires a large amount of knowledge; the rater has to know each trait, its distribution, and its relation to attractiveness (i.e., either positive or negative).

Our final approach was to apply an information reduction procedure in order to explore the organization of the feature space. A principal components factor analysis (varimax rotation) was carried out on all 36 measurements. The Kaiser-Meyer-Olkin Measure of Sampling Adequacy equals 0.59. This is mediocre, but not unacceptable. A four-factor solution explains only 56% of the

Table 4.3. The four factors, their Eigenvalues, the loading of the single traits on the factors, and the rank-spearman correlations of the attractiveness ratings with the factors (N = 70).

	Babyness	Color	Obesity	Nubility
Eigenvalue	5.19	3.77	3.05	2.65
Areolar color value	.88	-.20	.11	.17
Areolar red color value	-.88	.20	-.12	-.18
Front view color value	.85	-.17	.03	.02
Back view color value	.84	-.19	.05	.04
Breast symmetry	-.68	-.10	.10	.28
Brow height	-.32	-.04	-.06	.01
Nose width	-.26	.09	-.17	.15
Lip color value	.16	-.90	-.02	.15
Face color value	.20	-.89	-.01	.15
Lip red color value	-.11	.89	.06	-.22
Skin homogeneity	-.06	.73	.06	.16
Face symmetry	-.02	.50	.02	.43
Brow curvature	-.08	.38	-.06	.05
Shoulder width	.09	.13	.10	-.06
Weight	.07	.01	.84	.14
Hip circumference	.06	-.02	.78	-.12
Waist circumference	.18	.08	.68	-.08
Breast circumference	.16	.03	.60	-.04
Buttock size	-.27	-.13	.57	-.23
Cheekbone height	.26	.22	.43	.16
Areolar size	-.14	-.14	.40	-.11

Jaw width	-.04	.23	.35	.20
Buttock symmetry	-.20	.26	-.35	-.18
Hair length	-.23	-.17	-.29	.06
Eye width	.19	.25	-.27	-.07
Pubic hair color value	-.01	-.06	-.19	.67
Breast size	.21	-.03	-.00	.55
Hair color value	-.05	-.12	.05	.53
Body height	.18	-.03	.36	.47
Angle of breast axis	-.21	-.11	.10	.43
Lower face length	.10	.27	.21	.37
Mouth width	.04	.20	-.18	.35
Eye height	.35	.17	-.10	-.35
Nose length	.04	-.00	.07	-.31
Mouth height	-.00	.19	-.17	.24
Forehead height	.13	.01	.01	-.14
Correlations of factors with attractiveness ratings				
Face	-.17	.14	-.09	.23
Front	.18	.06	-.30*	.39*
Back	-.23	.05	-.43*	.37*
Total	-.24*	.10	-.37*	.41*

*$p < 0.05$

variance, but factor loadings are reasonably high (see Table 4.3). This result might reflect that the choice of variables is exploratory.

In order to visualize the factors, the 10 pictures with the highest regression scores on one factor were morphed together. Factors 3 and 4 are easy to interpret. Factor 4 (column d in Figure 4.3) reflects nubility. Smaller eyes and a lower forehead contrast with high values for breasts, breast axis, mouth width, and height. Also note the high loadings of face and breast symmetry. Factor 3 (column c in Figure 4.3) seems to be a weight and size factor. Values are high in weight, breast, hip, and waist measures. This factor could be interpreted as a general body mass factor. These signal combinations on the senders' side have a correspondence in the attractiveness ratings on the receivers' side. Factor 4 correlates significantly positively with attractiveness, and Factor 3 correlates significantly negatively (Table 4.3).

Factors 1 (babyness) and 2 (color) are mainly dominated by color values. Factor 1 loads high on color values, and moderate on asymmetrical breasts, eye size, small buttocks, and a small nose. This factor correlates significantly negatively with total attractiveness (see Table 4.3). Factor 2 contains light colors and a symmetrical face. This factor does not correlate with attractiveness (Table 4.3). These results indicate that the feature space has an internal structure where different features are linked and have a positive or negative relation to attractiveness. This would greatly simplify processing.

When we apply the best of, or worst of, strategy to the four regressed factor scores (with Factor 1 and Factor 3 reverse scored), we find relatively high correlations for the positive decision (use the best factor) and the negative decision (use the worst factor, see Table 4.2). This suggests that there are at least two templates—an attractiveness template and an unattractiveness template—used for decision-making.

As a final step, we wanted to know whether there is any connection between the deviance from the mean and these templates. This is not the case—correlations range from 0.04 to 0.13. Only complexity shows a significant correlation to the regressed factor scores from Factor 1 ($rs = .25, p = .04$). Overall these results indicate that it is possible to extract trait combinations from the sender, which are rated as either attractive or unattractive.

DISCUSSION

The results of our approach show that it is possible to extract features that are related to metatheoretical evolutionary explanations for trait values in attractiveness ratings. Not all traits correlate in the predicted ways, but many do. However, the absence of some predicted correlations does not prove that there is no general relationship in the predicted direction.

We show that the n-dimensional feature space of attractiveness is coherent and unidirectional, that is, features tend to point in the same direction, and low variability in attractiveness between features of a woman is attractive. This

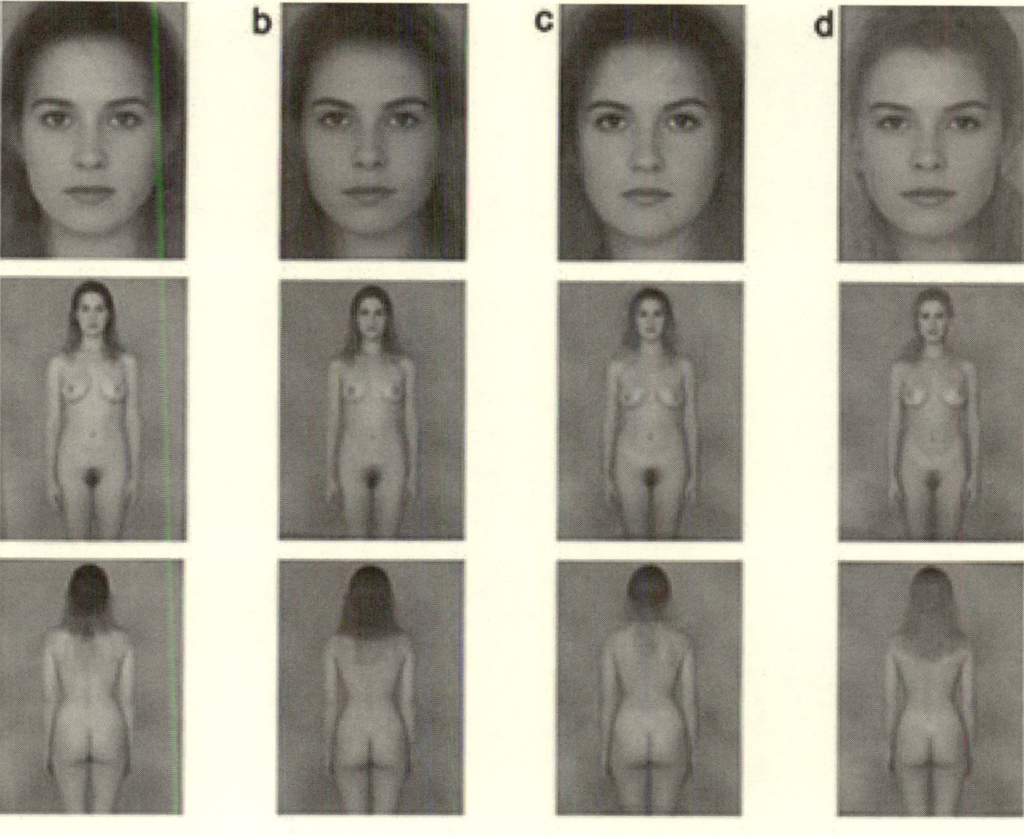

Figure 4.3. This shows the morphs of the 10 females that loaded highest in the regression scores for each factor.

is difficult to explain with cultural relativistic theories of attractiveness. If it is an arbitrary learning paradigm, why then should the sender signal coherently?

When we look at the single correlations of traits with attractiveness, we find several cases where the direction of the correlation contradicts correlations found in other studies. One trait where the actual correlation contradicts the predicted direction is breast circumference. If we take a closer look at the data, this measure might be confounded by breast form because breast form with large distances between lower breast fold and nipple correlates positively with attractiveness. Another result we did not find was correlations of attractiveness with all measures that are supposed to be a part of the babyness scheme. This replicates the findings of Grammer and Atzwanger (1994) on a different data set, where they assumed that babyness features are associated with incompetence and childishness. This is why males possibly would avoid those features and prefer traits of maturity.

Color values were analyzed in an attractiveness study for the first time. The results did not support our prediction. Lighter skin was not preferred. The males in our study preferred darker, apparently possibly tanned skin in this sample. Tanning of skin is also associated with more homogenous skin. There could be an interaction between these two parameters.

Our results indicate that bodies and faces can be considered as a whole. The fact that a unidirectional, n-dimensional feature is suggested allows us to use all traits (and their values) from face and body in simple fast and frugal algorithms in order to come to an attractiveness decision. But this decision-making approach may coexist with other strategies. The results indicate that simple strategies like avoidance of extremes, idiosyncratic learning, or simple deviations from the average explain the least variance in decision-making. In order to come to a decision, it seems to be necessary to have knowledge about the relation between traits and attractiveness. The question, then, is if and how this knowledge is gathered. In our approach, this could be solved easily, as long as the sender signals coherently in a unidirectional, n-dimensional feature space. If this n-dimensional feature space does not exist, it would be much harder to gather or accumulate any knowledge on what is attractive. This means that the starting point for any learning and flexible adjustment of attractiveness templates to an existing population (needed to maintain the chances of finding a suitable partner) could be provided by the coherently signaling sender. The sender's appearance would foster learning in an *attractiveness direction.*

The only approach without the need of some knowledge prerequisites that worked was the use of stimulus complexity. This complexity could be related to variability and thus noncoherence in the n-dimensional feature space. This is one of the most interesting results.

We did not find a relation between total averageness and attractiveness, although we were able to replicate the finding by Grammer and Thornhill (1994) that facial averageness correlates positively with attractiveness.

Another major result is that it seems to be possible (although the factor analysis is preliminary) to create attractiveness templates from body and facial features, that is, the sender's whole appearance is coherent. We do not assume that the prototypes we generated with morphing are the actual templates, nor that prototypes like this are represented in the brain; they are simple examples in order to visualize the findings. This result is not the foundation for a new constitution typology. It is simply the construction of prototypes to show that our approach is possible.

Basically, we show that taking knowledge on all traits into account would work as reliably as using prototypes. But, in both cases, we find a surprising result. Current literature describes beauty as a positive concept, but a negative concept works as well, if not better. If this is the case, research should consider redefining beauty as the *avoidance of ugliness.* When we take the principle of parsimony into account, we could favor the prototype solution. This solution would require less knowledge than a single trait solution where the relation between all traits and attractiveness has to be known to the decision-maker.

Our study itself has considerable shortcomings. Primarily, we conducted a simple correlation analysis. No corrections were applied for the number of tests carried out. The variance of the sample might not be high enough in some traits, and there might be curvilinear relations between traits and attractiveness ratings. We also did not use proportional measures. This was done for methodological reasons in order to keep the measured distances small and comparable in size. Actually, the prototype approach would not create problems with curvilinear relations and proportions, because a deviation or fitting on the prototype is measured. In fact, there also could be other strategies for information reduction, which use parallel distributed processing. There are still other alternatives like a hierarchical decoding approach where features are processed one after the other, as, for instance, take the best, then take the worst, and so on. We will address these possible strategies using different stimulus material in our forthcoming work. Future directions of research might benefit from use of 3D-meshes or wire frames, instead of predefined distances, in order to avoid possible bias in distance selection.

SUMMARY

Many studies show that female attractiveness plays an important role in human mate selection. Research in the past has focused on the influence of single features, for example, eye size or breast size, in attractiveness judgments. In recent years, bilateral symmetry and averageness or prototypic appearance have been discussed as possible general principles of attractiveness. The puzzle remaining is which features actually contribute to the perception of attractiveness and how these are integrated to result in attractiveness attributions. In this chapter we propose that attractiveness perception and judgment take place in a multidimensional feature space. If attractiveness signals mate quality honestly, the single features making up the multiple dimensions should actually correlate positively and thereby compose a single ornament of mate value.

In our rating study, three sets of males (each $n = 10$) rated three views (face alone, nude back, and nude front with face covered) of digital images of women ($n = 92$) in Austria as well as in the United States. Symmetry, averageness, skin color, hair color, stimulus complexity, and surface texture were assessed with digital image analysis. Thirty-six features on the digital images were measured by hand at anatomically defined points. A principal component analysis revealed that the n-dimensional feature space can be reduced to four main dimensions.

Computer simulations of the possible underlying cognitive decision-making implied that a fast and frugal algorithm, which uses the rule *simply avoid the worst*, best explains attractiveness ratings. Thus, beauty could be a negative concept, which finds its expression in the avoidance of ugliness.

APPENDIX

The notation will be as follows: if distances are used, the points are presented; xP1xP3 would indicate width of right eye for example (see Figure 4.1a). If regions are used, the notation is top/left/bottom/right; 27/2/3/28 would describe the rectangle where hair color has been measured (see Figure 4.1c). A value behind a point number describes a positive or negative offset to this point in pixels. For example, 27(10)/2 (-10)/3 (-10)/ 28(-10) would indicate that the rectangle from above was scaled down by a value of 10 pixels. Zero point for the coordinate system is the upper left corner of the picture.

Features: Pixel Dimension from Photographs.

1. Forehead height (Figure 4.1a: ((P21y-P14y)+(P23y-P14y))/2).
2. Brow height (Figure 4.1a: P21y-P16y) and curvature (Figure 4.1a: ((P3x-P16x)+(P19x-P4x))/2).
3. Lower face length (Figure 4.1a: P13y-P3y), nose width (Figure 4.1a: P8x-P7x) and length (Figure 4.1a: P29y-((P3y+P4y)/2)), chin length (Figure 4.1a: P13y-P29y), and jaw width (Figure 4.1a: P10x-P9x).
4. Eyes width (Figure 4.1a: ((P3x-P1x) +(P2x-P4x))/2) and height (Figure 4.1a: ((P22y-P21y)+(P24y-P23y))/2).
5. Mouth width (Figure 4.1a: P12x-P11x) and height (Figure 4.1a: P35y-P32y), cheekbone height (Figure 4.1a: $(((P13x-P5x)^2+(P13y-P5y)^2)^{0.5} + ((P6x-P13x)^2+ (P13y-P6y)^2)^{0.5})/2$).
6. Breast height (Figure 4.1b: ((P11y-P9y)+(P12y-P10y))/2). High values would indicate high amount of body fat and thus optimal sex hormone profiles (Frisch, 1975).
7. Areola size (Figure 4.1b: ((P51y-P49y)+(P52y-P50y))/2) and angle of breast axis (Figure 4.1b: P11x-P9x)+(P10x-P12x)).

8. Buttock size (Figure 4.1c: P15y-P12y).
9. Hair length (Figure 4.1c: P26y-P1y).
10. Shoulder width (Figure 4.1b: P4y-P3y).

Features: Digital Image Analysis

11. Face, breast, and buttock asymmetry (Face: Figure 4.1a: P16/P1/ P35/P2; Breast: Figure 4.1b: P7/P7/P12+10/P8; Buttock: Figure 4.1c: P12/P13/ P25+10/P14). High values are unattractive (see Introduction). This method was done with a digital image analysis algorithm for the detection of asymmetry. The program developed by the first author created a window on the facial picture that was defined by left and right outer eye corner, top of the brows, and the lower lip. This window then was divided in *n* horizontal, 1-pixel-wide symmetrical slices. Each slice was then moved to the left for 50 pixels and moved back in one-pixel steps. For every step the difference between left and right part of the slice was calculated. The symmetry point is reached when the difference between the two halves of each slice reaches a minimum. Thus, *n* symmetry points were calculated as the minimum difference between the sum of pixels of the left and the right half of the respective slice. In an ideal symmetrical face the line through all symmetry points is a straight line and equals the distance between the top of the brows and the lower lip. The symmetry index was calculated as the length of the symmetry line divided by the height of the window. This results in measures of asymmetry greater than 1, where 1 depicts absolute symmetry. Compared to the distance measure, this method does not only measure the symmetry of tissue and bone structure as expressed in landmarks, it also uses skin disturbances for determination of asymmetry, which might indeed play a crucial role for the perception of symmetry.
12. Skin texture (Face: Figure 4.1a: P22/P1/P35/P2). The region was the center of the face. Co-occurrence-matrix: For the analysis of texture, classification, and image segmentation, we used a method based on co-occurrence-matrices (for the source code, see Bässmann & Besslich; 1993, pp. 150–155; Davis, Johns, & Aggarwal, 1979; Dhawan & Sicsu, 1992; Haralick, Shanmugam, & Dinstein 1973). Co-occurrence-matrices are based on the spatial relationships of pairs of gry values of pixels in digital texture images. They count how often pairs of gry levels of pixels, which are separated by a certain distance and lie along a certain direction, occur in a digital image of texture. Co-occurrence-matrices are not used directly, but features based upon them are being computed. The aim is that these features capture some characteristics of textures, such as homogeneity, coarseness, periodicity, and others. Out of Haralick's original 14 features, we chose homogeneity. High values of homogeneity are supposed to be attractive. Texture was measured in a region of interest in the central face.
13. Skin color (Face: Figure 4.1a. P22+20/P1/P7/P3; Front: Figure 4.1b: P14+15/P14/P14/P15; Back: Figure 4.1c: P10+15/P10/P10/P11). We determined skin color in an RGB-color space and separately in an HSV-color space. Color was measured by calculating the mean hue and value. Colors in the RGB-color space are represented as values between 0 and 65,535 for red, green, and blue. The hue of the HSV-color space component is an angular measurement,

analogous to a position in a color wheel. A hue value of 0° indicates the color red; the color green is a value corresponding to 120°, and the color blue is at a value corresponding to 240°. The value component describes brightness or luminance. A value of 0 represents black; a maximum value means that the color appears brightest. For more information on the use of HSV-color spaces see *Advanced Color Imaging on the MacOS* (Apple Computer Inc., 1995). Body brightness, back brightness, and front brightness were measured by calculating the value of the following picture regions: face color in a rectangle on the right cheek determined by left and right corner of the eye, the point of maximum cheekbone protrusion, and the end of the nose; back and front in a 15-pixel-wide rectangle reaching from left to right waist in the front view and in the back view. High values are supposed to be attractive.

14. Hair color (value) (Figure 4.1c: P27/P27/P27+20/P28), pubic hair color (value) (Figure 4.1b: P20-10/P20-10/P20/P20+10).
15. Nipple color (Figure 4.1b: P9-5/P9-5/P9+5/P9+5). Light red areolars and nipples are supposed to signal nubility (Symons, 1979). High values of the red component and brightness are supposed to be attractive.
16. Lip color (Figure 4.1a: P34/P34-10/P35/P34+10). High values of the red component and brightness are supposed to be attractive.

Global Stimulus Descriptors (Face Only)

17. Averageness (all views) (Face: Figure 4.1a: P16/P15/P13/P20; Front: Figure 4.1b: P7/P7/P16/P17; Back: Figure 4.1c: P6/P6/P25/P7). Amount of necessary form warp to obtain the average picture. The mean coordinates for all females were calculated. Then each face was form-warped to these coordinates using an algorithm by Anderson and Anger (1995). If a face is average, then the individual pixels do not move very much, but if the form deviates considerably from average, many pixels have to be moved in order to reach the average form. Necessary pixel movement was calculated as the sum of all movements in pixels performed to reach average form. When averageness is considered attractive, low values would indicate attractiveness (see Introduction).
18. Stimulus complexity (all views) (Face: Figure 4.1a: P16/P15/ P13/ P20; Front: Figure 4.1b: P7/P7/P16/P17; Back: Figure 4.1c: P6/ P6/P25/P7). The complexity of a stimulus is represented in the amount of possible compression of the picture. The higher the stimulus complexity, the less it can be compressed. Here we used run-length encoding. This is a simple compression approach, which seeks strings of like pixels within the image and assigns a single value. High complexity would result in larger file sizes. High values of compression are predicted to be attractive because they would indicate low complexity and low complexity is more easily processed (see Introduction).

NOTE

There are a lot of methodological problems with the making of computer composites. Thus, some prior research is questionable. The first problem is scaling of the faces using nonstandard methods that result in distortion, although there are morphometric procedures that have been tested and verified (see Methods section).

The second problem is in the method of morphing itself. Exact morphing requires establishing many landmarks. The reliability for placement of landmark point locations often is not reported in published studies. We would assume that the placement of landmarks may sometimes be biased, because it is done by hand, and often not by a person who is blind to the hypothesis. Third, when commercial programs are used, the exact algorithms used for warping and morphing are often unknown and undocumented. Therefore, it may be completely unclear whether artifacts were created. Fourth, calculating the mean value of two colors (even on a grayscale) requires transformation of the colors in a color space. This can be done in many different ways, and in many programs it is unclear how this conversion is achieved. We must assume that color correction is done in many cases, leaving it unclear if the actual result is the mean or not. Fifth, the nature of the applied morphing algorithms leads inevitably to an artifact, which could be responsible for the high attractiveness of composites. Usually, there are differences between neighboring pixel values in a picture. By calculating the mean values, these differences disappear and are smoothed out. Thus, a morphed picture is reduced in terms of three dimensionality in that it is flatter than the original faces. This is an artifact, which has to be controlled for by raising the picture contrast. Sixth, this applies to color and grayscale pictures equally. The composite will automatically have less contrast and be lighter than the individual pictures. None of the studies reported in the literature addresses this problem.

REFERENCES

Anderson, J. L., Crawford, C. B., Nadean, J., & Lindberg, T. (1992). Was the Duchess of Windsor right? A cross-cultural review of the sociobiology of ideals of female body shape. *Ethology and Sociobiology, 13*, 197–227.

Anderson, S. & Anger, S. (1995). *PC-Graphik fuer Insider.* München, Germany: SAMS.

Apple Computer Inc. (1995). *Advanced color imaging on the MacOS.* New York: Addison-Wesley.

Bässmann, H., & Besslich, P. W. (1993). *Bildverarbeitung Ad Oculus* (2nd ed.) Berlin: Springer-Verlag.

Baugh, S. G., & Parry, L. E. (1991). The relationship between physical attractiveness and grade point average among college women. *Journal of Social Behavior and Personality, 6*, 29–228.

Bookstein, F. L. (1997). *Morphometric tools for landmark data; geometry and biology.* Cambridge, UK: Cambridge University Press.

Cosmides, L., Tooby, J., & Barkow, J. H. (1992). Introduction: Evolutionary psychology and conceptual integration. In J. Barkow, L. Cosmides, & J. Tooby (Eds.), *The adapted mind* (pp. 3–18). New York: Oxford University Press.

Crogan, S. (1999). *Body image: Understanding body dissatisfaction in men, women and children.* London: Routledge.

Cunningham, M. R. (1986). Measuring the physical in physical attractiveness: Quasi experiments on the sociobiology of female beauty. *Journal of Personality and Social Psychology, 50*, 925–935.

Cunningham, M. R., Druen, P. B. & Barbee, A. P. (1997). Angels, mentors, and friends: Trade-offs among evolutionary, social, and individual variables in physical appearance. In J. A. Simpson & D. T. Kenrick (Eds); *Evolutionary social psychology*. Hove, UK: Erlbaum.

Cunningham, M. R., Roberts, A. R., Wu, C.-H., Barbee, A. P., & Druen, P. B. (1995). Their ideas of beauty are, on the whole, the same as ours: Consistency and variability in the cross-cultural perception of female attractiveness. *Journal of Personality and Social Psychology, 68*, 261–279.

Darwin, C. (1872). *The descent of man and selection in relation to sex*. London: John Murray.

Davis, L. S., Johns, A., & Aggarwal, J. K. (1979). Texture analysis using generalized cooccurrence matrices. *IEEE Transactions on Pattern Analysis and Machine Intelligence, PAMI-1, 3*, 251–259.

Dhawan, A. P., & Sicsu, A. (1992). Segmentation of images of skin lesions using colour and texture information of surface pigmentation. *Computerized Medical Imaging and Graphics, 16*, 163–177.

Eibl-Eibesfeldt, I. (1997). *Die Biologie des menschliche Verhaltens*. Weyarn, Germany: Seehamer Verlag.

Ellis, H. (1926). *Studies in the psychology of sex*, (Vol. IV). Philadelphia: F. A. Davis.

Ellison, P. T. (1999). Reproductive ecology and reproductive cancers. In C. Panter-Brick, & C. Worthman (Eds.), *Hormones, health and behavior: A socio-ecological and lifespan perspective*. Cambridge, UK: Cambridge University Press.

Enquist, M., & Arak, A. (1994). Symmetry, beauty and evolution. *Nature, 372*, 169–172.

Fink, B., & Grammer, K. (under review). *Skin texture and female facial beauty*.

Fisher, R. A. (1930). *The gentical theory of natural selection*. London: Oxford University Press.

Folstad, I., & Karter, A. J. (1992). Parasites, bright males, and the immunocompetence handicap. *American Naturalist, 139*, 603–622.

Friedlund, A. J., & Loftis, J. M. (1990). *Sex-differences in smiling to babies and animals: Do females show a greater preference for juvenescence?* Unpublished manuscript.

Frisch, R. E. (1975). Critical weights, a critical body composition, menarche and the maintenance of menstrual cycles. In E. S. Watts (Ed.), *Biosocial interrelations in population adaption*. The Hague, Netherlands: Mouton.

Frost, P. (1988). Human skin color: A possible relationship between its sexual dimorphism and its social perception. *Perspectives in Biology and Medicine, 32* (1), 38–58.

Furnham, A., & Baguma, P. (1994). Cross-cultural differences in the evaluation of male and female body shapes. *International Journal of Eating Disorders, 15(1)*, 81–89.

Galton, F. (1879). Composite portraits, made by combining those of many different persons in a single resultant figure. *Journal of the Anthropological Institute, 8*, 132–144.

Gigerenzer, G., & Goldstein, D. G. (1996). Reasoning the fast and frugal way: Models of bounded rationality. *Psychological Review, 103*, 650–669.

Grammer, K. (1995). *Signale der Liebe: Die Biologischen Gesetze der Partnerschaft*. München, Germany: Deutscher Taschenbuch Verlag.

Grammer, K., & Atzwanger, K. (1994). Der Lolita-Komplex: Sexuelle Attraktivität und Kindchenschema. In K.-F. Wessel & F. Naumann (Eds.), *Kommunikation und Humanontogenese: Berliner Studien zur Wissenschaftsphilosophie und Humanontogenetik* (Vol. 6.) Bielefeld, Germany: Kleine Verlag.

Grammer, K., & Thornhill, R. (1994). Human (*Homo sapiens*) facial attractiveness and sexual selection: The role of symmetry and averageness. *Journal of Comparative Psychology, 108*, 233–242.

Hamilton, W. D., & Zuk, M. (1982). Heritable true fitness and bright birds: A role for parasites? *Science, 218*, 384–387.

Haralick, R. M., Shanmugam, K., & Dinstein, I. (1973). Textural features for image classification. *IEEE Transactions on Systems, Man, and Cybernetics, SMC-3, 6*, 610–621.

Hatfield, E., & Sprecher, S. (1986). *Mirror, mirror . . . : The importance of looks in everyday life.* Albany: State University of New York Press.

Henss, R. (1987). Zur Beurteilerübereinstimmung bei der Einschätzung der physischen Attraktivität junger und alter Menschen. *Zeitschrift für Sozialpsychologie, 18*, 118–130.

Henss, R. (1988). " . . . wer ist der / die Schönste im ganzen Land?" Zur Beurteilerübereinstimmung bei der Einschätzung der physischen Attraktivität. *Annales—Forschungsmagazin der Universität des Saarlandes, 1*, 54–58.

Hess, E. H., Seltzer, A. L., & Shlien, J. M. (1965). Pupil response of hetero- and homosexual males to pictures of men and women. *Journal of Abnormal Psychology, 70*, 165–168.

Iliffe, A. H. (1960). A study of preferences in feminine beauty. *British Journal of Psychology, 51*, 267–273.

Johnston, V. S., & Franklin, M. (1993). Is beauty in the eye of the beholder? *Ethology and Sociobiology, 14*, 183–199.

Johnstone, R. A. (1994). Female preferences for symmetrical males as a by-product of selection for mate recognition. *Nature, 372*, 172–175.

Jones, D. (1996). *Physical attractiveness and the theory of sexual selection.* Ann Arbor: Museum of Anthropology, University of Michigan.

Kalkofen, H., Müller, A., & Strack, M. (1990). Kant's facial aesthetics and Galton's composite portraiture—are prototypes more beautiful? In L. Halasz (Ed.), *Proceedings of the 11th International Congress on Empirical Aesthetics* (pp. 151–154). Budapest: International Association for Empirical Aesthetics.

Kowner, R. (1996). Facial attractiveness and judgement in developmental perspective. *Journal of Experimental Psychology: Human Perception and Performance, 22*, 662–675.

Kirchengast, S., & Huber, J. (1999). Body composition characteristics, sex hormone levels and circadian gonadotropin fluctuations in infertile young women. *Collegium Anthropologicum, 23(2)*, 407–423.

Langlois, J. H., & Roggman, L. A. (1990). Attractive faces are only average. *Psychological Science, 1*, 115–121.

Langlois, J. H., Roggman, L. A., & Musselmann, L. (1994). What is average and what is not average about attractive faces? *Psychological Science, 5*, 214–220.

Langlois, J. H., Roggman, L. A., & Reiser-Danner, L. A. (1990). Infant's differential social responses to attractive and unattractive faces. *Developmental Psychology, 26*, 153–159.

Lorenz, K. (1943). Die angeborenen Formen möglicher Erfahrung. *Zeitschrift für Tierpsychologie, 5*, 235–409.

Møller, A. P., & Pomiankowski, A. (1993). Why have birds got multiple sexual ornaments? *Behavioral Ecology and Sociobiology, 32*, 167–176.

Müller, A. (1993). Visuelle Prototypen und die physikalischen Dimensionen von Attraktivität. In R. Niketta & M. Hassebrauck (Eds.), *Physische Attraktivität*. Göttingen, Germany: Hogrefe.

Perrett, D. I., Burt, D. M., Penton-Voak, I. S., Lee, K. J., Rowland, D. A., & Edwards, R. (1999). Symmetry and human facial attractiveness. *Evolution and Human Behavior, 20*(5), 295–307.

Perrett, D. I., May, K. A., & Yoshikawa, S. (1994). Facial shape and judgement of female attractiveness. *Nature, 386*, 239–242.

Rensch, B. (1963). Versuche über menschliche Auslösermerkmale beider Geschlechter. *Zeitschrift für Morphologische Anthropologie, 53*, 139–164.

Rhodes, G., Proffitt, F., Grady, J. M., & Sumich, A. (1998). Facial symmetry and the perception of beauty. *Psychonomic Bulletin and Review, 5*(4), 659–669.

Rhodes, G., Sumich, A., & Byatt, G. (1999). Are average facial configurations attractive only because of their symmetry? *Psychological Science, 10*(1), 52–58.

Rhodes, G., & Tremewan, T. (1996). Averageness, exaggeration, and facial attractiveness. *Psychological Science, 7*(2), 105–110.

Rich, M. K., & Cash, T. (1993). The American image of beauty: Media representations of hair color for four decades. *Sex Roles, 29*(1/2), 113–123.

Rikowski, A., & Grammer, K. (1999). Human body odour, symmetry and attractiveness. *Proceedings of the Royal Society of London, Series B, 266*, 869–874.

Ronzal, G. I. (1996). *Physische Charakteristika weiblicher Schönheit*. M. A. thesis, Natural Sciences, University of Vienna, Austria.

Rosch, E. H. (1978). Principles of categorization. In E. Rosch & B. B. Lloyd (Eds.), *Cognition and categorization* (pp. 27–47). Mahwah, NJ: Erlbaum.

Samuels, C. A., Butterworth, G., Rogerts, T., Graupner, L., & Hole, G. (1994). Facial aesthetics: Babies prefer attractiveness to symmetry. *Perception, 23*, 823–831.

Schiavone, F. E., Rietschel, R. L., Sgoutas, D., & Harris, R. (1983). Elevated free testosterone levels in women with acne. *Archives of Dermatology, 119*, 799–802.

Schleidt, W. M., & Crawley, J. N. (1980). Patterns in the behaviour of organisms *Journal of Social and Biological Structure, 3*, 1–15.

Singh, D. (1993). Adaptive significance of female physical attractiveness: Role of waist-to-hip ratio. *Journal of Personality and Social Psychology, 65*, 293–307.

Steinberger, E., Rodriguez-Rigau, L. J., Smith, K. D., & Held, B. (1981). The menstrual cycle and plasma testosterone level in women with acne. *Journal of the American Academy of Dermatology, 4*(1), 54–58.

Stoddart, D. M. (1995). *The scented ape: The biology and culture of human odor*. Cambridge, UK: Cambridge University Press.

Swaddle, J. P., & Cuthill, I. C. (1995). Asymmetry and human facial attractiveness: Symmetry may not always be beautiful. *Proceedings of the Royal Society of London, Series B, 261*, 111–116.

Symons, D. (1979). *The evolution of human sexuality.* Oxford: Oxford University Press.

Symons, D. (1995). Beauty is in the adaptations of the beholder: The evolutionary psychology of human female sexual attractiveness. In P. R. Abramson & S. D. Pinker (Eds.), *Sexual nature/sexual culture* (pp. 80–118). Chicago: University of Chicago Press.

Thelen, T. H. (1983). Minority type human mate preference. *Social Biology, 30*, 162–180.

Thornhill, R. (1992). Fluctuating asymmetry and the mating system of the Japanese scorpionfly (*Panorpa japonica*). *Animal Behaviour, 44*, 867–879.

Thornhill, R., & Gangestad, S. W. (1993). Human facial beauty: Averageness, symmetry, and parasite resistance. *Human Nature, 4*, 237–269.

Thornhill, R., & Gangestad, S. W. (1996). The evolution of human sexuality. *Trends in Ecology and Evolution, 11*, 98–102.

Thornhill, R., & Gangstad, S. W. (1999a). Facial attractiveness. *Trends in Cognitive Science, 3*, 452–460.

Thornhill, R., & Gangestad, S.W. (1999b). The scent of symmetry: A human sex pheromone that signals fitness? *Evolution and Human Behavior, 20*, 175–201.

Thornhill, R., & Grammer, K. (1999). The body and face of woman: One ornament that signals quality? *Evolution and Human Behavior, 20*, 105–120.

Valentine, T. (1991). A unified account of the effects of ditinctiveness, inversion, and race in face recognition. *Quarterly Journal of Experimental Psychology, 43A*, 161–204.

Van den Berghe, P. L., & Frost, P. (1986). Skin color preference, sexual dimorphism and sexual selection: A case of gene-culture co-evolution? *Ethnic and Racial Studies, 9*, 87–118.

Wedekind, C., & Folstad, I. (1994). Adaptive or nonadaptive immunosuppression by sex hormones? *American Naturalist, 143*, 936–938.

Westermarck, E. (1921). *The history of human marriage.* London: MacMillan.

Wildt, L., & Sir-Peterman, T. (1999). Oestrogen and age estimations of perimenopausal women. *Lancet, 354*, 224.

Wolberg, G. (1990). *Digital image warping.* Los Alamitos, CA: IEEE Computer Society Press.

Zahavi, A. (1975). Mate selection. A selection for a handicap. *Journal of Theoretical Biology, 53*, 205–214.

Zebrowitz, L. A. (1998). *Reading faces: Window to the soul?* Boulder, CO: Westview Press.

CHAPTER 5

An Ethological Theory of Attractiveness

Magnus Enquist, Stefano Ghirlanda, Daniel Lundqvist, and Carl-Adam Wachtmeister

INTRODUCTION

Faces play a very important role in human social life. With our faces we can communicate emotions, species and individual identity, sex and age. The ability to read and remember faces is also highly developed. One intriguing fact is that we experience considerable variation in facial attractiveness, and this influences our behavior. We seek sexual partners who are attractive, we are more likely to vote for an attractive politician, and beautiful faces make an advertisement more persuasive (Chaiken, 1979; Efran, & Patterson, 1974; Zebrowitz, 1997), to take just a few examples. It is important here to point out that judgments of attractiveness emerge within the person that observes the face stimuli (the "receiver"). Unlike physical features such as shape or size, attractiveness is not a property of the face itself. An extraterrestrial being would not be able to tell what faces we find attractive without knowledge of our nervous systems. On the other hand, the same being could easily measure physical features of faces.

Attempts have been made to explain the variability in perceived attractiveness using evolutionary biology, arguing that reproducing with a more attractive partner will increase an individual's biological fitness (see e.g., Andersson, 1994; Bradbury & Vehrencamp, 1998, for theory and empirical data in favor or against such views). Choosing, for instance, the right species is crucial for successful reproduction, so that reliable mechanisms of species recognition are favored by evolution. Sex and sexual maturity are also important. Assessment of these characteristics in a potential mate is not necessarily a trivial task, and mistakes occur (Gray, 1958). However, current thinking suggests that mate choice is about finer details of partner quality, making the problems of species, sex, and age recognition appear simpler than they are. According to this view, the genetic and sometimes the phenotypic quality of the partner is assessed during mate choice (Andersson, 1994; Trivers, 1972). The advantage of choosing a mate with high genetic quality is that the offspring inherit these high-quality genes. If such a mate-quality hypothesis is correct, we expect a correlation between attractiveness of a face and the person's genetic or phenotypic quality. So far, studies of facial attractiveness have not revealed such a relationship (Shackelford, & Larsen, 1999: Kalick, Zebrowitz, Langlois, & Johnson, 1998).

In this chapter, we present an alternative hypothesis combining theories of signal evolution that emphasizes coevolution between signals and receiver mechanisms (Arak & Enquist, 1995, Dawkins & Krebs 1978; Enquist & Arak, 1993, 1998; Jones & Hill, 1993), ethological theories of sexual imprinting (e.g., Shettleworth, 1998) and theories of stimulus control (Mackintosh, 1974; Pearce, 1994). The hypothesis recognizes that some basic communication is needed and mechanisms have evolved enabling recognition of, for instance, species, sex, and age. On the other hand, the hypothesis does not assume the existence of cues enabling assessment of finer details of mate quality. Variation in attractiveness emerges in our model partly as a by-product of how recognition mechanisms work. We refer to such by-products as receiver biases. We show that this model is a viable alternative that can explain a wider range of phenomena than can theories based on communication of mate quality.

The chapter is organized according to three levels of causation, following ethological thinking (Tinbergen, 1963). At the first level, we consider attractiveness as the response of a behavior mechanism to stimulation from faces. Thus, variation in attractiveness can be investigated using models of stimulus control, which summarize our knowledge about how stimuli are coded into memory and how variation in stimulation influences behavior (Mackintosh, 1974, Pearce, 1997). We suggest that simple principles of stimulus control can explain many major findings about human facial attractiveness. To understand diversity and uniformity of preferences among people we need to consider the other levels of causation. At the second level, we consider developmental mechanisms—how judgments of attractiveness develop during an individual's lifetime. Finally, at the third level, we investigate cultural and genetic evolution of preferences, focusing on the interplay between behavioral mechanisms, development, and evolutionary mechanisms.

DISCRIMINATION AND GENERALIZATION

Communication requires evolution of signals as well as identification and discrimination abilities. Although we do not know the evolutionary history in detail, it is fair to assume that many characteristics of faces have evolved for communication. There have been many suggestions of messages that faces might communicate. However, an important aspect of our model is that even if we consider just one or two messages, such as sex and age, several phenomena arise. To see this we must consider how signals are recognized. A signal (in the present context, a face) is first received by a sense organ and then processed by the nervous system, eventually producing a behavioral response. This process has been extensively studied at the behavioral level both in animals and humans and some very general rules have been described (Baerends, 1982; Mackintosh, 1974; Pearce, 1994; Shanks, 1995). Judgments of attractiveness are behavioral responses (choice or ratings by subjects) and may thus follow general rules of stimulus control. Note also that many issues lurk behind the meaning of "attractive," and the reader should be aware that there is no unambiguous definition of attractiveness. Studies of attractiveness have considered sexual and other partner preferences, as well as pure aesthetic judgments and ratings of femininity and/or masculinity. In this chapter we mainly consider sexual preferences.

A basic principle of stimulus control is that if an organism reacts to a particular stimulus, it will also react to stimuli that are similar. This phenomenon is called *generalization*. It allows organisms to respond consistently to stimuli even though they are perceived differently (object or perceptual constancy, e.g., Walsh & Kulikowski, 1998). It also allows organisms in novel situations to try out those responses that functioned well in similar situations. However, the rules for generalization are largely independent of context, stemming from basic properties of the nervous system (Enquist & Arak, 1998). Because of this, and because old responses are not always appropriate in a new situation, generalization is not perfectly tuned to each situation (Enquist, Arak, Ghirlanda, & Wachtmeister, 2000).

Below we show how generalization and discrimination processes can explain general empirical results from studies of face perception.

Extreme Faces

An important determinant of generalization is the need for discrimination between stimuli. This can shift our preferences toward more exaggerated appearances. There is ample evidence that many animals prefer modifications of familiar stimuli that are outside the natural range of variation (Baerends, 1982; Tinbergen, 1951;). These effects can be understood from the results of simple generalization experiments (Mackintosh, 1974). The first step is to train an animal to discriminate between two stimuli along a particular dimension (e.g., frequency of sound). In the second step, the generalization gradient is determined by testing the animal's response toward a number of stimuli along the same dimension. This gradient will often show a response bias (Figure 5.1) resulting from the interaction between the memories of the positive and nega-

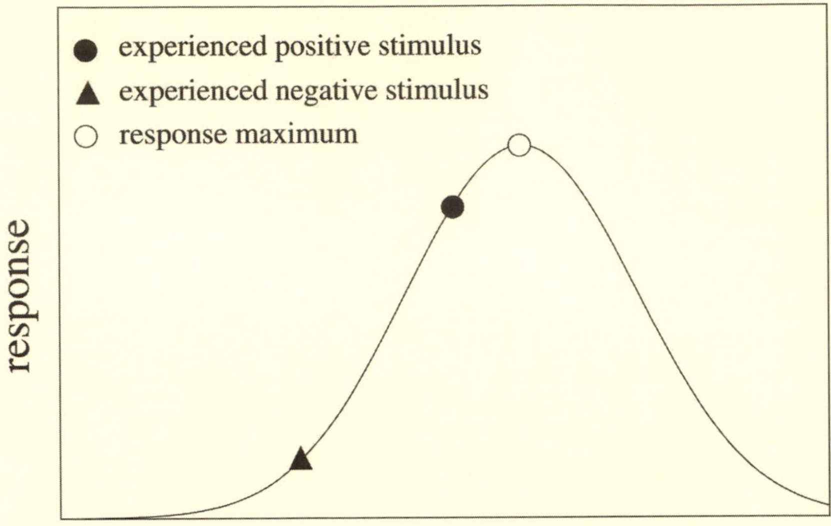

Figure 5.1. The generalization gradient shows how response strength typically is generalized along a stimulus dimension (e.g., sound frequency) after experiences of two similar stimuli when it is advantageous to react to one of them but not to the other (see, e.g., Mackintosh, 1974). Observe that the strongest response is not elicited by the positive stimulus. Instead, the response peak is shifted toward the right due to the interaction between the memory of the positive stimuli and the memory of the negative stimulus.

tive stimuli (we refer to such phenomena as memory interactions). Such a bias in responding is known as peak shift or supernormal stimulation and has been shown in humans and animals (Baerends, 1982; Baron, 1973; Mackintosh, 1974).

Several studies have shown that perception of faces is biased in this way—the impact a face has can often be magnified by exaggerating those components that make that face unique among other faces. The studies on recognition of individual faces firmly establish the existence of such biases (Rhodes, 1996; Rhodes, Brennan, & Carey, 1987). Caricatures of faces exploit this principle (Rhodes 1996). Sexual preferences, judgments of beauty, femininity, or masculinity seem also biased. Rensch (1963) showed that Europeans' preferences for faces do not match the actual appearance of Europeans. Discrimination between faces may be one factor behind such biases, by favoring characteristics in both sexes that make them more different from each other. In Figure 5.2, such an effect is demonstrated along the male—female dimension.

Several studies show that femininity is beneficial to female attractiveness (Gillen, 1981; Keating, 1985; Perrett et al., 1998; Rhodes, Hickford, & Jeffrey, 2000). Data about the effect of masculinity on male attractiveness are

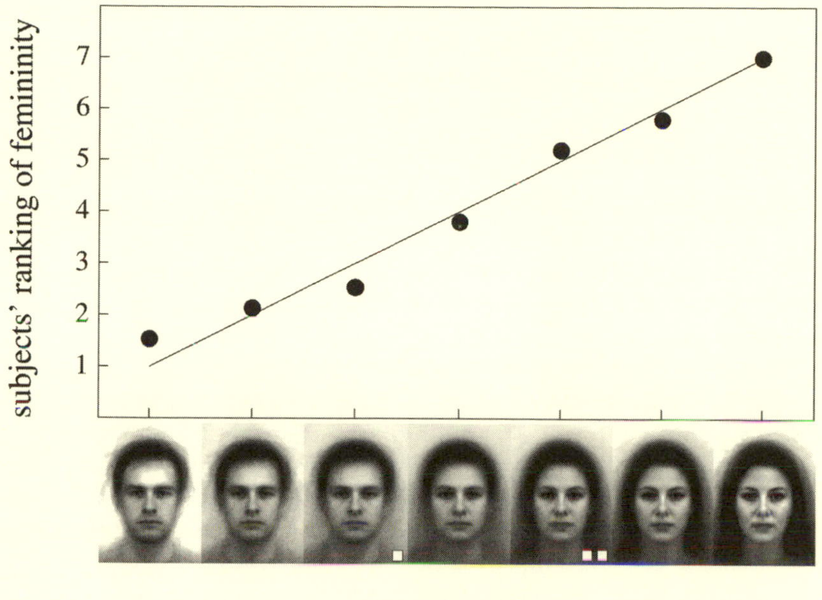

Figure 5.2. Subjects (17 biology students) were asked to rank 7 faces with respect to femininity. The figure shows average rank for each face (SE varied between 0.0 and 0.2). The pictures were constructed using two composites, one of male faces and one of female faces. Defining the value of each pixel in the figure as a dimension in a space, the positions of the two composites can be located in this space as two points. We construct a new dimension in this space by defining a line that travels through these two points. Five additional faces were picked along this line, one located exactly between the two composites and two located on each side of the composites. The aim is to demonstrate a response bias caused by the interaction between memories of female and male faces: exaggerated faces are rated as more feminine or masculine than average faces. The averages faces used are from the "averaged Karolinska directed emotional faces" (Lundqvist & Litton 2001).

less clear. Gillen (1981) reported that attractive males are rated high in masculinity. However, Perrett and colleagues (1998) and Rhodes and colleagues (2000) found that a masculinized male face, obtained by moving away the average male face from the average female face, is not preferred to the average male face.

Biased responding has also been shown for reactions to infants (i.e., stimuli for parental care in humans). It was noted by Lorenz (1950) that big eyes, a rounded head, a big forehead, and a small nose contributed to elicit parental care (for more precise studies, see Gardner, & Wallach, 1965; Sternglanz,

Gray, & Murakami, 1977; Maier, Holmes, Slaymaker, & Reich, 1984; Zebrowitz, 1997). Some of these findings are consistent with a peak shift in responding resulting from the need of discriminating infants from adults.

In reality, recognition of sexual partners is not based on sex only. For instance, age is also important: children and old individuals should not be preferred. The many discriminations involved in partner choice result in a more intricate organization of the memory than explored here, and whose effect on preferences remains to be fully understood.

We conclude this section with a technical note concerning the difficulty of predicting reactions to complex stimuli such as faces. In the simple, one-dimensional case in Figure 5.1, it was clear that stronger responses should occur on the right of the positive stimulus. This was in fact the only way of departing from the negative stimulus. In multidimensional spaces, such as the various spaces used to represent faces, it is far from trivial to predict in which direction to expect the stronger preferences. If we consider a case with just one positive and one negative stimulus, theories of generalization (e.g., Ghirlanda, & Enquist, 1998; Spence, 1937) predict that the strongest preferences lie somewhere on the line joining the positive and negative stimuli (beyond the positive stimulus). At the simplest level, this result can be applied to pixel patterns representing faces (as in Figure 5.2). Other techniques such as caricature generation by morphing (Benson & Perrett, 1991; Brennan, 1985; Rhodes, 1996) can be understood as applications of this result to various abstract spaces. If we have more than one negative stimulus and possibly more than one positive stimulus, we know of no simple method to predict the preference gradient, with one exception. If experiences fall into two well-defined clusters (e.g., male and female faces), we may use the two centers (averages) as single positive and negative stimuli and study how preferences vary along the line that goes through the two averages (cf. Figure 5.2). However, if we want to add additional factors to the discrimination, this technique does not work because the gradient can no longer be satisfactorily described along a line. For instance, if we want to consider partner preferences based on both sex and age, we need to include old and young faces as negative stimuli as well as faces of the same sex. It should be possible, though, to use artificial neural networks to make predictions (Enquist & Arak, 1998; Ghirlanda & Enquist, 1998). Such a network would need to be trained not only to recognize individuals but also to recognize sex and age.

Average Faces

In attempts to link appearances of faces with personality traits, Francis Galton developed in 1878 the technique of multiexposure photography, allowing him to blend several faces together. This had a surprising effect: the composite faces turned out to be more attractive than the individual ones used to produce the composites (Galton, 1878, 1883). Galton also mentioned that

A. L. Austin from Invercargill, New Zealand, had reported the same result using stereoscopic viewing of pairs of faces (Rhodes, 1996). This result has now been confirmed in several studies (Langlois & Roggman, 1990; Langlois, Roggman, & Musselman, 1994; Rhodes, Sumich, & Byatt, 1999; Rhodes, & Tremewan, 1996).

A preference for the average of many stimuli can be predicted from stimulus control theory (Enquist & Arak, 1994, 1998; Enquist & Johnstone, 1997; Ghirlanda & Enquist, 1998; Johnstone, 1994; Swaddle & Cuthill, 1994). What we have to consider is how subjects generalize among many similar stimuli requiring the same response. For instance, after training pigeons to react in the same way to the light of two different wavelengths, the resulting generalization gradient is bell-shaped with a maximum at the average wavelength (see Figure 5.3). This finding is relevant to questions about symmetry as well, since average stimuli are typically more symmetrical than the stimuli that enter the average (Enquist & Arak, 1998; Enquist, & Johnstone, 1997; Ghirlanda & Enquist, 1999). Applied to faces, this means that one may tend to prefer the average of those faces requiring similar responses, for example, adult male faces. One useful interpretation of the x-axis in Figure 5.3 is that it measures some difference between the left and right halves of the face. If there is no difference, the face is symmetrical with respect to this measure. Note that our model assumes memory interaction even after extensive experience (Enquist & Arak, 1998). Such an interaction is the hallmark of many popular memory models, such as prototype and exemplar theory (Shanks, 1995).

Averages and Extremes Combined

The reader may have noted that from the two types of memory interaction described above, a contradiction may arise. An extreme face is not an average face, and vice versa. It is possible to reconcile these two factors and show that in reality they both affect responding. In Figure 5.4, we have combined the gradients from Figure 5.1 and Figure 5.3 and obtained a gradient that is a function of two dimensions. The first dimension is the male–female dimension. The second dimension is some other dimension along which faces vary. The height of the gradient is the judgment of sexual attractiveness of male and female faces by receivers of one sex. Along the male-female dimension the gradient shows a peak shift in the direction of extreme traits. Along the second dimension a preference for the average is present.

Note that Figure 5.4 is idealized. In reality, faces vary along many more dimensions, and indeed we do not know how the brain represents faces. The two-dimensional model, however, allows us to make some detailed predictions (see Figure 5.4b). First, a minority of faces will be more attractive than the average face, which has been shown by Alley and Cunningham (1991). Another prediction is that an average of attractive faces of one sex will be more attractive than the average of all faces of the same sex, which has been empirically dem-

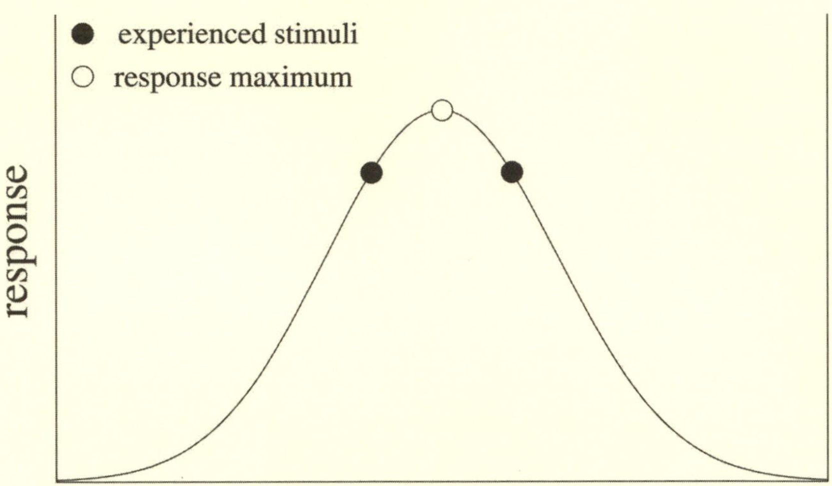

Figure 5.3. Experience of two similar stimuli requiring the same response can also create a peak shift. In contrast with Figure 5.1, the response maximum is now located between the two experience stimuli.

onstrated by Perrett, May, and Yoshikawa (1994) for female faces. The model also predicts that making a face more extreme in the male–female dimension does often make the face more attractive, but not always. It can be seen in the gradient in Figure 5.4 that attractiveness eventually decreases when faces become very extreme.

Symmetry

Symmetry has often been considered an important aspect of beauty in general as well as for faces (Gombrich, 1984; Zebrowitz, 1997). Before we deal with preferences for symmetry, let us consider why faces are bilaterally symmetrical (viewed from the front). Symmetries can usually be traced back to fundamental physical phenomena such as gravitation and the three dimensions of space (Stewart & Golubitsky, 1992). For land-living animals balance with respect to gravitation is necessary, and this will favor symmetry in form. As a further example, if one wants to minimize the surface-to-volume ratio in a three-dimensional world, a sphere (possessing complete rotational symmetry) is the solution. In addition, in many organisms the developmental process is based on a bilateral development plan established very early in embryonic life. Communication as well may favor symmetries. For instance, a signal may gain by looking the same from different directions, meaning that it must have the

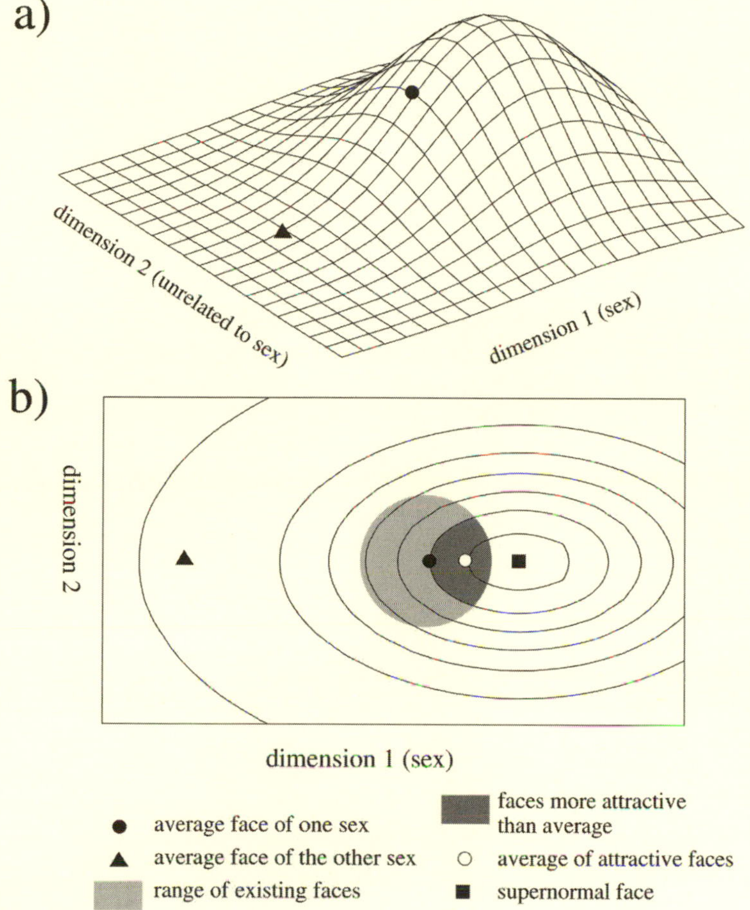

Figure 5.4. A simplified model of judgment of the sexual attractiveness of faces judged by one sex. The model combines the need for discriminating between sexes (see Figure 5.1) and responding similarly to variation within a sex (see Figure 5.3). It can be applied to either male of female preferences. Dimension 1 is the male–female dimension (see Figure 5.2) and dimension 2 is a trait that varies independently of sex. Part a) shows the gradient in a three-dimensional plot with the height of the surface describing the strength of the response to the face (attractiveness). Part b) shows contours of equal attractiveness of the gradient in a). In the right half, the existing variation in faces for one sex is indicated. The average face is more attractive than most faces but even more attractive faces exist. These faces are located near the average but further away from faces of the opposite sex. Supernormal (exceptionally attractive) faces may occur outside the range of existing faces.

corresponding symmetries (Enquist & Arak, 1993). The latter may be less important for faces since we usually interact face to face.

An important point is that average faces are typically more symmetrical than individual ones. Even if a high degree of symmetry is present in all individual faces (and possibly maintained by selection), we see some random deviations (fluctuating asymmetry), possibly due to stress during development (Ludwig, 1932; Møller & Swaddle, 1997; Parsons, 1990; Van Valen, 1962). What is important here is that such fluctuations are random in size and direction. By combining many faces, these random asymmetries cancel out each other and the composite face is more symmetrical. Thus, a preference for an average, thereby symmetrical, face may not reveal a general preference for symmetry. A fair question is whether symmetry per se is an aspect of facial attractiveness independent of preference for the average. If we make a face more symmetrical, will it be more attractive? Our simple model does not predict this. It seems also intuitively clear that faces can be symmetrical but at the same time unattractive (see Figure 5.5 for an example).

At the heart of the problem lies the fact that a face can be made symmetrical in an infinite number of ways, whereas "averaging" is a unique operation. If symmetry is not an independent component of attractiveness it can be conceived that a particular symmetrization will enhance the sexual attractiveness of a face only insofar as it brings the face closer to the average or away from other faces of the subject's own sex. To understand the predictions of our model with respect to symmetry, note first that all faces that lie on the line join-

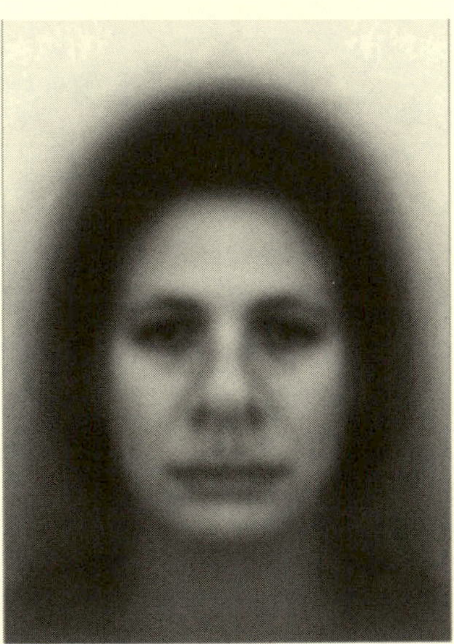

Figure 5.5. An example of a symmetrical but unattractive face.

ing the averages of the two sexes are perfectly symmetrical. Any modification that brings a face closer to this line increases its symmetry but not necessarily its attractiveness (see Figure 5.6). However, the most attractive faces lie close to the line and are thus highly symmetrical. We arrive at this result without any assumptions about symmetry. Instead, the result arises from combining stimulus-control theory with the fact that faces are on average symmetrical.

Empirically, symmetrical faces have been produced chiefly with two different techniques. One consists of mirror imaging one half of the face along the central vertical axis of the face. Using the left and right halves, two symmetrical faces can thus be constructed (so called "chimeras"). The second technique yields a single symmetrical face by averaging the two (already symmetrical) faces obtained with the first method. The same face can also be obtained by first averaging the original face and its mirror image. The first technique produces faces that in comparison with the original are not closer (on average) to the average face. In contrast, the face obtained with the second technique is

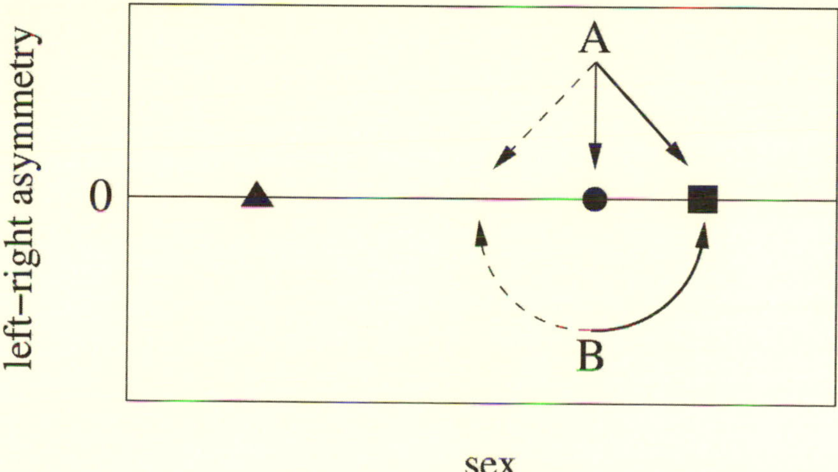

Figure 5.6. Examples of face modifications that increase symmetry but have different effects on sexual attractiveness (recall the model outlined in Figure 5.4). The first dimension is sex and the second dimension is some measure of the difference between the left and the right halves of a face. Zero difference means that the face is bilaterally symmetric with respect to this measure. The averages of the two sexes are indicated with the triangle and circle, respectively (the square is the peak of the gradient in Figure 5.4). Faces A and B are somewhat asymmetric faces. For face A, three modifications are indicated that all give rise to more symmetrical faces, but with different effects on sexual attractiveness, according to the model in Figure 5.4. Dashed lines indicate a decrease in attractiveness, whereas continuous lines indicate an increase in attractiveness (the thicker, the bigger the increase). For face B, two modifications are shown that both increase symmetry while keeping constant the distance from the same-sex average.

closer to the average face. Thus, we predict that the second technique but not the first should produce more attractive faces. Indeed, experiments indicate that symmetrical faces obtained with the first technique are not on average rated more attractive (Langlois, Roggman, & Musselman, 1994; Kowner, 1996; Samuels, Butterworth, Rogerts, Graupner, & Hole, 1994), while faces obtained with the second technique are perceived as more beautiful than the original faces (Langlois, Roggman, & Musselman, 1994; Rhodes, Proffitt, Grady, & Sumich, 1998; Rhodes, Roberts, & Simmons, 1999; but see also Swaddle & Cuthill, 1995).

The impact of facial symmetry per se on attractiveness can also be studied using individual faces directly. When both symmetry and attractiveness are rated by subjects, significant correlations have been found (Mealey & Townsend, 1999; Rhodes, Proffitt, Grady, & Sumich, 1998; Rhodes, Roberts, & Simmons, 1999a; Zebrowitz, Voinescu, & Collins, 1996). However, when face symmetry is measured objectively rather than judged, significant correlations have not been obtained. Shackelford and Larsen (1997) report overall correlations of -0.01 and -0.02 in two studies. Jones and Hill (1993) report only two significant correlations out of 28 in samples of faces of Ache Indians, Brazilians, and people from the United States. These results may suggest that attractiveness enhances perceived symmetry, rather than vice versa.

Existing studies are thus consistent with the view that symmetry per se is not a powerful determinant of attractiveness. However, it is also possible that experiences of symmetries in general could interact with particular memories and produce preferences for symmetries (Enquist & Arak, 1994). Also, special cognitive abilities to deal with symmetries may exist that could produce preferences for symmetry in general. A greater understanding of how symmetrical faces, and perhaps symmetries in general, are represented in the brain is needed to settle these questions.

DIVERSITY AND UNIFORMITY OF PREFERENCES

By considering how recognition mechanisms operate, it seems possible to explain biases in judgment of attractiveness within an individual, but what about patterns of variation within and between societies or populations? To answer this, we have to consider developmental (ontogenetic) and evolutionary processes. We start with development.

Development

In principle, we are faced with three possibilities for development. The first is that judgments of attractiveness are mainly under genetic control. This would fit with the view that sexual preferences have been finetuned by genetic evolution to allow an individual to choose a mate of high genetic quality. This view is also consistent with empirical studies showing that such judgments agree among individuals to a considerable extent (but not completely), both within and between populations (e.g., Buss 1989; Cunningham, Roberts, Barbee, Druen, & Wu, 1995; Rhodes, Harwood, Yoshikawa, Nishitani, & McLean, Chapter 2, this volume; Cunningham, Barbee, & Pillhower, Chapter 7, this volume; Dion, Chapter 8, this volume).

If genetic control dominates, variation between individuals must be due to genetic variation. However, it seems to us that it is difficult to explain in this way all diversity that we see. That variations in preferences for "natural" features such as skin, eye, and hair color or facial form have a genetic background may not pose any logical problems, but it seems implausible that preferences for recent cultural innovations can be explained in this way. Humans have been very creative when it comes to manipulating facial appearance in order to increase their attractiveness or status. Innovations include makeup, jewelry, haircut, tattoos, piercing, scarves, and hats. Some of these alterations simply exaggerate natural features such as eyebrows and lips. Other modifications are more remote from natural appearance and thus particularly difficult to reconcile with the idea of genetically coded recognition. Preference for individuals wearing eyeglasses is an interesting example. Glasses were originally designed not to enhance attractiveness but once they were used they became a part of faces and thus experienced by observers. As a consequence we now have some people who prefer partners with glasses and in some individuals this preference has reached the level of fetishism (self-reports from individuals on the Internet). Note also that glasses could be considered an indicator of bad quality. For similar reasons, the hypothesis that preferences are under genetic control is difficult to reconcile with cultural diversity. It is not uncommon to find facial adornment from a different culture funny and unattractive (Zebrowitz, 1997). A classic example is lip enlargement occurring in some African and South American tribes (Zebrowitz, 1997). We guess that within these cultures these features are very sexy, although this is hard to imagine for people from other cultures. Another reason why the genetic hypothesis seems less likely is the fact that we learn to recognize individual faces. If judgments of face attractiveness were under genetic control, that would mean that these two systems need to be independent.

The second hypothesis is that preferences are under no or little genetic control. While this could explain diversity, it leaves us with problems of a different kind. Without genetic guidance it would be impossible to know what to pay attention to and what to learn. A completely naive individual surrounded by massive amounts of more or less biologically relevant stimuli would not be able to know that it should learn about such things as sex and age.

The third hypothesis is that both genes and learning are important. Indeed, in reality most behavioral systems often seem to develop in a complex interaction between genes and learning (e.g., Hogan & Bolhuis, 1994). The process we envision most likely for reading faces is a learning process that is guided by genetic predispositions (Hogan & Bolhuis, 1994). Such guided learning is consistent both with the observation of individual and cultural diversity and the fact that we need to pay attention to certain properties such as age and sex. It is also consistent with patterns of generalization and discrimination, as discussed above. Since experiences will differ, individuals will learn different things. This may lead to more extreme preferences that in some contexts are called fetishes (Steele, 1996). Guided learning can also, perhaps surprisingly, explain why some preferences are shared by many human societies (Buss, 1989; Cunningham et al. 1995; Jones, & Hill, 1993; Rhodes, Harwood, Yoshikawa, Nishitani & McLean, Chapter 2, this volume). Such universalities in general are often regarded as genetic, adaptive, and due to common ancestry, but this may not always be the case. We can distinguish between universalities that stem from sharing the same genes and those stemming from other shared factors. For faces, such a shared factor may be that faces look alike in different populations, due to shared genes responsible for face morphology. Thus, universal preferences may derive from learning based on the faces we see and not from genetic control of preferences. It would be illuminating here to know more about differences between societies or populations. According to our theory, a bias toward experienced faces is often expected due to a preference for the average. In a comparison of several human populations, Jones and Hill (1993) showed that subjects within a population agree to a larger extent when rating familiar faces (from the same population) than unfamiliar ones (from different populations). They also showed that different populations may have different standards of attractiveness. For example, Ache and Hiwi Indians did not agree with people from the Unites States and Russia when rating faces of females from Brazil, the United States and the Ache tribe (correlations varied between -0.04 and 0.13).

Insight about development of facial preferences may be gained by considering how perceptual mechanisms develop in some animals. Ethologists have studied how animals learn sexual preferences through imprinting (see reviews by Bolhuis, 1991; Clayton, 1994; Kruijt, 1985; ten Cate, 1994). In the beginning, this developmental process was considered as a very unique and stable form of learning of species-specific characteristics, occurring only during a short and restricted period early in life (Eibl-Eibesfeldt, 1975; Lorenz, 1935). Recent studies have provided a more dynamic picture and demonstrated similarities with other forms of learning (see e.g., Bolhuis, 1991; Shettleworth, 1994). Still, imprinting-like processes are characterized by preprogrammed sensitive periods in which learning occurs more easily, often independent of the contexts in which it is later to be used. However, modifications later in life are possible (Bolhuis, 1991). In sexual imprinting, information about which stimuli sexual behavior will be directed to is learned. This has been studied in male zebra finches using cross-fostering experiments, in which Bengalese finches acted as foster parents. These experiments reveal the importance of experience in the development of partner preferences: zebra finches that have been raised by Bengalese finches develop a preference for Bengalese finches (ten Cate, 1994). An important finding is that social interactions and attention are decisive factors in these learning processes, that is, young are particularly prone to be imprinted on adults that interact with them (e.g., Bolhuis, 1991; Hofer, 1987; Kraemer, 1992; ten Cate, 1994). Observing the actions of others might also influence preferences. Recently, it has been shown that females of some bird species copy the mate preferences of other females (see, e.g., Andersson, 1994; Gibson, Bradbury, & Vehrencamp, 1991).

We suggest that learning processes similar to those observed in birds occur in humans as well. Unfortunately, our knowledge about ourselves is less precise than that we have for birds. Note, however, that many theories of human behavior and personality consider, in one way or the other, early experiences as important or fundamental to the ontogeny of perceptual mechanisms (e.g., Bandura, 1977; Bowlby, 1969; Money, 1986). Empirical studies of face reading in infants seem to suggest that we are born with coarse information about faces and a mechanism that guides development through learning (e.g., Johnson, 1994; Johnson & Morton, 1991). With increasing experience, the child pays more and more attention to both details and real faces (Johnson, 1992). However, exactly when sexual preferences become established and how genetic factors and individual experiences interact is poorly known. We are not aware of any studies that have tried to correlate mate preferences with appearance of parents or peers of the opposite sex. For instance, will a man with an older mother prefer older women than a man with a younger mother? Studies of this kind, relating childhood experiences with adult preferences, would be very enlightening.

Coevolution

We now turn to coevolution between facial appearances (regarding faces as signals or signaling devices) and receivers' preferences. By considering evolution, we should be able to understand why preferences and appearances vary among populations and in time. Both genetic and cultural evolution are important in shaping the appearance of faces. Face morphology (form and position of facial features) is primarily under genetic control. On top of this an individual may add things in a diversity of ways using makeup, jewelry, haircut, tattoos, or other means.

Let us first consider facial attributes that are under genetic control. Genetic evolution promotes those recognition mechanisms and those faces that produce most offspring. Over the last million years we can observe some significant changes in the skull of hominids (e.g., Boyd & Silk, 1997). This evolution may to some degree have been caused by receivers' preferences favoring certain appearances. Due to a combination of isolation and genetic evolution, we also see variation in facial appearance between populations in different parts of the world today.

To the extent that faces are signals, these changes and differences must have some meaning in a communication context. There are two major determinants of genetically coded signals. One is related to the problem of transmitting the signal to the receiver. This is an important problem for many signals, but faces are signaling devices used mainly for short-range communications so we ignore this problem here. The other main factor is related to the impact the signal has on the receiver. One idea is that receivers respond to sexual signals in a "rational way," reflecting the information they contain (e.g., Andersson, 1994; Bradbury & Vehrencamp, 1998; Grafen, 1990; Zahavi, 1975). Thus, if one sex prefers certain individuals of the opposite sex, this would indicate that potential partners vary in mate quality and that the preferences allow individuals to make adaptive choices.

The second hypothesis maintains that signals sometimes get their form because of their ability to manipulate the receivers by exploiting receiver biases (Dawkins, & Krebs, 1978; Enquist & Arak, 1998; Ryan, 1998; Staddon, 1975). By manipulation we mean that the receiver can be persuaded, to its disadvantage, to respond in a way beneficial to the sender. That is, judging one face more attractive than another may just mean that the preferred face is a stronger stimulus for the receiver, without any associated benefits. Indeed, the analysis of attractiveness presented above reveals that significant selection pressures could emerge directly from mechanisms responsible for generalization and discrimination of faces (see "Discrimination and Generalization," above). In the course of evolution, biases can act both as a "repulsion force" (making signals more different) and an "attraction force" (making signals more similar). Repulsion occurs in connection with discrimination (see Figure 5.1), attraction when different stimuli require the same response (Figure 5.3). Thus, biases in the nervous system could be directly responsible for the evolution of signal form, in particular if there are conflicts between senders and receivers, which give an incentive for manipulation (Enquist & Arak, 1998). Note that even in the presence of manipulation, signals may contain some important information (e.g., about the age and sex of the person).

Both hypotheses predict that receivers are influenced by senders. To evaluate these two hypotheses with respect to human faces, we need to know how the variation in facial attractiveness influences responses. Some support for the manipulation hypothesis comes from studies showing that attractive individuals of all ages are attributed more positive traits, by adults as well as children (e.g., Zebrowitz, 1997). For instance, attractive infants are judged by adults as easier and more rewarding to care for, as causing less trouble, and as being more competent, at the same time that expectations of competence are lower (Ritter, Casey, & Langlois, 1991; Stephan, & Langlois, 1984). Attitudes influence behavior, and mothers of attractive infants are shown to be more attentive, affectionate, and playful with their children (Langlois, Ritter, Casey, & Sawin, 1995). Although this may be interpreted as the mother caring more for offspring of higher quality (under the hypothesis that attractiveness signals quality), this can only explain variable investment within a family. Responses to attractiveness in some other situations are even more difficult to understand as reflecting some quality. For instance, attractiveness is advantageous when applying for a job, in communication and persuasion, when in trouble with the law, and when in need of aid (see references in Zebrowitz, 1997). People with attractive faces are also perceived as having higher socioeconomic status (Kalick, 1988).

To distinguish between the two hypotheses we must consider whether the receiver benefits from his or her reactions. One possibility is that these reactions to attractive faces are advantageous to the receiver, the other that they are not. Thus, we need to ask whether there are any indications that receivers actually benefit from their preferences. Particularly important for evolution is whether choosing attractive partners increases reproductive success. In the only study we are aware of, Kalick, Zebrowitz, Langlois, and Johnson (1998) find no significant correlations between number of children and attractiveness of partner (r=0.03 for males, n=116, and r=0.11 for females, n=127). In the same study, the authors correlated adolescent attractiveness with individual health, an important aspect of mate quality. The sample consisted of 169 females and 164 males, whose health was assessed in adolescence, middle adulthood, and late adulthood. No significant correlations were found (r scores varying from -0.10 to 0.10). Shackelford and Larsen (1999), based on health reports from 100 subjects over 4 weeks, report similar results. For men and women combined, the r scores varied between 0.02 and 0.17. Only one of eight health variables considered was significant. In summary, these two studies suggest that at most a few percent of the variation in attractiveness (estimated by r^2) can be explained by variation in health, or vice versa.

Some recent evolutionary thinking about mate preferences both in humans and in other animals have centered on symmetry (see "Symmetry," above). It is hypothesized that symmetry is an honest signal of mate quality (Møller & Swaddle, 1997). In particular, this idea has been embraced in studies on humans (Buss, 1999), whereas it remains controversial among biologists studying other species (e.g., Palmer, & Strobeck, 1997). Shackelford and Larsen (1997) studied correlations between facial asymmetry and a number of psychological and physiological measures in two samples (see also above). How these relate to mate quality is in many cases uncertain. However, most of the measures did not correlate with degree of symmetry. In one sample, 5 out of 48 correlations were significant and in the other sample 4 out 54. In both samples, there was no correlation between symmetry and reports of health parameters (referred to as "physiological complaints and events").

In summary, while being attractive clearly has advantages, it is unclear whether there are any benefits associated with being sensitive to facial attractiveness when reacting to people. Our preferences may not be perfectly tuned to always choose high-quality partners. Instead, facial attributes under genetic control may have evolved partly to manipulate rather than to provide accurate information to the receiver.

When studying human evolution, we cannot avoid cultural processes, and it is possible that findings about attractiveness need such considerations to be fully understood. The same might apply to preferences. To end the discussion about coevolution, we consider what culture can tell us. As we have already mentioned, facial appearance has been subject to significant cultural evolution. In almost all human societies, considerable amounts of time and effort are used to change facial appearance, including haircuts, colors, cosmetic surgery, and use of artifacts such as jewelry, hats, and masks (Alford, 1996; Gröning, 1997). Humans long ago discovered the power of appearance (e.g., Zebrowitz, 1997), and it seems clear that one purpose of these manipulations is to enhance sexual attractiveness and social status. However, what drives cultural evolution is not always clear (e.g. Boyd & Richerson, 1985) and other factors may also be important.

In cultural evolution, as in genetic evolution, we need to understand how a trait spreads and how innovations arise. Cultural traits spread when individuals mimic others. Such processes are often biased (Boyd & Richerson, 1985), that is, certain traits are more likely to be copied than others. For instance, it seems possible that receiver biases similar to those influencing judgment of attractiveness also influence what is copied from other individuals, but many other biases are certainly also important. Innovations are due to our creativity; people inventing new ways of modifying the face will supply the raw material for cultural evolution. Some innovations may primarily have another purpose. Hats were invented for protection but once used, they become a part of faces and stored in memory and thus affect judgment of faces. Soon it was discovered that hats, in addition to giving protection, could also have some impact on how a person is perceived by others. Such processes are referred to as ritualization. The exact direction evolution will take depends on preferences, and here signal repulsion and attraction are potentially very important. In addition, preferences may be transferred by imitation from one individual to another.

It is easy to see that cultural evolution can produce a lot of diversity between cultures. Innovations are partly random and depend also on local circumstances such as availability of artifacts. Two isolated groups of people will quickly enter different tracks that will be self-reinforcing as new receiver biases emerge partly caused by the particular innovations that occur. This process will lead to considerable change over time. That standards of beauty have varied considerably with respect to body adornment is well documented in the case of fashion. In contrast, we expect beauty standards for facial features that are under genetic control to be much more stable (see above).

Culture may also give rise to considerable variation within a particular society. Subgroups may want to look different. Young may want to look different from the older generation. Many different innovations may occur at the same time. All this may reinforce individual differences in preferences, because young individuals will have partly different experiences when preferences are established.

DISCUSSION

In this chapter, we have suggested an alternative theory for why we experience faces (and possibly many other things) as varying in attractiveness. First we presented a model of recognition, based on basic mechanisms for generalization and discrimination. This model seems to be able to explain major empirical findings about judgment of attractiveness (see Table 5.1). The model we applied is not particular to faces or humans, suggesting that judgments of attractiveness emerge by mechanisms similar to those controlling reactions to other stimuli. Thus, there may be nothing particular about reading faces, with the possible exception of resolution and memory capacity (e.g., Young 1998). We continued by suggesting that individual learning plays an important role in the formation of our preferences, although this process must to some extent be genetically guided. We discussed the relevance of ethological models. The hypothesis of guided learning is consistent with variation observed within societies and including extreme or unusual preferences. Combined with evolution, this hypothesis can also explain diversity between societies.

Evolution of genetically determined facial attributes as well as cultural traits is likely to be influenced by receiver bias. Two scenarios are particularly important (Enquist & Arak, 1998). One mechanism, signal attraction, is related to the problem of many different stimuli (for example, all individuals of one sex) requiring the same behavioral response. This favors average appearance. Our opinion about preferences for certain symmetries is that they are just a by-product of preference for the average. We suspect that many correlations obtained with symmetry would also be obtained by correlating with degree of deviation from the average appearance. In fact, the latter variable is probably much more informative. The second mechanism favors extremes and is related to discrimination (different behavior to different stimuli, e.g., individuals of different sex). Due to learning, any changes in the appearance of senders will directly affect receiver preferences and biases, and thus influence further evolution. This can lead to substantial diversity between societies with respect to preferences for facial attributes that are culturally inherited.

How does the theory that has been suggested here compare to a mate-quality hypothesis? Remember that both theories agree that sexual signals contain information about things like sex and species identity. However, mate-quality hypotheses continue further and predict that even details of the signal are informative and that the receiver responses are finetuned to this information; hence, the receiver responses are rational in all details (rational choice). In Table 5.1, we have tried to compare the two hypotheses based on the discussion in this chapter. Two variants of the "receiver bias hypothesis"

Prediction	Hypothesis		
	Receiver bias and guided learning	Receiver bias and genetic determination	Rational choice (genetic determination)
Existence of preferences	Yes *	Yes *	Yes *
Correlation between mate quality and attractiveness	-	-	Yes †
Receivers may respond not to their own advantage (manipulation)	Yes	Yes	No
Universality (not necessarily complete)	Yes *	Yes *	Yes *
Preferences for cultural innovations	Yes *	No †	No †
Individual variation in preferences	Yes *	-	-
Unusual preferences (e.g. fetishism)	Yes *	No †	No †
Geographical differences in preferences	Yes *	-	-
Preferences change during lifetime	Yes	No	No
Direction of bias predicted from theories of stimulus control	Yes *	Yes *	-

* Prediction agrees with empirical data.
† Prediction disagrees with empirical data.
(If empirical data is lacking or unclear no symbol is given)
- Prediction unknown or may go any direction

Table 5.1. Comparison of hypotheses for why faces vary in attractiveness.

are considered: one in which receiver preferences are due to genetically guided learning and the other in which preferences are genetically determined. As the table shows, the existence of culture in humans provides us with additional possibilities for distinguishing between hypotheses. Judging from the table, the hypothesis of biased receivers in combination with guided learning has the most support.

We would like to end the chapter by pointing out that it is not possible to rule out the possibility that faces or other sexual signals actually contain more information about partner quality than just species, sex, and age. However, we have presented a model that is a viable alternative hypothesis to theories based on rational choice. It is the task of future research to evaluate what is the exact mix of information and manipulation in sexual signals, and in particular in faces. Two kinds of empirical studies could be particularly illuminating. One is to explore individuals' ratings of attractiveness and compare them to the gradient in Figure 5.4. A possibility is to produce faces that vary in the male–female dimension and in an independent dimension in which the degree of asymmetry varies (note that there are many such dimensions, but it should be possible to choose one for which attractiveness varies considerably). The second kind of studies would investigate whether experiences of evolutionarily novel facial atributes such as earrings and haircuts could be encoded in an individual's preferences. Such studies would be important in determining how much of our preferences are genetically coded.

REFERENCES

Alford, R. (1996). Adornment. In D. Levinson & M. Ember (Eds.), *Encyclopedia of cultural anthropology* (pp. 7–9). London: Macmillan.

Alley, T. R., & Cunningham, M. R. (1991). Averaged faces are attractive. *Psychological Science, 2*, 123–125.

Andersson, M. (1994). *Sexual selection*. Princeton, NJ: Princeton University Press.

Arak, A., & Enquist, M. (1995). Conflict receiver bias and the evolution of signal form. *Philosophical Transactions of the Royal Society of London, Series B, 349*, 337–344.

Baerends, G. P. (1982). The herring gull and its eggs: General discussion. *Behaviour, 82*, 276–411.

Bandura, A. (1977). *Social learning theory*. Upper Saddle River, NJ: Prentice-Hall.

Baron, A. (1973). Postdiscrimination gradients of human subjects on a tone continuum. *Journal of Experimental Psychology, 101*, 337–342.

Benson, P. J., & Perrett, D. I. (1991). Perception and recognition of photographic quality facial caricatures: Implications for the recognition of natural images. *European Journal of Cognitive Psychology, 3*, 105–135.

Bolhuis, J. J. (1991). Mechanisms of avian imprinting: A review. *Biological Review, 66*, 303–345.

Bowlby, J. (1969). *Attachment and loss*. New York: Random House.

Boyd, R., & Richerson, P. J. (1985). *Culture and the evolutionary process*. Chicago: University of Chicago Press.

Boyd, R., & Silk, J. B. (1997). *How humans evolved*. New York: W. W. Norton.

Bradbury, J. W., & Vehrencamp, S. L. (1998). *Principles of animal communication*. Sunderland, MA: Sinauer Associates.

Brennan, S. E. (1985). The caricature generator. *Leonardo, 18*, 170–178.

Buss, D. M. (1989). Sex differences in human mate preferences: Evolutionary hypothesis testing in 37 cultures. *Behaviour and Brain Sciences, 12*, 1–14.

Buss, D. M. (1999). *Evolutionary psychology: The new science of the mind*. Boston: Allyn and Bacon.

Chaiken, S. (1979). Communicator physical attractiveness and persuasion. *Journal of Personality and Social Psychology, 37*, 1387–1397.

Clayton, N. S. (1994). The influence of social interactions on the development of song and sexual preferences in birds. In J. A. Hogan & J. J. Bolhuis (Eds.), *Causal mechanisms of behavioural development* (pp. 98–115). Cambridge, UK: Cambridge University Press.

Cunningham, M. R., Roberts, A. R., Barbee, A. P., Druen, P. B., & Wu, C.-H. (1995). "Their ideas of beauty are, on the whole, the same as ours": Consistency and variability in the cross-cultural perception of female physical attractiveness. *Journal of Personality and Social Psychology, 68*, 261–279.

Dawkins, R., & Krebs, J. R. (1978). Animal signals: Information or manipulation? In J. R. Krebs & N. B. Davies (Eds.), *Behavioural ecology* (pp. 282–309). Oxford, UK: Blackwell Scientific.

Efran, M. G., & Patterson, E. W. (1974). Voters are beautiful: The effect of physical appearance on national election. *Canadian Journal of Behavioral Science, 6*, 352–356.

Eibl-Eibesfeldt, I. (1975). *Ethology: The biology of behavior.* New York: Holt, Rinehart & Winston.

Enquist, M., & Arak, A. (1993). Selection of exaggerated male traits by female aesthetic senses. *Nature, 361*, 446–448.

Enquist, M., & Arak, A. (1994). Symmetry, beauty and evolution. *Nature, 372*, 169–172.

Enquist, M., & Arak, A. (1998). Neural representation and the evolution of signal form. In R. Dukas (Ed.), *Cognitive ecology* (pp. 21–87). Chicago: University of Chicago Press.

Enquist M, Arak A., Ghirlanda, S., & Wachtmeister, C.-A. (In prep.). Spectacular phenomena and limits to rationality in genetic and cultural evolution.

Enquist, M., & Johnstone, R. (1997). Generalization and the evolution of symmetry preferences. *Proceedings of the Royal Society of London, Series B, 264*, 1345–1348.

Galton, F. (1878). Composite portraits. *Journal of the Anthropological Institute of Great Britain and Ireland, 8*, 132–142.

Galton, F. (1883). *Inquiries into human faculty and its development.* New York: Macmillan.

Gardner, B. T., & Wallach, L. (1965). Shapes of figures identified as a baby's head. *Perceptual and Motor Skills, 20*, 135–142.

Ghirlanda, S., & Enquist, M. (1998). Artificial neural networks as models of stimulus control. *Animal Behavior, 56*, 1383–1389.

Gibson, R. M., Bradbury, J. W., & Vehrencamp, S. L. (1991). Mate choice in lekking sage grouse revisited: The roles of vocal display, female site fidelity, and copying. *Behavioral Ecology, 2*, 165–180.

Gillen, B. (1981). Physical attractiveness: A determinant of two types of goodness. *Personality and Social Psychology Bulletin, 7*, 277–281.

Gombrich, E. H. (1984). *The sense of order: A study in the psychology of decorative art.* London: Phaidon.

Grafen, A. (1990). Biological signals as handicaps. *Journal of Theoretical Biology, 144*, 517–546.

Gray A. P. (1958). *Bird hybrids, a check-list with bibliography.* Commonwealth Agriculture. Bureaux, Alva, Scotland.

Gröning, K. (Ed.). (1997). *Decorated skin: A world survey of body art.* London: Thames and Hudson.

Hofer, M. A. (1987). Early social relationships: A psychobiologist's view. *Child Development, 58*, 633–647.

Hogan, J. A., & Bolhuis, J. J. (Eds.). (1994). *Causal mechanisms of behavioural development.* Cambridge, UK: Cambridge University Press.

Johnson, M. H. (1992). Cognition and development: Four contentions about the role of visual attention. In D. J. Stein & J. E. Young (Eds.), *Cognitive science and clinical disorders* (pp. 43–60). San Diego, CA: Academic Press.

Johnson, M. H. (1994). Cortical mechanisms of cognitive development. In J. A. Hogan & J. J. Bolhuis (Eds.), *Causal mechanisms of behavioural development* (pp. 267–288). Cambridge, UK: Cambridge University Press.

Johnson, M. H., & Morton, J. (1991). *Biology and cognitive development: The case of face recognition.* Oxford, UK: Blackwell.

Johnstone, R. (1994). Female preferences for symmetrical males as a by-product of selection for mate recognition. *Nature, 372,* 172–175.

Jones, D., & Hill, K. (1993). Criteria of facial attractiveness in five populations. *Human Nature, 4,* 271–296.

Kalick, S. M. (1988). Physical attractiveness as a status cue. *Journal of Experimental Social Psychology, 24,* 469–489.

Kalick, S. M., Zebrowitz, L. A., Langlois, J. H., & Johnson, R. M. (1998). Does human facial attractiveness honestly advertise health? *Psychological Science, 9,* 8–13.

Keating, C. (1985). Gender and the physiognomy of dominance and attractiveness. *Social Psychology Quarterly, 48,* 61–70.

Kowner, R. (1996). Facial attractiveness and judgement in developmental perspective. *Journal of Experimental Psychology: Human Perception and Performance, 22,* 662–675.

Kraemer, G. W. (1992). A psychobiological theory of attachment. *Behavioral and Brain Sciences, 15,* 493–541.

Kruijt, J. P. (1985). On the development of social attachments in birds. *Netherlands Journal of Zoology, 35,* 45–62.

Langlois, J. H., Ritter, J. M., Casey, R. J., & Sawin, D. B. (1995). Infant attractiveness predicts maternal behaviors and attitudes. *Developmental Psychology, 31,* 464–472.

Langlois, J. H., & Roggman, L. A. (1990). Attractive faces are only average. *Psychological Science, 1,* 115–121.

Langlois, J. H., Roggman, L. A., & Musselman, L. (1994). What is average and what is not average about attractive faces? *Psychological Science, 5,* 214–220.

Lorenz, K. Z. (1935). Der Kumpan in der Umwelt des Vogel. *Journal of Ornithology, 83,* 137–413.

Lorenz, K. Z. (1950). Ganzheit und Teil in der tierischen und menschlichen Gemeinschaft. *Studium Generale, 9,* 555–599.

Ludwig, W. (1932). *Das recht-links problems im Tierrich und beim Menchen.* Berlin: Springer.

Lundqvist, D., & Litton, J.-E. (In preparation). *The essence of human facial emotions—the averaged Karolinska directed emotional faces.*

Mackintosh, N. J. (1974). *The psychology of animal learning.* London: Academic Press.

Maier, R. A., Holmes, D. L., Slaymaker, F. L., & Reich, J. N. (1984). The perceived attractiveness of preterm infants. *Infant Behavior and Development, 7,* 403–414.

Mealey, L., & Towsend, G. C. (1999). The role of fluctuating asymmetry on judgements of physical attractiveness: A monozygotic co-twin comparison. *Perspectives in Human Biology, 4,* 219–224.

Møller, A. P., & Swaddle, J. P. (1997). *Asymmetry, developmental stability, and evolution.* Oxford: Oxford University Press.

Money, J. (1986). *Love maps: Clinical concepts of sexual/erotic health and pathology, paraphilia, and gender transposition in childhood, adolescence, and maturity.* New York: Irvington.

Palmer, A. R., & Strobeck, C. (1997). Fluctuating asymmetry and developmental stability: Heritability of observable variation vs. heritability of inferred cause. *Journal of Evolutionary Biology, 10*, 39–49.

Parsons, P. A. (1990). Fluctuating asymmetry: An epigenetic measure of stress. *Biological Review, 65*, 131–145.

Pearce, J. M. (1994). Discrimination and categorization. In J. Mackintosh (Ed.), *Animal learning and cognition* (pp. 109–134). San Diego, CA: Academic Press.

Pearce, J. M. (1997). *Animal learning and cognition.* (2nd ed.). Hove, UK: Psychology Press.

Perrett, D., Lee, K., Penton-Voak, I., Rowland, D., Yoshikawa, S., Burt, M., Henzi, S. P., Castles, D., & Amakatsu, S. (1998). Effects of sexual dimorphism on facial attractiveness. *Nature, 394*, 884–887.

Perrett, D. I., May, K. A., & Yoshikawa, S. (1994). Facial shape and judgements of female attractiveness. *Nature, 368*, 239–242.

Rensch, B. (1963). Versuche über menschliche “Auslllöser-Merkmale” beider Geschlechter. *Zeitschrift für Morphologie und Anthropologie, 53*, 139–164.

Rhodes, G. (1996). *Superportraits: Caricatures and recognition.* Hove, UK: Psychology Press.

Rhodes, G., Brennan, S., & Carey, S. (1987). Identification and ratings of caricatures: Implications for mental representations of faces. *Cognitive Psychology, 19*, 473–497.

Rhodes, G., Hickford, C., & Jeffery, L. (2000). Sex-typicality and attractiveness: Are supermale and superfemale faces super-attractive? *British Journal of Psychology, 91*, 125–140.

Rhodes, G., Proffitt, F., Grady, G. M., & Sumich, A. (1998). Facial symmetry and the perception of beauty. *Psychonomic Bulletin and Review, 5*, 659–669.

Rhodes, G., Roberts, J., & Simmons, L. W. (1999). Reflections on symmetry and attractiveness. *Psychology, Evolution and Gender, 1*, 279–295.

Rhodes, G., Sumich, A. & Byatt, G. (1999). Are average facial configurations attractive only because of their symmetry? *Psychological Science, 10*, 52–58.

Rhodes, G., & Tremewan, T. (1996). Averageness, exaggeration, and facial attractiveness. *Psychological Science, 7*, 105–110.

Ritter, J. M., Casey, R. J., & Langlois, J. H. (1991). Adult’s responses to infants varying in appearance of age and attractiveness. *Child Development, 62*, 68–82.

Ryan, M. J. (1998). Sexual selection, receiver bias, and the evolution of sex differences. *Science, 281*, 1999–2003.

Samuels, C. A., Butterworth, G., Rogerts, T., Graupner, L., & Hole, G. (1994). Facial aesthetics: Babies prefer attractiveness to symmetry. *Perception, 23*, 823–831.

Shackelford, T. K., & Larsen, R. J. (1997). Facial asymmetry as an indicator of psychological, emotional, and physiological distress. *Journal of Personality and Social Psychology, 72*, 456–466.

Shackelford, T. K., & Larsen, R. J. (1999). Facial attractiveness and physical health. *Evolution and Human Behavior, 20*, 71–76.

Shanks, D. S. (1995). *The psychology of associative learning.* Cambridge, UK: Cambridge University Press.

Shettleworth, S. J. (1994). The varieties of learning in development: Towards a common framework. In J. A. Hogan & J. J. Bolhuis (Eds.), *Causal mechanisms of behavioural development* (pp. 358–376). Cambridge, UK: Cambridge University Press.

Shettleworth, S. J. (1998). *Cognition, evolution, and behavior.* New York: Oxford University Press.

Spence, K. W. (1937). The differential response in animals to stimuli varying in a single dimension. *Psychological Review, 44*, 430–444.

Staddon, J.E.R. (1975). A note on the evolutionary significance of "supernormal" stimuli. *American Naturalist, 109*, 541–545.

Steele V. (1996). *Fetish: Fashion, sex and power.* Oxford, UK: Oxford University Press.

Stephan, C. W., & Langlois, J. H. (1984). Baby beautiful: Adult attributions of infant competence as a function of infant attractiveness. *Child Development, 55*, 576–585.

Sternglanz, S. H., Gray, J. L., & Murakami, M. (1977). Adult preferences for infantile facial features: An ethological approach. *Animal Behaviour, 25*, 108–115.

Stewart, I., & Golubitsky, M. (1992). *Fearful symmetry: Is God a geometer?* London: Penguin Books.

Swaddle, J. P., & Cuthill, I. C. (1994). Female zebra finches prefer males with symmetrically manipulated chest plumage. *Proceedings of the Royal Society of London, Series B, 258*, 267–271.

Swaddle, J. P., & Cuthill, I. C. (1995). Asymmetry and human facial attractiveness: Symmetry may not always be beautiful. *Proceedings of the Royal Society of London, Series B, 261*, 111–116.

ten Cate, C. (1994). Perceptual mechanisms in imprinting and song learning. In J. A. Hogan & J. J. Bolhuis (Eds.), *Causal mechanisms of behavioural development* (pp. 116–146). Cambridge, UK: Cambridge University Press.

Tinbergen, N. (1951). *The study of instinct.* Oxford, UK: Clarendon Press.

Tinbergen, N. (1963). On aims and methods of ethology. *Zeitschrift für Tierpsychologie, 20*, 410–433.

Trivers, R. L. (1972). Parental investment and sexual selection. In B. Campbell (Ed.), *Sexual selection and the descent of man* (pp. 136–179). London: Heinemann.

Van Valen, L. (1962). A study of fluctuating asymmetry. *Evolution, 16*, 125–142.

Walsh, V., & Kulikowski, J. (1998). *Perceptual constancy.* Cambridge, UK: Cambridge University Press.

Young, A. W. 1998. *Face and mind.* Oxford, UK: Oxford University Press.

Zahavi, A. (1975). Mate selection: A selection for a handicap. *Journal of Theoretical Biology, 53*, 205–214.

Zebrowitz, L. A. (1997). *Reading faces: Window to the soul?* Boulder, CO: Westview Press.

Zebrowitz, L. A., Voinescu, L., & Collins, M. A. (1996). "Wide-eyed" and "crooked-faced": Determinants of perceived and real honesty across the life span. *Personality and Social Psychology Bulletin, 22*, 1258–1269.

CHAPTER 6

Charismatic Faces: Social Status Cues Put Face Appeal in Context

Caroline F. Keating

Human communication depends upon the face as a platform for the production of speech and expression. But faces speak even when silent and motionless. Large eyes communicate submissiveness, warmth, and trust (e.g., Keating, 1985a; Zebrowitz & Montepare, 1992). Prominent, square jaws convey dominance and strength (e.g., Cunningham, Barbee, & Pike, 1990; Keating, Mazur, & Segall, 1981). By influencing social judgments like these, physiognomy helps guide decisions about whom to approach, help, mate, follow, fight, and avoid. What cognitive foundations do faces rely on for their charismatic and influential ways?

In humans and other mammals, aspects of facial growth are imbued with social status information. Mature facial traits signal dominance, threat, and power. Immature facial features convey submissiveness, appeasement, and receptivity. The premise of this chapter is that elements of facial morphology evolved as social status displays patterned after developmental changes in facial structure (Guthrie, 1970; Keating, 1985b; Lorenz, 1943). Status messages from the face activate cognitive biases in perceivers that combine to attract or repel social interaction.

Faces are "attractive" in that they draw us into relationships. But the appeal of a face is partly determined by what we seek in it. Thus, facial images of attractive starlets differ from those of attractive mothers. What is appealing about a face can shift, based on social context and role expectations. For instance, facial cues conveying dominance may be attractive in a political leader but not in a sales clerk. The appeal of status cues may also differ depending upon whether the leader or clerk is a man or a woman. In this chapter, attractiveness is conceptualized not as an absolute standard applicable to every face, but as a cognition influenced by social context. The critical messages that faces deliver are social in nature, and the fit between social status messages and social expectations or context is responsible for cognitions about facial attractiveness.

OVERVIEW

This chapter begins by developing the conceptual significance of social status cues for context-dependent face appeal, first by briefly comparing the status cues approach to alternative theoretical perspectives (introduced below), and then by developing arguments for the social status signals interpretation of attractiveness. Embedded in these deliberations are research questions that become the focus of empirical inquiry in the second half of the chapter. The research explores the influence of status cues on facial attractiveness in different social contexts. Included are studies of facial types that are attractive because they inspire caregiving, invite heterosexual relationships, or entice a following.

Alternative Approaches

There are many ways to think about facial attractiveness and, throughout this chapter, I mention some alternatives to the social status cues perspective. Included in the array of proposals advanced by researchers to explain facial attractiveness are:

Averageness Is Attractive

Mathematically averaged facial configurations are most attractive because averageness or prototypicality is pleasing in and of itself, has the advantage of looking relatively familiar, and may reflect physical and genetic adaptability, which is ideal in a mate (e.g., Langlois & Roggman, 1990; Rhodes, Sumich, & Byatt, 1999; Rubenstein, Kalakanis, & Langlois, 1999).

Symmetry Is Attractive

Symmetrical faces are most attractive, because symmetry is linked to pathogen resistance, health, good genes, and, ultimately, reproductive potential (e.g., Gangestad, Thornhill, & Yeo, 1994; Thornhill & Gangestad, 1993).

Cues For Hormonal Status Determine Attractiveness

Sexually dimorphic features like facial shape, which are believed to be influenced by hormone levels at puberty, express relative degrees of masculinity and femininity, and predict judgments of heterosexual attractiveness (Perrett et al.,

1998) in concert with the hormonal status of perceivers (Penton-Voak et al., 1999).

Affordances Influence Judgments of Attractiveness

Consistent with the ecological approach to perception (McArthur & Baron, 1983), facial structures express affordances (opportunities for certain types of interactions). Sensitivity toward these signals is adaptive but can overgeneralize. Affordances proffered by babyish facial cues, for example, overgeneralize when displayed by adults and influence cognitions about face appeal (Berry & McArthur, 1986; Montepare & Zebrowitz, 1998; Zebrowitz & Collins, 1997).

Multiple Fitness Messages Determine Attractiveness

Facial attractiveness incorporates messages along multiple biological and cognitive dimensions, including those reflecting biological fitness, social traits, and aspects associated with self-presentation (Cunningham, 1986; Cunningham, Barbee, & Pike, 1990; Cunningham, Roberts, Wu, Barbee, & Druen, 1995).

These approaches share several foundations with each other and with the social status cues perspective. Each links facial cues to underlying, biological substrates such as hormones and the eruption of secondary sex characteristics, morphological adaptation, immune system functioning, or other ontogenetic factors. Each considers biological fitness and implications for mate selection. Most are grounded in cross-species models and incorporate predictions of cultural universality in facial attractiveness.

The proposals diverge in the importance placed on the face's ability to convey messages about biological fitness versus social traits. Propositions advancing structural symmetry and cues for hormonal status emphasize the way attractive faces directly convey good-faith messages about biological fitness. In contrast, the social status cues, affordances, and multiple fitness propositions emphasize the way attractive faces advertize desirable social traits, honestly or otherwise. Some approaches focus relatively sharply on facial attractiveness in the context of mate preferences (i.e., the symmetry, hormonal cues, and multiple fitness perspectives). Others readily lend themselves to considering facial attractiveness within different social realms (i.e., the status cues and affordances perspectives). The averageness and symmetry perspectives each project a different, universal, context-free standard for facial attractiveness, whereas the status cues, affordances, and multiple fitness approaches entertain more complex, context-dependent notions of relationships between facial cues and face appeal.

ATTRACTIVENESS IN CONTEXT

In what sense are faces "attractive?" Faces are attractive, appealing, or "charismatic" in that they have the power to draw people into a relationship, whether it be as mates, lovers, friends, caregivers, fans, or followers. The relationship sought and the expectations surrounding it influence perceptions of attractiveness. As Feingold (1992) asserted, cognitions about physical attractiveness exist not in isolation but as part of a constellation of valued social traits. A similar appreciation of context on judgments of attractiveness can be found in the affordances approach (e.g., Zebrowitz & Collins, 1997).

In this chapter, "context" comprises a host of social expectancies manifested in status relationships and social roles. We examine in particular how status cues relate to facial attractiveness when perceivers' expectancies are driven by cognitions about helping and forming heterosexual attachments, and by gender and leadership roles.

As every casting director knows, what audiences seek or expect in a character should be reflected in the social messages projected by an actor's physiognomy. Tom Hanks would not make an appealing James Bond despite his versatility as an actor. Can you picture Goldie Hawn in the role of Queen Elizabeth or Joan of Arc? In each case, social messages from the face are at variance with what we expect the character to portray. These Hollywood examples conspire to make a point: an attractive physiognomy in one context may be unattractive in another.

THE SOCIAL STATUS CUES APPROACH TO FACIAL ATTRACTIVENESS

It is not by mistake that humans use static facial appearance to draw inferences about each other's abilities and traits. The arrangement of features in the front of the face evolved partly by communicating just such information (Gregory, 1929/1965; Guthrie, 1970). The visibility of human facial structures, their metamorphosis over the lifespan, and the effectiveness with which they signal social status information is consistent with the idea that facial morphology helps regulate human social attraction.

Ontogeny, Phylogeny, and Status Messages from the Face

A tapestry of shapes, sizes, and spatial arrangements of features characterize faces at different stages of development. Prepubescent morphological traits (or "pedomorphic" characteristics) include proportionately large eyes, a large, protruding forehead, a small chin, pudgy lips, and thin, arched brows (Alley, 1988; Eibl-Eibesfeldt, 1975; Lorenz, 1943; Mark, Shaw, & Pittenger, 1988). After puberty, brows thicken and apparent eye size diminishes (Enlow, 1982; Gray, 1948; Guthrie, 1970). Vascular changes thin the lips and jaws square with the advent of adult dentition (Gray, 1948; Guthrie, 1970). Pedomorphic and mature facial appearances help perceivers gauge responses appropriately during social interactions with individuals of different ages (Berry & McArthur, 1986; Keating, 1985b; Zebrowitz & Collins, 1997). We can judge from faces who requires our protection and who does not, and who is a potential threat and who is not.

Thus, the importance of ontogenetic cues from the face lies in the social status messages they convey. In animal and human social groups, maturity generally corresponds with dominance, whereas immaturity is associated with submissiveness. Dominance is age-graded, with older individuals typically wielding more social power than younger ones (Van Den Berghe & Barash, 1977; Wilson, 1975). Age and dominance share a curvilinear rather than a linear relationship, with individuals at each end of the age continuum diminished in status (Guthrie, 1970). Theorists working from the affordances (ethological) perspective account for the curvilinear relationship between status and age by differentiating between cues that signal physical maturity and those that signal senescence (Montepare & Zebrowitz, 1998). The status cues perspective identifies dominance and submissiveness as the important signaling dimensions underlying both maturity and senescence. This emphasis on signaling social status as opposed to "age-related physical qualities" (Montepare & Zebrowitz, 1998, p. 95) helps distinguish the status cues perspective from the affordances approach.

From the status cues perspective, maturity and age set the stage for physiognomic status messages but are not the same as those messages. Natural selection transformed cues that relay information about development into social status signals. These signals can be displayed or mimicked by any face. Thus, status cues evolved a ritualized signaling system of their own, which operates somewhat independently of maturity and age cues. In other words, status cues can produce submissive-looking adults and dominant-looking children. An adult face may mimic pedomorphic (youthful) traits and look unusually submissive, or display exaggerated maturity cues and appear particularly dominant (Guthrie, 1970). Similarly, a child's face may display exaggerated pedomorphy and look unusually submissive or project enhanced maturity and appear unusually dominant (Zebrowitz & Montepare, 1992). The status messages are consistent across age groups. From the perceiver's point of view, enhanced maturity cues invoke dominance-related attributions such as power and threat, while enhanced immaturity cues convey submissiveness, warmth, and social receptivity (Keating, 1985b).

Research confirms that, when displayed by adults, mature and immature facial aspects generate attributions consistent with the social status messages that underlie them. Pedomorphic-looking facial traits transmit qualities associated with submissiveness, including warmth, weakness, femininity, and honesty (e.g., Berry & McArthur, 1986; Keating, 1985b; Montepare & Zebrowitz, 1998; Perrett et al., 1998; Zebrowitz & Montepare, 1992). Mature-looking facial characteristics relay attributions associated with dominance, such as strength, cunning, masculinity, and sexual potency (e.g., Cunningham, Barbee, & Pike, 1990; Keating, 1985b; Penton-Voak et al., 1999; Zebrowitz, Montepare, & Lee, 1993). Researchers differ in the signaling dimensions they presume are central to these facial messages. For instance, some view sexually dimorphic facial aspects (like shape) as conveyors of critical messages about the relative masculinity and femininity of facial appearances (Penton-Voak & Perrett, 2000; Penton-Voak et al., 1999; Perrett et al., 1998). However, messages of masculinity/femininity and social status overlap (Williams & Best, 1994). Signaling masculinity may essentially convey dominance, while signaling femininity may fundamentally transmit submissiveness. Thus, the emphasis on signs of sexual dimorphism intersects with the idea that social status themes underlie the cognitive biases triggered when adult faces are perceived.

Early Sensitivity to Status-Related Facial Traits

Perceptual biases that guide the processing of status-related facial information are evident early in life. Twenty-week-old infants tend to gaze longer at immature than mature adult female faces (Kramer, Zebrowitz, San Giovanni, & Sherak, 1995). The gazes of young infants are also drawn to "attractive" adult female faces (Langlois et al., 1987; Rubenstein, Kalakanis, & Langlois, 1999), due perhaps to the immature physiognomic qualities often exhibited by pretty women worldwide (Cunningham, 1986; Jones, 1995).[1] Though the data are not entirely consistent, they suggest that infants may be biologically prepared to prefer pedomorphic-looking facial characteristics over mature-looking ones (Montepare & Zebrowitz, 1998).[2] Are babies naturally drawn to pedomorphic facial appearances? Or do they avoid mature facial appearances that seem threatening?

There is evidence indicating that infants and young children do perceive mature faces as threatening. Stranger anxiety, a behavioral tendency that appears to have genetic underpinnings (Plomin & Rowe, 1979) and a maturational trigger at around 7 months of age (Kagan, 1976), occurs in response to adults' but not to children's faces (Bigelow, MacLean, Wood, & Smith, 1990; Brooks & Lewis, 1976). Perceptions of facial maturity are fine-tuned. Infants and children not only discriminate adult from juvenile faces, they also differentiate the degree to which faces exhibit mature and immature-looking traits (Gross, 1997; Montepare & Zebrowitz-McArthur, 1989). Preschoolers associate adults who have relatively mature physiognomies with social dominance. Consistent with cross-cultural findings for adult perceivers (Keating et al., 1981), 4-year-old U.S. children selected adult faces with large jaws and receded hairlines as people who "tell others what to do" (Keating & Bai, 1986).

Thus, biased reactions to mature and immature faces are important enough to be expressed early in life. These biases may reflect a biologically based, perceptual guidance system for social responding akin to the mechanisms Bowlby (1969) proposed to explain the onset of infant attachment. Early tendencies to approach pedomorphic stimuli and avoid mature stimuli may be reinforced by growing up in societies with age-graded, male dominance hierarchies.

Benefits of Displaying and Perceiving Facial Status Cues

What are the proximate and ultimate benefits of displaying and interpreting facial status cues? By displaying pedomorphic characteristics, young organisms elicit care and stem aggressive responses (Lorenz, 1943; McCabe, 1988). The protective value of such facial cues is very real: McCabe (1984) discovered that children who were abused had a less pedomorphic shape to their faces compared to nonabused children. A lack of pedomorphic facial cues may contribute to a child's risk for abuse (McCabe, 1988).

Advantages are also bestowed on perceivers who are drawn to babyfaces. Early ethologists concluded that the appeal of a baby's face evolved by inspiring successful parenting (Eibl-Eibesfeldt, 1975; Lorenz, 1943). Parents captured by the faces of their infants became devoted caregivers whose genes benefited in the long run. Genetic influences underlying this cognitive bias were favored by natural selection and retained. Thus, infantile characteristics strike us as cute and garner our help.

The ability to detect maturity and dominance is also beneficial to individuals throughout development. As they become mobile, infant wariness in response to unfamiliar mature faces keeps them at a distance from adult strangers who could pose a threat (Bigelow et al., 1990; Brooks & Lewis, 1976). Later in life, individuals benefit by using status cues to assess other's dominance and power (Keating, 1985b). Assessments enable individuals to avoid confrontations they are likely to lose and to selectively establish coalitions with those who appear to have just "the right stuff."

The display of facial maturity is associated with social benefits. Facial maturity and dominant appearances have been linked to social influence and status in juvenile and adult males (Berry & Landry, 1997; Cherulnik, Turns, & Wilderman, 1990; Mazur & Keating, 1984; Mueller & Mazur, 1997). In male children, however, mature facial characteristics correspond with social costs as well as benefits (Montepare & Zebrowitz, 1998), and patterns for mature-faced girls and women are hard to decipher (Berry & Landry, 1997).

The advantages—and costs—associated with displaying facial maturity and immaturity relate to social contexts and expectancies, issues we take up later in the chapter. The fact that outcomes from signaling a particular status may be positive or negative suggests that the signal in only the high or low status direction may be less attractive than the signal in both directions.

Facial Cues: Truth or Dare?

The social status cues perspective draws from the cross-species literature in anticipating that human individuals benefit both from sending and receiving status messages. Physiognomic signaling systems are viewed along with other nonverbal channels as a means by which individuals *manipulate* (rather than communicate with) each other (Dawkins & Krebs, 1976; Keating, 1994).

Successful manipulation may entail deceptive as well as honest signaling. Either way, physiognomy functions in combination with other nonverbal channels to attract or deter interactions and relationships.

From the social status cues perspective, the important "truth" about physiognomy may be that its signal value exists by design; it *functions* to help regulate social interchange (Guthrie, 1970). Physiognomy is not simply an *effect* or secondary consequence of other biological requirements or events like puberty. A square jaw is, in part, designed to signal dominance on a man or woman. Immature-looking facial structures are meant to convey submissiveness.

Others describe physiognomic cues more as effects than functions. From the affordances approach, for example, the stimulus value of adult babyfaceness derives from a process of overgeneralization, whereby babyish attributes are erroneously overdetected in adult faces (Berry & McArthur, 1986; Montepare & Zebrowitz, 1998). Detecting babyfaceness in adults is described as a consequence of heightened sensitivity to infantile cues and a perceptual error (Montepare & Zebrowitz, 1998). In contrast, the premise of the social status cues perspective is that facial elements evolved similar signal value whether displayed (or mimicked) by juveniles or adults. Big eyes express submissiveness/receptivity for all faces and not by mistake. Sensitivity to morphological status cues exists because it *functions* to regulate social interchange as it does for other species (Keating, 1985b). Also similar to the signaling systems of other species, the effectiveness of human physiognomic cues does not depend on complete veracity in their message.

Some theorists view faces as honest brokers of traits associated with reproductive value and potency (e.g., Mueller & Mazur, 1997; Penton-Voak et al., 1999; Perrett et al., 1998; Thornhill & Gangestad, 1993). After all, hormone levels and genetic factors underlie the development of secondary sex characteristics that relate to the immaturity and maturity of facial appearances. It may be that square jaws and high cheekbones accurately index pubescent androgen levels associated with reproductive functioning (Cunningham, 1986; Penton-Voak et al., 1999; Thornhill & Gangestad, 1993). But from a social status cues perspective, such displays need not be faithful messengers of underlying biological substrates or traits. Potentially, one need only fool most of the people much of the time for deceptive strategies to confer a communicative advantage (Otte, 1974). Deceptive signals will be constrained, however, by the extent to which such bluffs can be called into question, and by the cost of being detected (Dawkins & Krebs, 1976; Johnstone & Grafen, 1993).[3] To the degree that facial status cues present opportunities for immediate, independent corroboration, they are likely to be "honest" signals of underlying traits.

Like any good con artist, the face probably lies about what it can get away with but honestly conveys what can be immediately and independently verified. This possibility was tested by asking college undergraduates to judge different types of traits from facial portraits of other, unfamiliar undergraduates. Height was chosen as an easily verifiable trait because impressions about height from the face can be immediately corroborated by viewing the body. Height had another advantage. Unlike other traits, it is resistant to a self-fulfilling prophecy: being treated like a tall person is not likely to make you grow. We compared the accuracy of height judgments made from facial images (controlled for size) to judgments of traits that were less immediately verifiable. When perceivers' impressions were matched with actual data, we found the anticipated difference. Height was accurately cued by faces, whereas traits with the potential to remain at least initially cloaked (i.e., wealth, academic success, athletic involvement) showed no reliable relationship to judgments made from facial morphology.[4]

The accuracy with which faces broadcast underlying traits is a crucial issue for those who regard attractiveness as the packaging of health (e.g., Gangestad & Buss, 1993; Grammar & Thornhill, 1994; Thornhill & Gangestad, 1993). According to the "symmetry" view, pathogens disrupt growth asymmetrically throughout development. Lack of resistance to pathogens is thus stamped into asymmetric face and body forms. Symmetry, therefore, is a faithful, phenotypic expression for pathogen resistance, good health, and good genes. Health histories reflected in facial morphology are seen through the human lens as "beautiful" or not because they signal reproductive value.

Underlying the symmetry/attractiveness connection is the more general premise that these facial cues do not lie. Some evidence corroborates the integrity of facial signals. There are significant correlations between trait ratings of people based on facial photographs and standardized measures of their personality (e.g., Berry & Finch Wero, 1993). Sneaky-looking undergraduates are more willing to volunteer for tasks requiring deception than honest-looking undergraduates (Bond, Berry, & Omar, 1994). Attractive people are routinely judged as both more popular and more socially skillful than others and, when measurements are taken, they are (Feingold, 1992).

Are these instances of the faces' ability to honestly reflect underlying traits or consequences of the faces' ability to propagate self-fulfilling prophecies? Snyder, Tanke, and Berscheid (1977) demonstrated that faces are capable of creating powerful self-fulfilling prophecies; believing that someone is attractive (based on a fictitious, facial photograph) can make that someone behave in a more attractive, engaging way. Other social traits that researchers have linked to facial appearance are also vulnerable to self-fulfilling prophecies (e.g., Langlois & Downs, 1979; Mazur, Mazur, & Keating, 1984) or to a reaction against such prophecies (e.g. Zebrowitz, Andreoletti, Collins, Lee, & Blumenthal, 1998).

Even a connection between health and attractiveness may reflect a self-fulfilling bias. Attractive people typically have more friends and social support (Feingold, 1992). Social support has a demonstrated health advantage: people with strong support networks are healthier, probably due to reduced stress. Thus, if attractive people have better health, they may owe it to a little help from their friends; resistance to disease may be the result of social support and its accompanying reduction of stress rather than to genetically influenced health histories reflected in facial symmetry and attractiveness. In fact, from an evolutionary point of view, it would behoove the selfish gene to disguise any signs of underlying bad health and reproduce early before the onset of disease symptoms—just as individuals with Huntington's Chorea apparently do (Barash, 1979).

Although some reports have coupled good health with facial appearances linked to attractiveness, other studies find no honest relationship between such measurements. Shackelford and Larson (1997) reported that people with fewer facial asymmetries suffered fewer psychological and physical symptoms over a two-month period of time. However, facial asymmetry was, at best, only tenuously related to qualities of attractiveness. Reis, Wheeler, Kernis, Spiegel, and Nelzlek (1985) failed to uncover a relationship between judgments of physical attractiveness and actual health. Kalick and his colleagues examined the lifespan health records of 164 men and 169 women and found that attractive people were no healthier than unattractive people; they just looked healthier (Kalick, Zebrowitz, Langlois, & Johnson, 1998). The appearance of good health is apparently no guarantee that a person is, in fact, healthy.

In sum, facial signals do not necessarily deserve your trust. Consistent with the evolution of communicative systems across species, human facial messages should involve deceptive signaling for some traits and honesty for others. The integrity of facial cues is partly dependent upon the cost and likelihood of getting trapped in a lie. Faces should honestly signal easily verifiable traits such as height, weight, gender, and *gross* differences in age. Faces should disguise signs of long-term health problems. Despite stereotypes linking facial attractiveness to family income (Kalick, 1988), faces are likely to be unreliable reflections of traits like wealth that can be initially cloaked and permit cheating. Faces accurately cue some traits due to self-fulfilling prophecies.

Social Status Cues and Attractiveness

Whether honest or not, facial status cues influence adult facial attractiveness. The status messages inherent in immature and mature appearances can make faces look either appealing or unappealing. Which status messages (or which combination of status messages) make faces look attractive depends upon whether social contexts and expectancies favor displays of dominance or submissiveness.

Neoteny and Attractiveness

In the right contexts, the submissiveness and receptivity conveyed by pedomorphic facial traits can be very appealing when mimicked by adults. Neoteny, defined as the mimicry of pedomorphic characteristics, generates bias and often favoritism in the treatment of adults who display such traits on their faces. Montepare and Zebrowitz (1998) reviewed instances of positive bias toward baby-faced adults. They reported that in laboratory simulations of employment decisions, baby-faced job applicants were preferred over mature-faced applicants for jobs requiring interpersonal warmth and sensitivity. Moreover, baby-faced women (but not men) were disproportionately found in jobs requiring these social skills (e.g., nurse, teacher). In small claims courts, the more baby-faced the defendant who proclaimed innocence, the less likely it was that a judge would find the defendant guilty. Judges apparently fell victim to attributional biases linking babyfaceness with honesty and warmth (Montepare & Zebrowitz, 1998). In contexts valuing attributes like these, having a babyface is associated with increased social appeal and positive outcomes.

These examples imply that immature-looking facial traits on adult faces trigger attributions related to submissiveness (e.g., approachability, helplessness, dependence) that engender the same type of sympathy a child receives. *In the context of helping, therefore, adults with neotenous faces should attract disproportionate numbers of people to come to their aid.* A test of this hypothesis appears later in the chapter.

Maturity and Attractiveness

Mature facial traits offer a different brand of social appeal: power. Mature traits convey dominance when displayed by men and women (Keating, 1985a). Men with mature, dominant-looking faces are socially influential and attractive (Cherulnik et al., 1990; Cunningham, Barbee, & Pike, 1990; Keating, 1985b; Mueller & Mazur, 1997; Penton-Voak et al., 1999). They report having more influence over peers during social interactions than less mature-faced men (Berry & Landry, 1997). In the military, men with dominant-looking faces and above-average mental and physical ability attain higher rank and father more offspring than their less dominant-looking cohorts (Mueller & Mazur, 1997; see Collins & Zebrowitz, 1995, for an exception). Little is known about the appeal of mature, dominant facial traits for women. In general, the connection between maturity of facial structure and social appeal, especially in the context of social influence, seems stronger for male than for female faces.

Neoteny, Maturity, and Gender

The gender of the face can shift the way in which status messages conveyed by neoteny and maturity relate to perceptions of attractiveness and related social judgments. Studies using schematic faces have found that perceivers judging attractiveness prefer fewer neotenous characteristics and more mature traits on male than on female faces (Friedman & Zebrowitz, 1992; Keating, 1985a; McArthur & Apatow, 1993–94). In addition, neotenous features have been linked to impressions of both trustworthiness and distrust, depending on the gender of the face. Babyish facial structures that inspired trust when displayed by men (Berry, 1991; Berry & McArthur, 1986; Zebrowitz &

Montepare, 1992) evoked suspicion when displayed by women (Berry, 1991; Cunningham, 1986). For these attributions, the consequences of being baby-faced differed for men and women.

Female phenotypes generally express more neotenous facial traits than do male phenotypes. Although elements of the basic, feature formula for neoteny and maturity are the same for men and women (e.g., large vs. small eyes, full vs. thin lips, rounded vs. square jaw and chin, thin vs. thick brows), the sexes are distributed differently along morphological scales of size, shape, and placement of these facial features.[5] Females begin and end life with more babyish facial characteristics than males (Gray, 1948; Guthrie, 1970, 1976; Zebrowitz, Olson, & Hoffman, 1993). In neonates, for example, the distance between the pupil and arch of the brow is larger for females than for males (Haviland, 1977), giving baby girls a wide-eyed, raised-brow, submissive-looking appearance (Keating, 1985b). Adult female faces are distinguished from adult male faces by relatively thin, arched brows, larger apparent eye size, smaller noses, more rounded jaws, and smaller chins (Bruce & Young, 1998; Burton, Bruce, & Dench, 1993; Enlow, 1982). These differences suggest that the display of neoteny is somehow advantageous to females. But why?

The adaptive significance of youthful displays may be the projection of a long, healthy reproductive future (Buss, 1987; Buss & Schmitt, 1993; Jones, 1995). Males in particular prefer young, fertile mates whose reproductive potential is high. The selection mechanism underlying human female neoteny may simply be sexual; the result of males preferring younger-looking females as mates (Buss, 1987; Buss & Schmitt, 1993; Jones, 1995). Thus, neotenous-looking females would be sought after as mates and perhaps also mistrusted, as their opportunities for infidelity would be relatively great (Cunningham, 1986).

A broader vision of neoteny's potential benefits emerges from the social status cues perspective. Sex differences in neoteny reverberate across nonhuman species: it is generally more common for adult females to mimic pedomorphic characteristics than it is for adult males (Eibl-Eibesfeldt, 1975; Wilson, 1975). Juvenile morphological features that facilitate predator avoidance offer survival benefits to female mimics in some species. However, the display of neotenous traits may also benefit females directly by sending signals that reduce the likelihood of male aggression and elicit caregiving, just as these signals do for the very young (Keating, 1985a; Perusse, 1995). In addition, the relatively long-term, familial nature of female primate social bonds (de Waal, 1989; Wilson, 1975) make it especially advantageous for females to display social receptivity and cloak aggressiveness toward kin and peers (Ostrov & Keating, 2000).

Finally, male responsiveness to neotenous cues in adult females may forecast responsiveness to pedomorphic characteristics in offspring, a reassuring prospect for female fitness. Females perhaps display neoteny partly to fish for "new-age sensitive guys," and not just in the 1990s. Konrad Lorenz reportedly contended that the Neanderthal genetic line was not eliminated by warfare but arrested by the cuteness of homo sapiens whom they fancied as mates (Schweder, 1995). Was neoteny's appeal equally great for Neanderthal females and males? Later in the chapter we fast-forward to the 1990s and test whether, *in the context of heterosexual relationships, neotenous cues conveying submissiveness make female faces appear attractive, and look less appealing when displayed by males than by females.*

The expression and detection of dominance-related maturity cues also contributes to fitness by improving the odds of attracting and selecting reproductively worthy mates, by projecting one's own and assessing potential rivals' dominance, and by forecasting the likely cost of intrasexual competition (Buss, 1987; Buss & Schmitt, 1993; Cunningham, 1986; Cunningham et al., 1990; Dijkstra & Buunk, 1998; Keating, 1985a,b; Keating et al., 1981; Penton-Voak et al., 1999; Wade & McCrea, 1996). Research indicates that the display of mature-looking facial traits which, lend a dominant appearance, can be advantageous to males. More mature features, including masculine-looking square jaws, look dominant and often characterize attractive male faces (Cunningham, 1990; Keating, 1985a; Keating et al., 1981; see Perrett et al., 1998, for an exception). Males with mature, dominant-looking facial characteristics are more likely to report early sexual activity (Mazur, Halpern, & Udry, 1994). Females are apparently most attracted to masculine facial shapes at times in their cycle when sexual liaisons would most likely result in conception (Penton-Voak et al., 1999; Penton-Voak & Perrett, 2000). Mature traits also add to the sexual appeal of a woman's face: the development of high cheekbones, which is influenced by pubescent hormonal activity, is a highly desirable phenotypic trait in Western women and characterizes the faces of international beauty queens (Cunningham, 1986).

In general, however, relationships between maturity of facial structure, dominance, and attractiveness seem stronger for male than for female faces. Because male reproductive value is more clearly linked to dominance than female reproductive potential (Buss & Schmitt, 1993), neoteny is believed to play less of a role in male than in female good looks (Guthrie, 1976; Keating, 1985a). Instead, males who appear to possess the dominance-related abilities needed to accumulate and control resources should be favored by females as mates (Keating, 1985a; Mueller & Mazur; 1997). We subsequently test whether, *in the context of heterosexual relationships, mature facial traits that convey dominance make male faces appear attractive, and look less appealing when displayed by females than by males.*

Perhaps we seek in relationships elements of status signaled by both neoteny and maturity: qualities of submissiveness and dominance, receptivity and threat, dependence and independence. Cunningham and his colleagues proposed that mixed social messages define the facial appearances of attractive mates (Cunningham, 1986; Cunningham et al., 1990, 1995). *This possibility is probed later by experimentally manipulating facial images to make them "speak" more extremely than normal in each status direction. By pushing the normal faces' social messages off-center, we provide a novel test of whether making faces more extreme in their social status messages improves or diminishes their attractiveness as mates, dates, and friends.*

Neoteny, Maturity, and Attractive Male and Female Leaders

As argued above, when judgments about heterosexual attractiveness are made, mature-looking facial cues signaling dominance are expected to have a more positive effect on male than on female attractiveness. Neotenous features conveying submissiveness, weakness, and naivete are predicted to look more attractive on female than male faces. Because social influence and leadership include aspects of interpersonal attractiveness as well as dominance (Carli, 1999; French & Ravin, 1959), the feature formula for attractive female and male leaders may differ. In later sections of this chapter, we investigate the possibility that, *in the context of leadership, facial status cues influence the attractiveness of male and female leaders differently.*

STUDIES OF FACIAL ATTRACTIVENESS IN DIFFERENT SOCIAL CONTEXTS

Three different social contexts in which status cues are likely to shift cognitions about facial attractiveness have been identified: helping, heterosexual relationships, and leadership. Each context inspires a different type of relationship, a different set of social expectancies, and, perhaps, a different cognitive solution for determining the attractiveness of status cues. The research questions posed earlier in this chapter are revisited here and put to the test.

These tests share basic methodological features. Different grades of social status cues were either experimentally induced by altering maturity cues on digitized facial images and/or by selectively sampling traits from target populations. Experimental manipulations used computer software to create a neotenous version of a face by proportioning eyes and lips 15% larger than normal, thus mimicking the big-eyed, pudgy-lipped look of babyhood.[6] As humans mature, eyes appear proportionately smaller and narrower, and vascular changes thin the lips (Guthrie, 1970). So, to make faces appear mature, the eyes and lips of a face were reduced by 15% in size. Figure 6.1 depicts exemplary stimulus faces. By experimentally manipulating features, we made normal faces "speak" more extremely in each status direction and provided a novel test of whether exaggerated status messages improved or diminished face appeal in different social contexts.

Our approach differed from that of researchers who applied software techniques to mathematically average many different faces (e.g., Langlois & Roggman, 1990; Rhodes et al., 1999). These techniques have been used to extract the effects that averaged or prototypical facial aspects have on attrac-

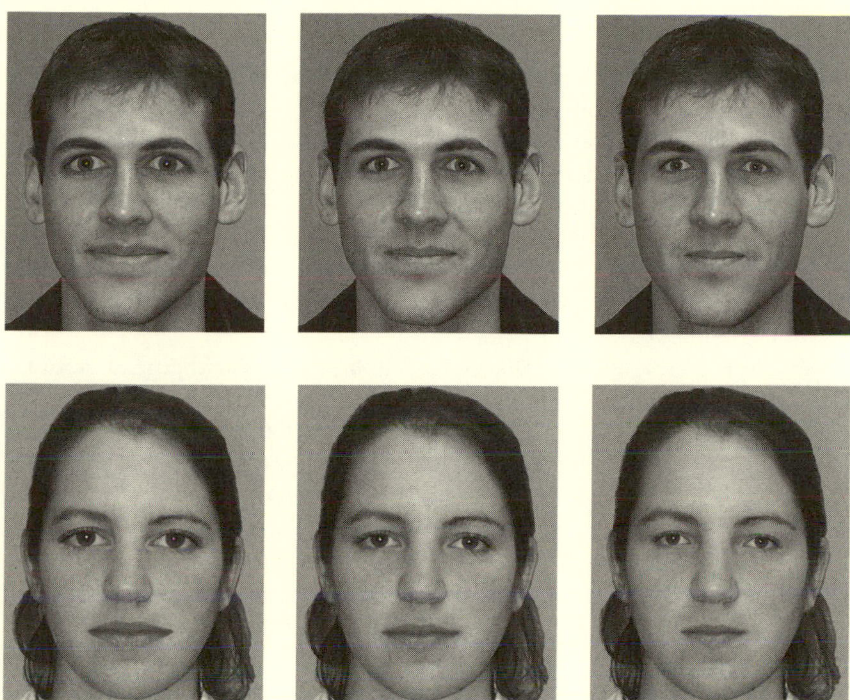

Figure 6.1. Exemplary stimulus faces. Faces on the left appear with enlarged eyes and lips, those on the right appear with diminished eye and lip sizes, and unaltered faces appear in the center.

tiveness. In contrast, we obtained nonnormative exemplars for each individual face by manipulating portraits away from their own unique, unaltered face, similar to the way Rhodes and Tremewan (1996) manipulated schematic faces by exaggerating their features. Using face as the unit of analysis, the question asked was this: Would making an individual's face look more mature or more neotenous shift its appeal in predictable ways? We searched not for an attractive "average," but for ways we could improve the appeal of normal faces by exaggerating the social status messages they sent.

There were notable limitations to our methods. In the studies reported here, only two features were systematically manipulated and alterations were restricted to a 15% size difference. Resizing features had multiple consequences. For example, making lips fuller by enlarging them increased the size of the entire mouth. Resizing also changed the spatial relationships among features. Thus, although our feature manipulations largely achieved the desired effects of altering attributions of status, maturity, and age, they really entailed more than changes in eye size and lip thickness.

Social Status Cues Attract Help

Research has shown that baby-faced adults are perceived as being relatively submissive, weak, dependent, and naive (e.g., Cunningham, Barbee, & Pike, 1990; Zebrowitz & Montepare, 1992). They apparently look like they need help, but whether they actually *attract* disproportionate amounts of help has not been directly tested. Rather, studies examining relationships between helping and facial maturity have generally surveyed whether adults who help others have babyfaces (Collins & Zebrowitz, 1995). We investigated whether, *in the context of helping, individuals with neotenous faces attract disproportionate numbers of people to come to their aid.*

Perceivers were given the chance to help adults whose digitized facial images were manipulated (as described above) to appear either neotenous or mature (Keating, Randall, Kendrick, & Gutshall, 2000). Images of black and white male and female faces of average attractiveness were used. Thus, two faces from each race/gender category were transformed to look more neotenous and more mature. The feature size transformations produced the desired effects: Faces with enlarged features were judged by undergraduate raters as less mature in structure than faces with features reduced in size (means = 3.6 and 4.3; $F(1, 7) = 12.58, p < .009$) and as younger (means = 22.16 and 25.13; $F(1, 7) = 10.82, p < .013$).

To see if face manipulations produced differences in status-related attributions, trait ratings for each manipulation of the eight faces were collected from U.S. undergraduates. Raters judged different subsets of the 16 facial images to ensure that they viewed only one version of a particular face. Because participants rated different subsets of faces, deviation scores were constructed to even-out within-subject differences in the use of scales. This technique essentially standardized trait ratings, making them comparable across faces (Rossi & Anderson, 1982). For each trait scale, deviation scores reflected differences from the overall mean rating across all faces and raters for that attribution. Faces received a deviation score for each trait, and face rather than rater was used as the unit of analysis. A deviation score of zero represented no difference from the mean rating of an attribute across all faces and raters. As expected, trait ratings revealed that neotenous feature substitutions made adults appear relatively submissive, babyfaced, young, weak, compassionate, feminine, naive, and honest compared to mature feature substitutions (see Table 6.1). Perhaps because our original faces were preselected to control for attractiveness, attractiveness ratings for their manipulated versions did not vary reliably or interact with gender or race (ps < .12). When used as a covariate, attractiveness ratings also did not generally account for differences in the perceptions of other traits.

A neotenous or mature face was printed at the top of a (fictitious) résumé, which described either "Susan Lawrence" (for female faces), or "David Lawrence" (for male faces), who claimed to be seeking employment in a bank and interested in "relocating near family." Résumés were attached to stamped en-

	Feature Size Manipulation		
	Enlarged	Reduced	p
Trait			
Submissive	.34	-.10	.01
Weak	.44	-.09	.03
Naïve	.26	-.07	.03
Feminine	-.05	-.21	.06
Compassionate	.02	-.41	.01
Honest	.15	-.23	.02
Attractive	-.20	-.41	ns

Table 6.1. Mean trait ratings for faces that were altered and printed on résumés (N = 16).

Note: Means represent deviations from average trait ratings across all faces and raters.

velopes printed with what appeared to be the potential employer's address, with a brightly-colored Post-It note that read, "Important! Mail Today!" affixed to it. Résumés were then "dropped" on sidewalks, in buildings, and near shopping areas in New York City (n = 409) and in Nairobi, Kenya (n = 176). "Helping" was indexed by whether résumés were posted (returned) or not.

Neotenous faces were expected to attract more help than mature faces, no matter where resumes were "lost." Preliminary results (depicted in Figure 6.2) were similar across nations and indicated that the motivation to help was influenced by facial structure. As predicted, resumes with baby-faced white male applicants and baby-faced black female applicants were returned at disproportionately high rates. Return rates for white females, though in the same direction, were not statistically significant. The pattern for black male faces differed for each country. These results provided partial support for the prediction that displays of neotenous facial cues motivate perceivers to help.

Some of the results from Kenya, however, countered predictions. Help from Kenyans (but not New Yorkers) was attracted by mature-faced black males. In Kenya, where jobs are scarce and ethnic minorities are distinguished by relatively fine-grained physiognomic cues, the motivations of participants may have been augmented by attempts to match faces with occupation (Montepare & Zebrowitz, 1998). It is possible that the manipulated black

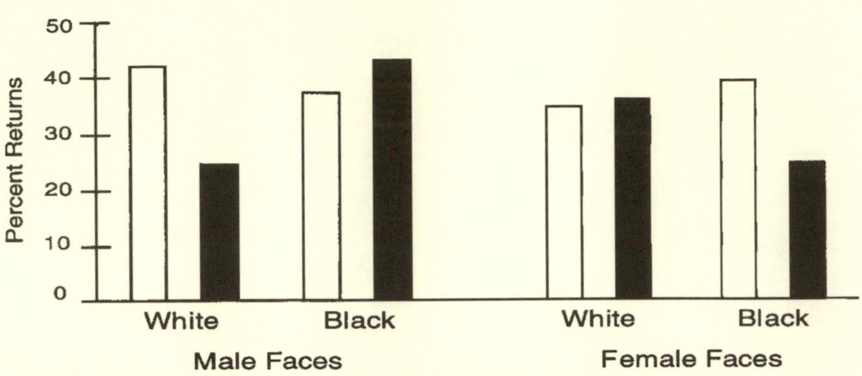

Figure 6.2. Percent of returned résumés depicting black and white, male and female applicants. Open bars report returns for applicants with enlarged facial features. Shaded bars report returns for applicants with reduced facial features.

male faces we used inadvertently resembled individuals from particular ethnic groups and biased which males received help.

Social Status Cues Affect Heterosexual Attractiveness

Two propositions from the social status cues perspective were made in the context of heterosexual relationships:

> Mature facial traits that convey dominance make male faces attractive, and these traits look less appealing when displayed by females than by males.
>
> Neotenous facial traits that convey submissiveness make female faces attractive, and these traits look less appealing when displayed by males than by females.

To investigate each proposition, we tested whether making normal faces more extreme in their social status messages improved or diminished their attractiveness as mates, dates, and friends. We applied the usual feature manipulation (described above) to a novel set of 24 undergraduates' portraits (evenly male and female) and tested how heterosexual attractiveness was affected (Keating & Doyle, 1999). Ratings from independent judges confirmed that enlarged features made faces appear less structurally mature and younger than unaltered faces and that reduced features made faces look more structurally mature and older.

Undergraduate perceivers rated subsets of the 72 stimuli so that they were never presented with more than one version of a particular face. Perceivers rated only other-sex faces. To capture multiple aspects of attractiveness, perceivers were asked to identify people they could imagine befriending, dating, or marrying, and to judge faces for attractiveness, sexiness, and other traits important to social bonds (e.g., honesty, caring, independence, faithfulness).

As before, face was used as the unit of analysis and ratings were transformed into deviation scores.

Which face type would appear most attractive and most desirable as a potential mate, date, or friend: mature, unaltered, or immature? We predicted that women would favor the dominance and power conveyed by mature-looking male faces and least prefer immature, nondominant versions of male faces (Buss & Schmitt, 1993; Guthrie, 1970; Keating, 1985a,b; Mueller & Mazur, 1997; Penton-Voak et al., 1999). Men were expected to value the receptivity and warmth expressed by neotenous traits in female faces and to perceive mature versions of female faces as least desirable (Guthrie, 1976; Keating, 1985a,b). It was possible, however, that faces incorporating messages of both power/maturity and warmth/immaturity would be perceived as more appealing than faces displaying the strong form of either single message (Cunningham, 1986; Cunningham et al., 1990, 1995). In this case, faces that conveyed aspects of both power and warmth would be preferred over those that emphasized one message over the other.

Differences in cross-sex judgments of the "attractiveness" of status cues were less than expected for male and female faces (see Table 6.2). Female faces with small, mature features looked less attractive than either unaltered faces or faces with enlarged features, as expected. However, enlarged features did not improve female attractiveness as we had predicted. For male faces, substitutions of enlarged features reduced attractiveness, as predicted, but so did the addition of diminished features. Thus, enhanced maturity diminished both women's and men's facial attractiveness, whereas enhanced neoteny diminished only men's attractiveness.

Despite some difference in which features made male and female faces look less "attractive," perceptions of their relationship potential converged: unaltered male and female faces were favored as mates, dates, and friends (Table 6.3).

We had no information about where our 24 unaltered faces stood in terms of a population average of faces, but exaggerating the features of actual faces may have resulted in face versions that appeared less normal or "more distinc-

	Feature Size Manipulation		
	Enlarged	Unaltered	Reduced
Male	$-.39^{a}$	$.45^{b}$	$-.05^{a}$
Female	$.01^{a}$	$.54^{a}$	$-.56^{b}$

Table 6.2. Mean attractiveness ratings for unaltered and manipulated images of male and female faces.

Note: Means represent deviations from average attractiveness ratings across all faces and raters. Row means with varied superscripts differ at $p < .05$ or better.

	Feature Size Manipulation		
	Enlarged	Unaltered	Reduced
Relationship			
Friend	-.08[a]	.33[b]	-.25[a]
Date	-.18[a]	.32[b]	-.11[a]
Mate	-.13[a]	.27[b]	-.16[a]

Table 6.3. Mean relationship ratings for unaltered and manipulated images of male and female faces.

Note: Means represent deviations from average across all faces and raters. Degrees of freedom for F-tests were (2,44). Row means with varied superscripts differ at $p < .05$ or better.

tive" (Rhodes et al., 1999) than other faces in the perceivers' universe. If so, then preferences for unaltered faces might be explained by their relative prototypicality (Langlois & Roggman, 1990; Rhodes et al., 1999).

Independent ratings confirmed that manipulated faces, as a group, looked less "normal" than unaltered faces. But relationship preferences for unaltered faces remained significant when assessments of how "normal" each face looked were covaried. Perhaps manipulated faces looked unhealthy (Thornhill & Gangestad, 1993), too masculine or too feminine (Penton-Voak et al., 1999; Perrett et al., 1998), or too old or too young (Buss & Schmitt, 1993) relative to unaltered faces. Each of these possibilities was tested using covariance analysis and none explained preferences for unaltered faces.

In fact, our "designer" faces largely failed to improve on Mother Nature: manipulated faces frequently produced trait ratings that were often no better than those for unaltered faces. For example, faces with enlarged eyes and lips received the same ratings as unaltered faces for traits such as "caring," "affectionate," and "good parent" (see Table 6.4). Faces with diminished eye and lip sizes elicited ratings for "dominant" and "strong" that were no different from those produced by unaltered faces. Moreover, manipulations designed to make faces look more powerful (i.e., dominant, independent, strong) mostly made them look less warm (i.e., affectionate, caring, good parent, faithful). Similarly, faces transfigured to look warmer instead looked less powerful. In other words, enlarging eyes and lips did not make faces look warmer but did make them look less powerful. Diminishing eyes and lips did not improve appearances of power but did reduce attributions of warmth. These patterns largely generalized across face gender (see Table 6.4).

Maybe the appeal of unaltered faces could be explained by the combined warmth and power messages they conveyed. Composite scores for warmth (i.e., the average rating for affectionate, caring, good parent, honest, faithful) and for power (i.e., the average rating for dominant, independent, strong) for

	Feature Size Manipulation			
	Enlarged	Unaltered	Reduced	F
Trait				
Dominant	-.53[a]	.08[b]	.38[b]	17.96***
Strong	-.59[a]	.22[b]	.36[b]	26.15***
Independent	-.33	.07	.25	9.76***
Masculine	-.38[a]	-.03[a]	.45[b]	16.44***
Caring	.30[a]	.15[a]	-.43[b]	13.78***
Affectionate	.22[a]	.22[a]	-.54[b]	14.00***
Good Parent	.14[a]	.14[a]	-.37[b]	8.41***
Faithful	1.37[a]	1.20[a]	.88[b]	5.37**
Honest	.37[a]	.11[b]	-.47[c]	13.59***
Sexy	-.28[a]	.44[b]	-.22[a]	6.75**
Rich	.10	.24	-.36	8.25***
Intelligent	.08[a]	.18[a]	-.28[b]	3.98*
Healthy	-.06	.20	-.16	1.93

Table 6.4. Mean trait ratings for unaltered and manipulated images of male and female faces.

Note: Means represent deviations from average trait ratings across all faces and judges. Degrees of freedom for F-tests were (2,44). Row means with varied superscripts differ at $p < .05$. Results for independent and rich were qualified by interactions with gender. $*p < .05$; $**p < .01$; $***\ p < .001$.

each face type were used as covariates in three, separate ANCOVAs with marriage, date, and friendship potential as dependent variables, and face manipulation and face gender as independent variables. The correlation between the warmth and power composites was -.43. Warmth, power, then warmth plus power were covaried from the face manipulation effect. If the combination of warmth and power explained social appeal, then only the latter test should diminish the face manipulation effect, while covarying warmth or power alone should spare the effect of manipulation. As Table 6.5 shows, the perceptions of power and warmth together dramatically reduced the effect of face manipulation on relationship potential: With warmth plus power controlled, the effect was no longer significant for dating and marriage potential, and was reduced in significance for friendship. In contrast, controlling for power or warmth alone failed to substantially reduce the face manipulation effect on judgments of rela-

	Covariate			
	No Covariate	Warmth	Power	Warmth + Power
Friend	.35***	.30***	.40***	.22**
Date	.25***	.27***	.26***	.11
Mate	.19**	.17*	.20**	.09

Table 6.5. Effect sizes for feature manipulation on relationship rating with covariates removed.

Note: Effect size measure = partial eta squared. **p* < .05; ***p* < .01; ****p* <. 005.

tionship potential. The combined messages of power and warmth largely accounted for the social appeal of faces.

We surmised that unaltered faces optimized both types of messages—power and warmth—rather than maximizing one message at the expense of the other. Regression analyses confirmed that perceptions of power and warmth combined (but not separately) explained the variance in preferences for unaltered male and female faces. We speculated that human faces were selected to display feature configurations that optimally combine social status messages conveying power and warmth (Keating & Doyle, 1999).

Some might interpret our study as a test of the averageness hypothesis. It is possible that making facial features more extreme in physical measurement moved some physiognomies away from the population average as well as from the individual's archetype (functional ideal), thereby eroding attractiveness (e.g., Carello, Grosofsky, Shaw, Pittenger, & Mark, 1989; Langlois & Roggman, 1990; Rhodes et al., 1999). However, whether our set of "normal" faces constituted anything close to a population average is unknown. Moreover, we were asking a very different question about what makes faces appealing.

Langlois and Roggman (1990) proposed that beauty materializes from faces with prototypical or "average" human features. Even if true (cf. Alley & Cunningham, 1991), a more essential question remains: "Why *that* average?" Why didn't a *different* human facial average evolve, say, one with bigger eyes or thinner lips? Why human faces converge on a particular average or prototype, and manifest a particular degree of variability, is a question that our approach may help to answer.[7]

Of course, variability (and prototypicality) in human faces is generally determined by functional considerations; constrained, for instance, by head shapes designed to accommodate the developing brain and jaw structures that permit effective chewing (e.g., Carello, Grosofsky, Shaw, Pittenger, & Mark, 1989; Mark, Shaw, & Pittenger, 1988). The social status cues approach suggests that the signal value of status messages imbued in facial structures over phylogenetic history may have also contributed to the evolution of human physiognomies and to what humans find becoming in a face (Guthrie, 1970; Keating, 1985b). Our data suggest that aspects such as eye size and lip thickness are among the stimulus elements that influence cognitions about attractiveness by sending social status messages. We found that the social messages conveyed by faces determined heterosexual appeal. Preferences could not be explained by variation in perceived health (Thornhill & Gangestad, 1993), by age (Buss, 1987), or by how feminine or masculine faces appeared (Penton-Voak et al., 1999; Perrett et al., 1998). Preferences were also independent of how normal faces looked. The best predictor of relationship preferences was a charismatic mix of warmth and power, and nature designed it. Thus, a combination of "good" social status messages made faces appealing, suggesting "what is good is beautiful," as well as the other way around (Dion, Berscheid, & Walster, 1972).

Social Status Cues and the Attractive Leader

When judgments about heterosexual attractiveness were made, facial cues signaling maturity and dominance diminished female attractiveness, whereas neotenous features conveying submissiveness, weakness, and naivete did not (Keating, 1985a; Keating & Doyle, 1999). In the context of leadership, women may be "faced" with a dilemma: Do cognitions about female facial attractiveness degrade women's ability to look influential (Zebrowitz, 1994)? Or, because social influence includes aspects of interpersonal attractiveness as well as dominance (Carli, 1999; French & Ravin, 1959), is the facial formula for attractive female and male leaders just different? We investigated whether, *in the context of leadership, facial status cues influence the attractiveness of males and females differently.*

Gender and the Attractive Leader

Faces convey social status with some accuracy; dominant-looking individuals are likely to assume positions of power, influence, and leadership. So far, support for this contention comes largely from data for men (e.g., Berry & Landry, 1997; Cherulnik, Turns, & Wilderman, 1990; Mazur et al., 1984), perhaps because associations between behavioral and physical aspects of attractiveness and leadership are closer for men than for women (Berry, 1991; Carli, 1999; Keating, 1985a; Sadalla et al., 1987).

We tested the influence of facial status cues on the attractiveness of male and female leaders (Keating, Oberting, & Weiss, 2000). Videotapes were made of college students who had babyish or mature facial characteristics and served as actors. Each actor portrayed leadership by appearing to speak to an audience. While speaking, actors conveyed either a direct, agentic, dominant leadership style (displaying facial and body dominance gestures that enhanced status) or an indirect, referential, submissive leadership style (displaying facial and body submissiveness gestures that diffused status). Perceivers viewed silent videotapes of these performances and assessed actors' attractiveness, warmth, likability, dominance, competence, leadership, and influence.

Cognitive appraisals of how attractive and powerful men and women with mature and immature facial structures looked when portraying different leadership styles were expected to be moderated by gender role expectations. Direct, agentic leadership is typically perceived as more appropriate for men while indirect influence tactics are regarded as more appropriate for women (e.g., Carli, 1999; Costrich, Feinstein, Kidder, Marecek, & Pascale, 1975). Eagly (1987) described how social roles, like gender roles, serve as lenses through which information is processed. Information that violates sex role expectations is evaluated differently from information that is role-consistent. Because female sex role stereotypes incorporate expectations of submissiveness, the cost of displaying indirect leadership (submissiveness) and neotenous facial traits was expected to be less for women than for men. The cost of displaying direct leadership (dominance) and mature facial traits was expected to be greater for women than men. Specifically, baby-faced females and/or females who displayed submissive, status-diffusing behavior were expected to receive higher ratings for social power and appeal than their baby-faced, submissive male counterparts. Mature-faced females and/or females who displayed dominant, status-enhancing behavior were expected to receive lower ratings for social power and appeal than their male counterparts who looked and acted similarly.

Undergraduate perceivers (91 men and 79 women) watched the videotapes and rated actors on scales for aspects of social attractiveness and social power. Their responses were submitted to a factor analysis to search for common dimensions among perceptions. We expected elements of power and warmth to load on two separate factors as they had when heterosexual appeal was judged for static faces. Instead, three factors emerged. The first factor reflected perceptions of power based on authority (dominance and competence) and was labeled "authority." The two remaining factors tapped different aspects of social attractiveness in the context of leadership: "approachability" (warmth and likableness) and "charisma" (attractiveness and influence). The elements of each factor were averaged and separate analyses were performed for each dependent measure (Figure 6.3).

Results showed that physiognomy was not destiny for the appearance of authority; regardless of models' facial structure, dominance behavior produced higher overall ratings for authority compared to submissive behavior (means = 5.17 and 2.36; $F(1,162) = 306.62, p < .001$). Physiognomy in interaction with gender also influenced impressions of authority, $F(1,162) = 9.54, p < .002$. Regardless of behavior, physiognomic cues that confirmed rather than countered sex-role expectations generated favorable impressions, as expected (see Figure 6.3 for means). Baby-faced women looked more authoritative than either

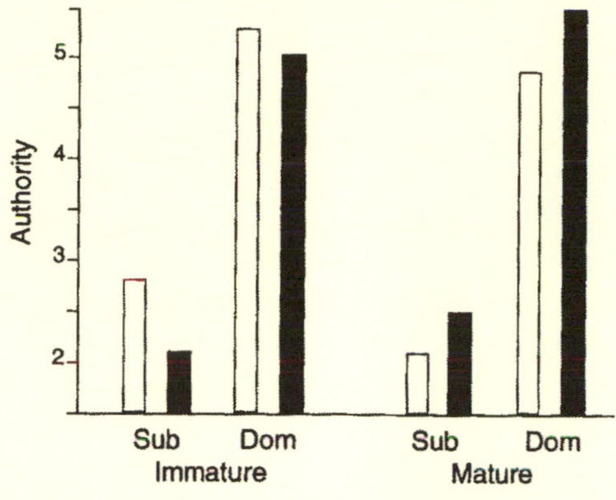

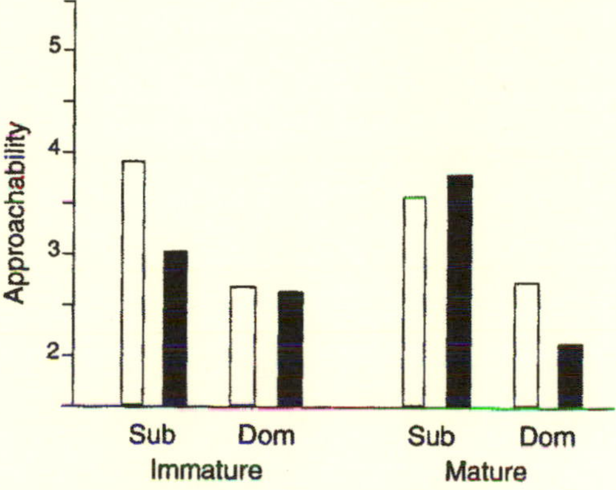

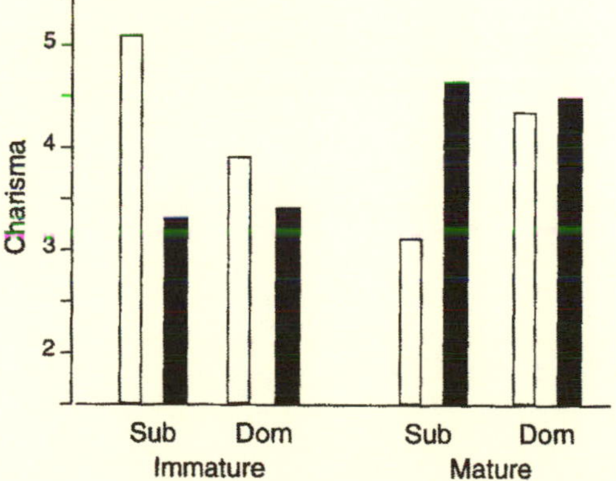

Figure 6.3. Social perceptions of men and women with immature or mature physiognomies who displayed submissive or dominant behavior. Open bars depict mean ratings for women. Shaded bars depict mean ratings for men. "Sub" designates submissive behavior. "Dom" designates dominant behavior.

baby-faced men or mature-faced women, *Fs*(1,162) = 4.75 and 3.92, respectively, *ps* < .05. Mature-faced men appeared more authoritative than mature-faced women or baby-faced men, *Fs*(1,162) = 8.20 and 9.08, respectively, *ps* < .01. None of these results could be explained by an attractiveness halo effect. Rather, they paralleled what other researchers have found for dominance behaviors: direct dominance is more effective when projected by men than by women (e.g., Butler & Geis, 1990; Carli, 1999; Costrich et al., 1975; Sadalla et al., 1987).

As for attributions related to aspects of the attractiveness of leaders, Figure 6.3 shows that both mature-faced men and women were more charismatic than their baby-faced counterparts when dominant, status-enhancing behavior was expressed, overall means = 4.47 and 3.67, $F(1,162) = 12.51$, $p < .007$. However, physiognomy influenced male and female charisma and approachability differently when their behavior diffused status (see Figure 6.3 for means). Under this gestural script, approachable, charismatic men were (again) mature-faced rather than baby-faced, *Fs*(1,162) = 3.78, $p < .05$, and 10.53, $p < .01$. In contrast, women of each physiognomic type were equally approachable, F(1,162) < 1.0, but charismatic only when baby-faced, $F(1,162) = 23.10$, $p < .001$. In other words, women were charismatic when status messages from physiognomy and behavior were consistent. Mature-faced men were charismatic regardless of how they behaved and approachable when portraying submissiveness.

Thus, in the context of leadership, the physiognomic standards used to judge aspects related to men's social attractiveness seemed relatively rigid. Men with mature physiognomies were charismatic (attractive and influential) no matter how they behaved, while baby-faced men were neither charismatic nor especially approachable (warm and likable). Baby-faced men could do little with gestures to improve their charisma. In contrast, the cognitive template for the physiognomic expression of women's charisma seemed relatively fuzzy. Charismatic females included baby-faced women who displayed submissive behavior and mature-faced women who expressed dominance. This apparent plasticity in cognitions about the appeal of female physiognomies may explain why researchers have had difficulty identifying female facial traits associated with social influence (Berry & Landry, 1997; Keating, 1985a; Zebrowitz-McArthur & Montepare, 1989). Consistent with behavioral studies of influence styles, female influence strategies may incorporate cues signaling submissiveness and receptivity as well as dominance and threat (e.g., Carli, 1989, 1990).

Someday soon, the first female U.S. president will be elected to office (Cannon, 1999). What will she look like? Our research suggests that she could be mature-faced or baby-faced, depending on her leadership style. We offer two physiognomic projections of the first, successful, female presidential candidate (see Figure 6.4). These projections represent an amalgam of what we have surmised from research findings and what we have observed among present-day,

Figure 6.4. Projections for the facial appearance of the first female U.S. president. The face on the left portrays the likely physiognomy for a woman with an indirect leadership style. The face on the right portrays the likely physiognomy for a woman with a direct leadership style.

charismatic female leaders. Based on our research, we offer separate projections for women characterized by indirect, status-diffusing and direct, status-enhancing nonverbal styles. The face on the left of Figure 6.4 comprises a morph of two current, female leaders selected for their relatively indirect, self-presentational nonverbal styles (Elizabeth Dole and, to a lesser degree, Hillary Rodham Clinton). In accordance with our research, this morph's chin was rounded to give it a slightly more neotenous appearance. The face on the right is a morph of two female leaders characterized by relatively direct, status-enhancing, self-presentational styles (Margaret Thatcher and Madeline Albright) (see Figure 6.4). The eyes of this morph were reduced slightly in size to give a slightly more mature appearance. The successful female candidate who exhibits a status-diffusing leadership style is projected to have a facial appearance close to the morph on the left; the candidate with a status-enhancing leadership style should resemble the face on the right.

Do Facial Status Cues Affect the Attractiveness of Real Presidents?

Laboratory studies like ours may exaggerate the influence facial appearance has on person perception: most use unfamiliar faces for which features provide the only basis for social judgments. We pursued the formula for charismatic physiognomies by using *familiar* faces. We tested whether the effects of neotenous and mature facial cues on social cognition were pervasive enough to alter judgments about the attractiveness of people with personal histories, specifically political leaders (Keating, Randall, & Kendrick, 1999).

This was hardly a new idea. All over the world, leaders attempt to enhance their influence by controlling their physical images. In the United States, White House officials promote favorable images of the president by carefully orchestrating photo-ops and by dispensing selected presidential photographs to the press and public (Adatto, 1993; Jamieson, 1984). In Iraq, portraits of President Saddam Hussein are commissioned by the government and typically portray a smiling Saddam who looks about half his actual age (Weiner, 1998). Are the efforts to "spin" a leader's physiognomy worth it? Can altering facial appearances improve the appeal of a president?

Researchers have documented the influence proximate nonverbal cues have on impressions made by politicians (e.g., Budesheim & DePaola,1994; Exline, 1985; McHugo, Lanzetta, Sullivan, Masters, & Englis, 1985; Way & Masters, 1996). Physical attractiveness in particular influenced evaluations of political candidates even when personality profiles were provided and political stances described (Budesheim & DePaola, 1994). Perceivers' agreement with the candidate's positions on issues mattered less when portrait photographs were provided than when they were withheld (Budesheim & DePaola, 1994). We therefore hypothesized that subtle changes in proximate, physiognomic cues would shift cognitions about familiar political leaders, over and above personal reputation and regardless of perceivers' political biases.

To test these ideas, we manipulated the famous facial images of real U.S. presidents (Keating et al., 1999). In one study, we applied our previous feature formula to three familiar presidential physiognomies: Bill Clinton, Ronald Reagan, and John F. Kennedy. Baseline photographic images depicted each president while he was in office. Each face was made more neotenous by enlarging eyes and lips by 15%, and made more mature by reducing the sizes of these features by the same amount (see Figure 6.5). Undergraduate perceivers viewed one version of each president and used scales to render social judgments about them. Trait ratings were transformed into deviation scores, as before.

Feature alterations were not consciously detected by perceivers. Virtually all perceivers identified each president correctly, by name, regardless of which version they saw. When queried about the faces, only two perceivers (out of a total of 207) indicated that the faces looked unusual in any way. The cognitive template for these well-rehearsed, famous physiognomies was notably flexible, at least when only one face version was seen. Rensink, O'Regan, and Clark (1997) seemed to tell it right: If perceivers are not privy to the transition, they often do not detect the change.

The impact of altering status cues on presidential images was expected to vary across the three presidents because of their distinctive physiognomies. Kennedy, the youngest U.S. president, was naturally baby-faced. His normal face was characterized by relatively neotenous facial features such as large eyes, thin brows, thick lips, and a round chin. Reagan, the oldest U.S. president, was naturally mature-faced and dominant-looking, with small eyes, bushy brows,

Figure 6.5. Neotenous, unaltered, and mature versions of the faces of Presidents Clinton, Reagan, and Kennedy. Neotenous versions appear to the left, unaltered in the center, and mature to the right.

Source: Figure 1 from "Presidential Physiognomies: Altered Images, Altered Perceptions," *Political Psychology*, v. 20, no. 3 (1999), pp. 593–610. Reprinted with permission from Blackwell Publishers.

thin lips, and a square jaw. President Clinton's face incorporated both mature-looking (small eyes, thin lips, and a prominent nose) and immature-looking (thin brows and a round chin) features. Thus, exaggerated maturity was hypothesized to primarily benefit impressions of Kennedy. Exaggerated neoteny was expected to be most advantageous to Reagan and Clinton.

Specific predictions were that enlarged, neotenous features would enhance impressions of attractiveness, honesty, and compassion, especially for the two presidents Clinton and Reagan, whose unaltered faces contained relatively few babyish cues. Neotenous features were generally expected to diminish perceptions of dominance, strength, and cunning. Substituting small, mature-looking features for normal ones was predicted to improve these ratings for Kennedy, who lacked many of the dominance features characteristic of his older, more mature-faced presidential peers. Enhancing the maturity of the oldest presidential physiognomy was expected to reduce perceptions of Reagan's power by conveying the diminished status of the elderly (Guthrie, 1970).

Results showed that replacing normal features with mature-looking ones had a different impact on ratings related to power for the three presidents (see Table 6.6). As predicted, facial maturity cues boosted ratings of Kennedy's cunning and, to some degree, his dominance (though not his strength), while neotenous cues reduced impressions of these three traits. Exaggerated neoteny also generally diminished perceptions of these power-related attributes for Reagan, and, particular to his physiognomy, so did enhanced maturity. However, perceptions of the sitting president's (Clinton's) dominance, strength, and cunning were unaffected by facial changes.

The pattern of results for aspects of presidential warmth differed from that of power (see Table 6.7). Impressions of Kennedy's honesty, attractiveness, and compassion were unaffected by facial manipulations. Judgments of Reagan's honesty and attractiveness were generally lowered by enhanced maturity, as predicted, but not raised by enlarged, neotenous features. Clinton was perceived as more honest and attractive with enlarged, neotenous eyes and lips, and less compassionate with reduced, mature features.

Altering the status messages inherent in mature and neotenous facial cues shifted character judgments about familiar leaders. The particular structure of each presidential face presumably determined the specific impact of facial status cues. However, the unique reputations and histories of leaders may have also moderated the impact of status cues. For example, increased neoteny primarily benefited President Clinton, whose honesty and personal attractiveness was under scrutiny at the time our data collection took place (during the Monica Lewinsky scandal in 1999) (Keating et al., 1999). Nevertheless, the take-home message is somewhat sobering. Depending on the face, status cues can be manipulated to improve perceptions of the attractiveness, honesty, and power of political leaders without the perceiver being aware.

	Feature Size Manipulation			
	Enlarged	Unaltered	Reduced	F
Clinton				
Dominant	-.06	-.29	-.15	--
Strong	-.06	-.58	-.15	--
Cunning	.43	.04	.32	--
Reagan				
Dominant	-.62[a]	.24[b]	-.56[a]	3.84*
Strong	-.24[a]	.18[a]	-.88[b]	3.44*
Cunning	-.76[a]	.54[b]	-.31[a]	4.04*
Kennedy				
Dominant	-.09[a]	.62[b]	.91[b]	3.84*
Strong	-.04[a]	.94[b]	.82[b]	3.40*
Cunning	-.85[a]	-.12[b]	.71[c]	6.47**

Table 6.6. Mean power-related ratings for unaltered and manipulated versions of presidential physiognomies.

Note: Means represent deviations from average trait ratings across all faces and raters. Degrees of freedom for F-tests were (2,46). Row means with varied superscripts differ at $p <. 08$ or better. $*p < .05$; $**\ p < .01$.

SUMMARY AND CONCLUSIONS

The basic premise of the social status cues perspective is that aspects of facial growth conveying social status information evolved as social display in humans as in other species. Status messages from the human face activate cognitive biases in perceivers and influence social attraction. Faces are "attractive" in that they draw us into relationships. The attractiveness of status cues depends on social context. Three different social contexts in which status cues were predicted to shift cognitions about facial attractiveness were probed: helping, heterosexual relationships, and leadership. Each context imposed a different set of social expectancies and a different cognitive solution for determining attractiveness.

Facial status cues were varied by selectively sampling faces and/or by altering the features of digitized, facial images. By enlarging eyes and lips, most faces appeared more neotenous, more babyish, and more submissive. By

	Feature Size Manipulation			
	Enlarged	Unaltered	Reduced	F
Clinton				
Honest	-.10[a]	-.76[b]	-1.17[b]	4.22*
Attractive	.29[a]	-.38[b]	-.78[b]	5.77**
Compassionate	.19[a]	-.18[a]	-.83[b]	5.56**
Reagan				
Honest	.58[a]	.50[a]	-.42[b]	4.30*
Attractive	-.84[a]	-.45[a]	-1.71[b]	5.51**
Compassionate	.56	.28	-.06	1.65
Kennedy				
Honest	.67	.52	.18	--
Attractive	1.22	1.42	1.22	--
Compassionate	.56	-.12	-.38	--

Table 6.7. Mean warmth-related ratings for unaltered and manipulated versions of presidential physiognomies.

Note: Means represent deviations from average trait ratings across all faces and raters. Degrees of freedom for F-tests were (2,46). Row means with varied superscripts differ at $p < .08$ or better. * $p < .05$; ** $p < .01$.

shrinking the sizes of these features, most faces looked more mature, less babyish, and more dominant.

In the context of helping, status messages inherent in facial neoteny were predicted to attract more help than those conveyed by facial maturity. In general, neotenous faces generated more help than mature faces. A notable exception to this pattern was found in Nairobi, where more help was given to mature-faced than to baby-faced black men.

In the context of heterosexual appeal, the attractiveness of status cues conveyed by neoteny and maturity were hypothesized to diverge for male and female faces. Exaggerated neoteny was predicted to improve female attractiveness but diminish male good looks. Enhanced maturity was expected to make male faces more attractive and female faces less so. Results partially supported predictions in that neoteny was more detrimental to male than to female attractiveness, while maturity was detrimental only to female attractiveness. Relationship appeal, however, was degraded by exaggerated maturity or neoteny in either sex, which suggested that the combination of status cues inherent in normal faces optimize messages promoting social bonds.

In the context of leadership, facial status cues that confirmed rather than countered sex-role expectations were expected to generate favorable impressions of leaders. Consistent with this idea, mature-faced males appeared influential and attractive (charismatic) no matter how they behaved. Influential, attractive female leaders displayed either a babyface and submissive behavior or a mature face and dominance behavior. Thus, charismatic women projected congruous status cues from physiognomy and behavior. Physiognomic status cues proved powerful enough to shift cognitions about familiar leaders, as well. Changes made to the digitized facial images of well-known presidents altered perceivers' assessments of their attractiveness, honesty, and power, even though the changes themselves went undetected.

Consistent with the social status cues approach to facial attractiveness, the critical messages that faces delivered were social in nature, and the fit between social status messages and social context was responsible for cognitions about attractiveness. The research reported here demonstrates that, in relationships and in politics, interpersonal appraisals are guided in important ways by responses to proximate, physiognomic social status cues. Human sensitivity to facial cues, whether conscious or otherwise, reveals that an "attractive" physiognomy is more than just a pretty face. Given the right social context, facial status cues convey charismatic qualities that motivate us to sacrifice, to love, to follow, and to trust some people more than others.

NOTES

1. This cognitive bias extends across species; puppies, kittens, and even baby rhinosaurus look "cute" in their own way. The human cute response even projects to inanimate objects and abstract stimuli, presumably explaining our attraction to teddy bears and Volkswagon beetles (Hinde & Barden, 1985; Pittenger, Shaw, & Mark, 1979).

2. The stimuli used by Kramer and colleagues (1995) distinguished attractiveness and babyfaceness and found effects for each when infant girls gazed at female faces. The results for male infants and faces were not statistically reliable.

3. The fitness value of any signal is limited by its *relative* advantage; if everybody's doing it, the relative value of a signaling tactic dissolves (Dawkins & Krebs, 1976). Whether deceptive signaling evolves as a strategy also depends upon the cost involved in producing the signal (Guilford & Dawkins, 1995; Otte, 1974).

4. Many "cloaked," psychological traits, including dominance and warmth, are believed to be accurately judged from facial appearances (e.g., Berry & Finch Wero, 1993; Mueller & Mazur, 1997; Zebrowitz and Collins, 1997).

5. There are discrepancies in reports of what characterizes a neotenous or babyish face. Zebrowitz & Montepare (1992) found that "baby-faced" males were characterized by relatively large eyes and thin brows, whereas "baby-faced" females were distinguished by a small nose bridge. Cross-cultural measurements of faces revealed that

females who appeared neotenous (operationalized as appearing younger than their actual age) had wide eyes, full lips, and a small nose (Jones, 1995).

6. Pilot studies revealed that a 15% change altered perceptions without arousing perceivers' suspicions that changes were made.

7. Feature configurations for human faces evolved to have many constraints. Using an identikit or software morphing program to create novel faces gives an appreciation for types of faces types that never develop.

REFERENCES

Adatto, K. (1993). *Picture perfect: The art and the artifice of public image making.* New York: Basic Books.

Alley, T. R. (1988). The effects of growth and aging on facial aesthetics. In T. R. Alley (Ed.), *Social and applied aspects of perceiving faces* (pp. 51–62). Mahwah, NJ: Erlbaum.

Alley, T. R., & Cunningham, M. R. (1991). Averaged faces are attractive, but very attractive faces are not average. *Psychological Science, 2*, 123–125.

Barash, D. (1979). *The whisperings within.* New York: Harper & Row.

Berry, D. S. (1991). Attractive faces are not all created equal: Joint effects of facial babyishness and attractiveness on social perception. *Personality and Social Psychology Bulletin, 17*, 523–531.

Berry, D. S., & Finch Wero, J. L. (1993). Accuracy in face perception: A view from ecological psychology. *Journal of Personality, 61*, 497–520.

Berry, D. S., & Landry, J. C. (1997). Facial maturity and daily social interaction. *Journal of Personality and Social Psychology, 72*, 570–580.

Berry, D. S., & McArthur, L. A. (1986). Perceiving character in faces: The impact of age-related craniofacial changes on social perception. *Psychological Bulletin, 100*, 3–18.

Bigelow, A., MacLean, J., Wood, C., & Smith, J. (1990). Infants' responses to child and adult strangers: An investigation of height and facial configuration variables. *Infant Behavior and Development, 13*, 21–32.

Bond, C. F., Berry, D. S., & Omar, A. (1994). The kernel of truth in judgments of deceptiveness. *Basic and Applied Social Psychology, 15*, 523–534.

Bowlby, J. (1969). *Attachment and loss (Vol. 1).* New York: Basic Books.

Brooks, J., & Lewis, M. (1976). Infants' responses to strangers: Midget, adult, and child. *Child Development, 47*, 323–332.

Bruce, V., & Young, A. (1998). *In the eye of the beholder.* Oxford, UK: Oxford University Press.

Budesheim, T. L., & DePaola, S. J. (1994). Beauty or the beast? The effects of appearance, personality, and issue information on evaluations of political candidates. *Personality and Social Psychology Bulletin, 20*, 339–348.

Burton, A. M., Bruce, V., & Dench, N. (1993). What's the difference between men and women? Evidence from facial measurement. *Perception, 22*, 153–176.

Buss, D. M. (1987). Sex differences in human mate selection criteria: An evolutionary perspective. In C. Crawford, D. Krebs, & M. Smith (Eds.), *Sociobiology and psychology: Ideas, issues, and applications* (pp. 335–351). Mahwah, NJ: Erlbaum.

Buss, D. M., & Schmitt, D. P. (1993). Sexual strategies theory: An evolutionary perspective on human mating. *Psychological Review, 100*, 204–232.

Butler, D., & Geis, F. L. (1990). Nonverbal affect responses to male and female leaders: Implications for leadership evaluations. *Journal of Personality and Social Psychology, 58*, 48–59.

Cannon, C. M. (1999). You go, girls. *National Journal, 30*, 2142–2147.

Carello, C., Grosofsky, A., Shaw, R. E., Pittenger, J. B., & Mark, L. S. (1989). Attractiveness of facial profiles is a function of distance from archetype. *Ecological Psychology, 1*, 227–251.

Carli, L. L. (1989). Gender differences in interaction style and influence. *Journal of Personality and Social Psychology, 56*, 565–576.

Carli, L. L. (1990). Gender, language, and influence. *Journal of Personality and Social Psychology, 59*, 941-951.

Carli, L. L. (1999). Gender, interpersonal power, and social influence. *Journal of Social Issues, 55*, 81–99.

Cherulnik, P. D., Turns, L. C., & Wilderman, S. K. (1990). Physical appearance and leadership: Exploring the role of appearance-based attribution of leader emergence. *Journal of Applied Social Psychology, 20*, 1530–1539.

Collins, M., & Zebrowitz, L. A. (1995). The contributions of appearance to occupational outcomes in civilian and military settings. *Journal of Applied Social Psychology, 25*, 129–163.

Costrich, N., Feinstein, J., Kidder, L., Marecek, J., & Pascale, L. (1975). When stereotypes hurt: Three studies of penalties for sex role reversals. *Journal of Experimental Social Psychology, 11*, 520–530.

Cunningham, M. R. (1986). Measuring the physical in physical attractiveness: Quasi-experiments on the sociobiology of female facial beauty. *Journal of Personality and Social Psychology, 50*, 925–935.

Cunningham, M. R., Barbee, A. P., & Pike, C. L. (1990). What do women want? Facialmetric assessment of multiple motives in the perception of male facial physical attractiveness. *Journal of Personality and Social Psychology, 59*, 61–72.

Cunningham, M. R., Roberts, A. R., Wu, C., Barbee, A. P., & Druen, P. B. (1995). "Their ideas of beauty are, on the whole, the same as ours": Consistency and variability in the cross-cultural perception of female physical attractiveness. *Journal of Personality and Social Psychology, 68*, 261–279.

Dawkins, R., & Krebs, J. R. (1976). Animal signals: Information or manipulation? In J. R. Krebs & N. B. Davies (Eds.), *Behavioural ecology: An evolutionary approach* (pp. 282–309). Sunderland, MA: Sinauer Associates.

de Waal, F. (1989). *Peacemaking among primates.* Cambridge, MA: Harvard University Press.

Dijkstra, P., & Buunk, B. P. (1998). Jealousy as a function of rival characteristics: An evolutionary perspective. *Personality and Social Psychology Bulletin, 24*, 1158–1166.

Dion, K., Berscheid, E., & Walster, E. (1972). What is beautiful is good. *Journal of Personality and Social Psychology, 24*, 285–290.

Eagly, A. H. (1987). *Sex differences in social behavior: A social role interpretation.* Mahwah, NJ: Erlbaum.

Eagly, A. H., & Wood, W. (1991). Explaining sex differences in social behavior: A meta-analytic perspective. *Personality and Social Psychology Bulletin, 17*, 306–315.

Eibl-Eibesfeldt, I. (1975). *Ethology: The biology of behavior* (2nd ed.). New York: Holt, Rinehart, & Winston.

Enlow, D. H. (1982). *Handbook of facial growth* (2nd ed.). Philadelphia: W. B. Saunders.

Exline, R. (1985). Multichannel transmission of nonverbal behavior and the perception of powerful men: The presidential debates of 1976. In S. L. Ellyson & J. F. Dovidio (Eds.), *Power, dominance, and nonverbal behavior* (pp. 183–206). New York: Springer-Verlag.

Feingold, A. (1992). Good-looking people are not what we think. *Psychological Bulletin, 111*, 304–341.

French, J.R.P., & Raven, B. H. (1959). The bases of social power. In D. Cartwright, (Ed.), *Studies in social power*. Ann Arbor: University of Michigan Press.

Friedman, H., & Zebrowitz, L. A. (1992). The contribution of typical sex differences in facial maturity to sex role stereotypes. *Personality and Social Psychology Bulletin, 18*, 430–438.

Gangestad, S. W., & Buss, D. M. (1993). Pathogen prevalence and human mate preferences. *Ethology and Sociobiology, 14*, 89–96.

Gangestad, S. W., Thornhill, R., & Yeo, R. A. (1994). Facial attractiveness, developmental stability, and fluctuating asymmetry. *Ethology and Sociobiology, 15*, 73–85.

Grammar, K., & Thornhill, R. (1994). Human facial attractiveness and sexual selection: The role of symmetry and averageness. *Journal of Comparative Psychology, 108*, 233–242.

Gray, H. (1948). *Anatomy of the human body*. Philadelphia: Lea & Febiger.

Gregory, W. K. (1965). *Our face from fish to man*. New York: Capricorn Books, G. P. Putnam's Sons. (Original work Published 1929.)

Gross, T. F. (1997). Children's perception of faces of varied immaturity. *Journal of Experimental Child Psychology, 66*, 42–63.

Guilford, T., & Dawkins, M. S. (1995). What are conventional signals? *Animal Behaviour, 49*, 1689–1695.

Guthrie, R. D. (1970). Evolution of human threat display organs. In T. Dobzhansky, M. K. Hecht, & W. C. Steere (Eds.), *Evolutionary biology, Vol. 4*, (pp. 257–302). New York: Appleton-Century-Crofts.

Guthrie, R. D. (1976). *Body hot spots: The anatomy of human social organ and behavior*. New York: Van Nostrand.

Haviland, J. M. (1977). Sex-related pragmatics in infant's nonverbal communication. *Journal of Communication, 27*, 80–91.

Hinde, R. A., & Barden, L. A. (1985). The evolution of the teddy bear. *Animal Behaviour, 33*, 1371–1373.

Jamieson, K. (1984). *Packaging the presidency*. New York: Oxford University Press.

Johnstone, R. A., & Grafen, A. (1993). Dishonesty and the handicap principle. *Animal Behaviour, 46*, 759–764.

Jones, D. (1995). Sexual selection, physical attractiveness, and facial neoteny: Cross-cultural evidence and implications. *Current Anthropology, 36*, 723–748.

Kagan, J. (1976). Emergent themes in human development. *American Scientist, 64*, 186–196.

Kalick, S. M., Zebrowitz, L. A., Langlois, J. H., & Johnson, R. M. (1998). Does human facial attractiveness honestly advertise health? *Psychological Science, 9*, 8–13.

Kalick, S. M. (1988). Physical attractiveness as a status cue. *Journal of Experimental Social Psychology, 24*, 469–489.

Keating, C. F. (1985a). Gender and the physiognomy of dominance and attractiveness. *Social Psychology Quarterly, 48*, 61–70.

Keating, C. F. (1985b). Human dominance signals: The primate in us. In S. L. Ellyson & J. F. Dovidio (Eds.), *Power, dominance, and nonverbal behavior* (pp. 89–108). New York: Springer-Verlag.

Keating, C. F. (1994). World without words. In W. J. Lonner & R. S. Malpass (Eds.), *Psychology and culture* (pp. 175–182). New York: Allyn & Bacon.

Keating, C. F., & Bai, D. (1986). Children's attributions of social dominance from facial cues. *Child Development, 57*, 1269–1276.

Keating, C. F., & Doyle, J. (1999). *The physiognomy of desirable mates, dates, and friends.* Unpublished manuscript.

Keating, C. F., & Heltman, K. R. (1994). Dominance and deception in children and adults: Are leaders the best misleaders? *Personality and Social Psychology Bulletin, 20*, 312–321.

Keating, C. F., Mazur, A. C., & Segall, M. H. (1981). A cross-cultural exploration of physiognomic traits of dominance and happiness. *Ethology and Sociobiology, 2*, 41–48.

Keating, C. F., Oberting, C., & Weiss, M. (2000). *Gender and the effects of physiognomy and gesture on social power: Is physiognomy destiny?* Unpublished manuscript.

Keating, C. F., Randall, D., & Kendrick, T. (1999). Presidential physiognomies: Altered images, altered perceptions. *Political Psychology, 20*, 593–610.

Keating, C. F., Randall, D., Kendrick, T, & Gutshall, K. (2000). *Do babyfaced adults receive more help? The (cross-cultural) case of the lost resume.* Unpublished manuscript.

Kramer, S., Zebrowitz, L. A., San Giovanni, J. P., Sherak, B. (1995). Infant preferences for attractiveness and babyfaceness. In B. G. Bardy, R. J. Bootsma, & Y. Girard (Eds.), *Studies in perception and action III* (pp. 389–392). Mahwah, NJ: Erlbaum.

Langlois, J. H., & Downs, A. C. (1979). Peer relations as a function of physical attractiveness: The eye of the beholder or behavioral reality? *Child Development, 50*, 409–418.

Langlois, J. H., & Roggman, L. A. (1990). Attractive faces are only average. *Psychological Science, 1*, 115–121.

Langlois, J. H., Roggman, L. A., Casey, R. J., Ritter, J. M., Reiser-Danner, L. A., & Jenkins, V. Y. (1987). Infant preferences for attractive faces: Rudiments of a stereotype? *Developmental Psychology, 23*, 363–369.

Lorenz, K. (1943). Die angeborenen Formen moglicher Erfahrung. *Zietschrift fur Tierpsychologie, 5*, 234–409.

Mark, L. S., Shaw, R. R., & Pittenger, J. B. (1988). Natural constraints, scales of analysis, and information for the perception of growing faces. In T. R. Alley

(Ed.), *Social and applied aspects of perceiving faces*, (pp. 11–49). Mahwah, NJ: Erlbaum.

Mazur, A., Halpern, C., & Urdy, J. R. (1994). Dominant looking teenagers copulate earlier. *Ethology and Sociobiology, 15*, 87–94.

Mazur, A., Mazur, J., & Keating, C. F. (1984). Military rank attainment of a West Point class: Effects of cadets' physical features. *American Journal of Sociology, 90*, 125–150.

McArthur, L., & Apatow, K. (1983–1984). Impressions of baby-faced adults. *Social Cognition, 2*, 315–342.

McArthur, L. Z., & Baron, R. M. (1983). Toward an ecological theory of social perception. *Psychological Review, 90*, 215–238.

McCabe, V. (1984). Abstract perceptual information for age level: A risk factor for maltreatment? *Child Development, 55*, 267–276.

McCabe, V. (1988). Facial proportions, perceived age, and caregiving. In T. R. Alley (Ed.), *Social and applied aspects of perceiving faces* (pp. 89–95). Mahwah, NJ: Erlbaum.

McHugo, G. J., Lanzetta, J. T., Sullivan, D. G., Masters, R. D., & Englis, B. G. (1985). Emotional reactions to political leader's expressive displays. *Journal of Personality and Social Psychology, 49*, 1513–1529.

Montepare, J. M., & Zebrowitz, L. A. (1998). Person perception comes of age: The salience and significance of age in social judgments. *Advances in Experimental Social Psychology, 30*, 93–161.

Montepare, J. M., & Zebrowitz-McArthur, L. (1989). Children's perceptions of babyfaced adults. *Perceptual and Motor Skills, 69*, 467–472.

Mueller, U., & Mazur, A. (1997). Facial dominance in *Homo sapiens* as honest signaling of male quality. *Behavioral Ecology, 8*, 569–579.

Ostrov, J. M., & Keating, C. F. (2000). *Differences in the aggressive tactics of preschool girls and boys: An observational study.* Unpublished manuscript.

Otte, D. (1974). Effects and functions in the evolution of signalling systems. *Annual Review of Ecological Systems, 5*, 385–417.

Penton-Voak, I. S., & Perrett, D. I. (2000). Female preference for male faces changes cyclically: Further evidence. *Evolution and Human Behavior, 21*, 39–48.

Penton-Voak, I. S., Perrett, D. I., Castles, D. L., Kobayashi, T., Burt, D. M., Murray, L. K., & Minamisawa, R. (1999). Menstrual cycle alters face preference. *Nature, 399*, 741–742.

Perrett, D. I., Lee, K. J., Penton-Voak, I., Rowland, D., Yoshikawa, S., Burt, D. M., Henzi, S. P., Castles, D. L., & Akamatsu, S. (1998). Effects of sexual dimorphism on facial attractiveness. *Nature, 394*, 884–887.

Perusse, D. (1995). Comments on "sexual selection, physical attractiveness, and facial neoteny." *Current Anthropology, 36*, 740–741.

Pittenger, J. B., Shaw, R. E., & Mark, L. S. (1979). Perceptual information for the age level of faces as a higher order invariant of growth. *Journal of Experimental Psychology: Human Perception and Performance, 5*, 481–492.

Plomin, R., & Rowe, D. C. (1979). Genetic and environmental etiology of social behavior in infancy. *Developmental Psychology, 15*, 62–72.

Reis, H. T., Wheeler, L., Kernis, M. H., Spiegel, N., & Nelzlek, J. (1985). On specificity in the impact of social participation on physical and psychological health. *Journal of Personality and Social Psychology, 48*, 456–471.

Rensink, R. A., O'Regan, J. K., & Clark, J. J. (1997). To see or not to see: The need for attention to perceive change scenes. *Psychological Science, 8*, 368–373.

Rhodes, G., Sumich, A., & Byatt, G. (1999). Are average facial configurations attractive only because of their symmetry? *Psychological Science, 10*, 52–58.

Rhodes, G., & Tremewan, T. (1996). Averageness, exaggeration, and facial attractiveness. *Psychological Science, 7*, 105–110.

Rossi, P. H., & Anderson, A. B. (1982). The factorial survey approach: An introduction. In P. H. Rossi & S. Nock (Eds.), *Measuring social judgments: The factorial survey approach* (pp. 15–67). Beverly Hills, CA: Sage.

Rubenstein, A. J., Kalakanis, L., & Langlois, J. H. (1999). Infant preferences for attractive faces: A cognitive explanation. *Developmental Psychology, 35*, 848–855.

Sadalla, E. K., Kenrick, D. T., & Vershure, B. (1987). Dominance and heterosexual attraction. *Journal of Personality and Social Psychology, 52*, 730–738.

Schweder, B. (1995). Comments on "Sexual selection, physical attractiveness, and facial neoteny." *Current Anthropology, 36*, 741.

Shackelford, T. K., & Larson, R. J. (1997). Facial asymmetry as an indicator of psychological, emotional, and physiological distress. *Journal of Personality and Social Psychology, 72*, 456–466.

Snyder, M., Tanke, E. D., & Berscheid, E. (1977). Social perception and interpersonal behavior: On the self-fulfilling nature of social stereotypes. *Journal of Personality and Social Psychology, 35*, 656–666.

Thornhill, R., & Gangestad, S. W. (1993). Human facial beauty: Averageness, symmetry, and parasite resistance. *Human Nature, 4*, 237–269.

Van Den Berghe, P. L., & Barash, D. P. (1977). Inclusive fitness and human family structure. *American Anthropologist, 79*, 809–823.

Wade, T. J., & McCrea, S. (1996, April). *Evolutionary theory and contrast effects on men's self-ratings of attractiveness and social dominance: Status, physical fitness, or looks.* Paper presented at the 67th Annual Eastern Psychological Association Meeting, Philadelphia.

Way, B. M., & Masters, R. D. (1996). Political attitudes: Interactions of cognition and affect. *Motivation and Emotion, 20*, 205–236.

Weiner, E. (Correspondent). (1998, March 17). All things considered [radio broadcast]. Washington, DC: National Public Radio.

Williams, J. E., & Best, D. L. (1994). Cross-cultural views of women and men. In W. J. Lonner & R. Malpass (Eds.), *Psychology and culture* (pp. 191–196), Boston: Allyn & Bacon.

Wilson, E. O. (1975). *Sociobiology: The new synthesis.* Cambridge, MA: Harvard University Press.

Zebrowitz, L. A. (1994). Facial maturity and political prospects: Persuasive, culpable, and powerful faces. In R. C. Schank & E. Langer, (Eds.), *Beliefs, reasoning, and decision making* (pp. 315–345), Mahwah, NJ: Erlbaum.

Zebrowitz, L. A., Andreoletti, C., Collins, M. A., Lee, S. Y., & Blumenthal, J. (1998). Bright, bad, babyfaced boys: Appearance stereotypes do not always yield self-fulfilling prophecy effects. *Journal of Personality and Social Psychology, 75*, 1300–1320.

Zebrowitz, L. A., & Collins, M. A. (1997). Accurate social perception at zero acquaintance: The affordances of a Gibsonian approach. *Personality and Social Psychology Review, 1*, 204–223.

Zebrowitz, L. A., & Montepare, J. M. (1992). Impressions of babyfaced males and females across the lifespan. *Developmental Psychology, 28*, 1143–1152.

Zebrowitz, L. A., Montepare, J. M., & Lee, H. K. (1993). They don't all look alike: Individuated impressions of other racial groups. *Journal of Personality and Social Psychology, 65*, 85–101.

Zebrowitz, L. A., Olson, K., & Hoffman, K. (1993). Stability of babyfacedness and attractiveness across the life span. *Journal of Personality and Social Psychology, 64*, 453–466.

Zebrowitz-McArthur, L., & Montepare, J. M. (1989). Contributions of a babyface and a childlike voice to impressions of moving and talking faces. *Journal of Nonverbal Behavior, 13*, 189–203.

CHAPTER 7

Dimensions of Facial Physical Attractiveness: The Intersection of Biology and Culture

Michael R. Cunningham, Anita P. Barbee, and Correna L. Philhower

The power of beauty, and the passion that it engenders to transcend all obstacles, has been celebrated in popular culture from the Song of Solomon and the Iliad in ancient times, to films such as *Cinderella* and *Pretty Woman* more recently. But Western culture also has substantial ambivalence about physical attractiveness. In the 1999 film *American Beauty*, 42-year-old Lester Burnham became obsessed with his daughter's 16-year-old friend, Angela. That event activated Burnham's testosterone to the point that he quit his job; confronted his cool, preoccupied wife; bought the red sports car he had craved as an adolescent; returned to working out, listening to hard rock music, and smiling. It was not Angela's narcissism or aspirations to become a model that enchanted Burnham, but rather her luminous eyes, beguiling smile, and lustrous blond hair, a fact that he acknowledged in his disclosure to her: "I've wanted you since the moment I first saw you."

Although a male awakening from midlife doldrums through attraction to a beautiful woman is a common film script (i.e., *Sabrina*, *Up Close and Personal*), the Western expectation is that the attraction must be based on something more than appearance alone. When that attraction involves an older man and a nubile adolescent, popular morality usually demands a tragic ending. The chance of Burnham living happily ever after with Angela was as unlikely as that of Humbert Humbert in Vladimir Nabokov's *Lolita*. In such cases, beauty is presented as a siren song, luring the smitten to shallow relationships at best and destruction at worst.

Scientific discussions of physical attractiveness are not bound by literary tradition or public morality. Nonetheless, social scientists also displayed some ambivalence toward the topic (Aronson, 1969) and toward the physically attractive (Dermer & Thiel, 1975). The twentieth century included commentators who either denied that physical appearance was meaningfully related to other personal or social variables; or recognized that physical attractiveness was linked to social outcomes, but assigned the cause to the vagaries of fickle culture; or asserted that a physically attractive phenotype is a valid indicator of a genotype that evolved to solve certain problems of adaptation. Each of those positions may be partially true.

This chapter describes an integrative, multidimensional model of physical attractiveness within the context of past and present approaches to appearance. First, we examine the origins of prejudice against the measurement of facial qualities. Next, we outline the Multiple Fitness model of physical attractiveness, which suggests that the perception of high physical attractiveness involves the assessment of a variety of desirable features and personal attributes. Third, we review controversy surrounding the possibility of the objective standards of beauty in light of the model's stipulation that the attractiveness of some elements of physical appearance is universal, but the attractiveness of other dimensions depends on the local physical and social ecology. We then consider each of the five major dimensions of the Multiple Fitness model. Fifth, we contrast the Multiple Fitness model with other approaches to physical attractiveness that focus on symmetry and averageness. Sixth, we discuss how physical appearance may involve substantial elements of natural artifice and deliberate deception, which may confound the relation between genotype, phenotype, and social outcomes (cf. Feingold, 1992). We conclude by discussing findings on the relative importance of physical attractiveness in mate choice, noting when other types of information about the perceptual target may override physical attractiveness in such decisions.

ORIGIN OF PREJUDICE AGAINST THE MEASUREMENT OF PHYSICAL APPEARANCE

Facial assessment has a long and controversial history, with a lineage that some trace to Aristotle. Formal measurement began with Lavater's (1797, 1860) pseudoscience of physiognomy, which involved assessments of character based on the morphology of the face. Lavater spoke with remarkable certainty about the inferential significance of such features as the chin and the eyebrows:

> I am, from numerous experiments, convinced that the projecting chin ever denotes something positive; and the retreating something negative. The presence or absence of

strength in man is often signified by the chin . . . . The angular chin is seldom found but in discreet, well-disposed, firm men. Flatness of chin speaks the cold and dry; smallness, fear; and roundness, with a dimple, benevolence (p. 396). Horizontal eyebrows, rich and clear, always denote understanding, coldness of heart, and capacity for framing plans. Wild eyebrows are never found with a mild, ductile, pliable character. (p. 470)

Physiognomy was popular in Europe and America from the eighteenth through the early part of the twentieth century. Dr. Katherine Blackford, (Blackford & Newcomb, 1919) made pronouncements about the relation of hair color to personality with a level of confidence that rivaled Lavater's:

In brief, always and everywhere, the normal blond has positive, dynamic, driving, aggressive, domineering, impatient, active, quick, hopeful, speculative, changeable, and variety loving characteristics; while the normal brunette has negative, static, conservative, imitative, submissive, cautious, painstaking, plodding, slow, deliberate, serious, thoughtful, and specializing characteristics. (p. 141)

Blackford's assertions rankled psychologists such as Paterson (1930), who believed that "such positive assertions ought to be put to a quantitative test" (p. 215). Paterson asked 94 judges to each select two blonds and two brunettes from among their acquaintances and indicate whether each one did or did not possess 26 traits, such as positive, dynamic, and driving. Paterson concluded that: "The percentage of brunettes possessing the blond traits is approximately as large as the percentage of blonds possessing blond traits. Likewise, the percentage of blonds possessing brunette traits is also very similar to the percentage of brunettes possessing brunette traits. This result is a flat contradiction to what one has a right to expect if Dr. Blackford's generalization is true" (p. 218).

Paterson's (1930) characterization of his study was accurate at one level, in that the difference between blonds and brunettes averaged only 3% across all 26 traits. But reexamination of Paterson's data revealed significant differences on such traits as changeable (53% of blonds; 43% of brunettes, $z = 1.95$), serious (58% of blonds; 72% of brunettes, $z = 2.84$); conservative (51% of blonds; 61% of brunettes, $z = 1.95$), deliberate (47% of blonds; 57% of brunettes, $z = 1.95$), and patient (43% of blonds; 52% of brunettes, $z = 1.743$, all $p < .05$ one-tail). Paterson may not have made a Type II error by failing to highlight the 5 results out of 26 that supported physiognomy, but his strong disapproval of such hypotheses may have discouraged other investigators from pursuing questions involving the relation between variations in Caucasian pigmentation and personality. Nearly half a century later, Worthy (1974) offered data indicating temperamental differences associated with eye color in both humans and animals. He suggested that those with light eye color (blue, gray, green, hazel) tended to outperform those with darker eye colors (brown, black) on self-paced tasks, such as stalking prey and self-paced sports such as golf and bowling, but not on reactive tasks, or sports such as boxing, defensive football, and hitting in baseball (cf. Jones & Hochner, 1973). More recently, Bassett and Dabbs (1999) reported that murderers tended to have a lighter eye color than those convicted of manslaughter in the Georgia correctional system, suggesting that light eyes are associated with planfulness rather than impulsiveness.

Paterson cannot be blamed for discouraging research on the relation of physical and psychological qualities, because other investigators were also reporting null results. Cleeton and Knight (1924) reported that they attempted to predict eight character traits (sound judgment, intellectual capacity, frankness, willpower, ability to make friends, leadership, originality, impulsiveness) using 13 to 36 physical measurements per trait taken from each of 28 college students, who presumably were Caucasian. Each of their subjects was subjectively rated in groups by casual observers for each trait, and also by members of the subjects' sorority or fraternity. Unfortunately, Cleeton and Knight's physical measurements did not appear to have been adjusted for the height, weight, or gender of the subject. Nonetheless, it is interesting to note that of the small number of Cleeton and Knight's physical measures that involved some standardization due to being expressed as ratios, all were predictive, such as anterior versus posterior head length (r = .29 with "judgment," the only trait for which full results were presented). Cleeton and Knight also found negative correlations, such as between nose width and judgment (r = -.27). Such outcomes could provide some support for physiognomist R. D. Stocker's (1900) speculation that "large wide nostrils show great coarseness of tastes and vulgarity of nature"(p. 19), if coarseness and vulgarity were regarded as the opposite of sound judgment. Cleeton and Knight, however, averaged their negative and positive correlations to produce a null average (r = -.005 for judgment), and concluded that "The average of 201 correlations between variations in character traits and our criteria was 0.000 with the correlations varying from 0.000 as chance would account for" (p. 216).

Cleeton and Knight (1924) may have been correct in their vigorous embrace of the null hypothesis concerning the relation between physiognomic signs and personality. But the impact of ideology on their analyses cannot be excluded. Hull (1928) reviewed the literature on the relation between anatomic signs and intellectual aptitude and provided a remarkably temperate summary:

> It cannot be denied that among academic psychologists there is a rather strong prejudice against placing any faith in the significance of anatomical signs as indicative of intellectual attitude. This is a perfectly natural reaction to the extravagance, dogmatism, and even charlatanism of the phrenologists and physiognomists. It has been known for a long time, however, that there is a positive relation between various dimensions of the brain case and academic aptitude . . . certain dimensions of the head, when combined with other indicators of aptitude such as samples of test behavior, may contribute unique and substantial increments to the prognosis of aptitudes. (pp. 137–138)

The dismissive attitude of Paterson was more influential than the moderate position of Hull concerning examination of the relation between physical and psychological qualities. For the next half-century, individuals who pursued such hypotheses were often portrayed as misguided, or worse (Goldstein, 1983; Gould, 1981; Secord, 1958). There has been a resurgence of interest in the relation between appearance and underlying personal qualities (Berry & Brownlow, 1989; Berry & Landry, 1997). The extent to which facial features accurately convey underlying personality is, however, extremely complex (Zebrowitz, Andreoletti, Collins, Lee, & Blumenthal, 1998; Zebrowitz, Voinescu, & Collins, 1996) and outside of the scope of this chapter. Yet, while it was possible to deny a relation between an individual's appearance and his or her objective ability or personality, it was impossible to deny a relation between physical appearance and the subjective responses of the perceiver, such as attraction.

THE MULTIPLE FITNESS MODEL OF PHYSICAL ATTRACTIVENESS

Cunningham and his associates (Cunningham, 1981, 1985; Cunningham, Barbee, & Pike, 1990; Cunningham, Roberts, Barbee, Druen, & Wu, 1995; Cunningham, Druen, & Barbee, 1997) drew upon social psychological (Berscheid & Walster, 1974), ethological (Guthrie, 1976), and evolutionary (Symons, 1979) analyses to offer an integrative theoretical account of the perception of physical appearance, called the Multiple Fitness model. The Multiple Fitness model was initially developed to account for the perception of attractiveness that ranges from romantically unappealing to the stunningly beautiful world-class model, but the approach has proven useful in accounting for a range of responses to appearance.

The Multiple Fitness model has several tenets: (1) Some, but not all, facial and bodily qualities are universally physically attractive to people; (2) Different categories of features suggest different forms of fitness in the perceptual target, which are desirable underlying personal qualities; (3) The perception of fitness as an ideal romantic partner is believed to involve a specific combination of features that simultaneously conveys youthfulness, sexual maturity, an absence of signs of advanced age, friendliness, and cultural similarity (see Figure 7.1); (4) Other combinations of facial features may convey different qualities about the target and stimulate a different form of attraction in the perceiver; (5) Culture and the local ecology may create predictable influences on the emphasis placed on some physical features and attributes; (6) Individual needs and personalities may cause differences in the relative emphasis placed on different categories of features, especially when evaluating targets who do not possess all ideal qualities; and (7) Targets may deceive perceivers, but perceivers may minimize the impact of physical attractiveness cues when making decisions, especially when

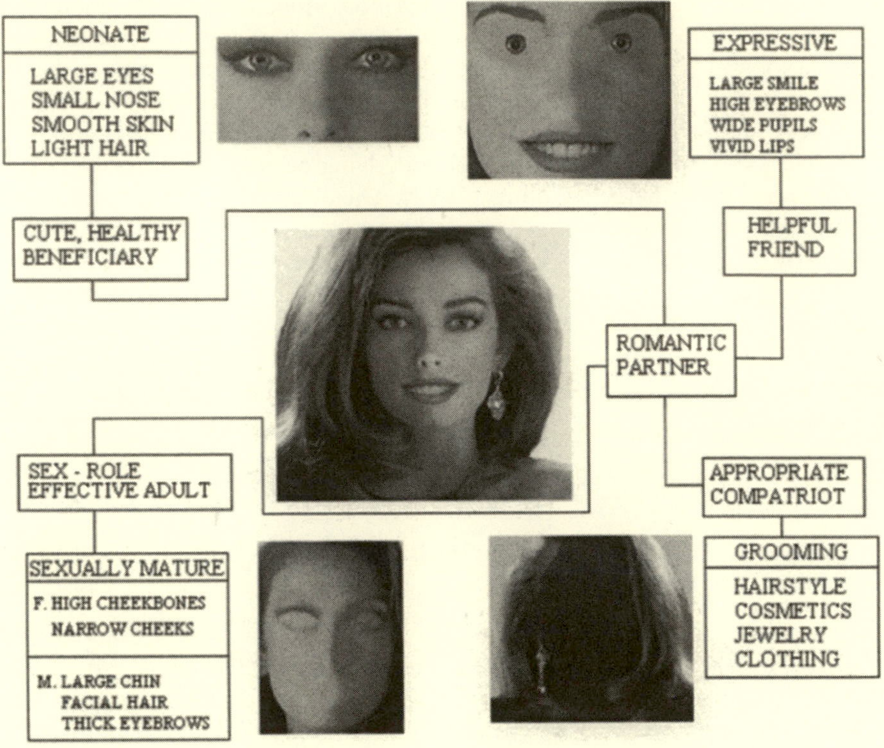

Figure 7.1. Multiple fitness dimensions for romantic partner.

better information about the target is available, or other considerations are paramount.

When young adults are evaluating the physical attractiveness of other young adults, they tend to focus on fitness as a romantic partner. But romantic interest is not the only form of attraction. The Multiple Fitness model suggests that each category of facial features, which will be explained in more detail below, conveys a different quality about the target and stimulates a different form of attraction in the perceiver. Although definitive evidence on these points is lacking, we speculate that babyish neonate features elicit nurturant attraction, or the desire to provide care and commitment to a worthy beneficiary (Alley, 1983). Ideal maturity features may arouse passionate attraction or sexual interest in a healthy and fertile or virile partner (Perper, 1985). Senescence features that convey seniority may stimulate respectful attraction, or the inclination to form an exchange or dependent relationship with a mentor (Muscarella & Cunningham, 1996). Expressive features that convey positive emotions may stimulate communal attraction (Clark & Mills, 1993), or the hope of forming an intimate friendship with a warm and supportive companion. Grooming features, such as cosmetics, hairstyle, body weight, and clothing, may accentuate other forms of attraction, including the desire to form a communal relationship with a person with similar values, tastes, and background to oneself, or the self that one would like to be (Aron & Aron, 1987). Evidence bearing on the assumptions of the Multiple Fitness model will be brought up within each section as appropriate.

Cultural Specificity Versus Universality in Attraction

The Multiple Fitness model suggests that physical attractiveness is complex and multidimensional. Other commentators have arrived at differing conclusions about the nature and universality of standards of attractiveness, in part by focusing on different aspects of appearance, such as grooming practices, body weight, costume, or facial features. Darwin (1871) suggested that "in civilized life, man is largely, but by no means exclusively, influenced in the choice of his wife by external appearances" (p. 738). But Darwin also was struck by cultural differences in preference for different skin colors, amounts of body hair, and grooming practices such as tooth filing and lip elongation. Ford and Beach (1951) reviewed the available anthropological literature and found wide variation across societies in preferences for different body weights, hip shapes, and breast sizes, leading them to conclude: "The cross-cultural evidence makes it clear that there are few if any universal standards of sexual attractiveness. Instead, the physical characteristics which are regarded as sexually stimulating vary appreciably from one society to another" (p. 86).

If the Chiricahua Indians valued a plump body build and the Chenchu Indians desired a slim body build, then culture and learning would seem to be paramount in the perception of physical appearance. Jackson (1992) summarized that view: "physical attractiveness itself has no inherent value. The culture imparts value to it" (p. 36). A survey of Western standards of beauty would seem to support the analysis that physical attractiveness is an arbitrary construct created by a capricious society. Prominent beauticians, whose primary focus was hairstyle, emphasized short and long, straight and curly in different decades. Banner (1983) traced seven distinct physical ideals in white female beauty in the period between 1800 and 1960:

> In the Antebellum years, the frail, pale, willowy woman . . . predominated. In the decades after the Civil War she was challenged by a buxom, hearty and heavy model who made her first appearance on the British music hall stage . . . the "voluptuous" woman. In turn, she was challenged by the tall, athletic, patrician Gibson girl of the 1890s, whose vogue was superseded in the 1910s by a small, model of beauty. . . . This "flapper" model of beauty was predominant throughout the 1920s. By 1930 a new, less youthful and frivolous beauty ideal came into being and remained popular throughout the 1960s, culminating in a renewed vogue of voluptuousness that bore resemblance to nineteenth-century types. That same decade, however, a youthful adolescent model reappeared and continued in popularity through the 1960s. (p. 5)

Commentator Naomi Wolfe (1991) saw a paternalistic conspiracy in changing ideas of physical attractiveness, asserting:

> Beauty is a currency system like the gold standard. Like any economy, it is determined by politics and in the modern age in the West it is the last best belief system that keeps male dominance intact. In assigning value to women in a vertical hierarchy according to a culturally imposed physical standard, it is an expression of power relations in which women must unnaturally compete for resources that men have appropriated for themselves. "Beauty" is not universal or changeless, though the West pretends that all ideals of female beauty stem from one Platonic ideal. (p. 12)

Not only did beauty ideals appear to change across time, but also differences in the ideal female physical form were evident between social groups within the same historical period. Black Americans, for example, rated women with higher body weight as more attractive than did white Americans (Cunningham, Roberts, Barbee, Druen, & Wu 1995), a preference to which we shall later return.

Yet while there is no doubt that culture contributes to judgments of beauty, the conclusion that there is no consistency across groups in the perception of attractiveness was premature. Darwin (1871) did not exclude the possibility of consistency in facial attractiveness judgments:

> Mr. Winwood Reade . . . who has had ample opportunities for observation . . . with the Negroes of . . . Africa . . . who have never associated with Europeans is convinced that their ideas of beauty are, on the whole, the same as ours; and Dr. Rohlfs writes to me the same effect with respect to Borneo and the countries inhabited by the Pullo tribes. . . . Capt. Burton, believes that a woman whom we consider beautiful is admired throughout the world (pp. 748–749).

Is it the case that similar standards of facial beauty are employed throughout the world? In fact, consistencies in judgments of attractiveness were shown by Chinese, Indian, and English females judging Greek males (Thakerar & Iwawaki, 1979); Cruzans and Americans rating white males and females (Maret & Harling, 1985); whites, blacks and Chinese evaluating white and Chinese males and females (Bernstein, Tsai-Ding, & McClellan, 1982); white South Africans and Americans judging white males and females (Morse, Gruzen, & Reis, 1976); whites, Asians, and Hispanics judging whites, blacks, Asians, and Hispanics (Cunningham et al., 1995); and whites, blacks, and Koreans judging whites, blacks, and Koreans (Zebrowitz, Montepare, & Lee, 1993).

Further supporting the notion that the perception of attractiveness is not solely attributable to cultural learning are the findings that 2- to-3-month-olds and 6- to 8-month-olds looked longer at attractive than unattractive faces (Langlois et al., 1987; Langlois, Ritter, Roggman, & Vaughn, 1991), that 12-month-old infants responded more positively to adults wearing attractive than unattractive masks, and played longer with attractive than unattractive dolls (Langlois, Roggman, & Rieser-Danner, 1990). It has been suggested that infants possess an innate facial schema (Morton & Johnson, 1991), which may provide the foundation for infants' attention to attractive faces. While it is valuable to document consistency in responses, neither the cross-cultural nor the developmental literature defined the specific feature stimuli that caused a target to be seen as physically attractive or unattractive.

It is interesting to note that comments about the inconsistency of perception of physical attractiveness emphasized variations in the appearance of the body, whereas studies of consistencies in the cross-age and cross-cultural perceptions of attractiveness generally emphasized the face (but see Singh, 1995). The Multiple Fitness model, described below, suggests that universal response dispositions have more impact on judgments of some facial structural features, such as those conveying youthfulness, whereas sociocultural and individual response dispositions have greater impact on judgments of other facial and bodily attributes, such as nonverbal expression, grooming, and weight. We will now consider the feature categories of the Multiple Fitness model.

Neonate Features

The Multiple Fitness model suggests that neonate features, which are characteristic of newborns, may convey an exaggerated appearance of youthfulness, freshness, naiveté, and openness. Ethologists such as Lorenz (1943) and Eibl-Ebesfeldt (1989) noted that the infants of a wide range of mammalian species tended to possess such characteristic neonate features as large eyes, a small nose, round cheeks, smooth skin and glossy hair, and light coloration. The fact that infant faces display stimulus regularities may have been the result of natural selection operating on both the target and the perceiver.

Exaggerations of key stimulus features can be more attractive than the normal version. A dummy egg with the correct shape and color for a species, but enlarged in size, termed a supernormal stimulus, tends to attract more attention from brooding birds than average-sized eggs (Baerends & Drent, 1982; Tinbergen, 1951). Similarly, exaggerated examples of infant features tend to be particularly attractive to human adults (Alley, 1983; Pittenger & Shaw, 1975; Todd, Mark, Shaw, & Pittenger, 1980). Those infants who were capable of eliciting more parental attention and care by displaying cute large eyes, small noses, and other exaggerated features may have been more likely to survive and produce offspring, who themselves received better care, down to the present age. Both mothers and fathers were found to respond more positively to cuter infants (Hildebrandt & Fitzgerald, 1983), whereas young children who were less cute were at risk for abuse (McCabe, 1984).

Conversely, those parents who, through random variation, were predisposed to respond with higher levels of affection and nurturance, and lower levels of aggression, to the large eyes, small noses and round cheeks of their infants may have provided better care, and left more surviving offspring, than those who were less partial to cute, babyish features. Such attunements may not be restricted to newborns. Adults who possess neonate features, such as large eyes or small noses, may elicit the attraction and nurturance responses that evolved for youngsters (Cunningham, 1981). Supporting the Multiple Fitness model's prediction that neonate features will be attractive is the finding that both male and female adults who possessed larger eyes and relatively smaller noses were rated as more attractive than adults with smaller eyes and larger noses (Cunningham, 1986; Cunningham, Barbee & Pike, 1990). In addition, adult female targets whose eyes were computer manipulated to be larger were rated as more attractive, and more often chosen as recipients of help than targets with normal eyes, or targets whose eyes had been manipulated to be smaller (Campbell, 1991). The preference for neotenous features was evident across a range of populations, including whites, African Americans, Hispanics, Japanese, and Taiwanese (Cunningham et al., 1995), homosexuals and lesbians (DeHart & Cunningham, 1993), heterosexual and homosexual pedophiles (Marcus & Cunningham, 2000), Brazilians, Ache Indians, and Hiwi Indians (Jones, 1995; Jones & Hill, 1993).

Similarly, drawings of adults with neotenous features, such as large eyes or short noses, were rated as more attractive than faces with small eyes or long noses (McArthur & Apatow, 1983–84). When Reidl (1990) provided subjects with the opportunity to construct faces using a computer program that allowed them to manipulate feature sizes and positions, the ideal female face created by males had larger eyes and smaller chins and jaws than typical female faces. It was not clear why subjects did not select smaller noses in the latter study, but this may be due to the specific nose shapes that were available to the subjects (cf. Fauss, 1986; Johnson & Franklin, 1993; Perrett, May, & Yoshikawa, 1994).

Responses to neonate features in adults may have capitalized on dispositions that evolved for childcare, but were adaptive for mate selection to the extent that youthfulness and health were associated with fertility (Symons, 1979). Subsequent research has added complexity to the picture by reporting that perceived youth is not reliably associated with attractiveness (Langlois, Roggman & Musselman, 1994; Musselman, Langlois, & Roggman, 1995), at least among samples of young adults with a relatively narrow range of ages. Across a wider range of ages, however, youthfulness is desirable (Miles & Cunningham, 1999). It is also interesting to note that the impact of babyish features can be separated from the effect of perceived age (Berry & McArthur, 1985, 1986), suggesting that the appearance of youthfulness may be desirable apart from its value in conveying remaining years of fertility or viability.

By suggesting brightness and openness (rather than mental retardation), and few medical problems (rather than unhealthiness), large eyes and a small nose may indicate that the person is a safe bet as a beneficiary of investments (Cunningham, 1981, 1986). Current research, however, has raised questions about whether attractive features reliably signify better than average medical status (Borkan, Bachman, & Norris, 1982; Kalick, Zebrowitz, Langlois, & Johnson, 1998; Shackleford & Larson, 1997, 1999). Recent advances in healthcare, however, may have reduced a relation between appearance and health that may have existed earlier in human history.

Other questions about the social perception of neonate features also require further research. Infant faces contain a complex set of features. Although the effects of some babyface features have been experimentally tested (Berry & McArthur, 1986; Keating, 1985; Zebrowitz, 1997), the differential impact of each feature, apart from all others, has not. This is a daunting challenge; not only does the large number of features make it tedious to conduct parametric variations, but there are natural confounds. Lowering the placement of features such as the eyes, nose, and mouth necessarily makes the chin smaller; narrowing the cheeks can make the mouth appear proportionately larger.

Establishing the effect of specific facial features on discrete social perception dimensions also can be complex. Large eyes, for example, may convey the appearance of youthfulness, which, in turn, may increase the perception of attractiveness. The perception of attractiveness may prime additional constructs within the attractiveness halo, such as friendliness or social skills (Eagly, et al., 1991), without large eyes directly influencing perceptions of friendliness. Disentangling such halo effects is important, because the social qualities that are seen as prototypical of infants, such as youthfulness, submissiveness, and friendliness (Zebrowitz, 1997) may vary independently in adults. It was previously noted that babyishness is distinguishable from age (Berry & McArthur, 1985, 1986). Similarly, research on the Interpersonal Circumplex (Wiggins, 1996) indicates that submissiveness can be distinguished from friendliness. Consistent with this reasoning, distinctions between features conveying youthfulness and openness, capability and dominance, and friendliness and warmth are maintained in the Multiple Fitness categories of neoteny, sexual maturity, and expressiveness, respectively.

Sexual Maturity Features

Although neonate features are charming, there are dimensions of attractiveness that are independent of babyishness (Berry, 1991). Evolution focused mating interest, in part, on signs of sexual maturity, which convey reproductive capability, strength, and ascendancy. Similar to the case of eggs and babies, features that convey sexual maturity often have more impact if they are exaggerated. Indicating the stimulus value of exaggerated maturity cues, female sticklebacks spent more time following a supernormally large dummy male, even though it exceeded the length of the largest males in the study population (Rowland, 1989). Similarly, male baboons responded more strongly to female conspecifics exhibiting exaggerated perineal swellings (Bielert & Anderson, 1985), and female swallows were more attracted to males with larger and more symmetrical tails (Moller & Swaddle, 1997).

In humans, sexual maturity is conveyed by features that, in part, exaggerate the differences between adults and children, and between males and females (Enlow, 1990). The Multiple Fitness model suggests that the appearance of full sexual maturity and extreme dominance requires more than simply the absence of neonate features. Sexual maturity in males is evident in such facial features as a large chin and thick eyebrows (Cunningham et al., 1990; Keating et al., 1981), and beardedness (Muscarella & Cunningham, 1996).

Keating (1985) used an IdentiKit to create line drawings of faces to test the effect of feature variations on perceptions of both dominance and attractiveness. She found that male faces with the individual features of small eyes and thin lips were associated with higher ratings of dominance than average faces. Faces with the individual mature features of a square jaw and thin lips were rated as more attractive than faces with round jaws or thick lips. Finally, females rated male drawings with the combination of four mature features of thick eyebrows, small eyes, thin lips, and square jaws as more dominant and more attractive than faces with thin eyebrows, large eyes, thick lips, and round jaws. Suggesting that maturity features influence the perception of male attractiveness, the attractiveness means for the mature and immature combination faces were 4.4 versus 3.9 on a 7-point scale. Such results also suggest that the most mature faces were not seen as extremely handsome.

Adult females retain more neotenous, babyish qualities in their faces than do males (Friedman & Zebrowitz, 1992), and mature facial qualities that may enhance male attractiveness may reduce that of females (Keating, 1985). Nonetheless, females may convey desirable sexual maturity qualities through some facial attributes. Cunningham, and colleagues (1995) reported higher attractiveness ratings of females with higher cheekbones and narrower cheeks. Suggesting greater ascendancy, women with such facial features were also seen as less modest and more sociable than others (Cunningham, 1986). Grammar and Thornhill (1994) also provided evidence suggesting that prominent cheekbones in women, and larger chins in men, were significantly associated with attractiveness ratings.[1] Further evidence suggesting that facial sexual maturity features are attractive even to those with minimal personal mating interest in the target are the findings that both gay males (DeHart & Cunningham, 1993) and pedophiles (Marcus & Cunningham, 2000) rated women with noticeable facial sexual maturity features more positively than they rated women with lower cheekbones and rounder cheeks.

The Balance of Neoteny and Sexual Maturity

The distinction between neoteny and sexual maturity has confused some commentators (Musselman, Langlois & Roggman, 1995), who did not recognize that physical feature growth does not always follow a linear continuum, but instead may involve discontinuous developmental stages. The chin of the newborn is quite small and receding, but generally grows to medium size during childhood (Enlow, 1990). We referred to small chins in females as a neotenous feature (Cunningham, 1986). During puberty, male chins and jaws may grow to be quite prominent. We referred to the distinction between medium chins and large, beard-stubbled chins as a male sexual maturity feature (Cunningham, Barbee & Pike, 1990). A second example, using the body rather than the face, might be helpful to clarify the discontinuity between neoteny and sexual maturity. A neonate body has a large head, short waist, and short limbs. Its developmental opposite during childhood is the juvenile body, with long limbs and androgynous flat chest. At puberty, the developmental opposite of the juvenile body takes two forms. A body with a .70 waist-to-hip ratio and developed breasts conveys female sexual maturity (Singh & Young, 1995; Tassinary & Hansen, 1998), whereas a body with prominent pectoral muscles, hair on the chest, and a 1.0 waist-to-hip ratio conveys male sexual maturity (Beck, Ward-Hull, & McClear, 1976; Singh, 1995).

If babyishness-maturity were conceptualized as a unitary bipolar dimension, that might suggest that the ideal face would bear a curvilinear relationship to that dimension, with the most attractive faces being neither the most neonate nor the most mature in overall appearance. Such a curvilinear relation was evident in McArthur and Apatow (1983–1984), Cunningham and colleagues (1990), and Perret and colleagues (1998). But a curvilinear relation between facial maturity and attractiveness may be an oversimplification. The Multiple Fitness model suggests that the most attractive male and female faces contain *both* highly neonate and highly sexually mature qualities.

As an alternative to a bipolar conception of babyishness versus sexual maturity, the two qualities might be conceptualized as roughly orthogonal. In addition, both neoteny and maturity involve features in the center (i.e., eyes and nose) and features at the periphery (i.e., chin, cheeks, and cheekbones) of the face. Based on this conception, Cunningham and colleagues (1990) suggested several alternate patterns of facial appearance. The Alpha pattern (shown on the left in Figure 7.2 with [top] and without [bottom] high expressiveness and grooming features) contains the high neonate features of large eyes and a small nose in the center of the face, plus the high mature features of prominent cheekbones and, in males, a large chin in the periphery of the face. The opposite type, labeled the Beta pattern (shown on the right in Figure 7.2 with [top] and without [bottom] low expressiveness and grooming features), has the low babyish features of small eyes and a large nose in the center of the face, combined with the low maturity features of round cheeks and, in males, a smallish chin at the periphery of the face. The Alpha and Beta patterns both convey intermediate maturity and comparable age, but the Alpha seems to be strongly preferred to the Beta pattern. Although explanation for that preference is speculative, the desirability of the Alpha pattern may stem from the potent impact of the eyes in conveying neoteny and expressing emotion. Eyes are the first feature that individuals scan when judging attractiveness (Hassebrauck, 1998).

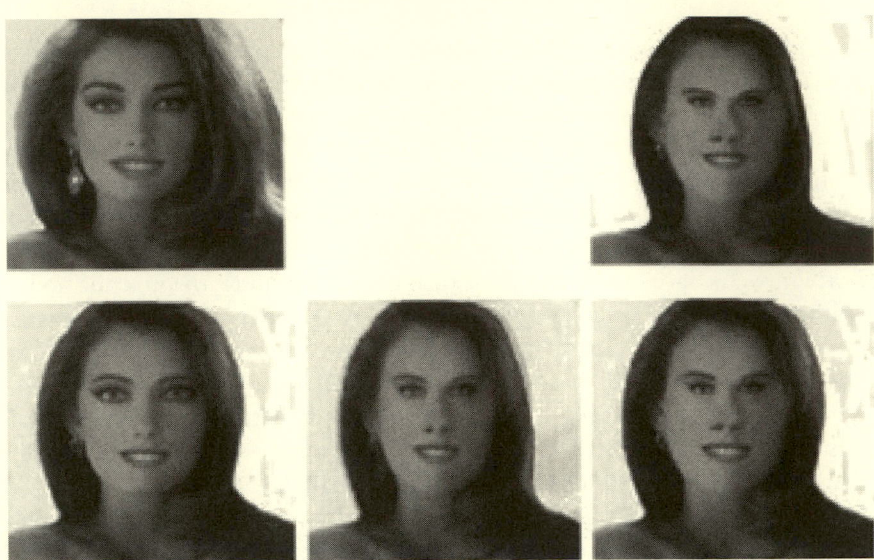

Figure 7.2. Alpha (*top left*: high neonate, high sexual maturity, high expressiveness, high grooming features), Beta (*top right*: low neonate, low sexual maturity, low expressiveness, low grooming features), Alpha- (*bottom left*: high neonate, high sexual maturity, medium expressiveness, medium grooming features), Gamma (*bottom center*: medium neonate, medium sexual maturity, medium expressiveness, medium grooming features), and Beta+ (*bottom right*: low neonate, low sexual maturity, medium expressiveness, medium grooming features) facial types.

Additionally, cheek size can be affected by overall body weight, so it may not be as reliable an indicator of neoteny as features in the center of the face, such as the eyes or nose. Finally, because the chin appears to be a potent signal of testosterone and masculinity (Enlow, 1990), it may be given some preference in the evaluation of men. A third facial type, termed the Gamma pattern (see Figure 7.2, center), also may convey intermediate maturity by having medium-size eyes, nose, cheekbones, and chin, and will be discussed in a later section on average features.

Directional and Stabilizing Selection

When a trait is perceived to be attractive, then individuals who possess that trait may enjoy greater mating success, and produce more offspring across generations, compared to those who do not. Among the offspring of the most attractive parents, those women with the largest eyes and cheekbones, and those men with the largest eyes and chins (and other positive qualities) may be favored, producing an increase in the trait's size in the population. This process is termed directional selection (Andersson, 1994), but there are upper limits to the desirability of any trait. Antlers that are too heavy for a caribou to carry, or a chin that is too large for a man to fit behind a normal automobile steering wheel, may impose costs to the bearer in the form of increased mortality and reduced reproduction rates. So, while directional selection creates a pressure for extreme traits, the costs associated with extreme traits create a contrary tendency, termed stabilizing selection pressure, that restrains a trait in the population (Andersson, 1994). As a consequence, the Multiple Fitness model stipulates that desirable features, such as a large chin and a muscular chest in men, and high cheekbones and prominent breasts in women (Lippa, 1983; Wiggins, Wiggins, & Conger, 1968), are most attractive at an optimal deviation from the average in the general population.

Although the hypothesis is well documented that features that are exceptional in size are attractive, the optimal deviation prediction is conjectural for human faces, in that no cases of female eyes or male chins that were too large to be attractive were observed (Cunningham et al., 1985, 1990, 1995). Nonetheless, we suspect that the supernormal facial features of Walt Disney's Tinkerbell or Hercules, although attractive on cartoons (Finch, 1975), might appear grotesque if encountered on living people. Experimental studies might be conducted to determine the catastrophe point, at which changing the size of a facial feature causes it to shift from attractive to awful (cf. Johnston & Franklin, 1993).

Support for the optimal deviation hypothesis can be derived from studies of body attractiveness. Large, muscular males, for example, are attractive, but the largest males are rated as less attractive than males who are simply above average in musculature (Beck, Ward-Hull, & McClear, 1976) or height (Graziano, Brothen, & Berscheid, 1978; Shepard & Strathman, 1989). Such above-average features might be more likely to occur under conditions of developmental stability, although the impact of genetics and prenatal and postnatal factors involved in the development of exceptional facial and body features remain to be established.

Senescence Features

The Multiple Fitness model notes that physical maturation continues after puberty (Enlow, 1990), and categorizes signs of additional aging as senescence cues. Senescence cues are often seen as undesirable. In males, visually estimated age predicted both physiological age and mortality (Borkan, Bachman, & Norris, 1982). Yet, the Multiple Fitness model suggests that there are several forms of attractiveness. Changes in the appearance of the face and head, such as graying hair and male pattern baldness, are genetically programmed and may be adaptive for their bearer. Such senescence cues are believed to convey social maturity, a nonthreatening form of dominance associated with wisdom and nurturance. Those cues may induce respect and supportiveness from the social community, while appeasing competitors.

Muscarella and Cunningham (1996) tested that interpretation by contrasting the social perception of men with full heads of hair with the same men who were computer-manipulated to display male pattern baldness. When they had full scalp hair, men were seen as younger and more aggressive. But when the men appeared to be bald, they were seen to possess more social maturity, indicated by such terms as "intelligent," "honest," "helpful," and "high in status," and also more appeasing, conveyed by terms such as "feminine" and "gentle". As a consequence, bald men seem to be less attractive as romantic partners, but more attractive as mentors.

In a second study on the impact of male senescence cues, Miles and Cunningham (1999) presented the same male targets as either 25, 40, or 60 years old by manipulating their hair color, skin smoothness, and wrinkles. The attractiveness of those targets was rated by three groups of females, with mean ages of 19.6, 39.9, and 59.2 years. The 60-year-old targets were seen as more trustworthy (loyal, honest, careful) but lower on surgency (active, self-confident, passionate) than the younger targets. Although all groups rated the apparently older men as less attractive than the younger targets, the 60-year-old females reported greater interest in dating their age mates than dating younger men.

Because signs of aging convey the onset of menopause and the loss of fertility, they may reduce the romantic attractiveness of females (Kenrick & Keefe, 1992). Studies of the perception of females have used targets of different age categories, and found inverse relations between actual age and rated attractiveness (Henss, 1991; McLellan & McKelvie, 1993; Zebrowitz, Olson, & Hoffman, 1993). But we know relatively little of the relations between specific female senescence cues and the perceptions (or self-perceptions, Cunningham, Barbee, & Druen, 1998) of the attractiveness and personalities of mature women.

Expressive Features

Structural features may convey physical development, but the movement of facial features also may be physically attractive, by conveying prosocial feelings, and fitness as a supportive friend and exciting partner. Agreeableness (Jensen-Campbell, Graziano, & West, 1995), social supportiveness (Cunningham & Barbee, 2000a) and sense of humor (Lundy, Tan, & Cunningham, 1998) are all desirable mate qualities. A small amount of friendliness may be conveyed by a small mouth or smile, whereas a large smile may convey happiness and eagerness to interact with the other person (Kraut & Johnston, 1979). The smile is the second feature that both males and females tend to view when evaluating the attractiveness of faces, after the eyes (Hassebrauck, 1998). The eyes may convey expressiveness as well as neoteny, because arousal and interest may be conveyed by dilated pupils (Hess, 1965).

Expressiveness seems to be particularly desirable in females (Deutsch, LeBaron, & Fryer, 1987), and female expressive features, which appear to be more pronounced than those of men, may have been selected to convey such qualities with particular intensity. Raised eyebrows convey a nondominant attitude (Keating, Mazur, & Segall, 1981), and highly set eyebrows are correlated with ratings of babyfacedness (Berry & McArthur, 1985; see also Zebrowitz & Montepare, 1992, for a distinction).[2] However, raised eyebrows may also signal happiness (Keating, et al, 1981), interest (Izard, 1971), and flirtatious attention (Eibl-Eibesfeldt, 1989), and eyebrows that are structurally set high on the forehead may facilitate such positive expressions. Lips are another feature that may convey several meanings. Large lips may appear less mature than thin lips (Keating, 1985; Keating, Mazur, & Sigall, 1981; Keating, Randall, & Kenrick, 1999). But female lips tend to grow during puberty to be larger and more everted than males (Farkas, 1981), so full lips also may indicate high levels of estrogen and female sexual maturity (Grammar & Thornhill, 1999; Johnson & Franklin, 1993). Because lips at rest mimic the expressive shape of a smile, with expansive lower curve and smaller upper curve, it seems appropriate to regard lip size as an expressive cue. In addition, lips tend to expand and flush red during arousal, conveying excitement and receptivity (Morris, 1985). Dilated pupils, smiles, arched eyebrows, and full, red lips seem to be similar in conveying some degree of submissive babyishness, but a larger degree of friendliness and warmth. The Multiple Fitness model classifies each as expressive features, and our research found that arched eyebrows, dilated pupils, full lips, and larger smiles all increased female attractiveness (Cunningham et al., 1995).

Although expressive features are highly important in evaluations of females, they are also consequential in evaluation of males. Contemporary females desire males who are warm, friendly, and supportive (Cunningham et al., 1999). Jensen-Campbell, Graziano, & West (1995) reported that females gave highest attractiveness ratings to men who behaviorally displayed the apparently inconsistent qualities of both high agreeableness and high dominance. A tradeoff of expressiveness and maturity may be made in the male face, such that maturely thick rather than expressively arched eyebrows are attractive. But a large smile is just as attractive in a male face as in a female face (Cunningham et al., 1990).

A number of other studies documented the attractiveness of expressive features. Reis and colleagues (1990) had 15 men and 15 women pose in smiling and neutral positions for photographs, which were rated by 100 subjects. Both males and females were rated as more attractive when smiling. Mueser, Grau, Sussman, and Rosen (1984) found that posing a sad expression reduced attractiveness ratings compared to neutral and happy expressions. Fauss (1986) had subjects create ideal faces of the opposite sex using a police IdentiKit. Ideal males and females both had wide mouths with full lips. Ideal females also had highly arched eyebrows. Farkas, Munro, and Kolar (1987) had 200 women, including 50 professional models, rated by 74 men and women on 7-point scales. The 34 faces that received ratings of 5 or 6 and the 21 faces that received a rating of 1 or 2 were measured by a single investigator. The authors reported that females with wide mouths and full lips were more attractive than females without these qualities. Johnson and Franklin (1993) allowed subjects to select features from a computer program, and reported that faces that were rated as more attractive had fuller upper and lower lips. Such studies suggest that female faces with the expressive features of arched eyebrows, dilated pupils, wide mouths, and full lips, and male faces with large smiles, are seen as more attractive than their less expressive counterparts. More research is needed, however, to determine the independent effects of expressive cues on social reactions.

Grooming Features

Grooming refers to selective modification of physical appearance. Such modifications often serve to accentuate features within the categories of attractiveness described earlier. Foundation makeup may recreate the smooth, healthy skin of infancy. Eyeliner and mascara may enhance eye size and neoteny. Blush may exaggerate the cheekbones, conveying maturity. Eyebrow pencil may raise the eyebrow line, and lipstick may simulate arousal, both of which may increase expressiveness and attractiveness (Osborne, 1996). Hair may be tinted blond to enhance the appearance of neoteny, or dyed brown to conceal signs of senescence. It may be worn long to attract attention, or elaborately coiffed to signal status and wealth. Cutting the nails and hair may be done simply to maintain hygiene and keep growth under control, or it may be part of an elaborate display. Clothing can be a language all its own, providing information about the wearer's age, gender, status, sexuality, interests, and aesthetics (Lurie, 1981). But whereas a makeup, hair, or clothing style may appear novel and intriguing when first introduced, the style may seem boring or silly after years of exposure. Discrepancies between past and present grooming styles may be a primary cause of the belief that standards of beauty are unpredictable or constantly changing.

Specific combinations of self-presentational display, including hair, clothing, and posture, may be linked to the Multiple Fitness dimensions. Ashmore, Solomon, and Longo (1996) had subjects sort 96 full-length photos of fashion models into self-generated categories. Multidimensional scaling analyses suggested underlying factors of Cute, Sexy, and Trendy. Although such findings do not provide definitive support for the Multiple Fitness model's categories, the similarity between Ashmore and colleagues' Cute and our neoteny, Sexy and female sexual maturity, and Trendy and grooming should be noted. Ashmore's dimension of Trendy emphasized the display of new and costly resources, including hairstyle, jewelry, and clothing, which may both capture attention and convey cultural fitness. Because Trendy grooming may be used to indicate group membership and status, it may create the appearance of social skills and popularity (cf. Eagly, Ashmore, Makhijani & Longo, 1991).

In a heterogeneous society, more than one form of Trendy grooming may be evident at a given time, such as glamour trendy, business trendy, athletic trendy, counterculture trendy, and ethnic trendy, to name just a few divergent styles. Individuals may use grooming cues to recognize other people who appear to have similar interests, and who conscientiously adhere to desired subcultural values. The perception that a target has compatible tastes in grooming, whether due to an impeccable haircut or alluring body piercing, may enhance perceived similarity and liking.

Selection and the Ecology

The Multiple Fitness model suggests that some features are attractive cross-culturally, but also proposes that some variation in grooming and in mate preference may occur as a function of the ecology and related social conditions (Cunningham et al., 1995). For example, a beard is a male sexual maturity feature that enlarges the appearance of the chin and jaw. Males wearing beards are seen as more aggressive and less attractive than men who are clean shaven (Muscarella & Cunningham, 1996). Thus, the grooming behavior of cutting off the beard reduces the appearance of male sexual maturity, but can be adaptive. The impact of the beard on attractiveness to the opposite sex may depend on whether aggressiveness and dominance, or cooperativeness and submissiveness, seem most adaptive in the individual's culture. Robinson (1976), for example, analyzed fashions in the shaving and trimming of the beard in London, and found intriguing patterns. Beard wearing was associated with wider skirts. Although the meaning of that association is not clear, longer female skirts have also been linked to poorer economic conditions (Richardson & Kroeber, 1940). Male beards, and female modesty, may be in greatest demand in a harsh, threatening ecology.

Female faces also may be more desirable if they appear to be optimally adapted to the challenges of their local environment. Pettijohn and Tesser (1999) hypothesized that facial maturity would be in greater demand during economic downturns than during times of prosperity. The investigators gathered social and economic indicators, such as changes in consumer prices and disposable income. They also measured the faces of the top 81 American actresses for each year between 1932 and 1995. They found that popular actresses had more neoteny and less maturity during good times, including larger eyes, rounder cheeks, and smaller chins. The converse was evident during economic downturns. It is important to note that female chin size, for example, was merely relatively larger during hard times; it likely did not fall into a range that would be considered unattractive during times of prosperity.

The appearance of the face, especially cheek roundness, is affected by overall weight. Regulation of weight is a grooming behavior, to the extent that it is under personal control and cultural mandate. When access to food is high, health and reproductive fitness may be indicated by conscientious self-control and slenderness, which may produce intrasexual competition for exceptional slimness (Silverstein, Peterson, & Perdue, 1986; Wiseman, Gray, Mosimann, & Ahrens, 1992). By contrast, in areas of the world besieged by famine and disease, health may be indicated by fleshiness (Anderson, Crawford, Nadeau, & Lindberg, 1992). Similar differences may be seen across cultures and ecologies within the same city. As noted earlier, whites and African Americans were found to have highly similar standards for evaluating faces, but differed in their standards for facial cheek width and body weight (Cunningham et al., 1995). However, it is not clear whether African Americans value body weight because they implicitly fear food shortages. The relation between positive evaluations of rounded faces and perceived resource scarcity requires additional research.

The prevalence of disease may affect the emphasis placed on physical attractiveness in general (Gangestad & Buss, 1993), and the use of grooming practices in particular. Singh and Bronstad (1997) used the Standard Cross-Cultural Sample of 186 societies to examine the relation between pathogen presence and the grooming behavior of facial and body scarification and tattooing. Such practices were expected to be more likely in areas of the world where disease was rampant as a means of drawing attention to fitness, and perhaps concealing evidence of unfitness. The investigators reported that females tended to scarify their faces more than men overall, perhaps due to a greater emphasis placed on female than male physical attractiveness. In addition, females were more likely to scarify their stomachs and breasts in areas of the world where pathogens were high compared to areas where pathogens were low, perhaps to draw attention to their fitness, potential fertility, and capacity to endure the pain of childbirth. Engaging in scarification practices to distinguish oneself in regions affected by pathogens might be psychologically equivalent to emphasizing thinness in a culture saturated with food.

Individual Differences in Preferences for Types of Physical Attractiveness

If ideal targets are unavailable, individual differences in personality and motive may cause variations in preferences for different varieties of moderately attractive people. People possessing the ideal combination of features for romantic attractiveness are rare, and most studies of the impact of physical attractiveness have used individual targets that ranged from moderately unattractive to moderately attractive (i.e., Reis et al., 1982). Just as it is possible to attain intermediate maturity through different combinations of features (Alpha, Beta, and Gamma), it is possible to attain moderate physical attractiveness through a variety of combinations of features. Such variations across the stimuli used in different studies of physical attractiveness may have caused some of the inconsistency in the social perception and attraction literature (cf. Berry, 1991; Dermer & Thiel, 1975; Eagly et al., 1991).

A target with high sexual maturity and stylish grooming, medium neoteny and low expressiveness, termed a Delta, for example, may look pretty and sophisticated, but also somewhat cool and rejecting. A target with high expressiveness, medium neoteny, but low sexual maturity, termed an Epsilon, may look more pleasant and friendly, but less dynamic and polished than the Delta (see Figure 7.3). Both the Delta and the Epsilon look fairly attractive, but they may appeal to different men.

The desire for maturity versus expressiveness in a date may vary as a function of the perceiver's own emotional state. Men experiencing elated affect might possess an increased aspiration level, plus an optimistic view of their capacity to handle the personality of such a challenging potential date as a Delta (Cunningham, 1988a, b), and might be more likely to approach her than would other men. By contrast, men experiencing induced negative affect might prefer warmth and nurturance over the risks associated with trying to attain a high-status, sexy date. Consequently, we expected that induced negative affect would be associated with a choice of a date with features conveying high expressiveness and low sexual maturity, like the Epsilon. Wong and Cunningham (1990; see Cunningham, Druen, & Barbee, 1997) examined these hypotheses, and found that males who were manipulated to be in a good mood preferred females with the Delta facial type over the Epsilon pattern. By contrast, men who were in a manipulated depressed mood preferred the woman with the Epsilon pattern. Men in a neutral mood were equally divided between the two. In an alternate experimental condition, men in induced positive, neutral, and negative moods all preferred an Alpha, who was high in both sexual maturity and expressiveness, over other types. The extent to which a partner with an expressive, attractive face can actually help to maintain another person's positive mood, or remedy a negative mood, remains to be determined.

Figure 7.3. Delta (*left*: medium neoteny, high sexual maturity, low expressiveness, high grooming) and Epsilon (*right*: medium neoteny, low sexual maturity, high expressiveness, medium grooming) facial types.

Females also may display some variability in their preferences. Females generally prefer a male face in which masculine sexual maturity is balanced by a degree of neoteny or femininity (Perrett et al., 1998). But when females are focusing on a short-term sexual relationship (Kenrick, Groth, Trost, & Sadalla, 1993) or are at the most fertile point of the menstrual cycle, their preferences may shift slightly to prefer a less feminine or more masculine face (Penton-Voak et al., 1999). Such results suggest that the meaning of facial qualities remains relatively constant, but individual trade-off decisions may fluctuate slightly, depending on motive and need.

OTHER CUES TO ATTRACTIVENESS

The Multiple Fitness model focuses on combinations of features and other characteristics that create impressions such as youthfulness, sexiness, and friendliness. Other approaches to facial attractiveness emphasize other qualities that may be related to attractiveness ratings, including symmetry and averageness. We review this literature with an emphasis on the extent to which an average or symmetrical appearance is necessary and sufficient to produce an ideally attractive face.

Symmetry

Fluctuating asymmetry (FA) refers to the extent to which pairs of features, such as ears and eyes, deviate from equal size, or are located an unequal distance from the centerline of the organism, excluding those traits for which bilateral asymmetry is normal, such as the size of the right bicep for right-handed people. Perfect symmetry indicates optimal expression of the genotype, whereas a high degree of asymmetry is associated with problems in development. Both genetic problems, such as recessive genes and homozygosity, and environmental stressors, such as parasites, pollutants, and extreme temperatures, can cause development to go askew, causing asymmetry (Livshits & Kobyliansky, 1991; Moller & Pomiankowski, 1993). As a consequence, low FA might be regarded as an indicator of developmental stability and the accurate translation of genotype into phenotype (Trivers, Manning, Thornhill, Singh, & McGuire, 1999). Low levels of FA also may serve as an indicator of fitness after puberty. Testosterone can reduce the effectiveness of the immune system, but it is essential for the development of some secondary sexual characteristics (Alexander & Stimson, 1988). A robust immune system may afford higher levels of testosterone, and allow the development of more prominent male features, such as a large chin. When secondary sexual characteristics are both large and symmetrical, the appearance may serve as an advertisement of immunocompetence (Thornhill & Gangestad, 1993). Low FA in males is correlated with greater body mass (Manning, 1995), physicality (muscularity, robustness, and vigor), and perceived social dominance (Gangestad &

Thornhill, 1997a, b), perhaps due to higher levels of testosterone in more symmetrical individuals.

The attractiveness of low FA has been tested across a range of species, including scorpionflies, swallows and humans (Thornhill & Gangestad, 1994). Ratings of human facial attractiveness tended to be negatively related to assessments of facial bilateral asymmetry (Mealy, Bridgestock and Townsend, 1999; Thornhill & Gangestad, 1994), and body asymmetry (Gangestad, Thornhill, & Yeo, 1994), and to ratings of the symmetry of the face (Zebrowitz, Voinescu & Collins, 1996). Ratings of the attractiveness of the face were correlated with independent ratings of the attractiveness of the body (Thornhill & Grammar, 1999), and lower levels of body asymmetry also were associated with younger age at first intercourse for men, and a greater lifetime number of sexual partners (Thornhill & Gangestad, 1994), including extra-pair partners. Low FA males more reliably stimulate female orgasms; smell more attractive to females who are in the fertile phase of their menstrual cycle; and boast about themselves while belittling their competitors, to obtain a date (Gangestad & Simpson, 2000; Simpson, Gangestad, Christensen, & Leck, 1999).

Although symmetry is associated with desirability, causality is unclear. When females rate a symmetrical male face as attractive, is it because: a) perceivers associate symmetry specifically with sturdiness and health, including mutation resistance and immunocompetence; or b) the symmetrical face has carried higher levels of sexual hormones, allowing the development of stronger maturity features, such as high cheekbones or a large chin, which then suggests a sexually mature body; or c) perceivers are drawn to the aesthetics of symmetry, per se? Perceived health is attractive, but its impact is difficult to disentangle from other variables, such as expressiveness, sexual maturity, and grooming cues (Cunningham, 1986). Similarly, as noted earlier, females tend to prefer males who exemplify sexual maturity features, who have large chins and are moderately large-chested (Beck, Ward-Hull, & McClear, 1976), and males tend to prefer females who exemplify sexual maturity features through high cheekbones and prominent hips (Singh & Young, 1995).

Although people with lower degrees of facial symmetry may be less attractive than those with higher degrees of symmetry, the literature on the inherent attractiveness of facial symmetry is inconsistent (Shackleford & Larsen, 1997). Perfectly symmetrical faces have not consistently produced increased attractiveness (Kowner, 1996; Rhodes, Sumich, & Byatt, 1999; Samuels, Butterworth, Roberts, Graupner, & Hole, 1994; Swaddle & Cuthill, 1995). Because of directional asymmetry in the expression of emotion (Davidson Mednick, Moss, Saron, & Schaffer, 1987; Sackheim, Gur, & Saney, 1978), some perfectly symmetrical faces may appear flat and uncongenial. It is possible that a perfectly symmetrical appearance simply looks too perfect, which may be intimidating to potential dates who are aware of their own imperfections. Perhaps that is why a bit of asymmetry, in the form of a facial mole, is called a beauty mark (The year of the mole, 1990). A symmetrical face created by mirroring the right side of the target's face on to her left side is shown in Figure 7.4 (left).

Rhodes, Proffit, Grady, and Sumich (1998) were unique in manipulating degrees of symmetry. These investigators contrasted ratings of normal faces with the same face whose symmetry was achieved by computer averaging the normal face with its mirror-image opposite. An illustration of that approach is also shown in Figure 7.4 (middle). The normal and perfectly symmetrical faces were contrasted with two other versions of the face. The symmetry of those faces was raised by increasing by 50% the similarity between the normal and the perfectly symmetrical versions of the face, or lowered in the same manner. Faces with perfect symmetry were rated as more attractive (mean = 4.9 on a 10–point scale) than the raised symmetry and normal faces (both 4.6), which were more attractive than the face with lowered symmetry (4.2). Such results suggest that enhancing symmetry may improve attractiveness, but a perfectly symmetrical face may still fall substantially short of the romantic ideal.

Averageness

During the nineteenth century, Francis Galton (1878) sought to present the defining characteristics of different types of faces, such as military officers versus criminals and meat eaters versus vegetarians. His approach was to copy eight portraits, one at a time, onto the same photographic plate. The portraits were centered so that the eyes of each were in the same position. Because of differences in the size of the individual faces, the superimposition processes produced an ethereal softness to the features and ghostly corona around the margins. Nonetheless, the composites looked fairly realistic, and sometimes appeared to Galton to be more attractive than the individual portraits.

Inspired by Galton, the team of Burson, Carling, and Kramlich (1986) brought superimposition to the computer. Burson and her associates devel-

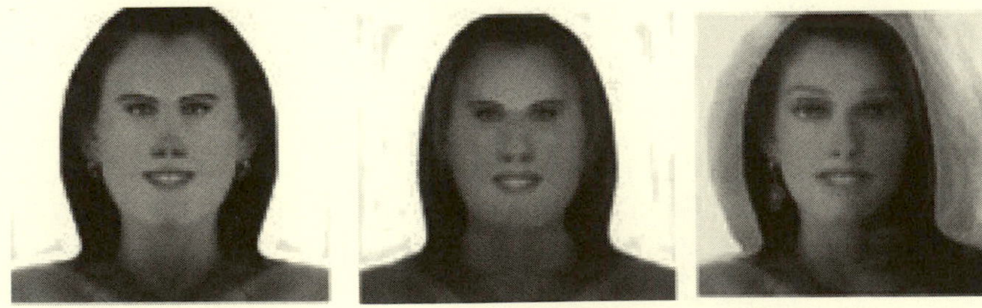

Figure 7.4. Mirrored symmetrical (*left*: reflexed right hemiface), morph-averaged symmetrical (*center*: composite of normal & mirror-imaged faces), and superimposed-averaged (*right*: composite of Alpha & Beta) faces.

oped procedures for digitally aging pictures of kidnapped children's faces by blending the photos of young victims with photos of their older siblings. When they were not assisting the FBI, Burlson and colleagues were creating composites to represent conceptions of beauty by averaging the portraits of film stars of the 1950s (Bette Davis, Audrey Hepburn, Grace Kelly, Sophia Loren, Marilyn Monroe) and those of the 1980s (Jane Fonda, Jacqueline Bisset, Diane Keaton, Brooke Shields, Meryl Streep). The description of their process acknowledged that the averaging process created a composite that is initially "blurry and ambiguous in places" (p. 17), but was cleaned up, pixel by pixel, under high magnification. An illustration of the superimposed faces, including redundant eyebrows, is shown in Figure 7.4 (right).

Langlois and Roggman (1990), using a similar procedure, combined 2, 4, 8, 16, and 32 college students' faces into a set of black and white composites. Separate composites were made of females and males. Before creating the composites, the definition and clarity of the features in the individual portraits were softened or "smoothed" by averaging the gray value of each pixel with each adjacent pixel. Composites were created by averaging adjacent pixels in pairs of photos. While doing so, those lines and edges that the authors regarded as "extra" were removed. After the composites were created, they were sharpened and contrast enhanced. Langlois and Roggman reported that composites that were based on 16 and 32 faces were rated as more attractive than composites based on fewer faces, and more attractive than the mean of individual faces, leading the authors to conclude that "social scientists may be less disturbed by studying the effects of attractiveness knowing that attractive faces, in fact, are only average" (p. 120).

Langlois and Roggman's (1990) concern about social scientists being disturbed by studying attractiveness echoes the mixed attitudes about studying physical appearance from the beginning of the twentieth century. Their consoling use of the phrase "only average" suggests the familiar connotation of the term "average" as "typical," "not out of the ordinary," and "midway between extremes" (*Webster's 3rd Unabridged*, 1986). It was previously noted that stabilizing selection pressure might produce preferences for traits that are less extreme than the maximum possible in a population, which could make averaged faces more attractive than those with conspicuous deviations from the average. But there is no evidence that stabilizing selection is dominant in humans, and that physical attractiveness is exempt from Darwinian competition and directional selection pressure. Indeed, directional selection tendencies are apparent in a wide range of human evaluations. From university admission criteria based on the highest intellectual test scores, to Olympic awards for greatest strength and speed, to females' preferences for males with large chest sizes (Beck, Ward-Hull, & McClear, 1976), to *Playboy* magazine attracting a large male readership by featuring females whose bodies were trimmer and more voluptuous (Wiseman, Gray, Mosimann, & Ahrens, 1992) and whose hair color was blonder than the population (Rich & Cash, 1993), people seem to prefer the "above average" to the unexceptional.

An alternate meaning of the term "average" is the mathematical mean, which may be skewed upward or downward from the median and mode as a function of outliers in the sample. Langlois and Roggman's (1990) sample of faces was limited to young, healthy college students, and excluded older faces, male faces with beards, and faces with the malformations that are characteristic of the mentally retarded (Jones, 1996). If a sample of faces is skewed by containing more portraits with exceptionally attractive features than exceptionally unattractive features, and if the averaging process itself tends to enhance appearance by removing facial blemishes and increasing symmetry (Alley & Cunningham, 1991; Pittenger, 1991), then a composite face may be more attractive than its constituents. But given the exclusion criteria and the cosmetic benefits of the averaging process itself, it is not clear that such a computer-averaged composite represents the prototypical face in a population.

Unexceptional Ratings of Averaged Faces

Langlois and her associates (Langlois, Roggman, Musselman, & Acton, 1991; Langlois, Roggman & Musselman, 1994) indicated that they meant the term "average" to refer only to the mean, and argued against methodological concerns about their averaging procedure. But they did not account for why averaged faces were not strikingly gorgeous or handsome. Langlois and Roggman (1990) included female faces with individual ratings ranging from 1.20 to 4.05 on a 5-point scale, and a group mean of 2.43. Their 32-face female composite received a rating of 3.25, which was higher than the group mean, but conspicuously lower than their most attractive individual woman. The male faces ranged from 1.8 to 3.8, with a group mean of 2.51; the 32-face male composite garnered a rating of 3.27, which again was higher than the group mean, but fell far short of the "5 = very attractive" scale endpoint. Such results suggest that technological processing of faces offers an outcome with modest benefits for the group, but perhaps at the expense of the most outstanding individuals.

Grammar and Thornhill's (1994) examination of averaged faces produced mixed results. Facial composites made from sets of 4, 8, and 16 women were rated more attractive by men than the group mean (3.26 vs. 2.79), but did not reach the midpoint of their 7-point scale. Facial composites of men tended to be rated as *less* attractive by women (2.88 vs. 3.12). Rhodes and Tremewan (1996) used computer-created line drawings based on facial photographs, and produced 32-face composites that were more attractive than their group means (3.7 vs. 2.8 for females; 4.0 vs. 3.0 for males on 7-point scales), but still not highly attractive. The authors reported that attractiveness ratings tended to be negatively correlated with ratings of distinctiveness, but their most attractive face was unexpectedly distinctive. They concluded: "This result reinforces the point that, although averageness is attractive, average faces are not the only attractive faces" (p. 108). Rhodes, Sumich and Byatt (1999) used a procedure that warped individual faces onto a configuration based on the mean location of multiple landmarks. Their composites again tended to be more attractive than individual portraits, but were not rated as exceptionally desirable, including a female composite mean of 5.2 and a male composite mean of 4.6 on a 7-point scale. The investigators also demonstrated that increasing symmetry, by blending each face with its mirror image, produced a small increase in attractiveness, but did not reduce the impact of averaging. Ratings of attractiveness were correlated with perceptions of averageness (r = .37), but no more strongly than with ratings of pleasant expression (r = .47) or symmetry (r = .40).

Pollard (1995) used Galton's photographic approach to produce composites using photos of New Zealand Caucasian students. Faces that "had gross defects or which had a shape which was not sufficiently common to combine readily with another five" (p. 79) were excluded. Subjects were asked to indicate which face in sets of seven faces they thought was most attractive. Female composite faces tended to be preferred more often than male composites. New Zealand Caucasian and Chinese preferred male composite faces, but Indian and Nigerian men showed only chance response to composites. Although Pollard found a preference for composite faces, he expressed reservations because the process produced composites with features that are larger than the median: "This is because the larger individual features will still be represented in the composite, albeit more faintly, and may add to its perceived size" (p. 81). Pollard concluded with concern about whether such a composite represents a category exemplar or prototype: "It remains to be shown that the composite face is an average face in any generally accepted prototypical sense or that it is regarded as typical of any particular class of faces" (p. 82).

Are Faces with Average Features Most Attractive?

The computer averaging process combines individuals to produce a composite that is supposed to represent the mean of the population at all points. If the enhancement in attractiveness of computer averaged portraits was not due to the averaging process itself, then individuals whose faces happened to represent the population mean should be exceptionally attractive. Two facial measurement studies examined whether faces whose features were closer in size to the population mean were seen as more attractive. Cunningham, Barbee and Pike (1990) correlated global facial attractiveness ratings with the extent to which 22 facial measurements deviated from the sample mean of 60 portraits, and found little relations with perceived attractiveness. Whereas that study tested averageness feature by feature, Pollard, Shepard, and Shepherd (1999) used all measures simultaneously. They took 19 measures of 240 men and 88 women, converted each measure to a z-score, and selected the 10 faces with the lowest combined z-score, who were closest to the population average, and the 10 faces with the highest combined z-score, who were most deviant. The authors found little difference in perceived attractiveness between the average and the deviant faces, for both male and female portraits. They concluded: "Tested. . . with actual rather than contrived faces, the hypothesis that average faces are attractive is not supported" (p. 101).

Other studies demonstrated that some of the parts are greater than the sum of the whole. Perrett, May and Yoshikawa (1994) suggested that if attractiveness is based on averageness, then a composite derived from faces that are rated as highly attractive should not differ from a composite based on a larger general sample of faces. Similarly, if averageness is ideal, then any exaggeration should reduce attractiveness. But if attractiveness involves a degree of directional selection, then some exaggerations may enhance attractiveness. To address these possibilities, the investigators created an "average" computer composite using 60 Caucasian female faces. A second "high" composite was created by averaging those 15 individual faces from the 60 who had received the highest attractiveness ratings by 36 judges. A third "high + 50%" composite was created by exaggerating the shape differences between the "average" and the "high" composites. Both male and female subjects displayed a strong preference for the "high" composite over the "average" composite, and the "high+50%" composite over the "high" composite. Perrett and colleagues conducted a replication using 342 Japanese faces for the "average" composite, and the most attractive 16 faces for the "high" composite, and found the same pattern of preferences among Japanese judges. Consistent with the Multiple Fitness model, the more attractive composite face had larger eyes, higher cheekbones, a shorter chin, and a more pronounced eyebrow shape than the average face. A third study, conducted with 59 Caucasian male faces, also found that the "high" composite was preferred over the average composite. The authors concluded that "our results show that highly attractive faces are systematically different in shape from average. . . . Attractive facial features may signal sexual maturity and fertility, emotional expressiveness or a 'cuteness' generalized from parental protectiveness towards young" (p. 241).

Although Langlois and Roggman's (1990) statement that "attractive faces . . . are only average" appeared definitive, they also acknowledged that: "a sample of movie stars might be rated as more attractive than our composites. It may be the case that although averageness is a necessary and critical element of attractiveness, other elements may also be important in influencing judgments of attractiveness" (p. 120). We concur that averageness is a necessary condition for moderate attractiveness, but may not be sufficient for the perception of extremely high physical attractiveness.

Our review of the literature on exceptional, symmetrical, and average features suggest that each quality may be effective in accounting for a segment of the continuum of physical attractiveness. Extreme asymmetry is unattractive, because it conveys developmental abnormalities, including mental retardation. Attractiveness increases with increasing symmetry, but perfect symmetry does not appear to produce the pinnacle of attractiveness. Computer averaging of a normal distribution of faces produces a composite that is more attractive than many individuals, both because asymmetries and facial irregularities are deleted, and because the mean of the population is familiar and unoffending. We suggest that a symmetrical and average face, which we call the Gamma pattern, is more attractive than the Beta, with small eyes, a large nose, and low cheekbones. But an averaged and symmetrical face is not, in our judgment, as attractive as the Alpha pattern of exceptional features, including large eyes, a small nose, high cheekbones, a small chin on females, and a large chin on males. The Alpha pattern is often seen in movie stars (Pettijohn & Tesser, 1999).

THE FALSIFICATION OF PHYSICAL APPEARANCE

Because physical attractiveness may appear to contribute to success in many domains of life (Jackson, 1992), individuals may spend many hours of labor and many dollars on their grooming. In order to further enhance their image, some individuals may be willing to engage in deception concerning their physical appearance. Rowatt, Cunningham, Rowatt, Druen, and Miles (2000) documented admissions of past deception by both males and females, and their willingness to provide misleading information in the future, about the attractiveness of their face, as well as their weight, height, age, physical condition, and hair color, in order to attract a date. Deceptive self-enhancement was particularly likely when a potential date was physically attractive (Rowatt, Cunningham, & Druen, 1998, 1999).

Cosmetic surgery also may be undertaken to increase attractiveness (Birtchnell,Whitfield, & Lacey, 1990). Cash and Horton (1983), for example, had different groups of judges rate photos of 14 preoperative or postoperative rhinoplasty patients. Sixty-four percent of the women who received nose resculpting received higher physical attractiveness ratings as a result of the procedure.

If it is not disclosed to a potential date, cosmetic surgery may be seen as a form of deception, in that the individual's phenotype does not reflect his or her genotype. Although studies have been conducted on those seeking cosmetic surgery, relatively little is known about the social perception of such individuals (Haiken, 1997; Harre, 1991). To explore that issue, Cunningham, Bettler, and Beggan (2000c) presented subjects with scenarios such as the following:

> A friend is about to introduce you to a woman whom you've never seen before. She is in her early 20s, white, and a college student. Your friend also tells you that the woman you're about to meet had plastic surgery to make her nose look smaller. What's your impression of this person before you ever actually meet her?

Subjects indicated their perceptions of the woman on such dimensions as physical attractiveness, happiness in romantic relationships, social climbing, and deceptiveness on 7-point scales. In addition to rhinoplasty, scenarios were presented concerning a woman who used cosmetic makeup to make her nose look smaller, who wore foam rubber pads inside her bra to increase her breast size from a 34B to a 36C, or who had surgical breast implants to increase her breast size by the same amount. Preliminary analyses were conducted on 51 males and 45 females surveyed to date. Both rhinoplasty and augmentation mammoplasty were associated with significantly greater perceptions of physical attractiveness, but not of increased happiness in romantic relationships. In addition, the self-enhancement procedures also entailed some stigma, including increased perceptions of social climbing and deceptiveness. The use of surgical procedures to enhance the attractiveness of the nose and breasts was seen as more deceptive than the use of nonpermanent procedures.

The social perception of surgical procedures to improve appearance depends, in part, on the motive and circumstances of the patient (Albino & Tedesco, 1988). An additional condition in Cunningham, Bettler, and Beggan (2000c) asked individuals' perceptions concerning a person who underwent surgical procedures to restore the appearance of the nose or breast after a disfiguring injury. A woman whose use of cosmetic surgery was due to events outside of her personal control was seen as substantially less deceptive than one who uses makeup, pads, or surgery for self-enhancement.

The effects of appearance-enhancing intention on the social perception of those who have plastic surgery are similar to the perception of those with suntans. Miller, Ashton, McHoskey, and Gimbel (1990) reported that those who happened to acquire a deep suntan as a result of playing tennis or softball outdoors were regarded as athletic, friendly, and attractive. But people who deliberately sought to acquire a suntan were seen as less attractive and more vain than their counterparts. Such results are reminiscent of Dermer and Thiel (1975), who found that exceptionally attractive women were perceived to be more vain, bourgeois, and likely to have a divorce or affair than less attractive women. Thus, while good grooming is desirable, those who engage in extraordinary levels of self-modifications to enhance their physical attractiveness may risk activating intrasexual competition among members of their own sex (Wolf, 1991), and suspicion of fraud by members of the opposite sex (Rowatt, Cunningham, Rowatt, Druen, & Miles, 2000), leading to repulsion rather than attraction.

VARIABLES THAT MODERATE THE IMPACT OF PHYSICAL APPEARANCE IN MATE SELECTION

The Multiple Fitness model suggests that neonate, sexual maturity, senescence, expressive, and grooming attributes all contribute to the perception of attractiveness. But an underlying premise of the model is that attraction is in the service of adaptation and increased inclusive fitness, including survival, well-being, and the reproductive success of oneself and one's offspring. Other information that has a bearing on fitness might override physical attractiveness cues, even in species regarded as less flexible than humans.

Social Information and Mate Copying

Female Trinidadian guppies, for example, prefer to mate with brightly orange-colored males, who often behave more boldly in the presence of predators than their muted conspecifics. Female guppies preferred bolder males, irrespective of their coloration, when given the opportunity to observe the male's behavior toward a potential fish predator (Godin & Dugatkin, 1996). Female guppies also tend to engage in "mate-copying" or displaying increased mating interest with a male who receives disproportionate attention from other females. In an experimental treatment in which less colorful males appeared to be "popular" with another female, female guppies preferred the less physically attractive male in two out of three conditions. When males differed by 40% orange body color, however, observer females preferred the more colorful male and did not copy the mate choice of other females. Thus, imitation can override genetic preferences when the differences in physical attractiveness are small to moderate, but genetically based preferences for ideal appearance may override imitation effects when the difference in physical attractiveness is large (Dugatkin, 1996).

Social information, including evaluations of a potential date's desirability made by other people, may be as influential as objective physical attractiveness in human mate choice. Graziano, Jensen-Campbell, Shebilski, and Lundgren (1993) reported that social influence caused attractiveness ratings to shift a few points, especially among females. Females may be more influenced by social information than males, because a portion of the criteria that females emphasize when selecting mates, such as a male's ambitiousness, reliability, and acceptance by the larger community, are intangible, which increases the need for social comparison information.

Cunningham, Dugatkin, and Lundy (2000d) directly examined mate-copying in humans. In Study 1, males and females reported their interest in short-term and long-term relationships and their social perceptions of six targets. The targets received high, medium, or low levels of attention from peers, and were high or low in physical attractiveness. Consistent with the mate-copying behavior of other species, subjects reported greater mating interest in popular members of the opposite sex, independent of the significant impact of physical attractiveness. This tendency was particularly evident in females, and was associated with the attribution of greater social skills, sense of humor, and wealth to the socially popular mate. Study 2 manipulated peer attention, physical attractiveness, and wealth due to a parent's luck. Peer attention again increased mating interest, especially for females. Physical attractiveness and wealth also influenced responses, but peer attention and perceived personality were more reliable predictors of mating interest.

The apparent plasticity of attraction responses is not in conflict with evolutionary interpretations of the perceptions of physical attractiveness. Evolved dispositions orient the individual to some basic dimensions of a fit mate, but awareness of the ecology, the behavior of other people, and one's own goals, all may influence responses to physical features. It is conceivable that the perceiver might be capable of ignoring neoteny features if the perceiver were certain about a target's youth and openness, or partially disregard sexual maturity cues if there was other evidence of strength, fertility or virility, and extroversion. Information about a target's friendliness and emotional stability might suffice instead of expressive features, and certainty about a target's social status, cultural adaptation, and conscientiousness might substitute for grooming cues. But because physical attractiveness is highly vivid, the alternative information would have to be equally salient to override the impact of appearance.

Gender and Care Variables

The mate copying results described above were consistent with contemporary discussions of mate selection, which often emphasize gender differences in the relative importance of physical attractiveness versus other mate selection variables. Ben Hamida, Mineka, and Bailey (1998), for example, recently suggested: "Men . . . tend to value attractiveness and youth in their mates much more than do women. These cues are likely to have been associated with higher fertility, reproductive potential, and health" (p. 955). That males rate physical attractiveness as more important than do women is well established (Buss, 1989; Feingold, 1990), even if the causes are not (Eagly & Wood, 1999; Howard, Blumstein, & Schwartz, 1987; Rosenblatt, 1974). But are the two genders really so different; is physical attractiveness truly valued "much more" by men?

In the Ben Hamida and colleagues study, physical attractiveness ranked number 14 out of 62 items in terms of what men were looking for in a woman. Using a similar approach, Cunningham and colleagues (1999) surveyed 157 men and 230 women on the importance of 195 mate selection criteria in 25 categories. They found that genders were much more similar than different in the value that they place on various qualities in a romantic partner. Across the 25 mate preference categories collected in this study, the correlation between male and female mean importance ratings for mate selection criteria was $r = .98$, $p < .0001$. Men were found to be more interested in care variables, such as social support (ranked 2nd of 25) than in physical appearance (ranked 5th). They valued a woman who "accepts you for who you are" more than one who is physically attractive. Similarly, they preferred a woman who "makes you feel unique and special" more than one with "physical attractiveness." Men also placed just as much importance on the characteristic of "honesty" and on someone who "tells you her innermost thoughts" as on physical attractiveness. Women also valued social support (ranked 2nd) as much as did men, and rated physical attractiveness (ranked 7th) nearly as important as affluence (ranked 5th) in a prospective mate. Similar analyses, conducted using Buss and colleagues' (1990) 37 culture data, produced similarities between male and female mate selection criteria rankings that ranged from r = .63 in Nigeria to r = .97 in Brazil, with a mean of r = .87 across cultures.

The foregoing is not to say that the genders do not differ somewhat in their mate selection criteria, or that physical attractiveness is unimportant. But these results suggest that males are not excessively preoccupied with physical attractiveness, nor are females indifferent to superficial charms. Similar conclusions were offered by Sprecher (1989), who experimentally manipulated written descriptions of an opposite sex target's physical attractiveness, earning potential, and expressiveness. She found that women and men were both most affected by physical appearance descriptions when judging the attractiveness of the person, but females believed that they were more affected by earning potential and expressiveness than by attractiveness. Using a comparable but forced choice approach, Cunningham and colleagues (2000b) manipulated physical attractiveness using photographs and written descriptions of personality and wealth. For a date and for marriage, both males and females were more likely to choose a person who was physically attractive and possessed a good personality, but was financially disadvantaged, over one who was physically attractive and wealthy but had an undesirable personality, or had wealth and a good personality but was physically unattractive.

CONCLUSION

This chapter outlined the Multiple Fitness model within the context of Western attitudes toward physiognomic assessment and physical attractiveness. The model suggests that the perception of physical attractiveness evolved to aid social decision-making, such as mate choice, through the perception of a variety of desirable features conveying possible fitness qualities in the target. Evidence was described that indicated that exceptional attractiveness for a romantic relationship involves a combination of features conveying youthfulness, sexual maturity, expressiveness, and cultural adaptation. The attractiveness of some facial qualities appears to be universal, but specific ecological and individual variables may influence the perception of other features and attributes, especially with targets lacking perfectly ideal qualities. The Multiple Fitness model suggests that perceivers often desire exceptional physical qualities, including those that might appear to be contradictory, such as neoteny and sexual maturity, or maturity and expressiveness. But the Multiple Fitness model also suggests that there is some variability in the importance placed on some attractiveness dimensions, due to personality, mood, or hormonal fluctuations.

The Multiple Fitness model was contrasted with approaches to attractiveness based on averageness and symmetry. Our review of the literature on optimally exaggerated, symmetrical, and average features suggests that each may contribute to attractiveness. Extreme asymmetry may cause extreme unattractiveness. Attractiveness appears to increase with increasing symmetry, but perfect symmetry does not appear to produce perfect attractiveness. Computer averaging of faces produces moderate-size facial features that are more attractive than a face containing such unattractive features as small eyes, a large nose, and low cheekbones. However, a symmetrical or averaged face does not appear to be as attractive as a face possessing specific exceptional features, such as large eyes and a small nose, which convey neoteny, and high cheekbones in women and a large chin in men, which convey sexual maturity. Given structural facial features that are optimally attractive, maximum physical attractiveness appears to be attained through a positive nonverbal facial expression, and grooming qualities that are prescribed by the culture.

The Multiple Fitness model notes that the relation between genotype, phenotype, and social outcomes may be confounded because appearance involves impression management and deception. In part because of such realities, and in part because of other priorities, neither males nor females rank physical attractiveness as most important when selecting a mate. And, the impact of physical attractiveness cues may be altered when other information about the target is available.

The Multiple Fitness approach suggested that different aspects of beauty might serve as indicators for different types of desirable qualities. Fitness as a reproductive partner, conveyed by neonate and sexual maturity cues, does not entail fitness as a life partner, which requires consideration of expressive, grooming, and even senescence cues, if the perceiver is older than 25 years of age. As a consequence, beauty may serve as an honest advertisement of reproductive quality (Thornhill & Grammar, 1999) but certainly not of personal compatibility. Lester Burnham and Humbert Humbert, to their detriment, were slow to realize that irony.

With its emphasis on the attractiveness of potentially contradictory facial dimensions; with its recognition of both universally desirable qualities and self-presentation elements that are unique to specific times and places; with its acknowledgment of some between-individual and intraindividual variability, the Multiple Fitness perspective may not satisfy the demands of parsimony. But it may explain why different commentators on the nature of beauty reach different conclusions, and serve to reflect a portion of the complex interaction of primitive needs, sophisticated preferences, and personal trade-offs (Cunningham, Druen, & Barbee, 1997) that influence the perception of human facial physical attractiveness.

NOTES

1. Grammar and Thornhill's (1994) study included other measurements such as eye size, but they were not reliable predictors of attractiveness. This may have occurred because only 16 targets of each gender were used. The use of a large number of targets is helpful to avoid weak results and confounds. Obtaining a linear relation between any individual feature measurement and a global attractiveness rating requires that the desirable features not be negatively correlated with each other, nor positively correlated with undesirable features. If only a few of the men in a sample of targets had large chins, and each of them happened to also have a large nose that lowered their attractiveness rating, for example, the relation between large chin size and male attractiveness would be attenuated. This potential problem can be prevented if a broad sample of targets is employed, and includes a substantial percentage with extremely high attractiveness ratings (ideally, 9 and 10 on a 10-point scale) and extremely low attractiveness ratings (Cunningham, Barbee, & Pike, 1990). Such an approach helps ensure that a wide range of feature sizes is included (very small to very large chins) and that artifactual confounds are minimized (i.e., there would be enough men with large chins who have both small and large noses).

2. The methods used to solicit ratings of faces sometimes can obscure the underlying social perceptions. In the nonverbal expression of anger, for example, the eyebrows are generally drawn down and the lips are often compressed tightly together (Izard, 1971). The expression of anger is often involved in the establishment of dominance. Perceptions of dominance are usually rated on a bipolar scale ranging from dominance at one end to submissiveness at the other. A photo of an unsmiling face with low eyebrows and thin lips tends to be rated, or dichotomously chosen, as more dominant than a face with higher eyebrows, fuller lips, or a large smile (Keating, 1985; Keating, Mazur, & Segall, 1981a; Keating et al., 1981b). But merely because ratings of faces with high eyebrows and uncompressed lips were rated as low in dominance does not mean that such faces conveyed submissiveness, in the sense of meekness and compliance. In Keating (1985), for instance, dominance ratings were higher on a 7-point dominance-submissiveness rating scale for faces with the "mature" individual features of small eyes (M = 4.66) than large eyes (M = 3.65), thin lips (M = 4.32) than thick lips (M = 3.53,) and the combination of thick eyebrows, small eyes, thin lips, and a square jaw (M = 5.8) than the opposite combination of thin eyebrows, large eyes, thick lips, and a round jaw (M = 3.2). Note, however, that ratings of the "immature" features were quite close to the midpoint of the bipolar rating scale, which was labeled "neither dominant nor submissive." Asymmetrical relations, such as the stronger impact of "mature" features on perceived dominance, and the weaker impact of "immature" features on that dimension, may not be apparent when data are reported in the form of correlations.

REFERENCES

Albino, J. E., & Tedesco, L. A. (1988). The role of perception in the treatment of facial appearance. In T. R. Alley (Ed.). *Social and applied aspects of perceiving faces* (pp. 217–238). Mahwah, NJ: Erlbaum.

Alexander, J., & Stimson, W. H. (1988). Sex hormones and the course of parasitic infection. *Parasitology Today, 4*, 189–193.

Alley, T. R. (1983). Infantile head shape as an elicitor of adult protection. *Merrill-Palmer Quarterly, 29*, 411–427.

Alley, T. R., & Cunningham, M. R. (1991). Averaged faces are attractive, but very attractive faces are not average. *Psychological Science, 2*, 123–125.

Anderson, J. L., Crawford, C. B., Nadeau, J., & Lindberg, T. (1992). Was the Duchess of Windsor right? A cross-cultural review of the socioecology of ideals of female body shape. *Ethology and Sociobiology, 13*, 197–227.

Andersson, M.B. (1994). *Sexual selection.* Princeton, NJ: Princeton University Press.

Aron, E., & Aron, A. (1987). The influence of inner state on self-reported long-term happiness. *Journal of Humanistic Psychology, 27*, 248–270.

Aronson, E. (1969). Some antecedents of interpersonal attraction. In W. J. Arnold & D. Levine (Eds.), *Nebraska Symposium on Motivation* (pp. 143–177). Lincoln: University of Nebraska Press.

Ashmore, R. D., Solomon, M. R., & Longo, L. C. (1996). Thinking about fashion models' looks: A multidimensional approach to the structure of perceived physical attractiveness. *Personality and Social Psychology Bulletin, 22*, 1083–1104.

Baerends, G. P., & Drent, R. H. (1982). The herring gull and its egg: II. The responsiveness to egg-features. *Behaviour, 82*, 416.

Banner, L. W. (1983). *American Beauty.* Chicago: University of Chicago Press.

Bassett, J. F., & Dabbs, J. M. (November 1999). *New directions in eye color research.* Paper presented at the annual conference of the Society for Southeastern Social Psychology, Richmond, VA.

Beck, S., Ward-Hull, C., & McClear, P. (1976). Variables related to women's somatic preferences of the male and female body. *Journal of Personality and Social Psychology, 34*, 1200–1210.

Ben Hamida, S., Mineka, S., & Bailey, J. M. (1998). Sex differences in perceived controllability of mate value: An evolutionary perspective. *Journal of Personality and Social Psychology, 75*, 953–966.

Bernstein, I. H., Tsai-Ding, L., & McClellan, P. (1982). Cross- vs. within-racial judgments of attractiveness. *Perception and Psychophysics, 32*, 495–503.

Berry, D. S. (1991). Attractive faces are not all created equal: Joint effects of facial babyishness and attractiveness on social perception. *Personality and Social Psychology Bulletin, 17,* 523–531.

Berry, D. S., & Brownlow, S. (1989). Were the physiognomists right? Personality correlates of facial babyishness. *Personality and Social Psychology Bulletin, 15*, 266–279.

Berry, D. S., & Landry, J. C. (1997). Facial maturity and daily social interaction. *Journal of Personality and Social Psychology, 72*, 570–580.

Berry, D. S., & McArthur, L. Z. (1985). Some components and consequences of a babyface. *Journal of Personality and Social Psychology, 48*, 312–323.

Berry, D. S., & McArthur, L. Z. (1986). Perceiving character in faces: The impact of age-related craniofacial changes in social perception. *Psychological Bulletin, 100*, 3–18.

Berscheid, E., & Walster, E. (1974). Physical attractiveness. In L. Berkowitz (Ed.), *Advances in experimental social psychology* (Vol. 7, pp. 158–216). New York: Academic Press.

Bielert, C., & Anderson, C. M. (1985). Baboon sexual swellings and male response: A possible operational mammalian supernormal stimulus and response interaction. *International Journal of Primatology, 6*, 377–393.

Birtchnell, S., Whitfield, P., & Lacey, J. H. (1990). Motivational factors in women requesting augmentation and reduction mammaplasty. *Journal of Psychosomatic Research, 34*, 509–514.

Blackford, K.M.H., & Newcomb, A. (1919). *The job, the man, the boss.* Garden City, NY: Doubleday.

Borkan, G. A., Bachman, S. S., & Norris, A. H. (1982). Comparison of visually estimated age with physiologically predicted age as indicators of rates of aging. *Social Science and Medicine, 16*, 197–204.

Burson, N., Carling, R., & Kramlich, D. (1986). *Composites: Computer-generated portraits.* New York: Beech Tree Books.

Buss, D. M. (1989). Sex differences in human mate preferences: Evolutionary hypotheses tested in 37 cultures. *Behavior and Brain Sciences, 12*, 1–49.

Buss, D. M., Abbott, M., Angleitner, A., Asherian, A., Biaggio, A., Blanco-Villasenor, A., Bruchon-Schweitzer, M., Ch'U, H.-Y., Czapinski, J., Deraad, B., Ekehammar, B., El Lohamy, N., Fioravanti, M., Georgas, J., Gjerde, P., Guttman, R., Hazan, F., Iwawaki, S., Janakiramaiah, N., Khosroshani, F., Kreitler, S., Lachenicht, L., Lee, M., Liik, K., Little, B., Mika, S., Moadel-Shahid, M., Moane, G., Montero, M., Mudy-Castle, A. C., Niit, T., Nsenduluka, E., Pienkowski, R., Pirttila-Backman, A. M., Ponce DeLeon, J., Rousseau, J., Runco, M. A., Safir, M. P., Samuels, C., Sanitioso, R., Serpell, R., Smid, N., Spencer, C., Tadinac, M., Todorova, E. N., Troland, K., Van Den Brande, L., Van Heck, G., Van Langenhove, L., & Yang, K. S. (1990). International preferences in selecting mates: A study of 37 cultures. *Journal of Cross-Cultural Psychology, 21*, 5–47.

Campbell, M. R. (1991). *The impact of facial feature attractiveness on helping behavior: A sociobiological examination of males' perception of female faces.* Unpublished master's thesis, University of Louisville.

Cash, T. F., & Horton, C. E. (1983). Aesthetic surgery: Effects of rhinoplasty on the social perception of patients by others. *Plastic and Reconstructive Surgery, 72*, 543–548.

Clark, M. S., & Mills, J. (1993). The difference between communal and exchange relationships: What it is and is not. *Personality and Social Psychology Bulletin, 19*, 684–691.

Cleeton, G. C., & Knight, F. B. (1924). Validity of character judgments based on external criteria. *Journal of Applied Psychology, 8*, 215–231.

Cunningham, M. R. (1981). Sociobiology as a supplementary paradigm for social psychological research. In L. Wheeler (Ed.), *Review of personality and social psychology* (Vol. 2, pp. 69–106). Beverly Hills, CA: Sage.

Cunningham, M. R. (1985). Levites and brother's keepers: A sociobiological perspective on prosocial behavior. *Humboldt Journal of Social Relations, 13*, 35–67.

Cunningham, M. R. (1986). Measuring the physical in physical attractiveness: Quasi-experiments on the sociobiology of female facial beauty. *Journal of Personality and Social Psychology, 50*, 925–935.

Cunningham, M. R. (1988a). Does happiness mean friendliness? Induced mood and heterosexual self-disclosure. *Personality and Social Psychology Bulletin, 14*, 283–297.

Cunningham, M. R. (1988b). What do you do when you're feeling blue? Affect, motivation, and social behavior. *Motivation and Emotion, 12*, 309–331.

Cunningham, M. R., & Barbee, A. P. (2000a). Social support. In S. Hendrick & C. Hendrick (Eds.), *Close relationships: A sourcebook* (pp. 273–286). Thousand Oaks, CA: Sage.

Cunningham, M. R., Barbee, A. P., & Druen, P. B. (1998). Passion lost and found. In J. Harvey (Ed.), *Perspectives on loss: A sourcebook* (pp. 153–169). New York: Wiley.

Cunningham, M. R., Barbee, A. P., Graves, C. R., Lundy, D. E., Lister, S. C., & Rowatt W. (2000b). *Can't buy me love: The effects of male wealth and personal qualities on female attraction.* Unpublished manuscript, University of Louisville.

Cunningham, M. R., Barbee, A. P., & Pike, C. L. (1990). What do women want? Facialmetric assessment of multiple motives in the perception of male facial physical attractiveness. *Journal of Personality and Social Psychology, 59*, 61–72.

Cunningham, M. R., Bettler, R., & Beggan, J. K. (2000c). *Perceptions of women who modify their appearance: Cosmetics, pads and surgery*. Manuscript in preparation, University of Louisville.

Cunningham, M. R., Dugatkin, L. A., & Lundy, D. E. (2000d). *Who's hot and who's not: Peer attention, physical attractiveness, wealth and mate copying in humans.* Manuscript in preparation, University of Louisville.

Cunningham, M. R., Druen, P. B., & Barbee, A. P. (1997). Angels, mentors, and friends: Trade-offs among evolutionary, social, and individual variables in physical appearance. In J. A. Simpson & D. T. Kenrick (Eds.), *Evolutionary social psychology* (pp. 109–140). Mahwah, NJ: Erlbaum.

Cunningham, M. R., Roberts, A. R., Barbee, A. P., Druen, P. B., & Wu, C. (1995). "Their ideas of beauty are, on the whole, the same as ours": Consistency and variability in the cross-cultural perception of female physical attractiveness. *Journal of Personality and Social Psychology, 68*, 261–279.

Cunningham, M. R., Rowatt, T. J., Shamblen, S., Rowatt, W. C., Ault-Gaulthier, L. K., Bettler, R., Miles, S. S, & Barbee, A. P. (1999). *Men and women are from Earth: Life-trajectory dynamics in mate choices.* Manuscript in preparation, University of Louisville.

Darwin, C. (1871, 1901). *The descent of man and selection in relation to sex.* New York: P. F. Collier & Son.

Davidson, R. J., Mednick, D., Moss, E., Saron, C., & Schaffer, C. E. (1987). Ratings of emotion in faces are influenced by the visual field to which stimuli are presented. *Brain and Cognition, 6*, 403–411.

DeHart, D. D., & Cunningham, M. R. (1993, April). *Perceptual correlates of attractiveness judgments and judgments of homosexuality by heterosexual and homosexual males and females.* Paper presented at the annual meeting of the Southeastern Psychological Association, Atlanta, GA.

Dermer, M., & Thiel, D. L. (1975). When beauty may fail. *Journal of Personality and Social Psychology, 31*, 1168–1176.

Deutsch, F. M., LeBaron, D., & Fryer, M. M. (1987). What is in a smile? *Psychology of Women Quarterly, 11*, 341–351.

Dugatkin, L. A. (1996). Interface between culturally based preferences and genetic preferences: Female mate choice in *Poecilia reticulata. Proceedings of the National Academy of Science, 93*, 2770–2773.

Eagly, A. H., Ashmore, R. D., Makhijani, M. G., & Longo, L. C. (1991). What is beautiful is good: A meta-analytic review of research on the physical attractiveness stereotype. *Psychological Bulletin, 110*, 109–128.

Eagly, A. H., & Wood, W. (1999). The origins of sex differences in human behavior: Evolved dispositions versus social roles. *American Psychologist, 54*, 408–423.

Eibl-Ebesfeldt, I. (1989). *Human Ethology*. New York: Aldine DeGruyter.

Enlow, D. M. (1990). *Handbook of facial growth (*3rd ed.). Philadelphia: W. B. Saunders.

Farkas, L. G. (1981). Anthropometry of the head and face in medicine. New York: Elsevier.

Farkas, L. G., Munro, I. R., & Kolar, J. C. (1987). Linear proportions in above- and below-average women's faces. In L. G. Farkas & I. R. Munro (Eds.), *Anthropometric facial proportions in medicine* (pp. 119–129). Springfield, IL: Thomas.

Fauss, R. (1986). Zur Bedeutung des Gesichts fur die Partnerwahl. *Homo, 37*, 188–201.

Feingold, A. (1990). Gender differences in effects of physical attractiveness on romantic attraction: A comparison across five research paradigms. *Journal of Personality and Social Psychology, 59*, 981–993.

Feingold, A. (1992). Good looking people are not what we think. *Psychological Bulletin, 111*, 304–341.

Finch, C. (1975). *The art of Walt Disney*. New York: Abrams.

Ford, C. S., & Beach, F. A. (1951). *Patterns of sexual behavior*. New York: Harper.

Friedman, H., & Zebrowitz, L. A. (1992). The contribution of typical sex differences in facial maturity to sex role stereotypes. *Personality and Social Psychology Bulletin, 18*, 430–438.

Galton, F. (1878). Composite portraits. *Journal of the Anthropological Institute of Great Britian and Ireland, 8*, 132–142.

Gangestad, S. W., & Buss, D. M. (1993). Pathogen prevalence and human mate preferences. *Ethology and Sociobiology, 14*, 89–96.

Gangestad, S. W., & Simpson, J. A. (2000). The evolution of human mating: Trade-offs and strategic pluralism. *Behavioral and Brain Sciences, 23*, 573–644.

Gangestad, S. W., & Thornhill, R. (1997a). The evolutionary psychology of extrapair sex: The role of fluctuating asymmetry. *Evolution and Human Behavior, 18*, 69–88.

Gangestad, S. W., & Thornhill, R. (1997b). Human sexual selection and developmental stability. In J. Simpson & D. Kenrick (Eds.), *Evolutionary social psychology* (pp. 169–196). Mahwah, NJ: Erlbaum.

Gangestad, S. W., Thornhill, R., & Yeo, R. A. (1994). Facial attractiveness, developmental stability, and fluctuating asymmetry. *Ethology and Sociobiology, 15*, 73–85.

Godin, J. J., & Dugatkin, L. A. (1996). Female mating preference for bold males in the guppy, *Poecilia reticulata. Proceedings of the National Academy of Science, 93*, 10262–10267.

Goldstein, A. G. (1983). Behavioral scientists' fascination with faces. *Journal of Nonverbal Behavior, 7*, 223–225.

Gould, S. J. (1981). *The mismeasure of man.* New York: W. W. Norton.

Grammar, K., & Thornhill, R. (1994). Human (*Homo sapiens*) facial attractiveness and sexual selection: The role of symmetry and averageness. *Journal of Comparative Psychology, 108*, 233–242.

Grammar, K., & Thornhill, R. (1999). The body and face of woman: One ornament that signals quality? *Evolution and Human Behavior, 20*, 105–120.

Graziano, W., Brothen, T., & Berscheid, E. (1978). Height and attraction: Do men and women see eye-to-eye? *Journal of Personality, 46*, 128–145.

Graziano, W. G., Jensen-Campbell, L., Shebilski, L., & Lundgren, S. (1993). Social influence, sex differences and judgments of beauty. Putting the "interpersonal" back in interpersonal attraction. *Journal of Personality and Social Psychology, 65*, 522–531.

Guthrie, R. D. (1976). *Body hot spots: The anatomy of human social organs and behavior.* New York: Van Norstrand Reinhold.

Haiken, E. (1997). *Venus envy: A history of cosmetic surgery.* Baltimore: Johns Hopkins University Press.

Harre, R. (1991). *Physical being: A theory for a corporeal psychology.* New York: Routledge.

Hassebrauck, M. (1998). The visual process method: A new method to study physical attractiveness. *Evolution and Human Behavior, 19*, 111–123.

Henss, R. (1991). Perceiving age and attractiveness in facial photographs. *Journal of Applied Social Psychology, 21*, 933–946.

Hess, L. H. (1965). Attitude and pupil size. *Scientific American, 212*, 46–54.

Hildebrant, K. A., & Fitzgerald, H. (1983). The infant's physical attractiveness: Its effects on bonding and attachment. *Infant Mental Health Journal, 4*, 3–12.

Howard, J. A., Blumstein, P., & Schwartz, P. (1987). Social or evolutionary theories? Some observations on preferences in human mate selection. *Journal of Personality and Social Psychology, 53*, 194–200.

Hull, C. L. (1928). *Aptitude testing.* Yonkers-on-Hudson, NY: World Book.

Izard, C. E. (1971). *The face of emotion.* New York: Appleton Century Crofts.

Jackson, L. A. (1992). *Physical appearance and gender: Sociobiological and sociocultural perspectives.* Albany, State University of New York.

Jensen-Campbell, L. A., Graziano, W. G., & West, S. G. (1995). Dominance, prosocial orientation, and female preferences: Do nice guys really finish last? *Journal of Personality and Social Psychology, 68*, 427–440.

Jones, D. (1995). Sexual selection, physical attractiveness, and facial neoteny: Cross-cultural evidence and implications. *Current Anthropology, 36*, 723–748.

Jones, D., & Hill, K. (1993). Criteria of facial attractiveness in five populations. *Human Nature, 4*, 271–296.

Jones, J. M., & Hochner, A. R. (1973). Racial differences in sports activities: A look at the self-paced versus reactive hypothesis. *Journal of Personality and Social Psychology, 27*, 86–95.

Jones, K. L. (1996). *Smith's recognizable patterns of human malformation.* (5th ed.). Philadelphia: W. B. Saunders.

Johnson, V. S., & Franklin, M. (1993). Is beauty in the eye of the beholder? *Ethology and Sociobiology, 14,* 183–199.

Kalick, S. M., Zebrowitz, L. A., Langlois, J. H., & Johnson, R. M. (1998). Does human facial attractiveness honestly advertise health? *Psychological Science, 9,* 8–13.

Keating, C. F. (1985). Gender and the physiognomy of dominance and attractiveness. *Social Psychology Quarterly, 48,* 61–70.

Keating, C. F., Mazur, A., & Segall, M. H. (1981a). A cross-cultural exploration of physiognomic traits of dominance and happiness. *Ethology and Sociobiology, 2,* 41–48.

Keating, C. F., Mazur, A., Segall, M. H., Cysneiros, P. G., Divale, W. T., Kilbride, J. E., Komin, S., Leahy, P., Thurman, B., & Wirsing, R. (1981b). Culture and the perception of social dominance from facial expression. *Journal of Personality and Social Psychology, 40,* 615–626.

Keating, C. F., Randall, D., &. Kendrick, T. (1999). Presidential physiognomies: Altered images, altered perceptions. *Political Psychology, 20,* 593–610.

Kenrick, D. T., & Keefe, R. C. (1992). Age preferences in mates reflect sex differences in human reproductive strategies. *Behavioral and Brain Sciences, 15,* 75–133.

Kenrick, D. T., Groth, G. E., Trost, M. R., & Sadalla, E. K. (1993). Integrating evolutionary and social exchange perspectives on relationships: Effects of gender, self-appraisal, and involvement level on mate selection criteria. *Journal of Personality and Social Psychology, 64,* 951–969.

Kowner, R. (1996). Facial asymmetry and attractiveness judgment in developmental perspective. *Journal of Experimental Psychology: Human Perception and Performance, 22,* 662–675.

Kraut, R. E., & Johnston, R. E. (1979). Social and emotional messages of smiling: An ethological approach. *Journal of Personality and Social Psychology, 37,* 1539–1553.

Langlois, J. H., Ritter, J. M., Roggman, L. A., & Vaughn, L. S. (1991). Facial diversity and infant preferences for attractive faces. *Developmental Psychology, 27,* 79–84.

Langlois, J. H., & Roggman, L. A. (1990). Attractive faces are only average. *Psychological Science, 1,* 115–121.

Langlois, J. H., Roggman, L. A., Casey, R. J., Ritter, J. M., Rieser-Danner, L. A., & Jenkins, V. Y. (1987). Infant preferences for attractive faces: Rudiments of a stereotype? *Developmental Psychology, 23,* 363–369.

Langlois, J. H., Roggman, L. A., & Musselman, L. (1994). What is average and what is not average about attractive faces? *Psychological Science, 5,* 214–220.

Langlois, J. H., Roggman, L. A., Musselman, L., & Acton, S. (1991). A picture is worth a thousand words: Reply to "On the difficulty of averaging faces." *Psychological Science, 2,* 354–357.

Langlois, J. H., Roggman, L. A., & Rieser-Danner, L. A. (1990). Infants' differential social responses to attractive and unattractive faces. *Developmental Psychology, 26,* 153–159.

Lavater, J. C. (1797). *Essays on physiognomy.* London: H. D. Lymonds.

Lavater, J. C. (1860). *Essays on physiognomy.* New York: R. Worthington.

Lippa, R. (1983). Sex typing and the perception of body outlines. *Journal of Personality, 51,* 667–682.

Livshits, G., & Kobyliansky, E. (1991). Fluctuating asymmetry as a possible measure of developmental homeostasis in humans: A review. *Human Biology, 63,* 441–466.

Lorenz, K. (1943). Die angeborenen Formen moglicher Arfahrung [The innate forms of potential experience]. *Zietschrift fur Tierpsychologie, 5,* 234–409.

Lundy, D. E., Tan, J., & Cunningham, M. R. (1998). Heterosexual romantic preferences: The importance of humor and physical attractiveness for different types of relationships. *Personal Relationships, 5,* 311–325.

Lurie, A. (1981). *The language of clothes.* New York: Random House.

Manning, J. T. (1995). Fluctuating asymmetry and body weight in men and women: Implications for sexual selection. *Ethology and Sociobiology, 16,* 145–153.

Marcus, D. L., & Cunningham, M. R. (2000). *Do pedophiles have aberrant perceptions of adult female facial attractiveness?* Unpublished manuscript, Sam Houston State University.

Maret, S. M., & Harling, C. A. (1985). Cross-cultural perceptions of physical attractiveness: Ratings of photographs of whites by Cruzans and Americans. *Perceptual and Motor Skills, 60,* 163–166.

McArthur, L. Z., & Apatow, K. (1983–1984). Impressions of babyfaced adults. *Social Cognition, 2,* 315–342.

McCabe, V. (1984). Abstract perceptual information for age level: A risk factor for maltreatment. *Child Development, 55,* 267–276.

McLellan, B., & McKelvie, S. J. (1993). Effects of age and gender on perceived facial attractiveness. *Canadian Journal of Behavioural Science, 25,* 135–142.

Mealy, L., Bridgestock, R., & Townsend, G. (1999). Symmetry and perceived facial attractiveness: A monozygotic co-twin comparison. *Journal of Personality and Social Psychology, 76,* 151–158.

Miles, S., & Cunningham, M. R. (1999, June). *Do older women find younger men attractive? The effects of target and participant age on male attractiveness ratings.* Paper presented at the International Network on Personal Relationships, Louisville, KY.

Miller, A. G., Ashton, W. A., McHoskey, J. W., & Gimbel, J. (1990). What price attractiveness? Stereotype and risk factors in suntanning behavior. *Journal of Applied Social Psychology, 20,* 1272–1300.

Moller, A. P., & Pomiankowski, A. (1993). Fluctuating asymmetry and sexual selection. *Genetica, 89,* 267–279.

Moller, A. P., & Swaddle, J. P. (1997). *Asymmetry, developmental stability, and evolution.* Oxford, UK: Oxford University Press.

Morris, D. (1985). *Body watching.* New York: Crown.

Morse, S. J., Gruzen, J., & Reis, H. T. (1976). The nature of equity-restoration: Some approval-seeking considerations. *Journal of Experimental Social Psychology, 12,* 1–8.

Morton, J., & Johnson, M. (1991). The perception of facial structure in infancy. In G. R. Lockhead & J. R. Pomerantz (Eds.), *The perception of structure: Essays in honor of Wendell R. Garner* (pp. 317–325). Washington, DC: American Psychological Association.

Mueser, K. T., Grau, B. W., Sussman, M. S., & Rosen, A. J. (1984). You're only as pretty as you feel: Facial expression as a determinant of physical attractiveness. *Journal of Personality and Social Psychology, 46*, 469–478.

Muscarella, F., & Cunningham, M. R. (1996). The evolutionary significance and social perception of male pattern baldness and facial hair. *Ethology and Sociobiology, 17*, 99–117.

Musselman, L. E., Langlois, J. H., & Roggman, L. A. (1995). Comment on Jones (1995). *Current Anthropology, 36*, 739–740.

Osborne, D. R. (1996). Beauty is as beauty does? Makeup and posture effects on physical attractiveness judgments. *Journal of Applied Social Psychology, 26*, 31–40.

Paterson, D. G. (1930). *Physique and intellect.* New York: Century.

Penton-Voak, I. S., Perrett, D. I., Castles, D. L., Kobayashi, T., Burt, D. M., Murray, L. K., & Minamisawa, R. (1999). Menstrual cycle alters face preference. *Nature, 399*, 741–742.

Perper, T. (1985). *Sex signals: The biology of love.* Philadelphia: Isi Press.

Perrett, D. I., Lee, K. J., Penton-Voak, I., Rowland, D., Yoshikawa, S., Burt, D. M., Henzil, S. P., Castles, D. L., & Akamatsus, S. (1998). Effects of sexual dimorphism on facial attractiveness. *Nature, 394*, 884–887.

Perrett, D. I., May, K. A., & Yoshikawa, S. (1994). Facial shape and judgments of female attractiveness: Preferences for non-average characteristics. *Nature, 386*, 239–242.

Pettijohn, T. F., & Tesser, A. (1999). Popularity in environmental context: Facial feature assessment of American movie actresses. *Media Psychology, 1*, 229–247.

Pittenger, J. B. (1991). On the difficulty of averaging faces: Comments on Langlois and Roggman. *Psychological Science, 2*, 351–357.

Pittenger, J. B., & Shaw, R. E. (1975). Aging faces as viscal-elastic events: Implications for a theory of nonrigid shape perception. *Journal of Experimental Psychology: Human Perception and Performance, 1*, 374–382.

Pollard, J., Shepard, J., & Shepard, J. (1999). Average faces are average faces. *Current Psychology: Developmental, Learning, Personality, and Social, 18*, 98–103.

Pollard, J. S. (1995). Attractiveness of composite faces: A cross-cultural study. *International Journal of Comparative Psychology, 8*, 77–83.

Reidl, B.I.M. (1990). Morphologisch-metrische Merkmale des mannlichen und weiblichen Partnerleitbildes in ihrer Bedeutung fur die Wahl des Ehegatten. *Homo, 41*, 72–85.

Reis, H. T., Wheeler, L., Spiegel, N., Kernis, M. H., Nezlek, J., & Perri, M. (1982). Physical attractiveness in social interaction, II: Why does appearance affect social experience? *Journal of Personality and Social Psychology, 43*, 979–996.

Reis, H. T., Wilson, I. M., Monestere, C., Bernstein, S., Clark, K., Seidl, E., Franco, M., Giogioso, E., Freeman, L., & Radoane, K. (1990). What is smiling is beautiful and good. *European Journal of Social Psychology, 20*, 259–267.

Rhodes, G., Proffitt, F., Grady, J. M., & Sumich, A. (1998). Facial symmetry and the perception of beauty. *Psychonomic Bulletin and Review, 5*, 659–669.

Rhodes, G., Sumich, A., & Byatt, G. (1999). Are average facial configurations attractive only because of their symmetry? *Psychological Science, 10*, 53–59.

Rhodes, G., & Tremewan, T. (1996). Averageness, exaggeration, and facial attractiveness. *Psychological Science, 7*, 105–110.

Rich, M. K., & Cash, T. F. (1993). The American image of beauty: Media representations of hair color for four decades. *Sex Roles, 29*, 113–124.

Richardson, J., & Kroeber, A. L. (1940). Three centuries of women's dress fashions: A quantitative analysis. *Anthropological Records, 5*, 111–153.

Robinson, D. E. (1976). Fashion in shaving and trimming of the beard: The men of the *Illustrated London News*, 1842–1972. *American Journal of Sociology, 81*, 1133–1141.

Rosenblatt, P. C. (1974). Cross-cultural perspective on attraction. In T. Huston (Ed.), *Foundations of interpersonal attraction* (pp. 79–95). New York: Academic Press.

Rowatt, W. C., Cunningham, M. R., & Druen, P. B. (1998). Deception to get a date. *Personality and Social Psychology Bulletin, 24*, 1228–1242.

Rowatt, W. C, Cunningham, M. R., & Druen, P. B. (1999). Lying to get a date: The effect of facial physical attractiveness on the willingness to deceive prospective dating partners. *Journal of Social and Personal Relationships, 16*, 209–223.

Rowatt, W. C., Cunningham, M. R., Rowatt, T. J., Druen, P. B., & Miles, S. S. (2000). *Tactical deception and the suspicion of deception to attract a date.* Unpublished manuscript, Baylor University.

Rowland, W. J. (1989). Mate choice and the supernormality effect in female sticklebacks (*Gasterosteus aculeatus*). *Behavioral Ecology and Sociobiolgy, 24*, 433–438.

Sackheim, H. A., Gur, R.C.J., & Saney, M. C. (1978). Emotions are expressed more intensely on the left side of the face. *Science, 202*, 434–436.

Samuels, C. A., Butterworth, G., Roberts, T., Graupner, L., & Hole, G. (1994). Facial asthetics: Babies prefer attractiveness to symmetry. *Perception, 23*, 823–831.

Secord, P. (1958). Facial features and inference processes in interpersonal perception. In R. Tagiuri & L. Petrullo (Eds.), *Person perception and interpersonal behavior* (pp. 300–315). Stanford, CA: Stanford University Press.

Shackleford, T. K., & Larsen, R. J. (1997). Facial asymmetry as an indicator of psychological, emotional and physiological distress. *Journal of Personality and Social Psychology, 72*, 456–466.

Shackelford, T. K., & Larsen, R. J. (1999). Facial attractiveness and physical health. *Evolution and Human Behavior, 20*, 71–76.

Shepard, J. A., & Strathman, A. J. (1989). Attractiveness and height: The role of stature in dating preference, frequency of dating and perceptions of attractiveness. *Personality and Social Psychology Bulletin, 15*, 617–627.

Silverstein, B. Peterson, B., & Perdue, L. (1986). Some correlates of the thin standard of body attractiveness for women. *International Journal of Eating Disorders, 5*, 895–905.

Simpson, J. A., Gangestad, S. W., Christensen, P. N., & Leck, K. (1999). Fluctuating asymmetry, sociosexuality, and intrasexual competitive tactics. *Journal of Personality and Social Psychology, 76*, 159–172.

Singh, D. (1995). Female judgment of male attractiveness and desirability for relationships: Role of waist-to-hip ratio and financial status. *Journal of Personality and Social Psychology, 69*, 1089–1101.

Singh, D., & Bronstad, P. M. (1997). Sex differences in the anatomical locations of human body scarification and tattooing as a function of pathogen prevalence. *Evolution and Human Behavior, 18*, 403–416.

Singh, D., & Young, R. K. (1995). Body weight, waist-to-hip ratio, breasts, and hips: Role in judgments of female attractiveness and desirability in relationships. *Ethology and Sociobiology, 16*, 483–507.

Sprecher, S. (1989). The importance to males and females of physical attractiveness, earning potential, and expressiveness in initial attraction. *Sex Roles, 21*, 591–607.

Stocker, R. D. (1900). *The human face*. London: H. J. Glaisher.

Swaddle, J. P., & Cuthill, I. C. (1995). Asymmetry and human facial attractiveness: Symmetry may not always be beautiful. *Proceedings of the Royal Society of London, Series B, 261*, 111–116.

Symons, D. (1979). *The evolution of human sexuality*. New York: Oxford University Press.

Tassinary, L. G., & Hansen, K. A. (1998). A critical test of the waist-to-hip-ratio hypothesis of female physical attractiveness. *Psychological Science, 9*, 150–155.

Thakerar, J. N., & Iwawaki, S. (1979). Cross-cultural comparisons in interpersonal attraction of females toward males. *Journal of Social Psychology, 108*, 121–122.

The year of the mole. (1990, Summer). *People*, p. 128.

Thornhill, R., & Gangestad, S. W. (1993). Human facial beauty: Averageness, symmetry, and parasite resistance.*Human Nature, 4*, 237–269.

Thornhill, R., & Gangestad, S. W. (1994). Human fluctuating asymmetry and sexual behavior. *Psychological Science, 5*, 297–302.

Thornhill, R., & Grammar, K. (1999). The body and face of woman: One ornament that signals quality? *Evolution and Human Behavior, 20*, 105–120

Tinbergen, N. (1951). *A study of instinct*. London: Oxford University Press.

Todd, J. T., Mark, L. S., Shaw, R. E., & Pittenger, R. E. (1980). The perception of human growth. *Scientific American, 242*, 132–145.

Trivers, R., Manning, J. T., Thornhill, R., Singh, D., & McGuire, M. (1999). Jamaican symmetry project: Long-term study of fluctuating symmetry in rural Jamaican children. *Human Biology, 71*, 417–430.

Websters 3rd Unabridged Dictionary. (1986). Springfield, MA: Merriam-Webster.

Wiggins, J. S. (1996). An informal history of the interpersonal circumplex tradition. *Journal of Personality Assessment, 66*, 217–233.

Wiggins, J. S., Wiggins, N., & Conger, J. C. (1968) Correlates of heterosexual somatic preference. *Journal of Personality and Social Psychology, 10*, 82–90.

Wiseman, C. V., Gray, J. J., Mosimann, J. E., & Ahrens, A. H. (1992). Cultural expectations of thinness in women: An update. *International Journal of Eating Disorders, 11*, 85–89.

Wolf, N. (1991). *The beauty myth: How images of beauty are used against women*. New York: Morrow.

Wong, D. T., & Cunningham, M. R. (1990, April). *Interior versus exterior beauty: The effects of mood on dating preferences for different types of physically attrac-*

tive women. Paper presented at the Southeastern Psychological Association, Atlanta, GA.

Worthy, M. (1974) *Eye color, sex and races: Keys to human and animal behavior.* Anderson, SC: Droke House.

Zebrowitz, L. A. (1997). *Reading faces: Window to the soul?* Boulder, CO: Westview Press.

Zebrowitz, L. A., Andreoletti, C., Collins, M. A., Lee, S. Y., & Blumenthal, J. (1998). Bright, bad, babyfaced boys: Appearance stereotypes do not always yield self-fulfilling prophecy effects. *Journal of Personality and Social Psychology, 75,* 1300–1320.

Zebrowitz, L. A., & Montepare, J. M. (1992). Impressions of babyfaced individuals across the life span. *Developmental Psychology, 28,* 1143–1152.

Zebrowitz, L. A., Montepare, J. M., & Lee, H. K. (1993). They don't all look alike: Differentiating same vs. other race individuals. *Journal of Personality and Social Psychology, 65,* 85–101.

Zebrowitz, L. A., Olson, K., & Hoffman, K. (1993). Stability of babyfaceness and attractiveness across the life span. *Journal of Personality and Social Psychology, 64,* 453–466.

Zebrowitz, L. A., Voinescu, L., & Collins, M. A. (1996). "Wide-eyed" and "crooked-faced": Determinants of perceived and real honesty across the lifespan. *Personality and Social Psychology Bulletin, 22,* 1258–1269.

CHAPTER 8

Cultural Perspectives on Facial Attractiveness

Karen K. Dion

Do cultural factors contribute to understanding the psychology of facial attractiveness? Among perceivers from different societies and from different ethnocultural groups within a given society, is beauty in the "eye of the beholder"? Or, do perceivers from diverse groups share a similar vision of beauty? To address these questions, this chapter examines the discriminability of facial attractiveness and degree of interjudge consensus among perceivers from diverse ethnocultural groups when judging members of their own and/or other groups. Not only do perceivers judge others' attractiveness, they may also form inferences about traits and other personal characteristics based on an individual's appearance. Considerable empirical evidence indicates that facial attractiveness affects evaluations of others. However, much of this research has been conducted in the United States and in Canada. Does facial attractiveness have the same evaluative impact across culturally diverse societies? This issue is the focus of subsequent sections of this chapter.

DISCRIMINATING DIFFERENCES IN FACIAL ATTRACTIVENESS

Several studies have found that perceivers from different ethnocultural groups discriminated differences in facial attractiveness within and across various social categories, such as age and/or sex of stimulus person (e.g., Cross &

Cross, 1971; Maret, 1983; Maret & Harling, 1985). Bernstein, Lin, and McClellan (1982) suggested that two components were relevant for examining perceivers' judgments of the attractiveness of members of their own and other groups; namely, perceived variation in the attractiveness of the stimulus faces and the criteria (e.g., specific facial features, facial dimensions) forming the basis for attractiveness ratings. They investigated whether a) greater variation in facial attractiveness was reported for judgments of own versus other group members and b) there were differences in the criteria used by perceivers from different groups to judge facial attractiveness. In their first experiment, white American university students and Chinese students from Taiwan studying in an American university rated four sets of 100 facial photographs (college yearbook photographs of Chinese males, Chinese females, white males, and white females). In a second experiment, the investigators compared the ratings made by black judges and white judges asked to evaluate the facial attractiveness of 100 stimulus persons from each of four groups (college yearbook photographs): black females, black males, white females, white males. The findings indicated that judges from different ethnic groups perceived comparable own-group versus other-group variability in facial attractiveness. According to Bernstein and his colleagues, the pattern of results also suggested that the criteria for making these judgments were somewhat different, particularly comparing the ratings made by white judges and Chinese judges. These researchers did not, however, specifically analyze what aspects of the facial stimuli contributed to the attractiveness ratings for each group of judges.

Zebrowitz, Montepare, and Lee (1993) also found that raters made differentiated judgments of the facial attractiveness of stimulus persons from diverse groups. These investigators asked university students from three groups (black and white undergraduates from the United States and undergraduate students in Korea) to judge male stimulus persons (slides of faces) from these three groups on two dimensions of facial appearance, one of which was attractiveness, and on several personality traits. Except for black judges who judged both black and Korean stimulus faces, all other groups of judges rated faces from one group of stimulus persons. One issue examined was whether perceivers might make greater differentiations (that is, use more levels of the rating scale) when judging faces from their own group compared to faces from other groups. On judgments of attractiveness, however, there were no differences in own-group versus other-group differentiation or in the variability of these judgments. In summary, there is evidence that among perceivers, differences in facial attractiveness are discriminable, not only when judging members of one's own group, but also when judging individuals from other groups.

JUDGING FACIAL ATTRACTIVENESS: CULTURAL DIVERSITY OR CONSENSUS?

The criteria for judging physical attractiveness may depend on culture-related preferences. If judgments of physical attractiveness are context-specific, the criteria used to judge attractiveness may emerge from particular cultural traditions and vary across societies. Consistent with this perspective, Ford and Beach (1951) examined ethnographic accounts of diverse cultural groups and concluded that there was little evidence of universal criteria for defining sexual attractiveness. Rather, the evidence suggested considerable variation in the physical features desired in a mate. The ethnographic material they cited in support of this conclusion for the most part documented different preferences for physical features such as weight or body build, but there were some references to culture-related differences in the desirability of specific facial features and skin color. For example, one ethnographer cited by Ford and Beach noted that "Europeans are most emphatically not envied for their blond coloring . . . condolences were offered to me on two occasions on account of my pallor . . ." (p. 88).

However, more recent conceptual accounts of the nature of facial attractiveness have contended that the criteria for judging attractiveness are the same or similar across perceivers, reflecting processes such as averaging and responses to supernormal facial features, as discussed in several chapters in the present volume. If the criteria for judging attractiveness are based on aspects of information processing and/or cues with adaptive significance from the perspective of human evolution, there should be a high degree of consensus about judgments of facial attractiveness among judges from different ethnocultural groups within a given society and among judges from different societies. Judgments of attractiveness should be relatively context-independent, since these judgments emerge from processes that do not depend on particular cultural traditions. Some cultural differences might be expected in this framework, but at the core, perceivers from different cultural traditions should agree in their judgments.

Several researchers have examined interjudge agreement by asking university students to rate the facial attractiveness of stimulus persons from their own and other cultural groups. Some of these comparisons have involved native versus foreign-born students or students from different ethnocultural backgrounds within a given society, while other studies have looked at interjudge agreement across raters in different societies. Thakerar and Iwawaki (1979) compared the ratings made by English females to ratings made by a combined sample of Chinese and Indian female judges. The latter group was studying in England. All judges rated the attractiveness of 10 facial black-and-white photographs of Greek men. The two samples agreed in their rankings of attractiveness (rho = .89).

Cunningham, Roberts, Barbee, Druen, and Wu (1995) conducted a series of studies to examine the degree of consensus in ratings of women's facial attractiveness among university students from different racial and cultural groups. In Study 1, the specific facial stimuli judged included photographs of female beauty pageant participants from different groups (Asian, black, Hispanic, and white) plus photographs of white college women. Judges in Study 1 consisted of white college students and students from other societies studying in the United States, specifically from Asian societies (predominantly Japan) and a small sample of Hispanic students. Interjudge agreement between groups was assessed based on the average rating of each photograph made by Asian, Hispanic, and white judges. There was a high level of agreement between these different groups of judges (mean correlation of .93). In a second study, Cunningham and his colleagues found that Taiwanese male and female university students similarly showed high levels of agreement with ratings made by the other three groups of judges (mean $r = .91$). Finally, in a third study, black and white male university students were asked to rate the facial attractiveness of black college-aged women. The two groups showed a high level of consensus ($r = .94$).

Other researchers also have found interrater agreement across judges from different groups. As described previously, Zebrowitz and her colleagues (1993) compared black, Korean, and white students' ratings of the facial attractiveness of stimulus persons from their own or other groups. The average correlation for within-group judgments of attractiveness was .78, compared to .64 for between-group ratings. The latter value, though lower than within-roup agreement, nonetheless indicates substantial agreement. These re - searchers also examined the structural features of the faces that contributed to attractiveness ratings. They concluded that there was little between-group consistency in the specific facial features that predicted attractiveness ratings, at least among the dimensions assessed.

The research presented so far has examined whether judges from different ethnocultural groups within a given society and/or judges from different societies agree on ratings of facial attractiveness. Those asked to judge the facial stimuli typically have been university students. It is likely that university students as a group experience greater exposure to diverse aspects of popular culture, including various media that present contemporary ideals of facial appearance. Exposure to Western media may be a factor contributing to high levels of interjudge agreement on ratings of attractiveness among students from different societies. In their sample of Taiwanese students, Cunningham and his colleagues (1995) compared interjudge agreement for students reporting lower versus higher Western media exposure and fluency with English. These two groups did not show differential consensus in their attractiveness ratings. As Cunningham and his coauthors acknowledged, however, it is difficult to completely eliminate the potential effect of Western media exposure on judgments of attractiveness. The investigation of judgments of attractiveness by participants from groups that are relatively isolated from Western cultural influences, either direct or indirect, is particularly important.

Research conducted by Jones (1996) addressed this issue. Jones examined several questions in his program of research, including the extent of agreement on judgments of facial attractiveness among respondents from five different societies: the United States, Brazil, Russia, Paraguay (specifically, the Ache Indians), and Venezuela (specifically, the Hiwi Indians). Judges from the United States and from Russia were university students. The Brazilian sample of judges was more diverse, including university students and respondents from the general population.

The two other samples are of particular interest. These groups were chosen because they had relatively little contact with other groups and therefore provided the opportunity to assess interjudge consensus on evaluations of facial attractiveness among communities that until recently have been comparatively isolated. As described by Jones (1996), the Ache Indians of Paraguay are a group of former hunter-gatherers, now residing in five communities that differ in degree of acculturation. Although at the time of his research, the Ache had seen the faces of non-Ache individuals, this contact was not extensive, and for the most part, consisted of missionaries and anthropologists working in the communities. Similarly, the Hiwi Indians from Venezuela, much like the Ache, had not been subject to outside influences until recently.

Facial photographs were taken of volunteers of both sexes from the United States, Brazil, and the Ache community. Various anthropometric measurements plus demographic background information were also collected from these volunteers. The stimulus photographs were rated by individuals from the five groups studied. Since it seemed likely that the Hiwi and Ache samples might have greater difficulty using a standard rating scale given their lack of familiarity with this type of task, a successive sorting procedure was employed across all five samples.

Each rater was asked for a series of judgments of a set of nine facial photographs at a time of persons of the other sex randomly chosen from a specific stimulus set (e.g., photographs of Brazilian males). The nine stimulus photographs were presented using the format of a 3 x 3 grid, with respondents successively ranking first each column and then each row of three photographs, ultimately resulting in a ranked sorting of these stimuli from 1 to 9. This procedure continued for each rater until fewer than nine photographs remained in the stimulus set.

Since there was a greater age range represented in the photographs of the Ache compared to that of the American and Brazilian photographs (university students), male and female Ache photographs were divided into four subgroups by age, with the ranking task conducted within each subgroup. As Jones (1996) acknowledged, one potential problem with this approach was that the attractiveness level of the other faces might systematically affect the ranking of a given photograph, leading to its being ranked either lower or higher than it might have been without this constraint. However, given the wide age range represented, some grouping by age group was necessary. Even with this age grouping, the age range in some of the subgroups of photos rated was substantial, for example, 14–33 years and 22–40 years, respectively, among two subgroups of Ache females (Table 3.3, p. 59). Thus, it is possible that even within each subgroup, the range of attractiveness differed for the

Ache stimulus persons (compared to American and Brazilian stimulus photographs). Finally, the Ache respondents who made the attractiveness judgments were from a different village from the Ache stimulus persons depicted in the photographs, and the village from which the raters came was described by Jones as "the most isolated and least acculturated."

Turning first to within-group agreement, the average Spearman's rank correlations indicated significant agreement within each group of raters (e.g., Russians, Americans, Hiwi) in standards of attractiveness, with *r*'s ranging mostly from .2 to .4. The magnitude of these correlations provides evidence for consensus among group members but also indicates a sizable amount of individual differences in the relative rankings.

Comparisons between groups of raters from different cultural contexts revealed an intriguing pattern (Jones, 1996, Table 3.4, pp. 60–61). As noted above, judges from five groups (United States, Brazil, Russia, Ache Indians, and Hiwi Indians) evaluated the attractiveness of Brazilian, American (United States), and Ache stimulus persons. The stimulus persons from the United States included in these analyses were mostly of European descent. Moreover, the number of raters for Hiwi Indians was small ($n = 12$); however, for the Ache, the overall sample was much larger ($n = 95$), though it should be remembered that a particular group of stimulus photographs (e.g., Ache males, Brazilian females) was judged by a subset of this sample. The three Western samples showed substantial agreement with each other in their judgments of attractiveness (average correlation of .66). Moreover, there was moderate agreement between the Ache and Hiwi samples (average correlation of .43). However, the two most culturally different groups of judges; namely, the Western cluster (consisting of the United States, Brazilian, and Russian judges) on the one hand and the Ache and Hiwi cluster on the other hand showed, on average, much less consensus in their judgments of attractiveness (average correlation of .14).

Jones (1996) acknowledged the occurrence of cross-cultural variability in standards of attractiveness. He suggested that this diversity was, however, compatible with the presence of "specialized naturally selected mechanisms" to evaluate attractiveness. Moreover, he contended that the agreement between the Ache and Hiwi samples was unlikely to be attributable to shared culture since these two societies had not been in contact with each other. Instead, Jones suggested that psychological mechanisms such as facial averaging might produce a similar ideal of facial attractiveness among groups whose members were physically similar but culturally distinct.

Given the pattern of findings, what are the implications for the question of cultural diversity versus consensus in judgments of facial attractiveness? Research comparing judgments made by university samples in several societies with different cultural traditions has provided support for moderate to high levels of interjudge consensus. To date, the number of different societies from which these samples have been drawn has been relatively small, but the level of consensus has been quite consistent across samples. These findings offer support for the view that judgments of attractiveness are not dependent on particular ethnocultural contexts.

The pattern of findings obtained by Jones (1996), however, suggests that this conclusion may need to be qualified. The average correlation among the three Western samples, two composed of university students and one composed of students and adults from two communities, was quite high, consistent with other research. However, the lower level of average interjudge agreement found between this group of three Western samples on the one hand and the two samples of indigenous peoples on the other hand suggests that judgments of facial attractiveness are affected by the social and cultural context of the perceiver. As noted earlier, there are some methodological limitations to Jones's study, but nonetheless, this research is distinctive for its inclusion of participants relatively isolated from Western cultural influences.

STEREOTYPING FACIAL ATTRACTIVENESS: A UNIVERSAL PHENOMENON?

There is now considerable evidence that facial attractiveness elicits evaluative inferences about individuals' traits and abilities (Dion, 1986; Eagly, Ashmore, Makhijani, & Longo, 1991; Feingold, 1992). The literature on the social psychology of physical attractiveness (in particular, facial attractiveness) is extensive. Research interest in the attributions elicited by differences in facial attractiveness was stimulated in part by an experiment conducted by Dion, Berscheid, and Walster (1972). We asked university students of both sexes to judge stimulus persons differing on facial attractiveness (see Dion, 1990, for a discussion of this experiment). Instructions given to participants mentioned that the study concerned "accuracy in person perception." Respondents were told that little was known about the factors related to the accuracy of first impressions. They were led to believe that the stimulus persons were participating in a longitudinal study of personality development so it would be possible to determine how accurate respondents' first impressions were.

The ostensible purpose of the research was to compare the accuracy of person perception of untrained university students with professionals trained in skills related to person perception (e.g., clinical psychologists). Two different categories of attributes assessed appearance-based inferences: a series of personality traits and a series of predicted life outcomes/events. The findings indicated that physically attractive men and women were inferred to have more socially desirable personalities and more favorable outcomes in several domains (greater marital competence; higher occupational status) than physically unattractive individuals. The one domain where attractive individuals were not more positively evaluated was expected parental competence.

Many subsequent studies have examined the phenomenon of stereotyping based on physical attractiveness. Two issues of relevance here concern the trait domains most likely to be affected by attractiveness and the robustness of the stereotype in the presence of instructional sets designed to weaken the impact of appearance on judgments of others. Turning to the first issue, based on the emerging literature, Dion (1981, 1986) suggested that attractiveness was most likely to affect inferences about social competence and interpersonal ease (e.g., warm, sociable). In their meta-analysis of research on attractiveness stereotyping, Eagly and her colleagues (1991) reached a similar conclusion after assessing effect size across several trait domains. They found that the effect size for differences in ratings of attractive compared to unattractive stimulus persons was largest for traits reflecting social competence (e.g., extraversion, popularity). They found intermediate effect sizes on the domains of intellectual competence (e.g., intelligence, career success); adjustment (e.g., self-esteem, psychological stability), and potency (e.g., interpersonal dominance). By contrast, the effect size for ratings of integrity (e.g., honesty) or concern for others (e.g., sensitivity, generosity) as a function of the stimulus persons' physical attractiveness was close to zero. Moreover, these effect sizes did not differ as a function of sex of target or sex of judge. In other words, facial attractiveness functioned as an evaluative cue for ratings of both women and men.

The person perception paradigm used in our research on appearance stereotyping (Dion et al., 1972) stressed the importance of accuracy. Despite this instructional set, attractiveness-based stereotyping occurred. Some subsequent researchers have used a version of this accuracy set, while others have asked participants to give their first impressions of the stimulus persons. The impact of instructional set (accuracy versus first impression) was examined in the meta-analysis conducted by Eagly and her colleagues (1991), in which the effect size was smaller in the presence of an accuracy set but was nonetheless still substantial in size. The mean effect size was .60 for studies ($n = 38$) categorized as using an "impression formation" instructional set compared to a mean effect size of .50 for studies ($n = 19$) classified as using an "accuracy set" (see Eagly et al., 1991, Table 4, p. 120).

Ellis, Olson, and Zanna (1983) investigated whether an "objective" versus a "subjective" instructional set affected appearance stereotyping. Male undergraduates were asked to rate women differing in physical attractiveness on several personality traits. In the "subjective" condition, the instructions stressed that judgments about women's attractiveness were "primarily matters of personal taste." In the "objective" condition, respondents were told that judgments of attractiveness were "primarily determined by the target's physical characteristics." (In addition, a control condition was used that contained no information about the factors presumed to affect ratings of attractiveness). Contrary to their prediction, the "subjective" instructional set did not result in weaker inferences based on appearance cues compared to the "objective" instructions. Instead, a main effect for physical attractiveness occurred on several of the personality traits in the two experiments conducted. Physically attractive women were judged more favorably than unattractive women. Moreover, the specific trait judgments reflected perceived social skills (e.g., interesting, outgoing, sociable) consistent with the above points concerning the trait domain(s) most strongly influenced by physical attractiveness.

In summary, the findings discussed in the preceding section indicate that facial attractiveness affects inferences about other personal attributes in several domains, and this effect is quite robust. Much of this research has been conducted with North American samples, and until relatively recently, studies of attractiveness stereotyping conducted elsewhere typically involved participants residing in other Western societies. Perhaps the interest in this topic by North American researchers has not been coincidental, but rather reflects the salience and importance in Western societies of physical attractiveness—in particular, facial attractiveness—as a basis for inferences about an individual's traits and abilities. Is the judgmental bias connoted by the phrase "What is beautiful is good" (or, more precisely, "What is beautiful is socially skilled, well-adjusted, and competent") as prevalent in other cultural contexts?

Cultural factors may be related to the prevalence of stereotyping based on facial attractiveness. Specifically, the relative importance of the individual as contrasted with the group in different societies might influence the type of personal characteristics likely to exert the greatest impact on person perception (Dion, 1986). Cross-cultural social psychologists have noted this differential emphasis on the person versus group in conceptual accounts of individualism/collectivism (see Kim, Triandis, Kagitcibasi, Choi, & Yoon, 1994). Individualism and collectivism can be analyzed at the societal level and at the individual level.

At the societal level, Hofstede (1984) found that individualism was one important work-related value orientation differentiating the nations and cultural groups studied. In Hofstede's research, conducted in the late 1960s and early 1970s, comparisons were based on the mean score for a particular value dimension, such as individualism, obtained within a given society. Examples of societies scoring high on individualism in Hofstede's research included the United States, Canada, Australia, and Great Britain. According to Hofstede, manifestations of individualism in these societies included an emphasis on personal autonomy, on individual achievement, and on initiative and, of most interest here, on identity based on personal attributes. By contrast, in other societies, an individual's identity was more likely to be defined by his or her place in the social system, and there was greater emotional dependence on groups and organizations. Examples of societies scoring lower in individualism in Hofstede's analysis included several Asian societies, such as Singapore, Taiwan, and Hong Kong.

What is the relation between individualism and stereotyping based on facial attractiveness? Physical, in particular facial, attractiveness may be a more individuating cue compared to other personal characteristics (e.g., age, sex). Cues such as age or sex are related to various roles and statuses, whereas facial attractiveness differentiates the individual from other group members and focuses attention on his or her distinctiveness. Therefore, stereotyping based on facial attractiveness should be more prevalent or occur more strongly among persons from societies in which individualism is a dominant cultural value, such as the United States, Canada, and Australia, compared to those from societies in which traditionally an individual's identity has been based on group allegiances, family, and social position, such as China or Japan (Dion, 1986).

In addition to cross-cultural comparisons, this hypothesis can also be tested at the individual level. As noted previously, individualism and collectivism can be examined at different levels of analysis. Persons in a given society will not necessarily endorse salient cultural values to the same degree. In societies such as Canada and the United States, factors such as ethnocultural diversity, immigration, and geographic mobility within these societies should increase the likelihood of individual differences in value orientations. Differences in endorsing individualism and collectivism may also relate to the occurrence and/or the strength of attractiveness stereotyping (Dion, 1986).

Dion, Pak, and Dion (1990) tested this hypothesis in a sample of individuals (university students) of Chinese ethnicity, born outside Canada or the United States, who were studying in Toronto, Canada. Most respondents were born in Hong Kong (77%) with the remainder from other Asian societies (e.g., Taiwan, Vietnam, Malaysia). We examined the relation between individual differences in reported participation in Toronto's Chinese communities and the tendency to exhibit stereotyping of own-group members based on the stimulus persons' facial attractiveness. We reasoned that greater community involvement would reinforce a more group-oriented set of values, which in turn would decrease attractiveness stereotyping, given the discussion in the preceding paragraphs. Those reporting higher levels of Chinese community involvement were hypothesized to show less attractiveness stereotyping compared to those reporting lower involvement.

A version of the person perception paradigm (Dion et al., 1972) described previously was used in this experiment. Participants were asked to give their first impressions of a stimulus person of Chinese ethnicity (either a male or female of high or low attractiveness) on a series of personality traits and expected life outcomes. The personality traits used were drawn from previous research on attractiveness stereotyping and from pilot testing with students of Chinese ethnicity to help ensure that the traits chosen were regarded as socially desirable. The trait ratings in this experiment were summed to provide an overall social desirability index for the personality attributes. Similarly, ratings on expected life outcomes were summed to form an overall index. After completing the person perception task, the participants responded to a measure of Chinese community participation that we had designed. The index of community participation used in this experiment reflected a student's reported involvement in leisure and social activities centered on the Chinese community. Scores on this index were negatively related to time in Canada, time in Toronto, and to reported proficiency with English. Finally, participants completed a background information questionnaire.

For the personality ratings, our hypothesis was supported. Attractive stimulus persons were rated as having more socially desirable personalities compared to their less attractive counterparts by respondents who reported lower levels of Chinese community involvement, but not those reporting higher involvement. Items contributing most strongly to this finding reflected perceived social character (kind, considerate, sincere, easy to communicate with). In other words, this form of stereotyping was less likely to occur in the latter group, who, we reasoned, would endorse collectivistic values more strongly. For these individuals we suggested that inferences about social character would be more likely to be based on information about a person's behavior in a network of social relationships. As we noted at the time of this research, since greater adherence to collectivism was inferred from our measure of community involvement, an important direction for future research would be to directly measure this construct and to examine the hypothesized relation to attractiveness stereotyping.

On the expected life outcomes index, however, both groups of Chinese participants gave more favorable ratings to more physically attractive individuals. In particular, attractive individuals were expected to have higher status occupations and be more popular than their less attractive peers. In summary, the pattern of findings provided partial support for our hypotheses. Individual differences in respondents' Chinese cultural involvement were related to their inferences about the social character but not the social prestige and popularity of stimulus persons who differed in facial attractiveness.

A similar pattern of findings occurred in Hui and Yam's (1987) research conducted in Hong Kong concerning the effects of stimulus persons' physical attractiveness and English-language proficiency when respondents rated hypothetical job applicants. Physical attractiveness affected fewer trait ratings (one of six trait dimensions) than did English language proficiency (four of the six traits) when Chinese university students evaluated Chinese female stimulus persons. However, physical attractiveness did affect hiring intention and expected job-related success, consistent with the results found for expected occupational status in Dion and colleagues' (1990) study.

Finally, Albright and her colleagues (1997) investigated within and cross-cultural consensus in interpersonal perception. Participants rated external characteristics (including physical attractiveness) and also rated personality traits. These traits were drawn from the Western "Big Five" as well as the Chinese "Big Five" (Yang & Bond, 1990) personality dimensions. Thus, the dimensions were of cultural relevance to the participants. University students were randomly assigned to five-person groups in which all members were unacquainted with each other. They rated themselves and the other four individuals on the above dimensions. In addition, photographs were taken of them. In Study 1, participants were Chinese students from different areas of the People's Republic of China who were studying at a university in Beijing. In Study 2, Chinese students from Study 1 and American university students were asked to form impressions of each other (based on stimulus photographs rather than face-to-face) using the same set of dimensions. There was within-group consensus among the participants on judgments of physical attractiveness.

For Chinese students rating other Chinese students, their ratings of each others' physical attractiveness were positively related to one of the five personality dimensions, namely, ratings of intelligence. By contrast, nonverbal behavioral cues, especially smiling, were related to several trait dimensions. In Study 2, when Chinese participants judged Americans, physical attractiveness was positively related to four of the five perceived personality dimensions. American respondents' ratings of Chinese stimulus persons showed a similar pattern of correlates for physical attractiveness. Thus, compared to other types of cues (e.g., nonverbal behavior such as smiling), attractiveness was associated with fewer perceived personality traits when Chinese students judged own-group members. However, more correlations between attractiveness and perceived personality traits occurred when the Chinese respondents judged members of a different cultural group.

There are several possible interpretations of this pattern of findings. As suggested previously, among members of traditionally collectivistic societies, physical attractiveness stereotyping may be less pervasive for within-group judgments compared to judgments made of persons from other groups. There were also differences in methodology between the two studies (face-to-face judgments versus photographs). A third possibility is that attractiveness stereotyping occurs across cultures, but its content may differ.

This last possibility has been proposed as an alternative to the sociocultural hypothesis of attractiveness stereotyping proposed by Dion (1986). It has been suggested (Wheeler & Kim, 1997; Zebrowitz et al., 1993) that attractiveness stereotyping occurs across diverse societies and is a widespread, perhaps universal phenomenon. However, the trait domains influenced by attractiveness may vary when comparing respondents from different societies, depending on the particular traits regarded as socially desirable by members of a given ethnocultural group (Wheeler & Kim, 1997).

Zebrowitz and her colleagues (1993) found that among black and white American students rating members of their own group, physical attractiveness was positively related to both perceived warmth and honesty. When Korean students judged Korean stimulus persons, ratings of the target's attractiveness were related to perceived honesty but not warmth. The authors suggested that honesty may be more universally valued across cultures than warmth.

Wheeler and Kim (1997) hypothesized that in a collectivistic society such as Korea, traits such as concern for others and integrity should be highly valued, given their implications for harmonious interpersonal functioning. They predicted therefore that attractiveness should affect inferences about these dimensions. Female and male undergraduates in a Korean university evaluated slides of Korean male and female stimulus persons preselected to represent three levels of attractiveness (low, medium, and high) on dimensions identified by previous meta-analyses of attractiveness stereotyping (e.g., Eagly et al., 1991; Feingold, 1992). Sex of target and attractiveness of target were within-subject variables.

The results revealed that facial attractiveness did influence stereotyping among Korean university students. More attractive persons were inferred to be more intellectually competent and better adjusted than less attractive stimulus persons, consistent with findings from North American research on appearance stereotyping. In addition, attractiveness also affected trait ratings on several other dimensions, with more pronounced effects depending on the target person's gender. Specifically, attributions of greater social competence, sexual warmth, and concern for others to more attractive people were particularly evident for judgments of female stimulus persons. Greater integrity was attributed to more attractive males. The findings on two dimensions—concern for others and integrity—are of interest, since, as noted above, these attributes were expected to be highly regarded in a traditionally collectivistic society, such as Korea. Wheeler and Kim (1997) concluded that the pattern of findings provided evidence for the universality of attractiveness stereotyping, but its content reflected the trait dimensions valued in a given society.

The relation between cultural values and attractiveness stereotyping merits further investigation. There is evidence of increasingly more individualistic value orientations in some traditionally collectivistic societies, particularly among university students (e.g., Yang, 1986). It is therefore important to assess the degree to which participants in a specific study endorse collectivism. University students from some traditionally collectivistic societies cannot be assumed to endorse this system of values to the same degree. Their values may be less collectivistic than prior cohorts of students and/or reflect a distinctive blend of individual and group-oriented values.

For example, Wheeler and Kim's (1997) research was conducted with undergraduate students from a university in Seoul, Korea. Cha (1994) found that based on Cha's earlier study of young adults in their 20s, level of education and area of residence were related to collectivistic values and beliefs. Individuals who were university educated and resided in an urban setting (specifically, Seoul) were less collectivistic compared to those with less education residing in nonurban areas. Cha (1994) commented that although Korean society could be categorized as collectivist, there were increasing signs of individualistic values among younger adults. Cha speculated that among this group, a "new brand of individualism" (1994, p. 172) was evident as of the 1980s.

Therefore, it is possible that the attractiveness stereotyping evident among university samples from some traditionally collectivistic societies, such as Korea, is related to psychological individualism—consistent with Dion's (1986) sociocultural hypothesis. The following research design strategies would help to clarify the nature of the relation between cultural value orientations and attractiveness stereotyping: 1) sampling several different collectivistic and individualistic societies in the same study, and 2) measuring psychological individualism and psychological collectivism and examining their relation to attractiveness stereotyping, as suggested previously (Dion et al., 1990).

ON THE IMPORTANCE OF FACIAL ATTRACTIVENESS: CULTURAL DIFFERENCES

Research evidence suggests that the importance of physical attractiveness as an evaluative cue differs across cultures. Individuals from diverse cultural groups can indeed recognize and, if asked, judge the extent to which a particular face or physique is considered to be attractive. However, interjudge agreement on attractiveness ratings does not necessarily indicate that physical attractiveness has the same cross-cultural importance in different domains of social interaction. For example, Rosenblatt and Cozby (1972) found that "impractical grounds" (mostly, physical attractiveness) when choosing a marital partner were positively related to degree of freedom of choice in selecting one's spouse. Rosenblatt suggested that in some cultural contexts, due to demographic factors or societal norms concerning arranged marriage, "strongly dominating standards of beauty may be maladaptive, disrupting the only possible relationships in some cases, or the most useful relationships in others" (Rosenblatt, 1974, p. 87).

As discussed earlier, Thakerar and Iwawaki (1979) found a high level of interjudge agreement comparing the attractiveness ratings of males made by women from different cultural groups. However, when these respondents also were asked to consider the importance of different characteristics in a potential date, English women ranked physical traits (e.g., height) more highly, while Chinese and Indian women ranked nonphysical qualities (e.g., intelligence, kindness) as more important.

A large-scale cross-cultural study of mate preferences conducted by Buss and his colleagues (1990) similarly found cultural variability in the relative importance of a variety of attributes—including physical attractiveness—desired in a potential mate/marriage partner. These researchers asked respondents from 37 samples in 33 countries to judge the importance of different characteristics, including "good looks." One of the major findings from this research was a pervasive gender difference across almost all samples in the rated importance of attractiveness. Compared to women, men from diverse cultural groups more highly valued good looks as a preferred attribute in a potential mate. The reasons for this and other gender differences have been the focus of considerable debate contrasting evolutionary versus social structural perspectives (see Buss, 1989, for numerous commentaries on this research).

By contrast, compared to the debate about the meaning of the observed gender differences, the findings from Buss and colleagues' (1990) research concerning the contribution of culture to mate preferences have received much less attention. However, in their study, culture accounted for more variance than gender across all the characteristics judged (an average of 14% versus 2.4%, respectively). Buss and his colleagues analyzed the "unique features" of each cultural group sampled by comparing the judged importance of each characteristic made by respondents from each group with the rest of the international sample. This procedure enabled them to identity which characteristics were valued more or less compared to the international average. Of relevance here, among respondents from the five Asian countries sampled (mainland China, Taiwan, Japan, Indonesia, and India), "good looks" were valued less (compared to the international average) in four of the five cultural groups (all except India).

Why might this pattern of findings have occurred? One possibility again focuses on societal individualism. An anonymous reviewer of this chapter suggested that it might be of interest to consider Buss and colleagues' (1990) findings in the context of Hofstede's (1984) indexing of societal individualism. An examination of the rank ordering of scores reveals that the three Asian societies also included in Buss and colleagues' research (Japan, India, and Taiwan) had lower individualism scores compared to countries such as the United States or Australia. As mentioned earlier, less individualistic (more collectivistic) societies in Hofstede's analysis were described as valuing identity based on various group-related attributes and emphasizing emotional dependence on groups and organizations. Attributing less importance to physical attractiveness in various domains of life—including a potential marriage partner—would be consistent with this value orientation. This explanation is speculative, and research is needed that directly assesses the relation between individualism/collectivism and the relative importance of physical attractiveness compared to other attributes desired in a marriage partner.

In summary, in addition to the gender differences found by Buss and his colleagues (1990), the other factor in this research—culture—revealed some distinctive patterns of mate preferences among respondents from different societies. The relative importance of physical attractiveness in a potential mate/marriage partner was one attribute that showed cultural differences.

Cultural differences in the importance of physical attractiveness are not limited to research on heterosexual attraction and mate preferences. Crystal, Watanabe, Weinfurt, and Wu (1998) compared the type of concepts used to differentiate peers among children (5th graders) and adolescents (11th graders) in the United States, Japan, and the People's Republic of China. Participants were asked in the context of a larger questionnaire to think about classmates and friends whom they knew and list "all the general ways that people are different from each other" to a maximum of 10 perceived differences. These differences were coded using eight categories considered valid across the three samples. Of particular relevance here, two of these categories concerned physical characteristics. One labeled "appearance and attractiveness" included explicit evaluative appraisals of others' physical features (e.g., ugly, cute, pretty). The other category, labeled "physical features" included references to physical features without explicitly evaluating these differences (e.g., hair, eyes, height).

American students were more likely to include references to appearance and attractiveness when asked about differences between people compared to students in Japan and in China (35% of the U.S. sample versus 6% of the Japanese sample and 12% of the Chinese sample). Japanese students were more likely to mention physical features per se compared to either Chinese or American students (76% versus 29% and 46%, respectively). It could be argued that the above finding reflects a reluctance to make evaluative distinctions among one's peers (i.e., a reluctance to evaluate appearance). However, Japanese children and adolescents did make frequent use of other categories that have an evaluative component, such as cognitive ability and personality traits. Thus, the pattern of findings suggests that physical attractiveness was a more important social cue for American children and adolescents, since it was more often spontaneously used to differentiate peers from each other.

Culture-related differences in the importance of physical appearance are not limited to interpersonal evaluation but also have been found for self-evaluation. Crystal, Kato, Olson, and Watanabe (1995) asked university students in Japan and in the United States to list three aspects of themselves that they would most like to change and to indicate the anticipated difficulty and strategy for making each change. For the first area for self-change mentioned, students also rated how strongly they wanted to change this aspect of self. Crystal and his colleagues predicted culture-related differences in the domains of desired self-change based on theories of culture and self (e.g., Triandis, 1989).

Among the seven categories identified in both samples was the category "physical appearance," which included references to desired changes in the face (e.g., change shape of nose) and/or body (e.g., be taller, lose weight). Across all seven domains, differences occurred between American and Japanese students. Of relevance here, American university students were more likely to indicate a desire to change aspects of their physical appearance (23%) compared to Japanese students (8%). (There were no gender differences nor an interaction with culture and gender in mentioning a desire to change aspects of the physical self.)

Also of interest, Japanese students (51%) were more likely than American students (34%) to want to change aspects of self pertaining to interpersonal harmony (e.g., "be more understanding and tolerant of other people"). American students (47%) mentioned individualistic aspects of self as needing change (e.g., "want to get more of what I deserve," "need to rely less on others for my happiness") more often than did Japanese students (22%). The above differences on these two categories of self-change suggest that in this sample of respondents, American students were more psychologically individualistic than Japanese students, while the reverse pattern occurred for psychological collectivism. Finally, American students indicated a stronger overall desire for self-change compared to Japanese students. This cultural difference was most evident on the desire to change aspects of one's physical appearance. This pattern of findings provides support for a link between psychological individualism and the personal importance of physical attractiveness.

FACIAL ATTRACTIVENESS AND CULTURE: SUMMARY AND CONCLUSIONS

Do perceivers from different ethnocultural groups discriminate comparable variation in the facial attractiveness of members of their own and other groups? The research discussed here indicates that perceivers are indeed capable of making this type of judgment within and across groups, an important precondition for assessing interjudge consensus on attractiveness ratings. These findings stand in contrast to the out-group homogeneity effect, which occurs when perceivers make less differentiated judgments of the traits and behaviors of members of other groups compared to own-group members (e.g., Linville, Fischer, & Salovey, 1989; Quattrone & Jones, 1980). As Zebrowitz and her colleagues (1993) noted, however, typically the out-group homogeneity effect has been found in studies using methods that focus on targets' social category membership rather than individuated information, such as targets' facial appearance.

Do perceivers from different cultural groups agree in their judgments of facial attractiveness? The findings discussed here indicate considerable convergence in ratings of attractiveness, particularly among university students from different societies and/or from different ethnocultural groups within the same society. In more culturally and geographically isolated samples, however, the average interjudge agreement between these respondents and the predominantly university student samples was found to be notably lower (Jones, 1996). Clearly, more research is needed that examines consensus on judgments of facial attractiveness among more diverse samples across a broader group of societies. This point is particularly important since the respondents in the societies where much of the research on attractiveness has been conducted have had ample opportunity to be exposed to a variety of media. Convergence of judgments might in part reflect agreement on extent to which stimulus faces approximate the images of attractiveness portrayed.

What is the relation between culture-related factors and stereotyping based on facial attractiveness? Here, the debate centers on the role played by cultural variables. Cultural values, such as individualism and collectivism, may contribute the strength and pervasiveness of stereotyping based on physical attractiveness. Alternatively, cultural values may be related to the content of attractiveness stereotyping; that is, the specific traits affected by attractiveness may differ across societies. On both sides of the debate, the importance of culture is acknowledged. What differs are the parameters of attractiveness stereotyping that are hypothesized to be related to cultural factors. Some possible directions for future research pertinent to this debate were suggested in a previous section.

Does facial attractiveness have the same social and psychological importance in every society? The evidence presented here suggests that the importance attributed to physical attractiveness as an evaluative cue may vary across different cultural groups. The findings discussed were from several areas of research, representing different aspects of interpersonal evaluation and self-appraisal.

The questions raised at the start of this chapter contrasted two perspectives on the psychology of facial attractiveness, namely, do perceivers share a similar vision of beauty, or is beauty in "the eye of the beholder"? This distinction is a version of the nature–nurture debate that often characterizes discussions of the etiology of psychological phenomena. Explanations of a particular phenomenon typically begin on one side of this debate, followed by a critical analysis and reinterpretation from the opposite side. As applied to the psychology of facial attractiveness, assumptions about the cultural relativity of evaluating physical attractiveness (that is, its context-specificity) have been more recently challenged by perspectives stressing the relative context-independence of these judgments. From the former perspective, the role of culture is central, while from the latter perspective, the main research focus is the search for cultural invariants. However, it is argued here that to understand the psychology of facial attractiveness, the relevant processes include not only perceptual and cognitive processes (nature), but of equal importance, interpersonal and intergroup processes (nurture).

The relation between the evaluation of facial attractiveness and culture is best conceptualized as *context-responsive* rather than either *context-specific* or *context-independent*. This conceptualization explicitly acknowledges the contribution of culture and has the potential to bridge earlier accounts that suggested cultural diversity in judgments of attractiveness and more recent theoretical frameworks based on perceptual and cognitive processes that predict cross-cultural similarity. The term *context-responsive* indicates that cultural factors contribute to the psychology of facial attractiveness. The nature of this contribution has been discussed in this chapter and is summarized at the beginning of this section. This perspective does not preclude acknowledging the contribution of perceptual and cognitive processes to the evaluation of facial appearance, but it does emphasize that facial attractiveness gains its meaning in a cultural context. The empirical literature on the impact of facial attractiveness is still largely based on North American samples, where the salience and importance of this cue have been documented in numerous studies. Cultural comparisons have begun to receive attention from researchers. Continuation of this trend will lead to a more comprehensive understanding of the psychology of facial attractiveness.

REFERENCES

Albright, L., Malloy, T. E., Dong, Q., Kenny, D. A., Fang, X., Winquist, L., & Yu, D. (1997). Cross-cultural consensus in personality judgments. *Journal of Personality and Social Psychology, 72*, 558–569.

Bernstein, I. H, Lin, T.-D., & McClellan, P. (1982). Cross- vs. within-racial judgments of attractiveness. *Perception and Psychophysics, 32*, 495–503.

Buss, D. M. (1989). Sex differences in human mate preferences: Evolutionary hypotheses tested in 37 cultures. *Behavioral and Brain Sciences, 12*, 1–49.

Buss, D. M., Abbott, M., Angleitner, A., Asherian, A., Biaggio, A., Blanco-Villasenor, A., Bruchon-Schweitzer, M., Ch'u H.-Y., Czapinski, J., Deraad, B., Ekehammar, B., El Lohamy, N., Fioravanti, M., Georgas, J., Gjerde, P., Guttman, R., Hazan, F., Iwawaki, S., Janakiramaiah, N., Khosroshani, F., Kreitler, S., Lachenicht, L., Lee, M., Liik, K., Little, B., Mika, S., Moadel-Shahid, M., Moane, G., Montero, M., Mundy-Castle, A. C., Niit, T., Nsenduluka, E., Pienkowski, R., Pirttila-Backman, A.-M., Ponce de Leon, J., Rousseau, J., Runco, M. A., Safir, M. P., Samuels, C., Sanitioso, R., Serpell, R., Smid, N., Spencer, C., Tadinac, M., Todorova, E. N., Troland, K., Van Den Brande, L., Van Heck, G., Van Langenhove, L., & Yang, K.-S. (1990). International preferences in selecting mates. *Journal of Cross-Cultural Psychology, 21*, 5–47.

Cha, J.-H. (1994). Aspects of individualism and collectivism in Korea. In. U. Kim, H. C. Triandis, C. Kagitcibasi, S.-C. Choi, & G. Yoon (Eds.), *Individualism and collectivism* (pp. 157–174). Thousand Oaks, CA: Sage.

Cross, J. F., & Cross, J. (1971). Age, sex, race, and the perception of facial beauty. *Developmental Psychology, 5*, 433–439.

Crystal, D. S., Kato, K., Olson, S., & Watanabe, H. (1995). Attitudes towards self-change: A comparison of Japanese and American university students. *International Journal of Behavioral Development, 18*, 577–593.

Crystal, D. S., Watanabe, H., Weinfurt, K., & Wu, C. (1998). Concepts of human differences: A comparison of American, Japanese, and Chinese children and adolescents. *Developmental Psychology, 34*, 714–722.

Cunningham, M. R., Roberts, A. R., Barbee, A. P., Druen, P. B., & Wu, C.-H. (1995). "Their ideas of beauty are, on the whole, the same as ours": Consistency and variability in the cross-cultural perception of female physical attractiveness. *Journal of Personality and Social Psychology, 68*, 261–279.

Dion, K. K. (1981). Physical attractiveness, sex roles and heterosexual attraction. In M. Cook (Ed.), *The bases of human sexual attraction* (pp. 3–22). London: Academic Press.

Dion, K. K. (1986). Stereotyping based on physical attractiveness: Issues and conceptual perspectives. In C. P. Herman, M. P. Zanna, & E. T. Higgins (Eds.), *Physical appearance, stigma, and social behavior: The Ontario Symposium on Personality and Social Psychology* (pp. 7–21). Mahwah, NJ: Erlbaum.

Dion, K. K. (1990). Stereotyping based on physical attractiveness. *Current Contents: Social and Behavioral Sciences, 22*, 26.

Dion, K. K., Berscheid, E., & Walster, E. (1972). What is beautiful is good. *Journal of Personality and Social Psychology, 24*, 285–290.

Dion, K. K., Pak, A. W.-P., & Dion, K. L. (1990). Stereotyping physical attractiveness: A sociocultural perspective. *Journal of Cross-Cultural Psychology, 21*, 378–398.

Eagly, A. H., Ashmore, R. D., Makhijani, M. G., & Longo, L. C. (1991). What is beautiful is good, but . . . : A meta-analytic review of research on the physical attractiveness stereotype. *Psychological Bulletin, 110*, 109–128.

Ellis, R. J., Olson, J. M., & Zanna, M. P. (1983). Stereotypic personality inferences following objective versus subjective judgments of beauty. *Canadian Journal of Behavioural Science, 15*, 35–42.

Ford, C. S., & Beach, F. A. (1951). *Patterns of sexual behavior*. Westport, CT: Greenwood Press.

Feingold, A. (1992). Good-looking people are not what we think. *Psychological Bulletin, 111*, 304–341.

Hofstede, G. (1984). *Culture's consequences: International differences in work-related values*. Thousand Oaks, CA: Sage.

Hui, C. H., & Yam, Y.-M. (1987). Effects of English language proficiency and physical attractiveness on person perception. *British Journal of Social Psychology, 26*, 257–261.

Jones, D. (1996). *Physical attractiveness and the theory of sexual selection*. Ann Arbor, MI: Museum of Anthropology, University of Michigan.

Kim, U., Triandis, H. C., Kagitcibasi, C., Choi, S.-C., & Yoon, G. (1994). Introduction. In U. Kim, H. C. Triandis, C. Kagitcibasi, S.-C. Choi, & G. Yoon (Eds.), *Individualism and collectivism* (pp. 1–16). Thousand Oaks, CA: Sage.

Linville, P. W., Fischer, G. W., & Salovey, P. (1989). Perceived distributions of characteristics of in-group and out-group members: Empirical evidence and a computer simulation. *Journal of Personality and Social Psychology, 57*, 165–188.

Maret, S. M. (1983). Attractiveness ratings of photographs of blacks by Cruzans and Americans. *Journal of Psychology, 115*, 113–116.

Maret, S. M., & Harling, C. A. (1985). Cross-cultural perceptions of physical attractiveness ratings of photographs of whites by Cruzans and Americans. *Perceptual and Motor Skills, 60*, 163–166.

Quattrone, G. A., & Jones, E. E. (1980). The perception of variability within ingroups and outgroups: Implications for the law of small numbers. *Journal of Personality and Social Psychology, 38*, 141–152.

Rosenblatt, P. C. (1974). Cross-cultural perspective on attraction. In T. Huston (Ed.), *Foundations of interpersonal attraction* (pp. 79–95). New York: Academic Press.

Rosenblatt, P. C., & Cozby, P. (1972). Courtship patterns associated with freedom of choice of spouse. *Journal of Marriage and the Family, 34*, 689–695.

Thakerar, J., & Iwawaki, S. (1979). Cross-cultural comparisons in interpersonal attraction of females toward males. *Journal of Social Psychology, 108*, 121–122.

Triandis, H. (1989). The self and social behavior in differing cultural contexts. *Psychological Review, 96*, 506–520.

Wheeler, L., & Kim, Y. (1997). What is beautiful is culturally good: The physical attractiveness stereotype has different content in collectivistic cultures. *Personality and Social Psychology Bulletin, 23*, 795–800.

Yang, K.-S. (1986). Chinese personality and its change. In M. H. Bond (Ed.), *The psychology of the Chinese people* (pp. 106–170). Hong Kong: Oxford University Press.

Yang, K.-S., & Bond, M. H. (1990). Exploring implicit personality theories with indigenous or imported constructs: The Chinese case. *Journal of Personality and Social Psychology, 58*, 1087–1095.

Zebrowitz, L. A., Montepare, J. M., & Lee, H. K. (1993). They don't all look alike: Individuated impressions of other racial groups. *Journal of Personality and Social Psychology, 65*, 85–101.

CHAPTER 9

Nature Let a Hundred Flowers Bloom: The Multiple Ways and Wherefores of Attractiveness

Leslie A. Zebrowitz and Gillian Rhodes

WHY STUDY FACIAL ATTRACTIVENESS?

People are ambivalent about facial appearance. We are enjoined not to "judge a book by its cover" and we are cautioned that "beauty is only skin deep." These warnings suggest that our natural proclivity is in fact to judge people by their appearance and to prefer those who are beautiful. Thousands of research articles have demonstrated that this is so. Facial attractiveness has a strong impact on our judgments about people as well as on their social outcomes. Social psychologists have shown that we attribute positive psychological traits to attractive individuals, including social and intellectual competence, dominance, and psychological adjustment. Moreover, more attractive individuals receive more positive social interaction outcomes in several life domains across the life span.

In infancy, more attractive babies are preferred by their own parents. They receive more kissing, cooing, smiling, eye contact, and close cuddling from their mothers than those who are less attractive (Langlois, Ritter, Casey, & Sawin, 1995). In childhood, more attractive children are more popular with their peers (e.g., Kleck, Richardson, & Ronald, 1974; Langlois & Styczynski, 1979; Lerner & Lerner, 1977). In young adulthood, those who are more attractive are preferred as dates and mates. A classic study matched college students with blind dates for a big dance and found that observers' ratings of the dates' physical attractiveness was the only predictor of whether their partners wanted to see them again (Walster, Aronson, Abrahams, & Rottman, 1966).

The high valuation of attractiveness in a date is paralleled by actual marriage patterns. More attractive people are more likely to marry and, among those who do marry, those who are more attractive marry sooner (e.g., Holmes & Hatch, 1938; Kalick, Zebrowitz, Langlois, & Johnson, 1998; Udry & Eckland, 1984). Strangers also show preferences for attractive people. Strangers of both sexes and all ages were more likely to come to the aid of an attractive man who fell down in a subway car than a similarly indisposed unattractive man, and people were also more likely to help an attractive than an unattractive person who lost an urgent letter containing a graduate school application form with an attached photograph (Benson, Karabenick, & Lerner, 1976; Sroufe, Chaikin, Cook, & Freeman, 1977; see Patzer, 1985, for a pertinent review). More attractive adults also have more occupational success. More attractive job applicants are ranked higher than their unattractive counterparts for a variety of jobs, particularly those that require face-to-face contact with others, and more attractive people command higher salaries (Cash, Gillen, & Burns, 1977; Dipboye, Arvey, & Terpstra, 1977; Dipboye, Fromkin, & Wiback, 1975; Hammermesh & Biddle, 1994; Waters, 1985). A preference for attractive political leaders has also been shown, although the small amount of research in this domain is less conclusive (e.g., Budesheim & DePaola, 1994; Efran & Patterson, 1974; Lewis & Bierly, 1990; Sigelman, Thomas, Sigelman, & Ribich, 1986; see also Keating, Chapter 6, this volume). Attractive individuals are favored even in the criminal justice system. Shoplifters with attractive clothing and facial appearance are less likely to be reported by other customers even when their actions are clearly observed (Mace, 1972; Steffensmeier & Terry, 1973). Physically attractive defendants are less likely to be convicted and, if convicted, they receive more lenient sentences than those convicted of equally serious crimes (e.g., Stewart, 1980). The evidence showing preferential treatment of attractive individuals that has been cited here is but a small fraction of the research literature documenting such effects. This research clearly shows that people are singularly unsuccessful in adhering to conventional wisdom about facial appearance (for more extensive reviews, see Bull & Rumsey, 1988; Hatfield & Sprecher, 1986; Langlois et al., 2000; Zebrowitz, 1997).

Despite the strong evidence that attractiveness has significant social consequences, this variable has remained at the periphery of social psychology. Indeed, no chapter was devoted to physical appearance in the most recent *Handbook of Social Psychology* (Gilbert, Fiske, & Lindzey, 1998), which is viewed by many as the final word on important research in the field. The lack of attention to attractiveness may reflect in part the ambivalence about appearance that researchers too experience. It also may reflect the tacit assumption that preferences for attractive individuals reflect cultural influences, since social psychologists have been more concerned with universal than cultural phenomena (cf. Bond, 1988). But, contrary to this assumption, recent research suggests that a cultural explanation is insufficient to explain the preference for attractive people. In particular, the finding that even young infants prefer attractive faces (Kramer, Zebrowitz, San Giovanni, & Sherak, 1995; Langlois et al., 1987; Langlois, Ritter, Roggman, & Vaughn, 1991; Langlois, Roggman, & Rieser-Danner, 1990; Rubenstein et al., Chapter 1, this volume), coupled with evidence for cross-cultural agreement in attractiveness judgments (Bernstein, Lin, & McClellan, 1982; Cunningham, Roberts, Wu, Barbee, & Druen, 1995; Cunningham et al., Chapter 7, this volume; Rhodes et al., Chapter 2, this volume; Zebrowitz, Montepare, & Lee, 1993), indicates that some universal process is involved. In view of these results, the study of facial attractiveness promises to provide important theoretical insights about basic psychological processes.

The potential of research on facial attractiveness to contribute to our understanding of fundamental psychological processes has been realized by researchers in other areas, including biologists, zoologists, and evolutionary theorists, who have developed accounts for facial preferences that draw on principles of sexual selection and genetically guided cognitive processes. By studying facial attractiveness in this broader biological context, it may be possible to understand how selection pressures during human evolutionary history have shaped our perception of facial attractiveness and our responses to it.

There is a satisfying symmetry to the interest modern evolutionary theorists have taken in facial attractiveness, for the father of evolutionary theory himself was once disadvantaged by his facial appearance. Darwin writes in his autobiography that the captain of the HMS *Beagle*, the ship from which he made many of the observations that spawned evolutionary theory, "was convinced that he could judge of a man's character by the outline of his features, and he doubted whether anyone with my nose could possess sufficient energy and determination for the voyage" (Darwin, 1974, p. 41). Theory and research on facial preferences has moved far beyond observational anecdotes like Darwin's, and this chapter considers research evidence bearing on the particular facial qualities that influence facial preferences as well as the explanations that have been offered for such preferences. This research reveals that beauty is not all in the eye of the beholder, but neither is it all in the face, and we also consider evidence bearing on perceiver qualities that influence facial preferences. First, however, we consider what is meant by "attractiveness."

HOW SHOULD "ATTRACTIVENESS" BE CONCEPTUALIZED AND MEASURED?

It is important to be clear about what we mean by "attractiveness." Although many researchers have focused on sexual attraction (e.g., Grammer, Thornhill, Fink, Juette, & Ronzal, Chapter 4, this volume; Little, Penton-Voak, Burt, & Perrett, Chapter 3, this volume), others have viewed attraction as a multifaceted phenomenon. In addition to sexual attraction, we are attracted to infants (nurturant attraction), to friends (communal attraction), and to leaders (respectful attraction) (cf. Cunningham et al., Chapter 7, this volume; Keating, Chapter 6, this volume). Although it is possible that the same facial qualities are attractive across all categories, it is also possible that different facial qualities may define different types of attractiveness. For example, neonatal qualities are essential to the facial attractiveness of infants, while they detract from the charisma of male leaders (Alley, 1981, 1983; Hildebrant & Fitzgerald, 1983; Sternglanz, Gray, & Murakami, 1977; Keating, Chapter 6, this volume). There may also be variations in the facial qualities that are attractive even within a category, such as sexual attractiveness. For example, "cute" individuals, with neonatal qualities, may be highly attractive to the opposite sex, and so may more mature-faced, "sexy" individuals (Berry, 1991; Wheeler & Eghrari, 1986).

Since there are different types of attractiveness, it would seem advisable to employ measuring instruments that differentiate them. In particular, research on facial attractiveness should include questions designed to see with whom the perceiver would want to have sex, with whom the perceiver would want to raise children, with whom the perceiver would want to be friends; from whom the perceiver would want to get advice, and so on. Some investigators have in fact used questions like these to tap specific behavioral affordances conveyed by a face, such as leadership, warmth, and attractiveness as a short-term mate versus a long-term mate, but most have relied on global "attractiveness" rating scales (cf. Keating, Chapter 6, this volume; Little et al. Chapter 3, this volume; Montepare & Zebrowitz, 1998; Penton-Voak et al., 1999). Theoretically puzzling findings may be clarified when more specific judgments are obtained (see McArthur & Baron, 1983; Zebrowitz & Collins, 1997, for a discussion of the utility of assessing behavioral affordances). For example, the finding that women prefer men with feminized faces (Perret et al., 1998) was attributed to a preference for men who appear to have the traits of good fathers. This explanation was bolstered by the subsequent finding that the preference is stronger when seeking a long-term mate than a short-term mate (Penton-Voak et al., 1999).

The finding that one or another type of attractiveness covaries with particular facial qualities does not necessarily provide a full explanation of facial attractiveness. As Cunningham and colleagues (Chapter 7, this volume) have noted, many studies report statistically significant differences among faces, all of which are judged to be close to the middle of the rating scale. To fully explain attractiveness requires that we can specify the attribute(s) that make a face extremely attractive. Interestingly, as discussed below, it may be easier to identify attributes that make faces extremely unattractive than to identify those that make them extremely attractive. More specifically, low levels of any one attractive attribute may make a person very unattractive, whereas high levels of many attractive attributes may be needed to make someone very attractive. Researchers need to heed this possibility.

IS THERE A GOLD STANDARD OF ATTRACTIVENESS?

The chapters in this book provide evidence that several qualities contribute to facial attractiveness. These include averageness, symmetry, a pleasant expression, youthfulness, and sexual dimorphism. Although most of the research investigating these qualities has been implicitly concerned with sexual attraction rather than other types, explicit specification of the type of attractiveness judges are being asked to rate has been rare. Rather, the effects of various facial qualities typically have been assessed with a rating of global attractiveness. Therefore, our knowledge of the effects of these facial qualities may or may not generalize to all types of attraction.

Faces closer to the population average are more attractive both when natural variations in averageness are correlated with attractiveness judgments (Light, Hollander, & Kayra-Stuart, 1981; Jones & Hill, 1993, some ethnic groups; Rhodes, Sumich & Byatt, 1999b; Rhodes & Tremewan, 1996) and also when averageness is manipulated experimentally by compositing a number of faces (Langlois & Roggman, 1990; Rhodes, Sumich & Byatt, 1999b; Rhodes & Tremewan, 1996). More symmetrical faces are more attractive both when natural variations in symmetry are correlated with attractiveness judgments (Grammer & Thornhill, 1994; Jones & Hill, 1993, for some ethnic groups; Mealy, Bridgestock, & Townsend, 1999; Zebrowitz, Voinescu, & Collins, 1996) and also when symmetry is varied experimentally, so long as the manipulation does not produce structural abnormalities, as when chimeras are used (Perrett et al., 1999; Rhodes, Proffitt, Grady, & Sumich, 1998; Rhodes, Roberts, & Simmons, 1999). Faces with more positive expressions are more attractive than those with less positive expressions (Cunningham, 1986; Cunningham, Barbee, & Pike, 1990, Cunningham et al., 1995; Mueser, Grau, Sussman, & Rosen, 1984; Reis et al., 1990; Rhodes, Sumich, & Byatt, 1999a). Younger faces are more attractive, as shown by an age-related linear decline in the judged attractiveness of the same individuals who were photographed from childhood to the late 50s(Zebrowitz, Olson, & Hoffman, 1993). Additional evidence for the attractiveness of more youthful faces is provided by positive correlations between neotenous facial qualities and attractiveness in some samples of faces (Cunningham, Chapter 7, this volume; Keating, Chapter 6, this volume; Zebrowitz & Montepare, 1992; Zebrowitz et al., 1993).

The evidence for greater attractiveness of faces with more extreme sexual dimorphism is less consistent than the evidence for effects of averageness, symmetry, positive expressions, and youthfulness. Faces showing more extreme sexual dimorphism are more attractive when natural or manipulated variations in certain secondary sexual features are correlated with attractiveness judgments, but not when others are. Consistent with the sexual dimorphism hypothesis, smaller jaws, smaller noses, and thinner eyebrows are more attractive in female faces, while larger jaws, thicker eyebrows, and thinner lips are more attractive in male faces (Cunningham, 1986; Cunningham et al., 1990, 1995; Grammer & Thornhill, 1994; Johnston & Franklin, 1993; Keating, 1985; McArthur &

Apatow, 1983–1984). However, contrary to the hypothesis, larger noses are not more attractive in male faces and thicker lips have not been consistently rated as more attractive in female faces (Cunningham, 1986; Cunningham et al., 1990, 1995; Keating, 1985; McArthur & Apatow, 1983–1984). The hypothesis that faces with more extreme sexual dimorphism are more attractive has also received mixed support in studies using morphing techniques to create faces that magnify the average differences between composited male and female faces and in studies using computer simulations to "evolve" attractive male and female faces from perceiver judgments. While extremely feminine *female* faces are more attractive than those less extreme in sexually dimorphic traits, extremely masculine *male* faces are not consistently judged more attractive than less masculine faces (Franklin & Johnston, 2000; Perrett et al., 1998; Rhodes, Hickford, & Jeffery, 2000a). However, women at the fertile phase of their menstrual cycle do show a consistent shift in preferences toward male faces that are less feminized (Penton-Voak et al., 1999) or more masculinized, albeit not extremely masculinized (Franklin & Johnston, 2000; Penton-Voak & Perrett, 2000). The failure to find a consistent preference for masculinized male faces may reflect a preference for more *youthful* faces, since, as discussed below, feminine faces retain more neotenous facial qualities.

Despite the evidence that each of the foregoing facial qualities can augment attractiveness, none is a necessary or sufficient condition for attractiveness. Counterexamples provide evidence against the sufficiency of various facial qualities to produce attractiveness. The existence of unattractive children and adolescents shows that young faces are not always attractive. Figure 5.5 in Chapter 5, by Enquist, Ghirlanda, Lundqvist, & Wachtmeister (Chapter 5, this volume), clearly shows that symmetry is not sufficient for attractiveness. Similar examples may show that male and female faces with extreme secondary sexual features are not all attractive. Although smiling faces are more attractive than unsmiling faces, a smile is not sufficient to turn a frog into a prince, since it produces only a negligible change in how people rank in attractiveness. When smiling pictures of people were compared to pictures of 29 others who had neutral expressions, the smilers tended to be ranked only about two places higher in attractiveness than they were ranked on the basis of a picture of them with a neutral expression (Reis et al., 1990). Averageness comes closest to meeting the criterion of sufficiency (cf. Rubenstein, Langlois, & Roggman, Chapter 1, this volume). However, the existing evidence rests on the attractiveness of average faces composited from a set of young adult faces (Langlois & Roggman, 1990; Rhodes, Sumich, & Byatt, 1999b; Rhodes & Tremewan, 1996). Not only is youthfulness an inherent quality in these composites, but moreover the composites look younger than the individual faces from which they have been created (Langlois, Roggman, & Musselman, 1994). Would an average face composited from 80-year-olds be more attractive than randomly selected 20-year-old faces? We think not, in which case averageness does not seem to be a sufficient condition for attractiveness.

Not only is averageness, symmetry, a pleasant expression, youthfulness, or sexual dimorphism insufficient to produce attractiveness, but each may also be unnecessary. One method that has been employed to determine the necessity of each facial quality has been to covary out its effects when assessing the impact of the others. Such research has revealed that averageness, symmetry, and a pleasant expression are each independent predictors of facial attractiveness (Rhodes, Sumich, & Byatt, 1999b; Rhodes et al., 2000). The fact that any one of these facial qualities can independently produce attractiveness indicates that none of them is necessary, at least within the range of facial stimuli studied. Research has not yet determined whether the attractiveness-enhancing effects of these three facial qualities and those of youthfulness and extreme sexual dimorphism are also independent of one another. It should be noted in this regard that if all of these attributes are highly correlated, then the covariance analyses required to establish their independent effects may not be feasible, and it may not make sense to argue that one quality is more basic than another.

In order to assess whether averageness, symmetry, positive expression, youthfulness, or sexual dimorphism are necessary conditions for facial attractiveness, other possible influences on facial attractiveness also must be considered. If other factors can influence attractiveness with averageness, symmetry, and so on, controlled, then the latter facial qualities are not necessary. One such influence is familiarity. Considerable research demonstrates that we prefer familiar stimuli, including faces (e.g., Bornstein, 1989; Zajonc, 1968). Indeed, people even like their own face better when they view it in a familiar way—the way it looks in a mirror—than when they view it the way it looks in a photograph. On the other hand, close friends prefer nonmirror, photographic images of these people's faces, the likeness that is familiar to friends (Mita, Dermer, & Knight, 1977). The appeal of familiar faces *does* contribute to the appeal of faces high in averageness (Langlois, Roggman, & Musselman, 1994), and it may also contribute to the appeal of faces high in symmetry, positive expression, and sexual dimorphism, although no research has examined this. Not only does familiarity contribute to the appeal of average faces, but moreover when familiarity is manipulated such that nonaverage faces are more familiar, then preferences shift in the direction of those nonaverage faces (Rhodes, Nakayama, & Halberstadt, 2000b). Nevertheless, the effects of averageness on facial attractiveness may not be identical to those of familiarity. For nonfacial stimuli, averageness remained attractive when the effect of familiarity was statistically controlled, and familiarity remained attractive with averageness controlled. Thus, neither familiarity nor averageness were necessary for attractiveness of these stimuli (Halberstadt & Rhodes, 2000). Future research is needed to determine whether the same is true for faces.

Another influence on facial attractiveness that argues against the necessity of any single facial quality is captured by the maxim "pretty is as pretty does." Consistent with this maxim, people who are judged to be physically attractive are expected to have positive personality traits (cf. Eagly, Ashmore, Makhijani,

& Longo, 1991; Feingold, 1992; Zebrowitz, 1997). Moreover, people who are known to have positive personality traits are judged to be more physically attractive. Seventy percent of college students judged an instructor's physical appearance as appealing when he behaved in a warm and friendly manner, whereas only 30% judged the same instructor to have an appealing appearance when he was more cold and distant (Nisbett & Wilson, 1977). Students also rated others as more physically attractive when they had received a favorable description of their personalities than when they had received no description or an unfavorable one (Graziano, Jensen-Campbell, Shebilski, & Lundgren, 1993; Gross & Crofton, 1977). Indeed, the large effect of personality on ratings of attractiveness was sometimes strong enough to outweigh the large effect of physical appearance (as reflected in the attractiveness ratings made by those who had no personality information). For example, unattractive women with a favorable personality were judged equal in physical attractiveness to average-looking women with an unfavorable or neutral personality, and average-looking women with a favorable personality were judged as more attractive than attractive women with an unfavorable personality (Gross & Crofton, 1977). Not only does behavior influence global judgments of attractiveness, but moreover it can influence judgments of particular facial qualities. For example, people are judged to have bigger eyes, shorter noses, fuller lips, and smoother skin when they have been described as kind rather than as mean (Hassin & Trope, 2000). The fact that personality traits can override facial qualities when people judge attractiveness strongly suggests that no single facial quality is a necessary condition for attractiveness.

Summary and Conclusions

It appears that there is no "gold standard" of attractiveness, but rather a variety of interchangeable currencies. Averageness, symmetry, a positive expression or behavior, youthfulness, familiarity, or certain sexual dimorphic qualities each can augment facial attractiveness. This can be viewed as adaptive for species survival, since it means that there will be a wider range of acceptable mates in the case of sexual attraction as well as a wider range of people who receive nurturant and respectful attraction. The fact that a wide range of faces is attractive not only is adaptive, but it also suggests that an interesting question may be "What makes a face unattractive?" Whereas attractiveness is not guaranteed by an extremely pleasant expression or by extremely high levels of symmetry, averageness, youthfulness, or sexual dimorphism, unattractiveness may be certain with a sufficiently unpleasant expression or a sufficiently low level of symmetry, averageness, youthfulness, or sexual dimorphism. As discussed below, this asymmetry in the prediction of attractiveness and unattractiveness may have implications for how we can explain facial preferences.

HOW CAN WE EXPLAIN ATTRACTIVENESS?

Evolutionary, cognitive, and social explanations have been offered to account for the greater attractiveness of certain faces. Evolutionary explanations include the "good taste" hypothesis that these preferences evolved simply because attractive individuals have attractive offspring, who are themselves preferred as mates, as well as the "good genes" hypothesis that preferences for certain faces evolved because attractive individuals are higher quality mates. Cognitive explanations include the hypothesis that facial preferences are by-products of general-purpose perceptual mechanisms, such as those used to abstract prototypes or to recognize age and sex, and the overgeneralization hypothesis that facial preferences reflect biases that derive from the evolutionary importance of recognizing infants, people who are markedly unfit, emotional expressions, and specific individuals.[1] Social explanations include the hypotheses that preferences for certain faces reflect similarities and differences in learning histories and in social goals that occur between cultures as well as among individuals within a culture.

Good Taste

Some evolutionary theorists, including Darwin, have viewed the preference for attractive faces as an aesthetic preference without necessary adaptive functions, such as signaling good genes. In this case, a preference for attractive faces may evolve because attractive individuals have attractive offspring, who are themselves preferred as mates (Fisher, 1915). Individuals without the preference will leave fewer descendants in subsequent generations than will individuals with the preference, because their offspring will be less successful in attracting mates. Evidence that animals, including humans, may copy the mate choices of their peers is consistent with such a "good taste" mechanism for the evolution of preferences (for a review, see Thornhill & Gangestad, 1999a). On this good taste evolutionary account, preferences enhance long-term reproductive success without the preferred traits signaling mate quality (see Cronin, 1991, for a discussion). This account of preferences for attractive faces assumes that facial attractiveness is heritable, an assumption that seems plausible, but which has not been empirically tested.

Good Genes

According to the "good genes" account, preferences may have evolved as an adaptation to the problem of choosing a high-quality mate (Miller & Todd, 1998; Thornhill & Gangestad, 1993, 1999a). On this view, preferred facial traits signal mate quality and the preferences enhance reproductive success (Andersson, 1994; Hamilton & Zuk, 1982; Møller & Swaddle, 1997; see Berry, 2000, for a review of pertinent theories). Some researchers have investigated whether attractive faces signal mate quality, as proposed by the good genes account, by examining the relationship between attractiveness and health. Existing research has provided little support for the thesis that attractiveness signals health (Kalick, Zebrowitz, Langlois & Johnson, 1998; Shackelford & Larsen, 1999).

Investigators also have considered the relationship to health of two contributors to facial attractiveness: averageness and symmetry. These qualities are associated with developmental stability (the ability to maintain normal development despite environmental and/or genetic stress) and health in nonhuman animals (Møller & Swaddle, 1997; Parsons, 1990; Thornhill & Møller, 1997). In humans, there is evidence that genetic and environmental stress can produce deviations from averageness and symmetry (minor physical anomalies) in the human face (Hoyme, 1994; Thornhill & Møller, 1997) and that facial asymmetry is elevated in a variety of disorders (Thornhill & Møller, 1997). Facial averageness also may be associated with the ability to resist parasites (Gangestad & Buss, 1993; Thornhill & Gangestad, 1993), because genetic heterozygosity, which tends to produce average forms, is associated with enhanced parasite resistance (Livshits & Kobyliansky, 1991). While Shackelford and Larsen (1997) reported correlations between facial symmetry and some measures of current health, Rhodes and colleagues (2000c) found only a marginal correlation between women's facial symmetry at 17 years of age and health in the 30s, although symmetry was significantly related to *perceived* health. Rhodes and colleagues also found strong relationships between facial averageness and perceived health, while links to actual health were modest. For males, facial averageness at 17 years of age reflected childhood health and for females it reflected current and adolescent health, although the latter correlation was only marginal.

In addition to investigating relationships of health to attractiveness, averageness, and symmetry, proponents of the good genes hypothesis have argued that health is positively related to another contributor to facial attractiveness, extreme sexual dimorphism (Thornhill & Gangestad, 1993). This argument rests on the Zahavian (1975) handicap hypothesis, which holds that traits whose development requires high levels of sex hormones are honest badges of fitness. This is because it is hypothesized that sex hormones inhibit immune responses with the result that only very fit individuals can "afford" these secondary sexual traits, which in humans include high cheekbones in men and women and large jaws in men. The immunocompetence hypothesis is intriguing and has been supported by animal research (Folstad & Karter, 1992; Thornhill & Gangestad, 1993; Thornhill & Møller, 1997). There is also some evidence that sex hormones have adverse effects on the human immune system (Ellison, 1999; Kanda, Tsuchida, & Tamaki, 1996; Yesilova et al., 2000). However, there is no evidence bearing on the immune functioning of humans whose faces show more exaggerated secondary sex characteristics.

In sum, there is at best modest evidence to support the claim that facial attractiveness, averageness, symmetry, or sexual dimorphism are preferred because they signal good health. The relationship between attractive facial qualities and health may be attenuated in modern societies, where the availability of health care reduces the impact of genetic fitness on appearance. Consistent with this argument, attractiveness has been found to be a stronger predictor of mate preferences in cultures that are high in pathogens (Gangestad & Buss, 1993). It thus remains possible that a preference for certain facial configurations could have evolved because they signal health.

While it is possible that attractiveness did evolve as an honest indicator of health, it is also possible that it evolved as an honest indicator of some other trait that would enhance reproductive success. Intelligence is one plausible contender. Miller (1992; see also Miller & Todd, 1998; Miller, 2000) argues that intelligence is desirable in a potential mate:

> the neocortex is largely a courtship device to attract and retain sexual mates . . . [and] just as the peahen is satisfied with nothing less than a visually brilliant display of peacock plumage, I postulate that hominid males and females become satisfied with nothing less than psychologically brilliant, fascinating, articulate, entertaining companions. (1992)

More intelligent mates would likely provide better parental care and would also confer survival benefits on their offspring, since intelligence has a heritable component (see Mackintosh, 1998, for a review). Other adaptive traits that may be signaled by attractiveness include warmth and dominance (cf. Cunningham et al., Chapter 7, this volume; Keating, Chapter 6, this volume), since warmer mates would likely provide better parental care and dominant or strong mates may confer survival benefits on their offspring by securing important resources. Attractive individuals are in fact perceived as more intelligent, warmer, and more dominant, and there is also some evidence for the accuracy of these perceptions (Langlois et al., 2000; Zebrowitz, Hall, Murphy, & Rhodes, in press; but see Feingold, 1992, for lack of evidence). However, such findings do not necessarily reflect the coevolution of facial attractiveness and these adaptive traits. Rather, these relationships, as well as a relationship between attractiveness and health, can also be explained by a variety of nonevolutionary mechanisms (cf. Zebrowitz, Collins, & Dutta, 1998; Zebrowitz, Hall, Murphy, & Rhodes, in press).

Although proponents of the good genes account of facial attractiveness have been very influential, they have not critically examined their preferred explanation for a link between attractiveness and some adaptive trait. As shown in Figure 9.1, there are at least three nonevolutionary mechanisms that can account for a relationship between attractiveness and some adaptive trait, such as health, warmth, dominance, or intelligence. The evolutionary mechanism is shown by Path A, where biology/genetic quality influences both attractiveness and an adaptive trait. One nonevolutionary mechanism is an influence of environmental factors, as shown by Path B. For example, the quality of nutrition and the health care that a person receives may have an impact on the development of both attractiveness and intelligence. Another nonevolutionary

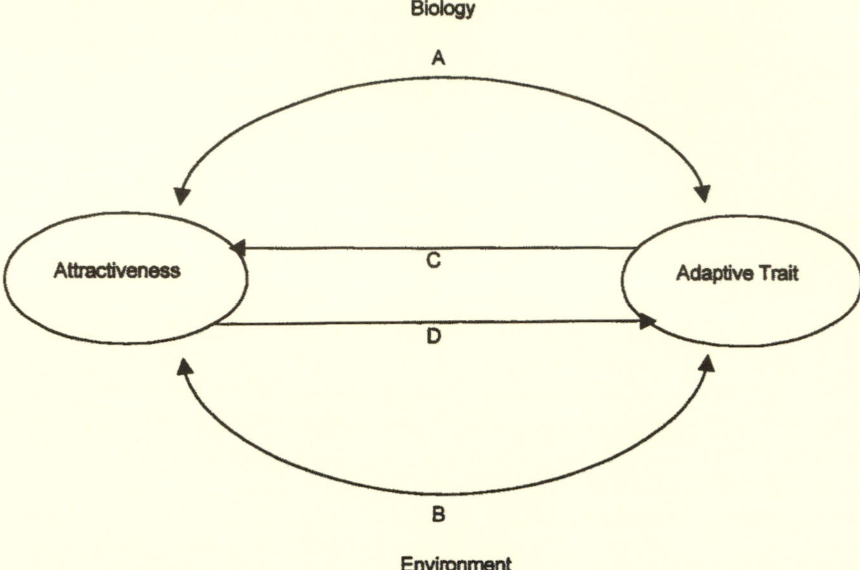

Figure 9.1. A model of attractiveness-trait relations. Path A represents an influence of the same biological factors on both attractiveness and some adaptive trait. Path B represents an influence of the same environmental factors on both attractiveness and some adaptive trait. Path C represents an influence of some adaptive trait on attractiveness. Path D represents an environmentally mediated influence of attractiveness on some adaptive trait. Although this model does not explicitly label all possible paths between the elements, the circular paths are intended to recognize the possibility of multiple bi-directional influences. For example, biological and environmental variables can influence each other via an influence on adaptive traits and/or attractiveness.

mechanism is that an adaptive trait influences attractiveness, as shown in Path C. For example, more intelligent individuals from puberty onward may increase their attractiveness through flattering makeup, better grooming, more stylish haircuts, or better health maintenance. A third non-evolutionary explanation for a relationship between attractiveness and some trait is a self-fulfilling prophecy effect, shown by Path D (cf. Snyder, Tanke, & Bersheid, 1977). As demonstrated in the introductory section of this chapter, there is considerable evidence that attractiveness influences people's social environments, and this in turn may influence their intelligence or other adaptive traits.

Zebrowitz and colleagues (in press) tested the various components of the model shown in Figure 9.1 in an attempt to explain observed correlations between attractiveness and intelligence. They found some evidence that genetic quality contributed to the relationship between attractiveness and intelligence in childhood and puberty. However, there was also evidence that socioeconomic status, an environmental explanation, contributed significantly to this relationship. Moreover, only a self-fulfilling prophecy mechanism could explain the relationship between attractiveness and intelligence for boys at adolescence and for women in middle and later adulthood; and only an influence of intelligence on the development of attractiveness could explain the relationship in later adulthood. Thus, the relationship between attractiveness and intelligence often reflects the operation of nonevolutionary mechanisms rather than the coevolution of these two traits. The same may be true for observed relationships between attractiveness and other adaptive traits.

In sum, there is at best weak evidence to support the "good genes" account of a relationship between facial attractiveness and adaptive traits, such as health and intelligence, within the sets of normal faces that have been studied. However, the fact is that extremely unattractive faces often mark people with congenital or genetic anomalies that severely impair their fitness. Individuals with anomalies such as Down syndrome, Williams syndrome, hydrocephaly, fetal alcohol syndrome, schizophrenia, and minor physical anomalies not only suffer from poor health and/or social and intellectual incompetence, but they are also marked by faces that are atypical or asymmetrical, two of the hallmarks of unattractiveness (see, e.g., Bell & Waldrop, 1982; Campbell, Geller, Small, Petti, & Ferris, 1978; Clarren et al., 1987; Cummings, Flynn, & Preus, 1982; Guy, Majorski, Wallace, & Guy, 1983; Krouse & Kauffman, 1982; Paulhus & Martin, 1986; Thornhill & Møller, 1997; Waldrop & Halverson, 1972). In view of this, a "bad genes" account of facial preferences may be more useful than the "good genes" account. Those who avoided mates with extremely unattractive faces would have increased their reproductive success as well as the survival of their offspring. Such a mechanism is consistent with the conclusion of Grammer and colleagues (Chapter 4, this volume) that the cognitive decision-making in attractiveness ratings may be best simulated by a strategy of "*simply avoid the worst.*" While a "bad genes" account may not explain all facial preferences, it provides a plausible account of judgments at the negative end of the attractiveness continuum. The available data that have been reviewed further suggest that mechanisms other than "good genes" should be sought to explain judgments at the positive end.

Perceptual By-Products

Several theorists propose that preferences for attractive faces may have evolved as the by-products of more general perceptual or recognition mechanisms (Endler & Basolo, 1998; Enquist & Arak, 1994; Enquist, Ghirlanda, Lundqvist & Wachtmeister, Chapter 5, this volume; Enquist & Johnstone, 1997; Johnstone, 1994). For example, a preference for symmetry could emerge as a by-product of mate recognition (Johnstone, 1994) or the need to generalize across a particular group of stimuli (Enquist & Johnstone, 1997; Enquist et al., Chapter 5, this volume). A preference for average faces may be a by-product of a general cognitive mechanism that abstracts prototypes from structurally distinct classes (Langlois & Roggman, 1990; Rhodes et al., Chapter 2, this volume; Rubenstein et al., Chapter 1, this volume). Evidence that average exemplars are attractive for nonface categories, such as dogs and birds, is consistent with this view (Halberstadt & Rhodes, 2000).

The general mechanisms, such as prototype abstraction mechanisms, would be useful in the classification and recognition of objects and may have evolved in that context, but the attractive traits themselves need not provide information about mate quality on these accounts. Instead, they are thought to trigger strong responses in perceptual or recognition systems, such as neural networks (e.g., Enquist & Arak, 1994; Johnstone, 1994). What these accounts lack, however, is an explanation of just why a trait that generates a strong response in a perceptual system is perceived as *attractive* (see Rhodes et al, Chapter 2, this volume, for further discussion).

In another perceptual by-product account, attractive traits *do* provide information about mate quality. More specifically, preferences for attractive faces may be a by-product of perceptual mechanisms that enable people to recognize age and sex (cf. Enquist, Ghirlanda, Lundqvist, & Wachtmeister, Chapter 5, this volume). Such mechanisms serve an adaptive function in the recognition of those who are potential mates, those who need care, and those who are potential sources of knowledge and wisdom, and they may have evolved in these contexts, where they would foster both individual and species survival. Consistent with this perceptual by-product account, facial qualities do reveal age and sex.

The growth process from birth to maturity and the aging process from maturity to senescence is accompanied by changes in the face that are reliable cues to age (cf. Montepare & Zebrowitz, 1998; Zebrowitz, 1997). Not only does the face change with age, but also there is a good deal of consensus and accuracy in guessing people's age from their facial appearance, and this ability develops early in life. Indeed, infants as young as 4 months old differentiate faces of babies from those of adults. This early development suggests that there is a biologically guided perceptual mechanism for age recognition (Brooks & Lewis, 1976; Edwards, 1984; Henss, 1991; Jones & Smith, 1984; Kogan, Stevens, & Shelton, 1961; Lasky, Klein, & Martinez, 1974; McCall & Kennedy, 1980; Montepare & McArthur, 1986; Todd, Mark, Shaw, & Pittenger, 1980).

There are also reliable facial cues to sex, with the adult female face retaining more infantile qualities (Enlow, 1990; Gray, 1985). More specifically, women retain the hairlessness and smoothness of skin that characterizes infants and children, as well as the smaller jaws and noses. Also, the forehead of a woman is relatively vertical, like that of a child, while men's foreheads tend to slope backward as well as protruding just above the nose and eyes in a brow ridge. Sex identification, like age identification, develops in early infancy, with accurate discrimination shown as early as 5 months of age, suggesting that there is also a biologically guided perceptual mechanism for this faculty (Lasky, Klein, & Martinez, 1974).

Consistent with the perceptual by-product account, not only do facial qualities accurately communicate a person's age and sex, but also the qualities that communicate these attributes affect attractiveness. An effect of age cues on attractiveness is shown by evidence that nurturant attraction is elicited by neonatal facial qualities, with such responses shown across a variety of species and even by human infants, thus arguing for a biologically guided perceptual mechanism (for pertinent reviews, see Eibl-Eibesfeldt, 1970; Zebrowitz, 1997). Sexual attraction also is affected by age cues, as shown by the positive effects of youthful facial qualities, such as smooth skin and large eyes, and it is affected by sex cues, as shown by the positive effects of sexually dimorphic traits, such as small jaws in women and large jaws in men (Cunningham, 1986; Cunningham et al., 1990, 1995; Grammer & Thornhill, 1994; Keating, 1985; McArthur & Apatow, 1983–1984; Zebrowitz & Montepare, 1992). Respectful attraction is elicited by facial qualities indicating advanced age, such as grey hair, baldness, lined skin, and small eyes (Cunningham et al., Chapter 7, this volume; Keating, Chapter 6, this volume; Muscarella & Cunningham, 1996).

The argument that preferences for attractive faces evolved as a by-product of the need to pick a mate of the correct age and sex implies that the facial qualities that influence sexual attraction to men and women will diverge. Consistent with this suggestion is the aforementioned evidence that men and women are more attractive when they have more extreme values of certain sexually dimorphic features, although the preference for such men may be most reliable for women who are at the fertile phase of their menstrual cycle (Cunningham, 1986; Cunningham et al., 1990, 1995; Grammer & Thornhill, 1994; Franklin & Johnston, 2000; Keating, 1985; McArthur & Apatow, 1983–1984; Penton-Voak & Perrett, 2000; Perrett et al., 1998; Rhodes et al., 2000).

Overgeneralizations

In addition to the possibility that facial attractiveness incorporates features that *accurately* identify mates of the appropriate age and sex, it also may reflect *overgeneralizations* that derive from the evolutionary importance of recognizing certain categories of faces. For example, the evolutionary importance of recognizing infants may have produced such a strong tendency to respond to neonatal facial qualities that responses are overgeneralized to "baby faced" adults. Considerable research has supported such a "babyface overgeneralization effect" (for reviews of this literature, see Montepare & Zebrowitz, 1998; Zebrowitz, 1997). People are judged as more baby-faced than their peers if they have facial qualities that differentiate real babies from adults. In particular, more baby-faced individuals have rounder and less angular faces, larger and rounder eyes, higher eyebrows, smaller noses, and lower vertical placement of features, which creates a higher forehead and a smaller chin. What is more, compared with peers of the same age, more baby-faced individuals are seen as more likely to have the childlike attributes of warmth, honesty, naiveté, and submissiveness. These perceptions have been documented across perceivers and faces of all races. Even young children show the babyface overgeneralization effect (Montepare & Zebrowitz-McArthur, 1989), and infants can differentiate baby-faced from mature-faced adults (Kramer, Zebrowitz, San Giovanni, & Sherak, 1995). This early development coupled with evidence of cultural universality suggests that there is a biologically based preparedness to associate certain traits with neonatal features. Such features may be preferred in mate selection because baby-faced individuals are perceived to have traits that augur a more devoted mate (cf. Cunningham et al., Chapter 7, this volume; Keating, Chapter 6, this volume; Perrett et al., 1998).[2]

Preferences for certain faces not only may reflect an overgeneralization of responses to infants, but also an overgeneralization of responses to those who are markedly unfit. As argued earlier, facial preferences may reflect an avoidance of those whose faces signal bad genes. But it must be acknowledged that facial preferences are more graded than this. Some faces are more preferred and some are more shunned even when they are not differentiated by any genetic anomaly. It may be that the evolutionary importance of recognizing individuals with "bad genes" has produced such a strong tendency to respond to their facial qualities that responses are overgeneralized to normal adults whose faces merely resemble those who are unfit. For example, the perception of normal individuals with somewhat asymmetrical or nonaverage faces as unattractive may be an overgeneralized response that is derived from an adaptive rejection of abnormal individuals who show marked asymmetry and nonaverageness and who do in fact lack health, intelligence, and/or other evolutionarily adaptive qualities.

Other overgeneralization effects also may contribute to the preferences for certain faces. An emotion overgeneralization effect may produce a preference for faces with structural features that resemble a positive emotional expression. An identity overgeneralization effect may produce a preference for faces with features that resemble significant others. Such overgeneralization effects could derive from an adaptive attraction to people who are pleasant or familiar (see Zebrowitz & Collins, 1997; see also Zebrowitz, 1997, for further discussion of overgeneralization effects).

Social Mechanisms

While the "good taste," "good genes," perceptual mechanisms, and overgeneralization accounts of facial attractiveness all predict culturally universal preferences, the adage 'beauty is in the eye of the beholder' suggests that attractiveness varies across individuals and cultures. Evidence for cultural differences has been provided by accounts of primitive cultures that practice exotic beautification practices, such as facial scarification, lip enlargement, teeth filing, and head deformation (see Zebrowitz, 1997). Even within modern cultures, one can observe changes in the ideal face. For example, the very high, thin eyebrows that characterized female movie stars in the 1920s and 1930s have given way to a more natural, less plucked ideal. Other evidence of social mechanisms is provided by research examining cross-cultural agreement in judgments of attractiveness. Although significant agreement has been found across a broad range of cultures, agreement is lower between cultures that are isolated from one another (cf. Dion, Chapter 8, this volume; Jones, 1996). The differences in ideals over time and place leave no doubt that social factors do have an influence on our facial preferences. However, the precise mechanisms for this influence remain to be determined.[3] Some possibilities, discussed below, derive from adaptive variations in attunements to particular stimulus information (cf. McArthur & Baron, 1983).

Effects of Learning Histories

Facial preferences may be influenced by people's learning histories—that is, the faces to which they have been exposed and the significant events that have been paired with various faces. Similar learning histories can explain universal facial preferences—for example, exposure to infants in all cultures may produce a preference for neonatal qualities across cultures. In this section, we consider how different learning histories can explain differences in facial preferences within or between cultures.

Cultural differences in learning histories may be important to consider when predicting effects of facial symmetry and averageness, which are assumed to be universal determinants of attractiveness. Since the likelihood of asymmetrical development is higher in cultures with a high incidence of parasites, the preference for symmetrical faces may be stronger in such cultures because there is a stronger correlation between symmetry and health. Although this has not been studied directly, indirect evidence is provided by research showing that attractiveness is more highly valued in such cultures (Gangestad & Buss, 1993).

Since, as discussed earlier, average faces are preferred and since the average face varies across cultures, it seems reasonable to predict that the most preferred faces would also vary across cultures. Some evidence consistent with this suggestion is provided by the finding that Asian Americans and Caucasians showed a preference for features typical of their own race when asked to rate the facial features that they find most attractive. In particular, compared with Caucasians, Asian Americans rated straight hair and black hair as more attractive and frizzy hair and a Roman nose as less attractive (Wagatsuma & Kleinke, 1979). Similarly, the relationship between black women's attractiveness and the "whiteness" of their features was weaker when the judges were African blacks than when they were American blacks or whites, both of whom showed an equivalent preference for "white" features (Martin, 1964). The preference of American blacks for white features may reflect their frequent exposure to such features. Consistent with this suggestion is the finding that members of isolated cultures show less cross-cultural agreement in their attractiveness judgments than members of cultures with more contact (cf. Dion, Chapter 8, this volume; Jones & Hill, 1993). Additional research is needed to fully document cultural differences in preferred facial features.

Individual differences in learning histories may also contribute to variations in facial preferences within a culture. As discussed above, facial preferences can be influenced by familiarity with the faces or with the behavior of those being judged (Graziano, Jensen-Campbell, Shebilske, & Lundgren, 1993; Gross & Crofton, 1977; Kniffin & Wilson, 2000; Mita, Dermer, & Knight, 1977; Nisbett & Wilson, 1977). Facial preferences not only are influenced by direct experience with the behavior of people whose faces are being judged, but they may also be influenced by experiences with the behavior of others with similar faces. More specifically, an identity overgeneralization effect (Zebrowitz, 1997) may cause people to prefer faces that resemble the faces of significant others. Although no research has directly assessed such effects on *facial* preferences, there is evidence for an effect on *social* preferences. Women expressed more positive emotions about a man who was physically similar to the type of man they had been attracted to in the past than about one who did not physically resemble an old flame, even if the latter was as attractive (Fiske, 1982). Even a brief encounter with someone may be sufficient to set in motion the "mistaken identity" effect. When people were asked to choose one of two women, A or B, for a job requiring a kind and friendly person, they were more likely to choose A if they had just been treated kindly by someone who resembled her than if they had not had such an interaction. Similarly, when others were required to interact with one of two people, C or D, they were more likely to approach D if they had just been treated irritably by someone who resembled C (Lewicki, 1985). In another experiment, students who were exposed to photos of short-faced professors who behaved fairly and long-faced professors who behaved unfairly subsequently judged an unknown short-faced professor to be more fair than an unknown long-faced one. They did so even though they were not consciously aware of the correspondence between facial length and fairness among the professors to whom they were initially exposed (Hill, Lewicki, Czyzewska, & Schuller, 1990). Since knowledge of a person's positive traits increases judgments of their attractiveness, the attribution of positive traits to strangers who physically resemble those known to have such traits should increase the physical attractiveness of those strangers.

Effects of Social Goals

Cultural differences in facial preferences may derive from variations in social goals as well as from differences in learning histories. Considerable evidence has shown that different facial qualities are perceived to be associated with different psychological traits and that there is a consensus in many of these perceptions both within and across cultures (cf. Zebrowitz, 1997). The faces that people find most attractive may be those perceived to offer traits that can fulfill their social goals. For example, the facial features of the most popular American movie actresses varied with the economic conditions of the United States from 1932–1995. When economic conditions were stagnant and pessimistic, popularity was greatest for mature-faced movie stars, whose faces offer security. On the other hand, when economic conditions were prosperous and optimistic, popularity was greatest for baby-faced movie stars, whose faces offer dependence (Pettijohn & Tesser, 1999). Extrapolating from these historical changes to cultural variations, one might predict a preference for more mature faces in cultures that are economically disadvantaged and a preference for babyfaces in those that are prosperous.

Cultural differences in some of the positive psychological traits that are associated with an attractive appearance (see, e.g., Wheeler & Kim, 1997) also suggest a possible effect of social goals on facial preferences. Evidence reviewed by Dion (Chapter 8, this volume) indicates that people in individualistic cultures attribute their culturally valued traits of dominance and extraversion to attractive individuals, whereas people in collectivist cultures attribute their culturally valued traits of integrity and intelligence. Insofar as the facial characteristics that signal dominance and extraversion differ from those that signal integrity and intelligence, different facial qualities may be preferred in these two types of cultures. Dion also argues that attraction among people may be more influenced by facial appearance in individualistic cultures, where the achievement of identity depends upon personal attributes, than in collectivistic cultures, where identity depends upon a person's place in the social system. More research is needed to assess this interesting hypothesis.

The desire to identify with individuals who are socially or culturally dominant is another social goal that can influence facial preferences (cf. Dion, Chapter 8, this volume). A cultural historian notes that there was a time when men of Irish descent had their noses surgically augmented to look more like the noses of English Americans, who were higher in status than the Irish. Many Jews, on the other hand, had their noses surgically diminished in order to look more like the noses of Irish or English Americans, who were higher in status than the Jews (Gilman, 1998). Jews as well as African Americans have their hair straightened in order to look more like members of the dominant culture, and Asians undergo eyelid surgery for the same purpose. The preference of American blacks for white facial features, which was discussed above, also may reflect a preference for features of the socially dominant group.

Differences in social goals may contribute not only to historical and cultural variations in facial preferences, but also to individual differences found within the same cultural and historical niche. For example, those who wish to dominate or protect others may prefer neonatal faces; those who wish to be protected may prefer mature faces. Consistent with this suggestion is the finding that men who scored high on personality tests of dominance expressed a greater preference for dating baby-faced women than those who were low in dominance (Hadden & Brownlow, 1991). Other evidence suggesting that social goals may moderate facial preferences is provided by the finding that men in a depressed mood showed a stronger preference for faces with positive expressions (cf. Cunningham et al., Chapter 7, this volume), and by evidence that women who are more willing to have short-term sexual relationships showed a stronger preference for attractive faces (Simpson & Gangestad, 1992).

Changes in facial preferences across the menstrual cycle (Franklin & Johnston, 2000; Little et al., Chapter 3, this volume; Penton-Voak & Perrett, 2000; Penton-Voak et al., 1999) may also be construed as an effect of social goals. Women who are at the fertile time of their cycle prefer more masculine male faces, suggesting that the implicit goal of conception may create a preference for such men. However, the *most* masculine-looking men are not the most preferred. This suggests that the goal of conception may also foster a preference for younger men or men who do not appear too cold or too dominant, since, as noted earlier, more feminized male faces are more neotenous, and research indicates that such "babyfaces" convey greater warmth and submissiveness (Montepare & Zebrowitz, 1998; Zebrowitz, 1997).

Recent evidence that facial preferences vary with women's assessment of their own attractiveness (Little et al., Chapter 3, this volume) may also reflect an effect of social goals. For example, women who perceive themselves as attractive prefer less feminized male faces than those who see themselves as less attractive (Little et al., Chapter 3, this volume). It remains to be determined whether the attractive women's greater preference for less feminized male faces reflects attractiveness matching (Aron, 1988; Feingold, 1988; Kalick & Hamilton, 1986, 1988; Price & Vandenberg, 1979; Terry & Macklin, 1977), stronger preferences for older-looking men, stronger preferences for the personality traits associated with more masculine faces (e.g., Franklin & Johnston, 2000; Friedman & Zebrowitz, 1992; Keating, this volume; Perrett et al., 1998), and/or some other difference between more and less attractive women.

Insofar as social goals influence facial preferences, one might expect variations as a function of perceiver sex or perceiver age. Although there has been considerable attention to sex differences in the valuation of attractiveness in a mate (cf. Buss, 1989; Buss & Schmitt, 1993; Eagly & Wood, 1999; Feingold, 1990), and some attention to age differences in preferences for youthfulness in a mate (Kenrick & Keefe, 1992), research has not systemically assessed sex or age differences in the particular facial qualities that are attractive. Typically, researchers have ignored perceiver age, and they have either studied only perceivers of the opposite sex from the faces being judged or they have demonstrated substantial male and female agreement in attractiveness judgments without probing further to see whether there are any dissimilarities in addition to the similarities. If face preferences are by-products of general perceptual mechanisms (e.g., prototype abstraction), then one would not expect them to vary with sex or age of rater. On the other hand, if face preferences have evolved to detect high-quality mates or friends, then there may be some interesting sex and age differences that have gone undetected. For example, men and women may have different social goals when judging the attractiveness of men, which could lead to different facial preferences. Intrasexual competition and communal goals may cause men to prefer less masculine-looking, baby-faced men, whom they may perceive as more cooperative and submissive, while the search for a high-quality mate may cause women to find men with more masculine features most appealing. Differences in social goals could also produce age differences in facial preferences. Insofar as younger individuals value status and dominance, they may find more masculine-looking, mature-faced men most appealing; insofar as older individuals value youthfulness, they may find baby-faced individuals most appealing.

In sum, there is considerable evidence indicating that beauty does indeed rest at least partly "in the eye of the beholder." Although there are facial qualities that reliably increase facial preferences for all or most perceivers, these effects can be moderated or eliminated by a perceiver's learning history and social goals, both of which produce cultural and individual differences in facial preferences. Our understanding of facial attractiveness would profit from additional research exploring how facial qualities and perceiver qualities interact to yield facial preferences (cf. Gangestad & Simpson, 2000, for a related discussion).

Summary and Conclusions

We have reviewed several mechanisms that could contribute to facial preferences. On the good genes account, preferences evolved because attractive facial traits provide reliable information about mate quality. On the perceptual by-product and overgeneralization accounts, attractive facial traits are seen as signals that exploit preexisting perceptual and cognitive mechanisms within the observer, without necessarily signaling mate quality. On the social mechanisms account, attractive facial traits depend on the learning history and social goals of the perceiver. It is important to realize that these mechanisms need not be mutually exclusive. Some attractive facial traits might exploit preexisting perceptual biases and others might have evolved because they signal mate quality. Still others might reflect the particular faces to which people have been exposed, the significant events that have been paired with those faces, and the psychological qualities being sought. Moreover, the information value of the signals and our attunement to them may both play a role. Of the many facial traits presumably reflecting mate quality, we may respond only to those that are readily processed by our perceptual and cognitive systems, and these may vary across perceivers. Multiple selection pressures operating during our evolutionary history, our personal learning histories, and our social goals all may combine to shape our facial preferences.

GENERAL CONCLUSIONS

Facial appearance influences sexual attraction as well as attraction to infants, peers, and leaders, and it influences the social interaction outcomes of people in all of these categories. These significant social consequences of appearance underscore the importance of understanding what makes a face attractive and why. Although the differential contributions of various facial qualities to each type of attraction require further research, it is clear that facial attractiveness can be enhanced by averageness, symmetry, positive expressions and behavior, youthfulness, familiarity, or certain sexually dimorphic qualities. However, high values of any one of these qualities are neither necessary nor sufficient to enhance facial attractiveness. The responsiveness of facial preferences to any one of these qualities reveals an adaptive flexibility that is likely to ensure a broad range of acceptable mates and recipients of nurturant and respectful attraction. Not only are none of these qualities necessary for facial attractiveness, but also none of these qualities alone seems to produce an extremely high level of attractiveness. Average faces are more attractive than nonaverage faces, but they are not necessarily beautiful. The same is true for faces that are symmetrical versus nonsymmetrical, smiling versus unsmiling, youthful versus older, familiar versus unfamiliar, or high versus low in sexual dimorphism. It may be that high values on *multiple* qualities are needed for very high levels of attractiveness, and additional research is needed to address this issue (cf. Cunningham, Chapter 7, this volume).

Whereas multiple positive qualities may be necessary to produce high facial attractiveness, we have argued that a low value on any one quality may be sufficient to produce an unattractive face. A greater ease of producing unattractiveness than attractiveness would be consistent with other evidence that people are highly responsive to negative cues. In particular, people show greater responsiveness to negative than to positive emotions (Hansen & Hansen, 1988) and to negative than to positive personality traits (e.g., Fiske, 1980; Hodges, 1974; Warr, 1974). These responses can be explained by the greater evolutionary importance of reacting to cues that signal danger, as might a lower bar for detecting unattractiveness than attractiveness.

Each of the explanations for facial preferences that has been offered is problematic. The hypothesis that attractiveness reflects an aesthetic preference without necessary adaptive functions begs the question of where that aesthetic preference comes from. The hypothesis that attractiveness signals "good genes" is at best weakly supported by the available evidence. The hypothesis that attractiveness is a by-product of correct age and sex identification suffers from inconsistent preferences for masculine-looking men. The hypothesis that attractiveness derives from an overgeneralization of responses to infants, unfit individuals, emotional expressions, or familiar people has not been empirically tested. A dearth of research evidence also plagues the hypotheses that perceptions of attractiveness derive from learning histories and social goals.

More research is needed to assess the power of the various explanatory hypotheses, which are not mutually exclusive. Although there has been much research testing the "good genes" hypothesis, little has tested the various perceptual by-product hypotheses or the hypotheses that overgeneralizations, learning histories, and social goals contribute to facial preferences. Efforts to explain preferences for certain faces also would do well to take into account the likely possibility that facial attractiveness serves *multiple* functions: It may advertise genetic quality, a desirable age and sex, nonthreatening familiarity, *and* desirable personality traits. Considering the possibility that several of the explanations for facial attractiveness are working in concert may lead to a better understanding of the facial qualities that produce very high levels of attractiveness. For example, the fact that masculine male faces are not always the most preferred, as predicted from the correct sex identification explanation, may reflect a countervailing influence of an averageness effect. Indeed, Franklin and Johnston (2000) found that the male face judged most attractive was in between that judged to be most masculine and that judged to be most average (which was in fact close to the true average). The multiple functions that attractiveness may serve underscore the important role of the perceiver. A face may offer nonthreatening familiarity, desirable personality traits, and a desirable age and sex to one perceiver, but not to another, depending on the perceiver's learning history and social goals. Even the genetic quality advertised by a face may depend upon the perceiver, since reproductive success is enhanced by an optimal level of genetic variation (Thornhill & Gangestad, 1993; Wedekind, Seebeck, Bettens, & Parpke, 1995).

Not only may facial attractiveness serve multiple functions, but also these functions may vary with the type of attraction. For example, the function of advertising a person's sex and genetic quality may be more relevant to sexual attraction than it is to respectful attraction, while the function of advertising a person's age and particular personality traits may be more relevant to respectful attraction. The functions served by attractiveness also may vary with the level of attractiveness. For example, the function of advertising genetic quality may be more relevant to very low attractiveness, than to very high attractiveness, insofar as health and fertility fall off significantly only at the very low end of the attractiveness continuum, a possibility that merits investigation.

In conclusion, we suggest that attractiveness may serve multiple functions, each of which can influence what makes a face attractive. A multipurpose attractiveness has at least three consequences that should be pursued in future research: 1) different facial qualities may contribute to different types of attraction; 2) multiple facial qualities may contribute to very high attractiveness, while a single quality may be sufficient for very low attractiveness; and 3) both qualities of the perceiver and qualities of the face may contribute to facial attractiveness. As this research agenda reveals, facial attractiveness is a complex phenomenon, even more so than suggested by a poet's wisdom:

Tis not a lip, or eye, we beauty call,
But the joint force and full result of all. (A. Pope, 1711)

NOTES

This work was supported by National Science Foundation Grant No. 97–08619 to the first author and by grants from the Australian Research Council and the University of Western Australia to the second author.

1. It should be noted that some perceptual by-product accounts are evolutionary, since they argue that signals from potential mates evolved to exploit a perceptual mechanism that itself evolved in a context other than mate choice.

2. The fact is that baby-faced individuals often do not have the traits they are perceived to have (e.g., Zebrowitz, Andreoletti, Collins, Young, & Blumenthal, 1998), which is consistent with the argument that these perceptions reflect an overgeneralization of accurate perceptions of real babies.

3. Many attribute cultural influences on standards of beauty to the media, but this simply begs the question of what cultural forces are operating *on* the media.

REFERENCES

Alley, T. R. (1981). Head shape and the perception of cuteness. *Developmental Psychology, 17*, 650–654.

Alley, T. R. (1983). Infantile head shape as an elicitor of adult protection. *Merrill-Palmer Quarterly, 29*, 411–427.

Andersson, M. (1994). *Sexual selection.* Princeton, NJ: Princeton University Press.

Aron, A. (1988). The matching hypothesis reconsidered again: Comment on Kalick and Hamilton. *Journal of Personality and Social Psychology, 54*, 441–446.

Battistich, V. A., & Aronoff, J. (1985). Perceiver, target, and situational influences on social cognition: An interactional analysis. *Journal of Personality and Social Psychology, 49*, 788–798.

Bell, R. Q., & Waldrop, M. F. (1982). Temperament and minor physical anomalies. In R. Porter & G. M. Collins (Eds.), *Temperamental differences in infants and young children: CIBA Symposium No. 89* (pp. 206–220). London: Pitman.

Benson, P. L., Karabenick, S. A., & Lerner, R. M. (1976). Pretty pleases: The effects of physical attrctiveness, race, and sex on receiving help. *Journal of Experimental Social Psychology, 12*, 409–415.

Bernstein, I. H., Lin, T. D., & McClellan, P. (1982). Cross- vs. within-racial judgments of attractiveness. *Perception and Psychophysics, 32*, 495–503.

Berry, D. S. (1991). Attractive faces are not all created equal: Joint effects of facial babyishness and attractiveness on social perception. *Personality and Social Psychology Bulletin, 17*, 523–531.

Berry, D. S. (2000). Attractiveness, attraction, and sexual selection: Evolutionary perspectives on the form and function of physical attractiveness. In M. P.

Zanna (Ed.), *Advances in experimental social psychology* (Vol. 32, pp. 273–342). San Diego, CA: Academic Press.

Bond, M. (Ed.). (1988). *The cross-cultural challenge to social psychology.* Newbury Park, CA: Sage.

Bornstein, R. F. (1989). Exposure and affect: Overview and meta-analysis of research, 1968–1987. *Psychological Bulletin, 106*, 265–289.

Brooks, J., & Lewis, M. (1976). Infants' responses to strangers: Midget, adult, and child. *Child Development, 47*, 323–332.

Budesheim, T. L., & DePaola, S. J. (1994). Beauty or the beast? The effects of appearance, personality, and issue information on evaluations of political candidates. *Personality and Social Psychology Bulletin, 20*, 339–348.

Bull, R., & Rumsey, N. (1986). *The social psychology of facial appearance.* New York: Springer-Verlag.

Buss, D. M., (1989). Sex differences in human mate preferences: Evolutionary hypotheses tested in 37 cultures. *Behavioural and Brain Sciences, 12*, 1–49.

Buss, D. M., & Schmitt, D. P. (1993). Sexual strategies theory: An evolutionary perspective on human mating. *Psychological Review, 100*, 204–232.

Campbell, M., Geller, B., Small, A. M., Petti, T. A., & Ferris, S. H. (1978). Minor physical anomalies in young psychotic children. *American Journal of Psychiatry, 135*, 573–575.

Cash, T. F., Gillen, G., & Burns, D. S. (1977). Sexism and "beautyism" in personnel consultant decision making. *Journal of Applied Psychology, 62*, 301–310.

Clarren, S. K., Sampson, P. D., Larsen, J., Donnell, D. J., Barr, H. M., Bookstein, F. L., Martin, D. C., & Streissguth, A. P. (1987). Facial effects of fetal alcohol exposure: Assessment by photographs and morphometric analysis. *American Journal of Medical Genetics, 26*, 651–666.

Cronin, H. (1991). *The ant and the peacock: Altruism and sexual selection from Darwin to today.* Cambridge, UK: Cambridge University Press.

Cummings, C. D., Flynn, D., & Preus, M. (1982). Increased morphological variants in children with learning disabilities. *Journal of Autism and Developmental Disorders, 12*, 373–383.

Cunningham, M. R. (1986). Measuring the physical in physical attractiveness: Quasi-experiments on the sociobiology of female facial beauty. *Journal of Personality and Social Psychology*, *50*, 925–935.

Cunningham, M. R., Barbee, A. P., & Pike, C. L. (1990). What do women want? Facialmetric assessment of multiple motives in the perception of male facial physical attractiveness. *Journal of Personality and Social Psychology, 59*, 61–72.

Cunningham, M. R., Roberts, A. R., Wu, C., Barbee, A. P., & Druen, P. B. (1995). "Their ideas of beauty are, on the whole, the same as ours": Consistency and variability in the cross-cultural perception of female physical attractiveness. *Journal of Personality and Social Psychology, 68*, 261–279.

Darwin, C. (1974). *Autobiographies: Charles Darwin, Thomas Henry Huxley.* Edited with an Introduction by Gavin de Beer. London and New York: Oxford University Press.

Dipboye, R. L., Arvey, R. D., & Terpstra, D. E. (1977). Sex and physical attractiveness of raters and applicants as determinants of resume evaluations. *Journal of Applied Psychology, 62*, 288–294.

Dipboye, R. L., Fromkin, H. L., & Wiback, K. (1975). Relative importance of applicant sex, attractiveness, and scholastic standing in evaluation of job applicant resumes. *Journal of Applied Psychology, 60*, 39–43.

Eagly, A. H., Ashmore, R. D., Makhijani, M. G., & Longo, L. C. (1991). What is beautiful is good: A meta-analytic review of research on the physical attractiveness stereotype. *Psychological Bulletin, 110*, 109–128.

Eagly, A. H., & Wood, W.(1999). The origins of sex differences in human behavior: Evolved dispositions versus social roles. *American Psychologist, 54*, 408–423.

Edwards, C. P. (1984) The age group labels and categories of preschool children. *Child Development, 55*, 440–452.

Efran, M. G., & Patterson, E. W. (1974). Voters vote beautiful: The effect of physical appearance on a national election. *Canadian Journal of Behavioral Science, 6*, 352–356.

Eibl-Eibesfeldt, I. (1970). *Ethology, the biology of behavior.* New York: Holt, Rinehart and Winston.

Ellison, P. T. (1999). Reproductive ecology and reproductive cancers. In C. Panter-Brick & C. M. Worthman (Eds.), *Hormones, health and behavior: A socio-ecological and lifespan perspective.* Cambridge, UK: Cambridge University Press.

Endler, J. A., & Basolo, A. L. (1998). Sensory ecology, receiver biases and sexual selection. *Trends in Ecology and Evolution, 13*, 415–420.

Enlow, D. H. (1990). *Facial growth* (3rd ed.). Philadelphia: Harcourt Brace Jovanovich.

Enquist, M., & Arak, A. (1994). Symmetry, beauty and evolution. *Nature, 372*, 169–172.

Enquist, M., & Johnstone, R. A. (1997). Generalization and the evolution of symmetry preferences. *Proceedings of the Royal Society of London, Series B, 264*, 1345–1348.

Feingold, A. (1988). Matching for attractiveness in romantic partners and same-sex friends: A meta-analysis and theoretical critique. *Psychological Bulletin, 104*, 226–235.

Feingold, A. (1990). Gender differences in effects of physical attractiveness on romantic attraction: Comparison across five research domains. *Journal of Personality and Social Psychology, 59*, 981–993.

Feingold, A. (1992). Good-looking people are not what we think. *Psychological Bulletin, 111*, 304–341.

Fisher, R. A. (1915). The evolution of sexual preference. *Eugenics Review, 7*, 184–192.

Fiske, S. T. (1980). Attention and weight in person perception: The impact of negative and extreme behavior. *Journal of Personality and Social Psychology, 38*, 889–906.

Fiske, S. T. (1982). Schema-triggered affect: Applications to social perception. In M. S. Clark & S. T. Fiske (Eds.), *Affect and cognition: The Seventeenth Annual Carnegie Symposium on Cognition* (p. 66). Mahwah, NJ: Erlbaum.

Folstad, I., & Karter, A. J. (1992). Parasites, bright males, and the immunocompetence handicap. *American Naturalist, 139*, 603–622.

Franklin, M., & Johnston, V. S. (2000, June) *Hormone markers and beauty.* Paper presented at the annual meeting of the Human Behavior and Evolution Society, Amherst College, MA.

Friedman, H., & Zebrowitz, L. A. (1992). The contribution of typical sex differences in facial maturity to sex role stereotypes. *Personality and Social Psychology Bulletin, 18*, 430–438.

Gangestad, S. W., & Buss, D. M. (1993) Pathogen prevalence and human mate preferences. *Ethology and Sociobiology, 14*, 89–96.

Gangstead, S. W., and Simpson, J. A. (2000). The evolution of human mating: Trade-offs and strategic pluralism. *Behavioral and Brain Sciences, 23*, 573–644.

Gilbert, D. T., Fiske, S. T., & Lindzey, G. (1998). *The handbook of social psychology* (4th ed.). New York: McGraw-Hill.

Gilman, S. (1998). *Creating beauty to cure the soul: Race and psychology in the shaping of aesthetic surgery.* Durham, NC: Duke University Press.

Grammer, K., & Thornhill, R. (1994). Human (*Homo sapiens*) facial attractiveness and sexual selection: The role of symmetry and averageness. *Journal of Comparative Psychology, 108*, 233–242.

Gray, H. (1985). *Anatomy of the human body* (30th ed.). Philadelphia: Lea & Febiger.

Graziano, W. G., Jensen-Campbell, L., Shebilski, L., & Lundgren, S. (1993). Social influence, sex differences and judgments of beauty: Putting the interpersonal back in interpersonal attraction. *Journal of Personality and Social Psychology, 65*, 522–531.

Gross, A., & Crofton, C. (1977). What is good is beautiful? *Sociometry, 40*, 85–90.

Guy, J. D., Majorski, L. V., Wallace, C. J., & Guy, M. P. (1983). The incidence of minor physical anomalies in adult male schizophrenics. *Schizophrenia Bulletin, 9*, 571–582.

Hadden, S. B., & Brownlow. S. (1991, March). *The impact of facial structure and assertiveness on dating choice.* Paper presented at the meeting of the Southeastern Psychological Association, New Orleans, LA.

Halberstadt, J., & Rhodes, G. (2000). The attractiveness of non-face averageness: Implications for an evolutionary explanation of the attractiveness of average faces. *Psychological Science, 11*, 285–289.

Hamilton, W. D., & Zuk, M. (1982). Heritable true fitness and bright birds: A role for parasites? *Science, 218*, 384–387.

Hammermesh, D., & Biddle, J. (1994). *Beauty and the labor market* (Working Paper No. 4518). National Bureau of Economic Research, Cambridge, MA.

Hansen, C. M., & Hansen, R. D. (1988). Finding the face in the crowd: An anger superiority effect. *Journal of Personality and Social Psychology, 54*, 917–924.

Hassin, R., & Trope, Y. (2000). Facing faces: Studies on the cognitive aspects of physiognomy. *Journal of Personality and Social Psychology, 78*, 837–852.

Hatfield, E., & Sprecher, S. (1986). *Mirror, mirror: The importance of looks in everyday life.* Albany: State University of New York Press.

Henss, R. (1991). Perceiving age and attractiveness in facial photographs. *Journal of Applied Psychology, 21*, 933–946.

Hildebrant, K. A., & Fitzgerald, H. (1983). The infant's physical attractiveness: Its effects on bonding and attachment. *Infant Mental Health Journal, 4*, 3–12.

Hill, T., Lewicki, P., Czyzewska, M., & Schuller, G. (1990). The role of learned inferential encoding rules in the perception of faces: Effects of nonconscious self-perpetuation of a bias. *Journal of Experimental Social Psychology, 26*, 350–371.

Hodges, B. (1974). Effect of valence on relative weighting in impression formation. *Journal of Personality and Social Psychology, 30*, 378–381.

Holmes, S., & Hatch, C. E. (1938). Personal appearance as related to scholastic records and marriage selection in college women. *Human Biology, 10*, 65–76.

Hoyme, H. E. (1994). Minor anomalies: Diagnostic clues to aberrant human morphogenesis. In T. A. Markow (Ed.), *Developmental instability: Its origins and evolutionary implications* (pp. 309–317). Hague, Netherlands: Kluwer Academic.

Johnston, V. S., & Franklin, M. (1993). Is beauty in the eye of the beholder? *Ethology and Sociobiology, 14*, 183–199.

Johnstone, R. A. (1994). Female preference for symmetrical males as a by-product of mate recognition. *Nature, 372*, 172–175.

Jones, D. (1996). *Physical attractiveness and the theory of sexual selection.* Ann Arbor: Museum of Anthropology, University of Michigan.

Jones, D., & Hill, K. (1993). Criteria of attractiveness in five populations. *Human Nature, 4*, 271–296.

Jones, G., & Smith, P. K. (1984). The eyes have it: Young children's discrimination of age in masked and unmasked facial photographs. *Journal of Experimental Child Psychology, 38*, 328–337.

Kalick, S. M., & Hamilton, T. E. (1986). The matching hypothesis reexamined. *Journal of Personality and Social Psychology, 51*, 673–682.

Kalick, S. M., & Hamilton, T. E. (1988). Closer look at a matching simulation: Reply to Aron. *Journal of Personality and Social Psychology, 54*, 447–451.

Kalick, S. M., Zebrowitz, L. A., Langlois, J. H., & Johnson, R. M. (1998). Does human facial attractiveness honestly advertise health? Longitudinal data on an evolutionary question. *Psychological Science, 9*, 8–13.

Kanda, N., Tsuchida, T., & Tamaki, K. (1996). Testosterone inhibits immunoglobulin production by human peripheral blood mononuclear cells. *Clinical and Experimental Immunology, 106*, 410–415.

Keating, C. F. (1985). Gender and the physiognomy of dominance and attractiveness. *Social Psychology Quarterly, 48*, 61–70.

Kenrick, D. T., & Keefe, R. C. (1992). Age preferences in mates reflect sex differences in human reproductive strategies. *Behavioral and Brain Sciences, 15*, 75–133.

Kleck, R. E., Richardson, S. A., & Ronald, L. (1974). Physical appearance cues and interpersonal attraction in children. *Child Development, 45*, 305–310.

Kniffin, K., & Wilson, D. S. (2000, June). *What is good is beautiful.* Paper presented at the annual meeting of the Human Behavior and Evolution Society, Amherst College, MA.

Kogan, N., Stevens, J., & Shelton, F. C. (1961). Age differences: A developmental study of discriminability and affective response. *Journal of Abnormal Social Psychology, 62*, 221–230.

Kramer, S. Zebrowitz, L. A., San Giovanni, J. P., Sherak, B. (1995). Infant preferences for attractiveness and babyfaceness. In B. G. Bardy, R. J. Bootsma, &

Y. Girard (Eds.), *Studies in perception and action III* (pp. 389–392). Mahwah, NJ: Erlbaum.

Krouse, J. P., & Kauffman, J. M. (1982). Minor physical anomalies in exceptional children: A review and critique of research. *Journal of Abnormal Child Psychology, 10*, 247–264.

Langlois, J. H., Kalakanis, L. E., Rubenstein, A. J., Larson, A. D., Hallam, M. J., & Smoot, M. T. (2000). Maxims and myths of beauty: A meta-analytic and theoretical review. *Psychological Bulletin, 126*, 390–423.

Langlois, J. H., Ritter, J. M., Casey, R. J., & Sawin, D. B. (1995). Infant attractiveness predicts maternal behavior and attitudes. *Developmental Psychology, 31*, 464–472.

Langlois, J. H., Ritter, J. M., Roggman, L. A., & Vaughn, L. S. (1991). Facial diversity and infant preferences for attractive faces. *Developmental Psychology, 27*, 79–84.

Langlois, J. H., & Roggman, L. A. (1990). Attractive faces are only average. *Psychological Science, 1*, 115–121.

Langlois, J. H., Roggman, L. A., Casey, R. J., Ritter, J. M., Reiser-Danner, L. A., & Jenkins, V. Y. (1987). Infant preferences for attractive faces: Rudiments of a stereotype? *Developmental Psychology, 23*, 363–369.

Langlois, J. H., Roggman, L. A., & Musselman, L. (1994). What is average and what is not average about attractive faces? *Psychological Science, 5*, 214–220.

Langlois, J. H., Roggman, L. A., & Rieser-Danner, L. A. (1990). Infants' differential social responses to attractive and unattractive faces. *Developmental Psychology, 26*, 153–159.

Langlois, J. H., & Styczynski, L. (1979). The effects of physical attractiveness on the behavioral attributions and peer preferences in acquainted children. *International Journal of Behavioral Development, 2*, 325–341.

Lasky, R. E., Klein, R. E., & Martinez, S. (1974). Age and sex discrimination in five- and six-month-old infants. *Journal of Psychology, 88*, 317–324.

Lerner, R. M., & Lerner, J. V. (1977). Effects of age, sex, and physical attractiveness on child–peer relations, academic performance, and elementary school adjustment. *Developmental Psychology, 13*, 585–590.

Lewicki, P. (1985). Nonconscious biasing effects of single instances on subsequent judgments. *Journal of Personality and Social Psychology, 48*, 563–574.

Lewis, K. E., & Bierly, M. (1990). Toward a profile of the female voter: Sex differences in perceived physical attractiveness and competence of political candidates. *Sex Roles, 22*, 1–12.

Light, L. L., Hollander, S., & Kayra-Stuart, F. (1981). Why attractive people are harder to remember. *Personality and Social Psychology Bulletin, 7*, 269–276.

Livshits, G., & Kobyliansky, E. (1991). Fluctuating asymmetry as a possible measure of developmental homeostasis in humans: A review. *Human Biology, 63*, 441–466.

Mace, K. C. (1972). The "overt-bluff" shoplifter: Who gets caught? *Journal of Forensic Psychology, 4*, 26–30.

Mackintosh, NJ (1998). *IQ and human intelligence*. Oxford: Oxford University Press.

Martin, J. G. (1964). Racial ethnocentrism and judgment of beauty. *Journal of Social Psychology, 63*, 59–63.

McArthur, L. Z., & Apatow, K. (1983–84). Impressions of babyfaced adults. *Social Cognition, 2*, 315–342.

McArthur, L. Z. & Baron, R. M. (1983). Toward an ecological theory of social perception. *Psychological Review, 90*, 215–238.

McCall, R. B., & Kennedy, C. B. (1980). Attention of 4-month infants to discrepancy and babyishness. *Journal of Experimental Child Psychology, 29*, 189–201.

Mealey, L., Bridgestock, R., & Townsend, G. C. (1999). Symmetry and perceived facial attractiveness: A monozygotic co-twin comparison. *Journal of Personality and Social Psychology, 76*, 151–158.

Miller, G. (2000). *The Mating Mind*. New York: Doubleday.

Miller, G. F. (1992, July). *Sexual selection for protean expressiveness: A new model of hominid encephalization*. Paper presented at the 4th annual meeting of the Human Behavior and Evolution Society, Albuquerque, NM. Cited in M. Ridley (1993). *The Red Queen: Sex and the Evolution of Human Nature*. New York: Penguin Books, p. 338.

Miller, G. F., & Todd, P. M. (1998). Mate choice turns cognitive. *Trends in Cognitive Sciences, 2*, 190–198.

Mita, T. H., Dermer, M., & Knight, J. (1977). Reversed facial images and the mere-exposure hypothesis. *Journal of Personality and Social Psychology, 35*, 597–601.

Møller, A. P., & Swaddle, J. P. (1997). *Asymmetry, developmental stability, and evolution*. Oxford: Oxford University Press.

Montepare, J. M., & McArthur, L. Z. (1986). The influence of facial characteristics on children's age perceptions. *Journal of Experimental Child Psychology, 42*, 303–314.

Montepare, J. M., & Zebrowitz, L. A. (1998) Person perception comes of age: The salience and significance of age in social judgments. *Advances in Experimental Social Psychology, 30*, 93–161.

Montepare, J. M., & Zebrowitz-McArthur, L. (1989). Children's perceptions of babyfaced adults. *Perceptual and Motor Skills, 69*, 467–472.

Mueser, K. T., Grau, B. W., Sussman, M. S., & Rosen, A. J. (1984). You're only as pretty as you feel: Facial expression as a determinant of physical attractiveness. *Journal of Personality and Social Psychology, 46*, 469–478.

Muscarella, F., & Cunningham, M. R. (1996). The evolutionary significance and social perception of male pattern baldness and facial hair. *Ethology and Sociobiology, 17*, 99–117.

Nisbett, R. E., & Wilson, T. D. (1977). The halo effect: Evidence for unconscious alteration of judgments. *Journal of Personality and Social Psychology, 35*, 250–256.

Parsons, P. A. (1990). Fluctuating asymmetry: An epigenetic measure of stress. *Biological Reviews, 65*, 131–145.

Patzer, G. L. (1985). *The attractiveness phenomenon*. New York: Plenum Press.

Paulhus, D. L., & Martin, C. L. (1986). Predicting adult temperament from minor physical anomalies. *Journal of Personality and Social Psychology, 50*, 1235–1239.

Penton-Voak, I. S., & Perrett, D. (2000). Female preference for male faces changes cyclically: Further evidence. *Evolution and Human Behavior, 21*, 39–48.

Penton-Voak, I. S., Perrett, D., Castles, D., Burt, M., Koyabashi, T., & Murray, L. K. (1999). Female preferences for male faces change cyclically. *Nature, 399*, 741–742.

Perrett, D. I., Burt, D. M., Penton-Voak, I. S., Lee, K. J., Rowland, D. A., & Edwards, R. (1999). Symmetry and human facial attractiveness. *Evolution and Human Behaviour, 20*, 295–307.

Perrett, D. I., Lee, K. J., Penton-Voak, I. S., Rowland, D. R., Yoshikawa, S., Burt, D. M., Henzi, S. P., Castles, D. L., & Akamatsu, S. (1998). Effects of sexual dimorphism on facial attractiveness. *Nature, 394*, 884–887.

Perrett, D. I., May, K. A., & Yoshikawa, S. (1994). Facial shape and judgments of female attractiveness. *Nature, 368*, 239–242.

Pettijohn, II., T. F., & Tesser, A. (1999). Popularity in environmental context: Facial feature assessment of American movie actresses. *Media Psychology, 1*, 229–247.

Pope, A. (1711). An essay on criticism, part II, line 45. Quoted in J. Bartlett (1980). *Bartlett's familiar quotations* (15th edition., p. 333). Boston: Little, Brown.

Price, R. A., & Vandenberg, S. G. (1979). Matching for physical attractiveness in married couples. *Personality and Social Psychology Bulletin, 5*, 398–400.

Reis, H. T., Wilson, I. M., Monestere, C., Bernstein, S., Clark, K., Seidl, E., Franco, M., Giogioso, E., Freeman, L., & Radoane, K. (1990). What is smiling is beautiful and good. *European Journal of Social Psychology, 20*, 259–267.

Rhodes, G., Hickford, C., & Jeffery, L. (2000a). Sex-typicality and attractiveness: Are supermale and superfemale faces super-attractive? *British Journal of Psychology, 91*, 125–140.

Rhodes, G., Nakayama, K., & Halberstadt, J. (2000b). [Perceptual adaptation affects attractiveness]. Unpublished raw data.

Rhodes, G., Proffitt, F., Grady, J. M., & Sumich, A. (1998). Facial symmetry and the perception of beauty. *Psychonomic Bulletin and Review, 5*, 659–669.

Rhodes, G., Roberts, J., & Simmons, L. (1999a). Reflections on symmetry and attractiveness. *Psychology, Evolution and Gender, 1*, 279–295.

Rhodes, G., Sumich, A., & Byatt, G. (1999b). Are average facial configurations attractive only because of their symmetry? *Psychological Science, 10*, 52–58.

Rhodes, G., & Tremewan, T. (1996). Averageness, exaggeration and facial attractiveness. *Psychological Science, 7*, 105–110.

Rhodes, G., Zebrowitz, L. A., Clark, A., Kalick, S. M., Hightower, A., & McKay, R. (2000c). Do facial averageness and symmetry signal health? *Evolution and Human Behavior, 21*, 1–16.

Shackelford, T. K., & Larson, R. J. (1997). Facial asymmetry as an indicator of psychological, emotional, and physiological distress. *Journal of Personality and Social Psychology, 72*, 456–466.

Shackelford, T. K., & Larsen, R. J. (1999). Facial attractiveness and physical health. *Evolution and Human Behavior, 20*, 71–76.

Sigelman, C. K., Thomas, D. B., Sigelman, L., & Ribich, F. D. (1986). Gender, physical attractiveness, and electability: An experimental investigation of voter biases. *Journal of Applied Social Psychology, 16*, 229–248.

Simpson, J. A., and Gangestad, S. W. (1992). Sociosexuality and romantic partner choice. *Journal of Personality, 60*, 31–51.

Snyder, M., Tanke, E. D., & Berscheid, E. (1977). Social perception and interpersonal behavior: On the self-fulfilling nature of social stereotypes. *Journal of Personality and Social Psychology, 35*, 656–666.

Sroufe, R. A., Chaikin, A., Cook, R., & Freeman, V. (1977). The effects of physical attractiveness on honesty: A socially desirable response. *Personality and Social Psychology Bulletin, 3*, 59–62.

Steffensmeier, D. J., & Terry, R. M. (1973). Deviance and respectability: An observational study of reactions to shoplifting. *Social Forces, 51*, 417–426.

Sternglanz, S. H., Gray, J. L., & Murakami, M. (1977). Adult preferences for infantile facial features: An ethological approach. *Animal Behavior, 25*, 108–115.

Stewart, J. E. (1980). Defendant's attractiveness as a factor in the outcome of criminal trials: An observational study. *Journal of Applied Social Psychology, 10*, 348–361.

Terry, R. L., & Macklin, E. (1977). Accuracy of identifying married couples on the basis of similarity of attractiveness. *Journal of Psychology, 97*, 15–20.

Thornhill, R., & Gangestad, S. W. (1993). Human facial beauty: Averageness, symmetry, and parasite resistance. *Human Nature, 4*, 237–269.

Thornhill, R., & Gangestad, S. W. (1999a). Facial attractiveness. *Trends in Cognitive Sciences, 3*, 452– 460.

Thornhill, R., & Gangestad, S. W. (1999b). The scent of symmetry: A human sex pheromone that signals fitness? *Evolution and Human Behaviour, 20*, 175–201.

Thornhill, T., & Møller, A. P. (1997). Developmental stability, disease and medicine. *Biological Reviews, 72*, 497–548.

Todd, J. T., Mark, L. S., Shaw, R. E., & Pittenger, R. E. (1980). The perception of human growth. *Scientific American, 242*, 132–145.

Udry, J. R., & Eckland, B. K. (1984). Benefits of being attractive. Differential payoffs for men and women. *Psychological Reports, 54*, 47–56.

Wagatsuma, E., & Kleinke, C. L. (1979). Ratings of facial beauty by Asian-American and Caucasian females. *Journal of Social Psychology, 109*, 299–300.

Waldrop, M. F., & Halverson, C. F. (1972). Minor physical anomalies: Their incidence and relation to behavior in a normal and a deviant sample. In R. C. Smart & M. S. Smart (Eds.), *Readings in child development and relationships* (pp. 146–155). New York: Macmillan.

Walster, E., Aronson, V., Abrahams, D., & Rottman, L. (1966). Importance of physical attractiveness in dating behaviour. *Journal of Personality and Social Psychology, 4*, 508–516.

Warr, D. (1974). Inference magnitude, range, and evaluative direction as factors affecting relative importance of cues in impression formation. *Journal of Personality and Social Psychology, 30*, 191–197.

Waters, J. (1985). Cosmetics and the job market. In J. Graham & A. Kligman (Eds.), *The psychology of cosmetic treatments* (pp. 113–124).Westport, CT: Praeger.

Waynforth, D. (1998). Fluctuating asymmetry and human male life-history traits in rural Belize. *Proceedings of the Royal Society of London, Series B, 265*, 1497–1501.

Wedekind, C., Seebeck, T., Bettens, F., & Parpke, A. J. (1995). MHC-dependent mate preferences in humans. *Proceedings of the Royal Society of London, Series B, 260*, 245–249.

Wheeler, L., & Eghrari, H. (1986). *Sexy, sophisticated, or wholesome: Perceptions of different types of attractive females.* Unpublished manuscript, University of Rochester, Rochester, NY.

Wheeler, L., & Kim, Y. (1997). What is beautiful is culturally good: The physical attractiveness stereotype has different content in collectivistic cultures. *Personality and Social Psychology Bulletin, 23*, 795–800.

Yesilova, Z., Ozata, M., Kocar, I. H., Turan, M., Pekel, A., Sengul, A., & Ozdemir, I. C. (2000). The effects of gonadotropin treatment on the immunological features of male patients with idiopathic hypogonadotropic hypogonadism. *Journal of Clinical Endocrinology and Metabolism, 85*, 66–70.

Zahavi, A. (1975). Mate selection: A selection for a handicap. *Journal of Theoretical Biology, 53*, 205–214.

Zajonc, R. B.(1968). Attitudinal effects of mere exposure. *Journal of Personality and Social Psychology, 9*, (Suppl. No. 2, Part 2).

Zebrowitz, L. A. (1997). *Reading faces: Window to the soul?* Boulder, CO: Westview Press.

Zebrowitz, L. A., Andreoletti, C., Collins, M. A., Lee, S. Y., & Blumenthal, J. (1998). Bright, bad, babyfaced boys: Appearance stereotypes do not always yield self-fulfilling prophecy effects. *Journal of Personality and Social Psychology, 75*, 1300–1320.

Zebrowitz, L. A., & Collins, M. A. (1997) Accurate social perception at zero acquaintance: The affordances of a Gibsonian approach. *Personality and Social Psychology Review, 1*, 204–223.

Zebrowitz, L. A., Collins, M. A., & Dutta, R. (1998). Appearance and personality across the lifespan. *Personality and Social Psychology Bulletin, 24*, 736–749.

Zebrowitz, L. A., Hall, J. H., Murphy, N. A., & Rhodes, G. (in press). Looking good and looking smart. *Personality and Social Psychology Bulletin.*

Zebrowitz, L. A., & Montepare, J. M. (1992). Impressions of babyfaced males and females across the lifespan. *Developmental Psychology, 28*, 1143–1152.

Zebrowitz, L. A., Montepare, J. M., & Lee, H. K. (1993). They don't all look alike: Individuated impressions of other racial groups. *Journal of Personality and Social Psychology, 65*, 85–101.

Zebrowitz, L. A., Olson, K., & Hoffman, K. (1993). Stability of babyfacedness and attractiveness across the life span. *Journal of Personality and Social Psychology, 64*, 453–466.

Zebrowitz, L. A., Voinescu, L., & Collins, M. A. (1996). "Wide-eyed" and "crooked-faces": Determinants of perceived and real honesty across the life span. *Personality and Social Psychology Bulletin, 22*, 1258–1269.

Index

Abrahams, D., 60
Abused children, 159, 201
Academic performance, 38
Ache Indians, 40–41, 138, 140, 242–244
Acton, S., 11
Adiposity, 20, 94–95, 200, 211–212
Adobe Photoshop, 42
Affordances, 155–156, 160, 264
Age. *See* Babyness; Youthfulness
Aging features, 198, 207–208
Alley, T. R., 12–13, 62, 133
Alpha pattern, 205–206, 221
American Beauty, 193
Amphipods, 75
Apatow, K., 205
Apocrine glands, 95–96
Approachability, 176, 178
Aronson, V., 60
Ashmore, R. D., 210
Ashton, W. A., 222
Asians: composites vs. component, 49, 50–52; cross-cultural preferences, 10, 40–41, 45–48; distinctiveness and attractiveness, 48–49; extreme features in, 17–18; feature preference, 277; importance of attractiveness, 252–253; preference experiments, 41–52; sexual dimorphism, 67–68
Assortative mating, 75, 80–81
Attractiveness: adaptive trait relationship model, 271–273; cultural specificity vs. universality, 199–201, 276–281; deception, 160–162, 185 n.3, 185 n.4, 221–222; definition, 92–93; extreme trait avoidance, 108–109, 273; factor analysis, 111–114; historical ideals of, 199, 279; learning histories and, 277–278; measurement of, 263–264; multiple fitness model, 99–102, 155, 197–214; n-dimensional vector approach, 99–102, 114–116; overgeneralizations, 275–276; paternalistic conspiracy in,

200; preferences given to, 5, 28, 142–143, 261–262; professional ambivalence about, 262; single feature approach, 93–96. *See also* Attractiveness, body; Attractiveness, facial; Attractiveness stereotyping; Preference judgments

Attractiveness, body: factor analysis, 111–114; feature measurements and, 105–107; n-dimensional vector approach, 99–102, 114–116; photograph standardization, 102–105; waist-to-hip ratio, 96–97

Attractiveness, facial: age, 20, 198, 207–208; averageness theory, 61–62, 96–98, 116, 132–135, 154, 219–221; babyness proportions, 93, 162–163, 170–175; criminal justice system and, 262; cross-cultural and cross-ethnic agreement, 10, 45–48; desire for self-change, 254–255; doll study, 4; effect of personality on, 267–268; facial extremes, 16–19; feminization, 19, 37–38, 66–68, 71–74, 158, 266; as fundamental characteristic, 2, 265–268; health and, 22–23, 99, 143, 161–162, 270–271; importance of, 252–256; in contexts, 155–156; in leaders, 175–183, 185; innate preferences for, 21–25, 200–201; mask study, 4; maturity, 163–166, 170–175; physical fitness and, 23; pleasant voices and, 5; preoccupation with, 92; reasons for studying, 261–263; self-perceived, 74–83, 254–255, 280; subjectivity of, 1–5; symmetry, 13–16, 62–65, 83, 154, 215–216, 265–266. *See also* Average faces; Preference judgments

Attractiveness stereotyping: collectivistic cultures, 248–252, 255, 279; expected life outcomes index, 249; individualistic cultures, 247–248, 251–252, 255, 279; person perception paradigm, 245–246, 248; research accuracy, 246; social desirability index, 248–249; trait domains, 246, 248

Atzwanger, K., 94, 116

Austin, A. L., 133

Authority, 176–178

Average faces: attractiveness of, 61–62, 96–98, 116, 132–135, 154, 219–221; average features, 219–221; averageness as fundamental, 21, 28; averages of attractive faces, 133–134, 220; biological basis, 35–55, 61–62; cross-cultural and cross-ethnic agreement, 10, 45–52; definitions, 217–218; evolutionary advantages, 21–22; extreme features vs., 16–19, 133–135; feminization, 19, 37–38, 66–68, 71–74, 158; geometrically, 54 n.2; multidimensional scaling, 19–21; natural variations in, 37; numbers of faces in composites, 7–8; preference by infants, 10–11; as prototypes, 25, 97, 109–111; stimulus control, 132–135; symmetry in, 13–16, 28, 136; unexceptional ratings of, 218–219; youthfulness, 13, 28

Average features, 219–221

Averaging techniques: biases in, 11–12; blurring and smoothing from, 12, 97–98; cognitive, 25–27; composites of mirror images, 64, 216; distortions, 11, 120; global stimulus descriptors, 120; image-warping, 15, 99, 120, 219; keypoint morphing, 9–10, 43, 121; mathematical, 11, 36–37; mirror-image, 14, 16, 64, 98–99, 137, 216; numbers of faces in composites, 7–8; optimal value argument, 11–12; photographic compositing, 6–7, 10, 36–37, 216–217; pixel averaging, 7–9, 11; procrustes approach, 103; psychological dimensions, 19–21; removal of blemishes, 42; sexual dimorphism, 67; symmetry from, 13–16, 63–65, 136–137, 219; youthfulness from, 13. *See also* Photographs

Avoidance, 101, 108–109, 116–117, 273

Babies. *See* Infants
Babyness: attracting help, 168–170, 184, 198, 202; body proportions, 205; caretaking response, 93; cute response, 185 n.1, 201, 264; gender and, 163–166, 170–175, 184–185, 202; in factor analysis, 112–114, 116; as indicator of medical status, 202–203; leadership qualities, 175–179, 182, 184–185, 264; multiple fitness model, 201–203; overgeneralizations, 275; parasite resistance and, 95; sexual maturity features and, 204–206; social status cues, 160, 162–163; stereotyping, 284 n.2; in U. S. presidents, 180–183; variations in characteristics, 185 n.5. *See also* Youthfulness
Bailey, J. M., 224
Baker, R. R., 69
Bakker, T. C., 76, 81
Baldness, 20, 207–208
Banner, L. W., 199
Barbee, A. P., 193–238, 241–242
Barn swallows, 75
Bassett, J. F., 196
Beach, F. A., 199, 241
Beards, 211
Beauty: cultural relativism, 91–92, 276–281; as currency, 200; Darwin on, 35, 54 n.1, 91, 199–200 health and, 22–23, 99, 143; historical ideals, 199, 279; in the eye of the beholder, 1–5. *See also* Attractiveness
Beauty marks, 216
Beetles, 75, 80, 82
Beggan, J. K., 221–222
Bellis, M. A., 69
Ben Hamida, S., 224
Bengalese finches, 140–141
Bernstein, I. H., 240
Berscheid, E., 161, 245
Beta pattern, 205–206, 221
Bettler, R., 221–222
Birds, 100
Black Americans: facial preferences, 240, 242, 277–278; ideal body weight, 200, 212
Blackford, Katherine, 195
Blind dates, satisfaction with, 60, 261
Blood pressure, 22–23
Blurring, from averaging, 12, 97–98
Body fat distribution, 23, 94–95
Body hair, 95
Body weight, 200, 211–212
Bomba, P. C., 25
Bower, T. G., 24
Bowlby, J., 158
Brazilian preferences, 242–244
Breast form, 112–113, 116
Bridgestock, R., 63
Bronstad, P. M., 212
Burson, N., 216–217
Burt, D. Michael, 59–90
Busey, T. A., 19–20
Buss, D. M., 225, 252–253
Byatt, G., 15, 62, 219

Caricatures, 17–19, 53, 130, 132. *See also* Extreme features
Carling, R., 216–217
Cash, T., 96, 221
Caucasian faces: extreme features in, 17–18; infant preferences, 10; menstrual cycle and, 72–73; sexual dimorphism, 67–68, 72–73
Cezilly, F., 75
Cha, J.-H., 251
Charisma, 176, 178–179
Children, 253–54, 266. *See also* Infants
Chimeras, 13–14, 64–65, 137, 265
Chinese preferences: attractiveness stereotyping, 248–252; Chinese vs. non-Chinese, 42, 45–49, 240; cross-cultural, 241; distinctiveness and attractiveness, 48–49; importance of attractiveness, 252, 253–254
Chins, 194–195, 204–205, 214
Clark, J. J., 180
Cleeton, G. C., 196
Clinton, William J., 180–182
Coevolution of preferences, 141–145

Cognitive theory, 25–27
Collectivist cultures, 248–253, 255, 279
Communication, evolution of facial features, 129, 142
Condition-dependent mate choice, 76–77
Cosmetic surgery, 221–222, 279
Cozby, P., 252
Crawley, J. N., 100
Criminal faces, 6
Criminal justice system, attractiveness and, 262
Crogan, S., 91
Cronin, D. L., 23
Cross-cultural ratings: Ache Indians, 40–41, 138, 140, 242–244; agreement in, 2–3, 93, 240–245, 255, 263; babyness, 185 n.5, 202; criteria differences, 240–241; cultural relativism, 91–92; in culturally isolated groups, 40, 242–245, 255; degree of differentiation, 240, 255; disagreement in, 199–200, 241; evidence for biological basis, 53; expert vs. nonexpert, 41, 45–48; exposure to Western media, 242–244; importance of attractiveness, 252–256; individualistic cultures, 247–248, 253–254, 279; in-group biases, 27; Multiple Fitness model, 211–212; photographic exposure differences, 10; social goals and, 278–281
Cross-ethnic ratings, 2–3, 10, 27
Crystal, D. S., 253–254
Cultural evolution, 144–146
Cultural relativism, beauty and, 91–92
Cunningham, M. R., 12–13, 62, 66, 100, 133, 165, 193–238, 241–242, 264
Cute response, 185 n.1, 201, 264. *See also* Babyness
Cuthill, I. C., 98

Dabbs, J. M., 196
Darwin, Charles, 35, 54 n.1, 91, 199–200, 263
Da Vinci, Leonardo, 6
Decision making. *See* Mate selection; Preference judgments
Delta pattern, 213
Dermatoses, 97–98
Dermer, M., 222
Desmots, D., 75
Developmental stability, 38, 97, 206–207
Digital image analysis, 105, 119–120
Dilated pupils, 208–210
Dimorphism. *See* Secondary sexual characteristics
Dion, K. L., 248
Dion, Karen K., 239–59, 279
Directional selection, 206–207, 217
Discrimination, 128–129, 132, 135, 142, 145, 274–275
Distinctiveness, facial, 38, 43, 48–49, 50–52, 61–62
Dominance: attractiveness in men, 170–175; attractiveness stereotyping, 246; early recognition of, 158–59; features associated with, 157–158, 204, 227 n.2, 271, 279; gender and, 178–179, 279–280; importance of behavior, 176–177; mature features and, 163, 165
Dot patterns, 25
Druen, P. B., 221, 241–242
Dugatkin, L. A., 223
Dunbar, R. I. M., 77

Eagly, A. H., 246
Economics, effect on attractiveness, 211, 279
Effective reliability, 29 n.1
Egg size, 201
Eibl-Ebesfeldt, I., 201
Ellis, H., 99
Ellis, R. J., 246
Ellison, P. T., 94
Employment, attractiveness preference in, 168–170, 249, 262
English preferences, 241, 252
Enquist, Magnus, 127–151
Epsilon pattern, 213
Estrogen, 66, 93–94. *See also* Hormones

Evolutionary theory: coevolution, 141–145; cultural evolution, 144–146; developmental stability, 38, 97, 206–207; directional selection, 206–207, 217; facial extremes and, 16–19; good genes benefits, 71–72, 74, 79, 83, 269–273, 276; good taste hypothesis, 269; heterozygosity, 38, 61, 70, 97; innate preferences for attractive faces, 21–25; mate quality, 36–38, 59–60, 71, 76; normalizing selection, 21–22; overgeneralizations, 275–276; prototype abstraction mechanism, 39, 97, 274; youthfulness in, 59–60
Expected life outcomes index, 249
Expressive features, 198, 208–210, 215
Extra-pair copulation (EPC), 69, 71–72, 74
Extreme features: avoidance of, 108–109, 116; caricatures, 17–19, 53, 130, 132; combined with preferences for averages, 133–35; discrimination and generalization, 129–132, 135; facial, 16–19, 61–62; as sexual maturity features, 203–204
Extremes, facial, 16–19, 53, 61–62, 130, 132
Eye color, 195–196
Eyebrows, 209–210, 277
Eyeglasses, preference for, 139
Eyes, size of, 166–167, 170–175, 202–203, 205–206, 227 n.1

Face shape, 47–48, 54 n.5, 68, 71–74
Facial attractiveness. *See* Attractiveness, facial
Facial characteristics: age differentiation, 274–275; Alpha, Beta, and Gamma patterns, 205–206, 221; Delta and Epsilon patterns, 213; intellectual aptitude and, 196–197; pedomorphic, 156; resistance to generalization about, 195–197
Facial extremes, 16–19, 53, 61–62, 130, 132
Factor analysis, 111–114
Familiarity, 26–27, 39, 267
Farkas, L. G., 209
Fauss, R., 209
Feature measurements, 105–107, 194–197
Feingold, A., 2–3, 156
Females. *See* Women
Feminist perspective, 200
Feminization of features, 19, 37–38, 66–68, 71–74, 158, 266
Fertility, signs of, 93–95
Fetishes, 139–140
Fink, Bernhard, 91–125
Fitness, attractiveness and, 23
Fluctuating asymmetry (FA), 62–63, 136, 214–215
Folstad, I., 95
Forced-choice measures, 18, 43
Ford, C. S., 199, 241
Franklin, M., 210, 283
Freedman, G., 23
Frequency maps, 11
Friendliness, 208, 224
Furi, S., 70
FUTON system, 50

Galton, Sir Francis, 6–7, 36, 61–62, 96, 132–133, 216
Gamma pattern, 206, 221
Gammarus insensibilis, 75
Gangestad, S. W., 61, 63, 71, 82, 97, 99
Gasterosteus aculeatus (sticklebacks), 76, 81, 203
Generalization, 129, 132
Gente, P., 75
Geometric averageness, 54 n.2
Ghirlanda, Stefano, 127–151
Gigerenzer, G., 101
Gillen, B., 131
Gimbel, J., 222
Golden Proportion, 6
Goldstein, D. G., 101
Gomi, Akira, 102, 105
Good genes benefits, 71–72, 74, 79, 83, 269–273, 276
Good taste hypothesis, 269
Grady, J., 64, 98, 216

Grammer, K., 14–15, 63, 66, 91–125, 204, 218, 227 n.1, 273
Grau, B. W., 209
Gray values, 7
Graziano, W. G., 223
Grooming features, 198–199, 210–211
Gryphon Morph program, 43
Guppies, 76, 223
Gyrodactylus turnbulli, 76

Hair characteristics, 20, 95–96, 113, 195, 207–208, 211
Hallam, M. J., 10
Hamilton, W. D., 74
Handbook of Social Psychology (Gilbert et al.), 262
Hansell, S. J., 22
Harwood, C., 10
Harwood, Kate, 35–58
Health: accuracy of facial cues, 159–162; attractiveness and, 22–23, 38, 99, 143, 161–162, 270–271; facial distinctiveness and, 38; neoteny and, 202–203; parasites, 38, 61, 66, 70, 74–76, 270; perception of, 270; physical anomalies and, 38; symmetry and, 38, 161–162, 270
Heart rate recovery, 22–23
Height, 160–161
Henss, R., 92
Heterozygosity, 38, 61, 70, 97, 270
Hickford, C., 19
High cheekbones, 94, 165, 204
Hill, K., 41, 138, 140
Hirundo rustica, 75
Hiwi Indians, 140, 243–244
Hofstede, G., 247, 253
Honesty, 225, 246, 250
Hormones: attractiveness and, 93–95, 154–155; facial deception, 160; immune function and, 95, 270; menstrual cycle, 69–74, 84, 214, 266, 275, 280; skin condition, 97–98
Horton, C. E., 221
Huber, J., 94
Hui, C. H., 249
Hull, C. L., 196–197
Hume, D. K., 64
Huntington's Chorea, 162
Hussein, Saddam, 180
Hyperactivity, 38

Idiosyncratic choice strategy, 108–109, 116
Iliffe, A. H., 92
Immune system function: major histocompatability complex, 70; mate selection and, 81–82; secondary sexual characteristics, 66, 74, 77; sex hormones and, 66, 95, 214, 270; social support and, 161–162. *See also* Parasites
Indian preferences, 241, 252
Individualism, 247–248, 253–55, 279
Infants: attractiveness of, 131–132, 142–143, 261; composites of unattractive faces, 39–40; effect of experimenters on, 24–25; faces vs. nonfacial pattern preferences, 24; facial characteristics of, 164, 201; familiarization, 26–27, 39; guided learning, 141; pleasant voices and attractiveness, 5; preferences for attractive faces, 3–5, 24–25, 200–201, 263; preferences for average faces, 10–11; prototype formation, 25–27, 39; rapid learning rates, 24; response to symmetry, 15; sensitivity to social status cues, 158, 185 n.2; visual preference procedure, 3–4; visual tracking procedure, 25
In-group biases, 27
Innate preferences, 21–25, 200–201. *See also* Infants
Intellectual aptitude, attractiveness and, 196–197, 246, 250–251, 271–273
Intermodal matching procedures, 5
Interpersonal Circumplex, 203
Ips pini, 76–77
Iwawaki, S., 241, 252

Jackson, L. A., 199
Japanese: averages of attractive faces, 220; desire for self-change, 254–255; distinctiveness and, 50, 52; importance of attractiveness,

253–254; menstrual cycle and, 72–73; own-race attractiveness, 49–52; sexual dimorphism, 67–68
Jeffery, L., 19
Jensen-Campbell, L., 223
Johnson, R. M., 23, 143
Johnson, V. S., 210, 283
Jones, D., 41, 93, 138, 140, 242–2145
Judicial system, attractiveness and, 262
Juette, Astrid, 91–125

Kalakanis, L., 9–10, 24–25
Kalick, S. M., 23, 38, 143
Karter, A. J., 95
Kato, K., 254
Keating, C. F., 227
Keele, S. W., 25
Kennedy, John F., 180–182
Kernis, M. H., 22, 162
Keypoint morphing technique, 9, 11, 43
Kim, Y., 250–251
Kirchengast, S., 94
Knight, F. B., 196
Kolar, J. C., 209
Korean preferences, 240, 242, 251
Kramer, S., 185 n.2
Kramlich, D., 216–17
Kunzler, R., 76

Langlois, Judith H., 1–33, 41, 55 n.7, 62, 97–98, 143, 174, 217–218, 220
Larsen, R. J., 38, 138, 143, 162, 270
Larson, A. D., 10
Lavater, J. C., 194–195
Leaders: gender and attractiveness, 175–179; importance of attractiveness, 262; neoteny and maturity cues in, 166, 182, 184–185; projections, 178–179; status cues in real, 179–183
Learning histories, 277–278
Lee, H. K., 240
Light, L. L., 62
Likert-scale judgment measures, 18
Lip enlargement, 139, 170–175, 209–210, 277
Little, Anthony C., 59–90
Longo, L. C., 210
Lopez, S., 76
Lorenz, K. Z., 131, 164–165, 201
Lundgren. S., 223
Lundqvist, Daniel, 127–151
Lundy, D. E., 223

Major histocompatability complex (MHC), 70
Makeup, 210
Male pattern baldness, 20, 207–208
Males. *See* Men
Market-value perceptions, 77–78, 80, 82–83
Masculinization, 67, 71–72, 82, 158, 265. *See also* Secondary sexual characteristics
Mate copying, 223–224
Mate selection: assortative mating, 75, 80–81; condition-dependent, 76–77; cultural processes, 144–145; dominance cues, 165, 170–175; evolutionary mechanisms, 36–38; feminization of male features, 38, 68, 71–74, 78–80, 82; freedom of choice vs. arranged, 252; genetic component, 81; good genes benefits, 71–72, 74, 79, 83, 269–273, 276; hair characteristics, 95–96; immunocompetence vs. paternal care, 81–82; importance of attractiveness, 224–225, 262; individual preferences, 212–214; intelligence, 271–272; long-term vs. short-term preferences, 72–74; male scent, 70; market-value perceptions, 59–60, 77–78, 80–83; mate-copying, 223–224; menstrual cycle and, 71–74; multiple fitness model, 100, 155, 198; n-dimensional vector approach, 99–102; neoteny, 170–175, 202, 276; parasites, 75–76, 97, 270; parental competence, 82, 173, 245, 271; phenotypic quality, 80–83; skin color, 96; social information, 223–224; stimulus control theory, 141–145, 274; symmetry, 78–80,

83, 98–99, 143, 215. *See also* Sexual activity
Maturity, sexual, 163–166, 182–183, 198, 203–206
May, K. A., 134, 220
Mazzi, K., 76
McArthur, L. Z., 205
McCabe, V., 159
McHoskey, J. W., 222
McLean, Ian, 35–58
Mealy, L., 63
Mean interrater reliability, 29 n.1
Memory interactions, 130, 133
Men: attractiveness stereotyping, 246–247, 251; body fat distribution, 94; distinctiveness of, 61–62; enhanced masculinization, 67, 71–72, 82, 158, 265; expressiveness, 209–210, 215; extreme features in, 16; facial distinctiveness and health, 38; feminization of features, 37–38, 62, 67–68, 71–74; importance of attractiveness, 224, 252–253; large jaws, 66–67, 165; leadership cues, 175–179, 185; masculinity and attractiveness, 71–74, 78–81, 83, 130–131; masculinity and dominance, 157–159, 163, 165, 170–175; mate quality of youthful females, 60; neoteny and maturity, 163–166, 169–170, 204; number of faces in composite, 47; personality, 68–69; scent of, 70; senescence cues, 207–208; sexual dimorphism, 66–69; symmetry in, 63–65, 78–80, 83, 214–215
Menstrual cycle: conception risk and attractiveness, 71–74; extra-pair copulation, 69, 71; male facial preferences, 71–74, 84, 214, 266, 275, 280; odor preferences, 70; tight clothing, 70. *See also* Hormones
MHC (major histocompatability complex), 70
Miles, S., 208, 221
Miller, A. G., 222
Millinski, M., 76
Mineka, S., 224
Mistaken identity effect, 278
Møller, A. P., 38, 75, 100
Montepare, J. M., 162–163, 185 n.5, 240, 242
Montgomerie, R., 64
Mueser, K. T., 209
Multidimensional scaling (MDS), 20–21
Multiple fitness model, 197–214; average features, 220–221, 226; cultural specificity vs. universality, 199–201; directional and stabilizing selection, 206–207, 217; ecology and social conditions, 211–212; expressive features, 198, 208–210, 215; falsification of appearance, 221–222, 226; grooming features, 198–199, 210–211; individual differences, 212–214; neonate features, 198, 201–203; neoteny and sexual maturity balance, 204–206, 226; overview, 99–102, 155, 197–198; senescence features, 198, 207–208; sexual maturity features, 203–204; symmetry, 214–216, 226; variables other than physical appearance, 222–225
Multiple message hypothesis, 100–102
Munro, I. R., 209
Muscarella, F., 208
Musselman, L., 11, 98

n-dimensional vector approach, 99–102, 114–116
Nelzlek, J., 162
Neoteny. *See* Babyness
Neuroaesthetics, 99
Newborns. *See* Infants
Nezlek, J., 22
Nishitani, Miwa, 10, 35–58
Normalizing selection, 21–22
Nose size, 266, 279
Nubility, 112–114

Obesity, 112–13. *See also* Body fat distribution; Body weight
Odor preferences, 70, 100

Offspring of attractive parents, 23, 36
Oget, E., 75
Olson, J. M., 246
Olson, S., 254
Ontogeny, 156–157
Optimal deviation hypothesis, 207
Oral contraceptives, 70
O'Regan, J. K., 180
Ovarian dysfunction, 97–98
Overgeneralizations, 275–276
Ovulation, 70

Pak, A. W.-P., 248
Parasites: assortative mating and, 75–76; attractiveness and, 38, 61, 66, 70, 74–75; averageness, 270
Parental competence, 82, 173, 245, 271
Paterson, D. G., 195–197
Pawlowski, B., 77
Pedomorphic characteristics, 156–159. *See also* Babyness; Social status cues
Penton-Voak, Ian S., 59–90
Perrett, D. I., 17–19, 59–90, 98–99, 131, 134, 205, 220
Person perception paradigm, 245–246, 248
Personality, 68–69, 249–250, 267–268. *See also* Attractiveness stereotyping
Pettijohn, T. F., 211
Pheromone distribution, hair and, 95–96
Philhower, Correna, 193–238
Photographs: artifacts, 121; compositing, 6–7, 10, 36–37, 216–217; digital image analysis, 105, 119–120; feature measurements, 105; resizing features, 166–167; standardizing methodology, 102–105, 118–119; world leaders, 180. *See also* Averaging techniques
Physical fitness, attractiveness and, 23
Physiognomy, 194–196
Pike, C. L., 219
Pine engraver beetles, 76–77
Pittenger, J. B., 11
Pixel averaging, 7–9, 11, 19–21
Pixel dimension measurement, 105, 118–119
Plastic surgery, 221–222, 279
Poecilia reticulata (guppies), 76, 223
Pollard, J. S., 10, 41, 219
Polycistic ovary syndrome, 98
Pomiankowski, A., 100
Popularity, 223
Posner, M. I., 25
Preference judgments: as behavioral responses, 129; cultural processes, 144–46; discrimination and generalization, 128–129, 132, 135, 142, 145, 274–275; diversity and uniformity of, 138–145; evolution and, 21–25, 141–145, 269–273; extreme trait avoidance, 108–109, 116; favoring differences, 130; forced-choice vs. Likert-scale, 18; genetic control of, 138–139, 146; guided learning, 139–140, 146; health and, 22–23, 38, 99, 162, 270–271; idiosyncratic choice strategy, 108–109, 116; in animals, 140–141; individual differences, 212–214; mistaken identity effect, 278; model of, 133–135; perceiver age, 280–281; prototyping, 109–111, 117; single features, 106–109; stimulus complexity, 111, 116, 120; stimulus control, 133; threshold model, 101; use the best trait strategy, 109; worst (or best) feature approach, 101. *See also* Attractiveness; Mate selection
Prepubescent characteristics, 156–159
Procrustes approach, 103
Proffitt, F., 64, 98, 216
Prototypes: abstraction mechanisms, 97, 274; definition, 25; infant preferences, 25–27, 39; preference for averageness, 25, 36, 97, 109–111

Reagan, Ronald, 180–182
Receiver biases, 128, 130, 142–143, 145–146

Recognition model, 128–129, 132, 135, 142, 273–275. *See also* Stimulus control
Redundant signal hypothesis, 100–102, 106–108
Reidl, B.I.M., 202
Reis, H. T., 22, 162, 209
Reliability measures, 29 n.1, 106
Renaud, F., 75
Rensch, B., 130
Rensink, R. A., 180
Repulsion, 142, 222
Rhodes, G., 9, 15, 19, 35–58, 62, 64, 98, 131, 167, 216, 218–219, 261–293
Rich, M. K., 96
Rieser-Danner, L. A., 4
Roaches, 66
Roberts, A. R., 241–242
Robinson, D. E., 211
Roggman, Lori A., 1–33, 62, 97–98, 174, 217–218, 220
Ronchi, D., 22
Ronzal, Gudrun, 91–125
Rosen, A. J., 209
Rosenblatt, P. C., 252
Rosenthal, R., 29 n.1
Rottman, L., 60
Rowatt, T. J., 221
Rowatt, W. C., 221
Rubenstein, Adam J., 1–33, 39
Russian preferences, 242–244
Rutilus rutilus, 66

Samuels, C. A., 15
Scarification, 212, 277
Scent preferences, 70, 100
Scheib, J. E., 63
Schleidt, W. M., 100
Scorpionflies, 98
Secondary sexual characteristics: attractiveness, 66–69, 71, 265–266, 275; extreme variations, 38, 66; handicap principle, 74–75, 95, 270; multiple ornaments hypotheses, 100–102; parasite resistance, 74–75; parental competence, 82, 173, 245, 271
Self-fulfilling prophecies, 161–162, 272–273
Self-rated attractiveness: immunocompetence vs. paternal care, 81–82; market-value concept, 77–78, 82–83; masculinity preferences, 78–81, 83, 280; mate choice and, 80–83; symmetry preferences, 78–80, 83
Senescence features, 198, 207–208
Sensory exploitation, 99
Sex hormones. *See* Hormones
Sexual activity: assortative mating, 75, 80–81; condition-dependent mate choice, 76–77; dominant features, 165; extra-pair copulation, 69, 71–72; long-term vs. short-term preferences, 72–74; market-value perceptions, 77–78, 82–83; menstrual cycle and, 69–72; symmetry and, 82–83
Sexual dimorphism, 66–69, 74. *See also* Secondary sexual characteristics
Sexual ornaments, 100. *See also* Secondary sexual characteristics
Shackelford, T. K., 38, 138, 143, 162, 270
Shape, facial, 47–48, 54 n.5, 68, 71–74
Shebilski, L., 223
Shepard, J., 219
Shepherd, J., 219
Signal recognition: deception, 160–162, 185 n.3, 185 n.4, 221–222; mechanisms, 129, 142; overgeneralizations, 275–276; receiver biases, 128, 130, 142–143, 145–146; relative advantages, 185 n.3; social status, 157, 160
Singh, D., 212
Single feature approach, 93–96
Siqueland, E. R., 25
Sir-Peterman, T., 93
Skin: color, 96, 112–114, 116, 119–120, 222, 241; digital image analysis, 119–120; texture, 97–99, 119, 208
Slater, A., 24
Smiling, 208–210, 250, 265–266

Smoothing, from averaging, 12, 97–98
Snyder, M., 161
Social desirability index, 248–249
Social goals, 278–281
Social status cues, 153–192; age and maturity, 156–158, 165–166; to attract help, 168–170, 184; benefits of, 159; deception and accuracy, 159–162, 185 n.3, 185 n.4, 221–222; desirability by others, 223; early sensitivity to, 158; height, 160–161; heterosexual attractiveness, 170–175, 184–185; importance of behavior, 176–178; importance of context, 155–156; infant perception of, 158; leadership and gender, 175–179; mate-copying, 223; neoteny, 162–166, 168–170; photograph manipulation, 166–167, 169; in U. S. presidents, 179–183
Social support, 224–225
Solomon, M. R., 210
Sparacino, J., 22
Spiegel, N., 22, 162
Spirduso, W. W., 23
Sprecher, S., 225
Stabilizing selection, 207, 217
Standard Cross-Cultural Sample, 212
Statistics: Bonferroni corrections, 45; correlation analysis, 106–108, 117, 227 n.1; Cronbach's coefficient alpha, 48; effective reliability, 29 n.1; feature uniformity, 106–107; mean interrater reliability, 29 n.1; measures of deviation from averageness, 54 n.3; power analyses, 18; principal components analysis, 111; reliability measures, 29 n.1, 106; sample size, 227 n.1; t tests, 45; variances, 54 n.4; z-scores, 220
Stereotyping. *See* Attractiveness stereotyping
Sticklebacks, 76, 81, 203
Stimulus complexity, 105, 111, 116, 120
Stimulus control: average faces, 132–133, 273–274; averages and extremes combined, 133–135; coevolution, 141–145; extreme faces, 129–132; manipulation by sender, 142; symmetry, 134–138, 273
Stocker, R. D., 196
Stoddard, J. T., 7
Stranger anxiety, 158
Submissiveness, 157, 163, 176–178
Sumich, A., 15, 62, 64, 98, 216, 219
Suntans, 222
Surgical procedures, 221–222
Sussman, M. S., 209
Swaddle, J. P., 98
Symmetry: attractiveness, 13–16, 62–65, 83, 154, 215–216, 265–266; from averaging, 136–137, 145; in compositing, 62; digital image analysis, 119; fluctuating asymmetry, 62–63, 136, 214–215; health and, 38, 98–99, 161–162, 270, 273; hypothesis, 98; male scent and, 70; mate recognition and, 98–99, 273; mirror image composites, 64, 98–99, 137; in monozygotic twins, 63; numbers of sexual partners, 82; perception of, 138; phenotypic and genotypic quality, 63, 143; physiological benefits of, 134–136; by remapping, 64–65; self-ratings and preferences for, 78–80; sensory exploitation, 99; stimulus control theory, 134–138; warping technique, 99
Symons, D., 99

Taiwanese preferences, 242
Tanke, E. D., 161
Tattooing, 212
Tesser, A., 211
Testosterone, 66, 94, 214–215. *See also* Hormones
Thakerar, J., 241, 252
Thelen, T. H., 96
Theocritus, 1
Thiel, D. L., 222
Thomas, F., 75
Thornhill, R., 14–15, 38, 61, 63, 66, 71, 82, 91–125, 204, 218, 227 n.1

Timarcha maritama, 75, 80
Townsend, G., 63
Tremewan, T., 9, 62, 167, 218
Trendy, 210–211
Twins, facial symmetry in, 63

Ugliness avoidance, 101, 117, 273
United States presidents, 178–183
Unreliable signal hypothesis, 100

Vegetarian faces, 6–7
Visual preference design, 3–4, 26
Visual tracking procedure, 25

Wachtmeister, Carl-Adam, 127–151
Waist-to-hip ratio (WHR), 96–97, 112–113
Walster, E., 60, 245
Walton, G. E., 24
Watanabe, H., 253–254
Wedekind, C., 70
Weight, body, 200, 211–212. *See also* Body fat distribution
Weinfurt, K., 253
Westermarck, E., 99
Wheeler, L., 22, 162, 250–251
Wildt, L., 93
Wolfe, Naomi, 200
Women: attractiveness stereotyping, 246–247, 251; body fat distribution, 94–95; enhanced feminization, 66, 266; expressiveness, 209–210, 215; extreme features in, 17–18; facial distinctiveness and health, 38; hair characteristics, 96; importance of attractiveness, 252; leadership cues, 175–179; male scent preferences, 70; mate quality of men, 68–69, 72–74, 83–84; maturity, 163–166; menstrual cycle shifts, 69–74, 84, 214, 266, 275, 280; neoteny, 163–166, 169–175; preferences in male faces, 47, 60–61, 66–69, 71–74, 80–83; scarification of, 212; secondary sexual characteristics, 66; self-ratings and masculinity preferences, 78–80, 83; senescence cues, 208; sexual maturity features, 204; social information about men, 223; symmetry in, 79; youthfulness in, 93–94
Wong, D. T., 213
Worst (or best) feature approach, 101, 117–118
Worthy, M., 195
Wu, C.-H., 241–242, 253

Yam, Y.-M., 249
Yoshikawa, S., 10, 35–58, 134, 220
Youthfulness: attractiveness, 13, 28, 202–203, 265–266; caricatures and, 53; cross-cultural preferences, 41, 93; facial characteristics, 156; in averaged composites, 37, 55 n.7; mate quality of, 59–60, 95; skin color, 96; submissiveness, 157

Zahavi, A., 270
Zanna, M. P., 246
Zebra finches, 140–141
Zebrowitz, L. A., 23, 143, 162–163, 185 n.5, 240, 242, 250, 261–293, 272
Zuk, M., 74

About the Editors and Contributors

ANITA P. BARBEE received her Ph.D. in 1988 from the University of Georgia in social psychology with an emphasis in family studies. She is currently an associate research professor at the Kent School of Social Work at the University of Louisville. Also, she is principle investigator on five grants including the evaluation of Child Welfare and Family Support Training for the Cabinet for Families and Children, the Governor's Early Childhood Initiative, the Jefferson County Domestic Violence Coordinated Response Team Program, and a training program for child welfare supervisors funded by the Department for Health and Human Services, Administration on Children Youth and Families, Children's Bureau. Her research interests also include the formation and maintenance of close relationships, social support, and women's health issues.

D. MICHAEL BURT is studying for a Ph.D. in the School of Psychology at the University of St. Andrews, UK. He graduated from the University of St. Andrews in 1995 with a B.Sc. in psychology. His current research includes using computer graphics to investigate emotion perception in clinical populations and perceptions of facial health and attractiveness.

MICHAEL R. CUNNINGHAM received his Ph.D. in 1977 from the University of Minnesota in social/personality psychology, where he began his research on the perception of physical attractiveness. He is currently a professor in the Department of Psychological and Brain Science at the University of

Louisville. His interpersonal research focuses on the process of attraction and relationship maintenance, mood and social support, and social allergies and the loss of liking and loving. His applied research focuses on attitudinal predictors of job performance in such domains as integrity, service, sales, and management potential, and social allergies among coworkers.

KAREN K. DION received her Ph.D. from the Universtiy of Minnesota and is now a professor of psychology at the University of Toronto. She is interested in social development and more recently, cultural perspectives on interpersonal processes. Her research on the psychology of facial attractiveness reflects both these perspectives.

MAGNUS ENQUIST is Professor of Ethology at the Zoology Institution of Stockholm University. His research interests include the evolution of social interactions and communication, and human cultural evolution.

BERNHARD FINK studied human ethology at the Ludwig-Boltzmann Institute for Urban Ethology in Vienna and is still enrolled for his master of psychology at the University of Vienna. His main areas of interest are human attractiveness, non-verbal communication, and their application to human modeling. He is currently a member of six scientific societies and shares several collaborations with biologists, psychologists, and computer scientists.

STEFANO GHIRLANDA graduated in physics at La Sapienza University in Rome, Italy. He is now a Ph.D. student in ethology at the Zoology Institution of Stockholm University. His research interests include the functioning and evolution of nervous systems, with particular interest in learning and memory mechanisms.

KARL GRAMMER studied zoology, anthropology, and physics in Munich, Germany. Received doctoral degree at the University of Munich in 1982. He was assistant professor at the Max-Planck Research Station for Human Behavior, 1985–1990. Since 1991, he has been the scientific and administrative director of the Ludwig-Boltzmann Institute for Urban Ethology in Vienna, Austria.

KATE HARWOOD graduated from the University of Western Australia with Honours in Psychology. Her Honours thesis focused on cross-cultural evidence for the attractiveness of average faces. She is now a combined master of psychology (clinical) and Ph.D. student at UWA.

ASTRID JUETTE studied zoology and anthropology at the Universtiy of Vienna, Austria. She wrote her masters thesis on human female pheromones in 1995. Since 1997, she has been an assistant at the Ludwig-Boltzmann Institute for Urban Ethology in Vienna. She is currently working on her Ph.D. on digital movement analysis of depressed patients.

CAROLINE F. KEATING is associate professor of psychology at Colgate University in Hamilton, New York. She received her Ph.D. from Syracuse University in 1979. She studies the elusive quality of charisma by investigating the nonverbal skills and physical appearances associated with social dominance and leadership in children and adults. Her research linking leadership and deception skill was funded by the Harry Frank Guggenheim Foundation.

JUDITH H. LANGLOIS is the Charles and Sarah Seay Regents Professor of Psychology at the University of Texas at Austin, where she has taught since receiving her Ph.D. in 1973. She is a fellow of the American Association for the advancement of Science, the American Psychological Society, and of Division 7 (Developmental) of the American Psychological Association. She has received grants from the National Science Foundation, the National Institute of Mental Health, and is currently funded by the National Institute of Child Health and Human Development. She studies social development, particularly the origins of social stereotypes associated with facial appearance.

ANTHONY C. LITTLE is currently studying for his Ph.D. in the school of Psychology at the University of St. Andrews, UK. He graduated from the University of Durham in 1998 with a B.Sc. in psychology and the University of Stirling in 2000 with an M.Sc. in psychological research methods. His current research includes work on personality perception from faces and individual differences in judgments of attractiveness.

DANIEL LUNDQVIST graduated in psychology at Uppsala University in Sweden. He is curently a Ph.D. student in the psychology section, Department of Clinical Neuroscience at the Karolinska Institute. His research focuses on the psychology of attention, emotion, and memory.

IAN MCLEAN obtained his first degree at the University of Auckland, New Zealand and his Ph.D. from the University of Alberta, Canada. His current research centers on the conservation psychology of endangered Australian wildlife and on the use of dogs as tools for clearing land mines.

MIWA NISHITANI obtained her B.A. at Keio University and her M.A. at Kyoto University in psychology. She is now a graduate student at Kyoto University and doing research on facial attractiveness and averageness.

IAN S. PENTON-VOAK is a lecturer in the School of Psychology at the University of Stirling, UK. He received his Ph.D. on "Evolutionary theories of human facial attractiveness: Computer graphic investigations" from the University of St. Andrews in 2000. His current work includes examining male and female facial attractiveness from an evolutionary perspective and cross-cultural studies of facial attractiveness.

DAVID I. PERRETT is a professor of psychology at the University of St. Andrews, UK. He received his Ph.D. from Oxford University in 1981. He studies the organization of higher visual processing. Current research focuses on how the visual system recognizes objects, individuals, their movements, and their actions as well as diverse work on face perception.

CORRENA L. PHILHOWER is graduate student in the Department of Psychological and Brain Science at the University of Lousiville. Her interests include the perception of physical attractiveness, mate selection strategies, social support, and health.

GILLIAN RHODES is professor of psychology at the University of Western Australia and is author of Superportraits: Caricatures and Recognition (1996), which explores how findings in experimental psychology, art, biology, and cognitive science can explain the power of caricatures. She is a recipient of the New Zealand Psychological Society's Hunter Award for Excellence in Research and is on the editorial boards of *Psychonomic Bulletin and Review*, *The British Journal of Psychology*, and the *New Zealand Journal of Psychology.*

LORI A. ROGGMAN is an associate professor in the Department of Family & Human Development at Utah State University. She received her B.S. in psychology (1972) and M.S. in human development (1981) from Utah State University and her Ph.D. in developmental psychology (1988) from University of Texas in Austin. Her research and teaching interests are mostly focused on social development in the early years of life, including infant reactions to facial stimuli varying in physical attractiveness. She has collaborated on a series of studies on the perception and effects of physical attractiveness with Judith Langlois and associates.

GUDRUN RONZAL studied zoology and anthropology at the University of Vienna, Austria and completed a thesis "Physical Characteristics of Female Beauty" at the Ludwig-Boltzmann Institute for Urban Ethology in Vienna.

ADAM J. RUBENSTEIN is an assistant professor of psychology at the College of William and Mary. He received his Ph.D. in developmental psychology from the University of Texas at Austin in 1999. His current research focuses on the perception of facial attractiveness, the formation and maintenance of appearance-based stereotypes, and the development of conceptual representations during infancy.

RANDY THORNHILL is Regents' Professor and professor of biology at the University of New Mexico. His research interests include insect, bird, and human behavior; characterizing the process of sexual selection; and the study of adaptation and methodology in evolutionary biology in general. Over the last 10 years, he has focused his research on human sexuality. He is co-author, with evolutionary anthropologist Craig T. Palmer of the recent *A Natural History of Rape: Biological Cases of Sexual Coercion* (2000).

CARL-ADAM WACHTMEISTER received his Ph.D. in ethology and has investigated the evolutionary significance of courtship displays and rituals, and how these relate to behavior mechanisms.

SAKIKO YOSHIKAWA is associate professor of cognitive psychology at Kyoto University and one of the coauthors with D. I. Perret of papers dealing with facial attractiveness (*Nature*, 1994 vol. 638; *Nature*, 1998 vol. 394). She also edited the book, *Face and Mind: Introduction to the Psychology of Face Processing* (1993), and is the author of *Psychological Research on Recognition Memory for Faces* (1999).

LESLIE A. ZEBROWITZ is Manuel Yellen Professor of Social Relations and professor of psychology at Brandeis University in Waltham, Massachusetts. She is the author of *Social Perception* (1990) and *Reading Faces* (1997), which provides a systematic account of the tendency to judge people by their appearance. She has been a visiting scholar at Seoul National University, the Murray Research Center at Harvard University, and the University of Canterbury, New Zealand. She has also served as program director for Social Psychology at the National Science Foundation.